PLANET, PLANTS & ANIMALS

Planet, Plants & Animals
Ecological Paradigms in Buddhism

ANAND SINGH

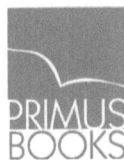

PRIMUS
BOOKS

PRIMUS BOOKS

An imprint of Ratna Sagar P. Ltd.

Virat Bhavan

Mukherjee Nagar Commercial Complex

Delhi 110 009

Offices at CHENNAI LUCKNOW
AGRA AHMEDABAD BENGALURU COIMBATORE DEHRADUN GUWAHATI
HYDERABAD JAIPUR JALANDHAR KANPUR KOCHI KOLKATA MADURAI
MUMBAI PATNA RANCHI VARANASI

First published 2019

ISBN: 978-93-5290-226-2 (hardback)
ISBN: 978-93-5290-227-9 (POD)

Published by Primus Books

Laser typeset by Mithu Karmakar
mithu.karma@gmail.com

Contents

Preface

Human beings since early age persistently enquire about habitable planet and their relationship with it. Sometimes thinking about divinity, man explores that the Earth as a conducive habitation for human and other animate beings, are purposefully created. The natural phenomenon like climate, rains, forests, and rivers influence the moral and socio-economic compositions of human beings or the humans have inadvertently induced the nature of physical environment. Till a few decades ago, the notion that human societies can change the structure of climatic conditions received relatively little systematic attention. When human impact on natural environment was examined, it was found that major transformation in nature has been done by their anthropogenic actions. Such contesting roles of humans are under scrutiny not only by geologists, geographers, and other scientists but also by the philosophers and scholars of religious studies.

Buddhism as a non-theistic religion seeks to explore the cause and cure of human suffering. The fundamental Buddhist teachings centred on interdependence, non-violence, and conditionality contribute to both practice and perception that augment and honour the ecological paradigms. The relationship between Buddhism and environmentalism unquestionably emerged as a subset of the correlation between religion and science. The scientific ideas are liable to produce disagreement with religious opinions and practices, predominantly when they challenged the philosophical notions derived from religious traditions. Secular hostility to religious worldviews and particularly to ancient ethical approaches, traditions, and practices continues to be voiced. Regarding the environment, the scholarly benchmark of a view hostile to religion is given by the scholars who were experts in neither religion nor the environment. The antagonism between science and religion is historic and well-known, but it is also multifaceted, increasingly challenging, and contested. A motivating development is a growing rapprochement between organized religions, especially Buddhism and studies in the field of environmentalism. The notion that Buddhism is influential enough to mould people more environmentally benign and sustainable, might seem whimsical but it can bring significant success to such an effort.

The domain of study of Buddhism and environmentalism show complexity of reactions to climate change. Such investigations can identify, outline, and document the main ethics of Buddhism to revitalize, preserve, and sustain essential planetary conditions. Buddhism sees its worldview as a rejection of hierarchical dominance of humans over nature and encourages empathetic compassion which respects biodiversity. There has been significant progress in this exchange and substantial research has emerged since the 1970s. This book has explored the possibilities for Buddhism to endorse ideas that address anthropogenic climate change. Many scholars have demonstrated to be savvy in their countering of religion-based environmentalism, drawing on invented stories, and the scientific publications that carefully promote a distrust in man-made climate change. It is especially risky to assume that greening of Buddhism represents an inclination in religion-based reactions to climate change. Although for many scholars the compassionate purpose of Buddhism in relation to their environmental concerns seems unproblematic and apparently, closer readings of Buddhist texts and more historically and philosophically informed explanations of traditional Buddhist thought have led to a great length of discussion and critique. There is a clear need for sustained research by all religions to examine and endorse non-anthropocentric climate policies. It is imperative that a range of religious perspectives are carefully considered and included within climate studies.

Buddhist practices revolve around the notion of Dhamma, which means attainment of precise knowledge and removal of suffering. It teaches that people are accountable for their actions and go through a cycle of rebirths before the final realization of *Nibbāna*. Buddhism cares for environment and teaches that the protection of biological diversity is essential. Certain rivers and mountains are sacred, as they give and sustain life. The teachings of the Buddha give a clear description of ecology and interdependence of all life forms. The relation between Buddhist thought and contemporary ecological concerns has become one of the most important dimensions to study contemporary issues. In general, the discourse on Buddhism and environmentalism takes place within a wider discourse of the social relevance of Buddhism, most commonly known as socially engaged Buddhism. Engaged Buddhism itself developed out of Buddhist modernism and integrates presumptions from late nineteenth- and twentieth-century broad-minded innovative experiments by the Buddhist scholars. This is in contrast to the institutional position of Buddhism during most of its history throughout Asia, where it was largely either in missionary role or in reclusive form.

The chance meeting and interaction with Professor Padmasiri de Silva, Monash University in Thailand encouraged me to carry out this work. I am thankful to him for his advice and references. I must take this opportunity to express my heartfelt gratitude to Professor S.Z.H. Jafri, who has always encouraged me to carry out this work. The Mahachulalongkornrajavidyalaya University (MCU), Thailand has organized number of conferences on this topic and I as a panellist in these conferences got wider opportunities to interact with prominent scholars working on this subject. I would like to record my thanks to the university and organizers for such a wonderful opportunity. Thanks are also due to Dr Dipti Mahanta of MCU for a whole lot of suggestions on this topic.

Professor Madagoda Abhayatissa, Professor Wasanta Priyadarshna, and Professor Anura Manatunga of Sri Lanka have helped me in collection of some of the valuable papers and books from libraries of different universities of Sri Lanka. I thank all of them for their kind help. Professor K.K. Thaplyal, Professor K.T.S. Sarao, Professor Siddharth Singh, Professor Prashant Srivastava, Dr Sushma Trivedi, Dr Gurmet Dorjey, Dr Akshay Kumar Singh, Dr Priyadarsini Mitra, Dr K.K. Mandal, Dr R.P.K. Singh, Dr Srikant Ganveer, Dr Mukesh Kumar Verma, and Dr Krishna Murari helped me to resolve issues and facilitating library work related to the book. My earnest thanks goes to each of them.

I would like to express my thanks to Archaeological Survey of India (ASI), New Delhi, India which has granted permission to use photographs used in this book. I pay sincere gratitude to Professor Irfan Habib for allowing me to use one map taken from his book. Finally, I owe a special debt of gratitude to my mother, and brothers for always encouraging me in my academic pursuits.

Gautam Buddha University   ANAND SINGH
Greater Noida, India

Introduction

Origin of Ecological Studies

When the German scientist Ernst Haeckel (1834–1919 CE) coined the term 'ecology' in 1866 to study the bio-physical relations of living organisms with each other and their surroundings, he would never have thought it to earn such judicious introspection and articulate inquiry in the twenty-first century. Man, since his evolution, persistently pondered over habitable earth and his relationship with it. How does it influence the moral and social nature of the individuals that mould the human character and its culture? Driven by uncontrolled ambitions, human societies have been involved in the ruthless anthropogenic exploitation of the natural resources since the beginning of time. This has led to the fundamental problem of the survival and growth of human existence in recent decades. Thanks to its ability to repair itself, Nature has so long been able to cope with the anthropogenic disturbances and restore the disrupted natural processes. Since the scientific revolution and the consequent industrialization, the intensity of human impact on the environment has, in fact, exceeded the latter's potential for restoration, leading to irreversible damages in many parts of the world. Consequently, at this moment humanity is grappling with the complex historical inheritance of a considerably disrupted natural environment and the growing negative impact of industrialization and urbanization on it. The anthropocentric attitude of man concedes his superiority over nature and this pre-supposition dominates human beings and encourages them to exploit the natural resources. During this fatal crisis, the 'ecology' with its primary domain in the biological sciences is playing major role in social sciences and religious studies to restrain the negative action of human propensities and accentuate prudent assumptions of the past to save the planet.

Contemporary environmental ethics was shaped up in the latter half of the twentieth century by the idea that moral consciousness should cover human-induced ecological problems. The human impact has been the most pertinent factor affecting changes in vegetation. With the advent of agriculture, the role of humans has changed from a passive component to active crusader who expoits Nature. Arable and pastoral farming, growing human settlements and consequent changes in the economy have all significantly altered natural vegetation and the geographical landscape. When Nature is exploited by unbridled greed and is wasted mercilessly, an eco-crisis emerges. Man's destructive propensity has led to forest fast depleting and sea level rising to such dangerous levels that some main lands are soon going to be submerged under water. The meadows once fertilized by irrigation are now wastelands and unproductive. The rivers once flowing with abundant water are slowly drying up. The elevation of beds of estuaries and consequently diminishing velocity streams which flow into them have converted thousands of leagues of shallow sea and fertile lowland into unproductive and miasmatic morasses.[1] Responding to this crisis, academia, philosophers, and theologians began to integrate different religious traditions as a possible resource for the development of environmental ethics. Though many see this manifestation of delusion as a crisis that is more ethical and religious than technological.[2] The ecological studies to check environmental degradation started with the criticism of the biblical account of creation. The Book of Genesis accepts the Hebrew belief of special status to human beings who were granted dominion status over nature, which indicates that humans are the custodian of Nature. The western hypothesis overwhelmed by Christian values substantiates the belief that the natural world exists for exploitation and for the benefit of the humans. The question of morality begins and ends with the human world. The destruction of any part of Nature is not wrong if no harm has been done to humans.[3] The Renaissance and the Reformation in the West accelerated the growth of applied sciences which, led by modern inventions, investigated the mysteries of Nature for human specifications and comforts. The ultimate aim was to put humanity above any natural constraint. This led to the genesis of scientific rationalism which in turn ushered in the notion that everything could be tamed and measured with the help of the physical sciences. The planet could not be controlled or tamed by any form of divinity and if god exists, then he acts like 'a good watchmaker' who creates a mechanically perfect world and leaves it to run on its own rhythm and cycle.[4] The scientific and technological development during and post-Renaissance period aggravated this attitude. The Copernican Revolution shifted science from geocentric to heliocentric. The Sun was given at the central stage and the Earth, the habitation of humans and non-humans, was relegated to the peripheries. With this peripheral status, man also seems to have lost his superiority and this has been compensated by anthropocentricism.[5] It is the means-ends nexus that perpetuates ecological degradation. The inventions, use and misuse of splendid technological resources, and the pervasive effects of immense technological means to inculcate the spectacular change the living environment have been the hallmark of the post-Renaissance human image on the planet. The entire human space is technologically structured with apparent motive to improve the condition of human life by making it more comfortable. But, at the same time, the planet is grappling with environmental degradation initiated and perpetuated by the most prudent species of the universe. Environmentalism and eco-friendliness are direct reflections of candid confession that humans are eco-insensitive.[6] Rationalism and scientific inquiry not only triggered the Industrial Revolution, it eventually led to a reaction against it in the form of Romanticism. The Romanticists revolted against a highly mechanized and industrialized life which broke down their joint families, encouraged the nuclear family, and isolation from man, Nature, and the society at large. They encouraged a simple life and a peaceful world with their rebellious remarks against industrial society.[7]

The idea of man's supremacy over Nature has dominated the Western thought to the extent that Western scholars have failed to look beyond the scientific temperament and are instead constantly engaged in unravelling the secrets of Nature. The anthropocentric thought pre-supposes man's superiority over

Nature on the ground that humans are the only rational being under the Sun and the resources of Nature exists to fulfil the insatiable appetites. Western ethics seek their environmentalism from Plato (427 BCE–347 BCE) and Aristotle (384 BCE–322 BCE) who describe cosmology as a teleological world in which Demiurge creates the universe on pattern of ideal world, guided by the idea of the good. Demiurge works like an architect who creates the world with pre-existed things consisting of earth, air, water, and an animated soul. Everything has been designed for man's appetite with an idea that plants are there to nourish him while animal bodies to serve as habitation for fallen souls. Plato divides his soul into rational, active, and appetitive and realizing the rational as the highest moral action. In this context, Plato speaks of virtue as a habit of choice and prescribes the parameters to make the right choice. The selection of right choice is the basis of means which avoids both excess and defect. Despite the most ethical position awarded to Demiurge and world soul, Plato's mind prescribed superiority of mankind in the universe.[8] Aristotle says that the end or purpose of every man is to show his special characteristics which distinguishes him from other creatures. The highest desire for man is to compete for that what makes him more satisfied. Aristotle calls this eudemonia or happiness which is not pleasure, rather it is an immediate result of a virtuous activity.[9] Charles Darwin's *Theory of Natural Selection* emphatically propounds that *Homo sapiens* is the fittest among all the species in the struggle for survival.[10] The Copernicus-Galileo-Newton era envisaged path-breaking researches which have broken the feudal order and religious superstitions of Europe, which was forced on humans since time immemorial. The 'free-bird attitude' of newly-liberated European society was dramatically supported by new inventions, modern machines, and geographical discoveries. This newfound love to rule and conquer the universe encouraged the humans to explore, conquer, and devastate Nature. This thought process was accelerated in the post-Einstein period when nations started competing for supremacy in nuclear warfare.

Benedict de Spinoza's (1632 CE–1677 CE) Pantheism and Gottfried Wilhelm Leibniz's (1646 CE–1716 CE) Monadology depict nature as a manifestation of God, but such views fail to guide human behaviour and they remained at the level of abstract speculations only. Spinoza's doctrine of modes has been determined by his rational pre-suppositions. The infinite intellect of god and motion system together constitute the universe which remains constant although parts of it undergo constant changes. Nature as a whole may be compared to an individual organism, the element of which comes and goes but its manfistation remains the same. Spinoza says that every human has a right to do what he can but it leads to conflict when he goes beyond his powers. It is demand that man should restrict their action to facilitate harmonious co-existence. In only organized society morality is possible on the ground that it makes social life flourishing.[11] Leibniz says that the universe is composed of an infinite number of immaterial unextended dynamic units or monads. He says that monad is not the same in stone, plant, and man. The monads differ among themselves and in its miniscule form they are obscure and confusing, resembling sleep, and spend their entire existence in a comatose state for example plants. In animals there is perception with some consciousness and in humans that consciousness becomes apperception or self-consciousness. Each such monad represents a world in miniature or a microcosm.[12] However, it is debatable if the plants can be in a comatose state. Immanuel Kant (1724 CE–1804 CE) says that humans are the only beings on the Earth who possess knowledge and understanding. He is reigning the Nature.[13] The egoistic hedonism of Jeremy Bentham (1748 CE–1832 CE)[14] popularizes that 'pleasure is the only food', justifying that pleasure earned by the human beings is supreme. It acknowledges desire for pleasure and aversion to pain as a sole motive of human action, and formulates the utilitarian model of the 'greatest good of the greatest numbers'. The utilitarians under J.S. Mills (1806 CE–1873 CE) emphasizes 'maximum pleasures for maximum numbers' and an ethical consideration for human that is limited to pleasure. He agrees with Bentham that happiness is the *summum bonum* of life but says that pleasure differs in quality as intellectual actions are higher than sensuous pleasures. He strives for the greatest happiness of the greatest numbers but with social bonds with mankind.[15] This negative realm of greed has been challenged everywhere and Darwin's *Theory of Evolution* gives way to the interdependence of living species and other elements of the ecosystem. The argument finds place with the argument that non-humans are also sentient beings and that the suffering of animals for benefits of humans is not judicious. It gives birth to biocentrism which looks beyond anthropocentrism. John Rawls says that:

The advantage of one being should not cause inappropriate disadvantage to others. This alliance between man and nature ought to be based on the inclusion of wide range of interest-present and future, human and non-human.[16]

Adam Smith's 'invisible hand' envisages free-market capitalism of scarce resources with no requirement of any regulation to ensure the multiplication of goods and services. The notion was free flow of goods even on the expense of Nature's loss. But any attempt to impose standards or values may invite unwarranted interference in Nature to access happiness.[17] Erich Fromm has given an interesting relation between personality type and ecology. In his hypothesis *To Have or To Be* he says that there are two modes of existence, 'having mode' and 'being mode'. The having mode expresses man's basic acquisitiveness, his ambition for power, aggression, greed, envy, and violence. The 'being mode' is an expression of man's desire to care for others and philanthropy. The latter mode encourages conservation of resources while 'having mode' can give way to callous and unsympathetic attitude towards Nature which in turn leads to ecological disasters.[18] Altogether, ecological studies should be evaluative or axiological which implies a reflective analysis of value preferences, behavioural norms, and code of conduct for humans in a particular space-temporal context.

Discussion on Ecological Studies

Environmental ethics needs a significant departure which can signify an all-pervasive system including both biotic and abiotic species. It implies an interrelationship of all these species and their environment which will sustain the human existence through balance of ecosystem by conserving and preserving natural resources. Since the beginning of environmental studies, controversies were also raised about its necessity, use, and nature.

The contemporary intellectual arena is sometimes learnt as an archical on account of hypothesis developed or declaration made. Sometimes it produces undesired controversies and complications. Such controversies exist not only between humans and non-humans but also between people of different regions and nations. Many people deplete the natural resources and dump the toxic wastes in the periphery of oceans, rivers, and hills, with a contemptuous attempt to human population residing in these regions. The acid rain, the defiled ground water, and the water-borne diseases kill millions of people in several developing nations every year. The increasing population, commercial cropping, and use of pesticides intensify land erosion, salinization, and deforestation. The waste generation and global toxification results in circulation of harmful materials worldwide by atmospheric and oceanic circulation.[19] The pragmatism and efficacy of such eco-ethics have been challenged by one core section of scientists who believe that creation and destruction of the universe is an evolutionary process governed mainly by Nature. Some scientists even challenged the United Nations report on environment which relates change in sea level, melting of glaciers and acid rains to inordinate industrialization and globalization. One of the studies state that the cause of alarming rate of recession of Gangotri glacier of Himalayan region is its own typical characteristics and not necessarily global warming. United Nations Intergovernmental Panel on Climate Change suggests decreasing in temperature in Ladakh (Jammu & Kashmir, India) by 0.4 °C per decade. But the glacier are still retreating which suggests the reason may be some internal geological features, not man-made causes.[20] However, such excuses cannot be accepted as justification for the wanton destruction meted out to Nature. The human world needs a middle path for sustainable approach. It requires cultural and rational models encompassing moral space which is a prelude to the social and economic justification of Nature's destruction. What desired is to have an ecocentric ethics dealing with man's relation with other animates and inanimates in a pragmatic manner. The dominant anthropocentric ethical tradition has been challenged by Spenglar who accepts extreme materialism as a cause for decline of the West.

Western culture, during its early centuries tinged with Magian influences, could not be considered fully 'born' until shortly before the year 1000. In naming it Faustian, Spengler both paid tribute to Goethe and suggested its basic character of limitless striving or aspiration. As the free-standing temple or nude statue had symbolically epitomized the Apollonian, and the 'vaulted cavern' or dome the Magian, so the Faustian found its plastic, its architectonic symbol in the soaring vaults and spires of a Romanesque or gothic cathedral. This had occurred in its springtime. In its summer (or maturity) the Baroque had dissolved the artistic canon into fluid shapes and the play of perspective and shadow-finally (and unavoidably) passing over into the contractual music of Johann Sebastian Bach. Then after an autumn intermezzo of Rococo refinement and daring philosophical speculation, it had reached its ultimate stage, its winter, in the century just past. To delineate this 'late phase' Spenglar drew on the familiar German distintion between 'culture' and 'civilization'. The former, which the Faustian model had enjoyed from its springtime through its autumn, manifested itself in a sure sense of 'form' and 'style'. The latter lacked such virtues. Its art became eclectic, its thought desiccated, and its politics a façade for the power of money. Still more, its people pile together into 'barrack-cities' figured as little better than a mob, a ready prey for demagogues and a thirst for religious revelation. Unending warfare would be its lot-warfare no longer between nations but between the armed followings of newly arisen Caesars.[21]

However, there is no such widespread pessimism. The human can reconcile with environment by showing a sympathetic attitude. The complexity, frequency, and rising magnitude of environmental problems are partly a result of rapidly increasing population and partly because of ever growing per capita consumption. Humans have imposed undesirable pressure on environment which cannot be reversed but specific measures can be taken for its conservation and preservation. Religious traditions, especially Buddhism, have such world views which may be used as antidotes for the pessimistic views on the world's future. Buddhism says that wild species and plants have the right to co-exist with humans on this planet; none can exterminate them. Nature is not to transform, modify, or destroy to meet our own utilitarian ends.

In the nineteenth century, the devastative effects of the Industrial Revolution could be felt across the globe and people began to ponder over proper solutions. In 1888, the renowned painter Vincent Van Gogh painted a self-portrait as a Zen monk with shaven head and orientalized eyes with the quotation 'a simple worshipper of the eternal Buddha'. He painted a halo of brushstrokes to depict himself as a divine monk. The environmentalists took inspiration from Romanticism and wrote articles and translated texts inspiring environmentalism. Henry David Thoreau translated a part of the *Lotus Sūtra* in English and John Muir wrote a eulogy *My First Summit in the Sierra* on Nature in 1911.[22] Since the beginning of such studies one group of scholars believed in proper management of natural resources for human progress while the other group initiates ecocentric ideas to save environment from human aggression. The decade between 1900 and 1960 was conceived as the decade of establishing national parks, and conservation movements for forest regeneration. Two world wars and the use of nuclear weapons compelled man to think of the implications of technology on the Earth and humans. In the 1960s, policies were shaped for ecological studies. In the 1980s, the discovery of ozone hole in Antarctica acknowledged the stand that eco-friendly policies will decide the future of man.[23] James E. Lovelock propounded the Gaia Hypothesis based on the idea that the earth, the atmosphere, and the oceans are well-wisher of humans and has compassion for sentient beings. This is an opposing view to the established belief that life is accommodated to planetary conditions.[24] He propounded the Gaia hypothesis to establish a mandatory self-regulating practice to protect the planet. Thereafter, it became synonymous with the mechanism of self-defining and self-organizing living planet of which humanity is an inseparable part.[25] Lovelock says that every person in the world could not be non-violent because of their food habits, geographical necessities, and local spatial requirements. The so-called violent and non-violent traditions, habitation, and distributive techniques should be observed with the eyes of existing traditions. Sometimes compulsive necessities requires hunting and killing for food and survival.

Environmental ethics became important in the early 1970s and was adopted as a part of the progressive philosophy curriculum in the West. It was assumed that traditional metaphysics will have some solutions to the environmental problem. It was an arduous task to frame some rules and regulations regarding environmental ethics which could be used as a normative guide to the human mindset, behaviour and action towards Nature. Callicott observes on such ongoing problems that:

The problem which, taken together, constitute the so-called 'environmental crisis' appear to be of such ubiquity, magnitude, recalcitrance, and synergistic complexity, that they force on philosophy the task not of applying familiar ethical theories long in place, but of completely reconstructing moral theory (and a supporting metaphysics) in order adequately and effectively to deal with them. Environmental ethics in other words, begins with the assumption that traditional metaphysics and moral theory are more at root of environmental problems than tools for their solution.[26]

The early phase of environmentalism started with debates over fundamental misunderstanding of Nature and the moral concerns relating to Nature as predicted in Western thought which focuses on the Judaeo-Christian tradition. The following points of this tradition became the bone of contention among scholars having pro- and anti-sentiments about Christian tradition in order to deplore Nature:[27]

1. God is the centre of divinity.
2. Nature is a profane phenomenon of God. He manages and divides various elements of life.
3. Man is born as an image of God and exclusive status has been manifested to him by his segregation from rest of Nature.
4. Man has superiority over Nature.
5. God consents for reproduction by humans.
6. The Judaeo-Christian metaphysical structure is hierarchal. God is supreme and he monitors human beings.
7. God is the ultimate source of human's intrinsic and moral values. Since non-humans lack such virtues, they are inferior to humans.

Ian McHarg says that the creation myth of Judaism was assimilated without any change into Christianity which boast of exclusive attributes of man, his divine dominion over Nature, and his willingness to conquer the earth by any means. The Book of Genesis clearly shows the human attitude towards Nature and its subjugation. It derives man's most exploitative and destructive characteristics towards unsustainable growth.[28] Callicott argues that the Graeco-Roman philosophy does not get such critical appraisal by the environmentalists as of the Judaeo-Christian tradition. The early environmental critics like Lyn White, Jr., J. Donald Hughes, and John Rodman find Greek mythology and metaphysics, Pagan naturalism, Milesian Hylozoism (living cosmos), Heraclitus (process ontology), and Pythagoras (human-animal kinship) environmentally moulded and helped to frame appropriate ethics.[29]

Beginning of Ecological Studies in Buddhism

The twentieth century saw some new approaches and dimensions to academic and theological interpretations of human relations with Nature and consequent ecological degeneration. Scholars engaging in interpreting and apply the teachings of the Buddha are also taking a keen interest in investigating and applying Buddhist doctrines to environmental concerns. In an article penned down in 1967 on Christianity and the environment, Lynn White Jr., while criticizing Christianity, commended Buddhism for its holistic and egalitarian world view in contrast to Christian ideology. In his essay, White argues that Buddhism promotes preservation and sustainability while Christianity encourages human domination over Nature which leads to environmental degradation.[30] He says:

I personally doubt that disastrous ecological backlash can be avoided simply by applying to our problem more science and more technology. Our science and technology have grown out of Christian attitude towards man's relation to nature which are almost universally held not only by Christians and neo-Christians, but also by those who fondly regard themselves as post-Christians. Despite Copernicus, all the cosmos rotates around our little globe. Despite Darwin, we are not in our hearts, part of the natural process. We are superior to nature, contemptuous of it, willing to use it for our slightest whim.[31]

This caused widespread furore among scholars of Christianity who challenged White's hypothesis and pointed out that Western ethical practices overwhelmed by Christian ethics encompass atleast five attributes towards Nature: (a) despotic, (b) dominion over, (c) stewardship, (d) subordination to, and (e) particular in.[32] It emboldened Donald K. Swearer to categorize Buddhist ecological studies into five taxonomical classifications: (a) eco-apologists, (b) eco-critics, (c) eco-constructivists, (d) eco-ethicists, and (e) eco-contextualists.[33]

The 'eco-apologists' support the theory that environmentalism is embedded in Buddhist texts and traditions. Some prominent monologues and books supporting this hypothesis are: *Dharma Gaia: A Harvest of Essays in Buddhism and Ecology*, ed. Allen Hunt Badiner, 1990; *Buddhism and Ecology*, ed. Martine Batchelor and Kerry Brown, 1992; and *Dharma Rain: Sources of Buddhist Environmentalism*, ed. Stephanie Kaza and Kenneth Kraft, 2000.[34]

The counter-arguments of the eco-critics proposed by the 'apologists' propound that Buddhist ethics and tradition are not compatible with modern environmentalism. They contend that modern ecological problems are new to humans, so the text compiled in the pre-Christian era cannot essentially explain and solve such problems. Ian Harris is the main proponent of this theory, he believes that soteriology of Buddhism is based on a negative assessment of Nature as fundamentally unsatisfactory (*dukkha*) and subject to change (*anicca*) which does not promote grounds for environmental ethics. He claims that the Buddhist tradition is primarily anthropocentric, not biocentric, and emphatically focuses on spiritual liberation.[35]

The 'eco-constructivists' believe that Buddhist environmental ethics can be constructed from Buddhist doctrinal tenets and recommend a critical analytical approach towards formation of a Buddhist environmental ethics based on normative commitments. Lambert Schmithausen proponds that a viable Buddhist environmental ethics depends upon realizing a positive value to Nature and natural diversity but in a way that the essentials of tradition are not lost. Schmithausen says that early Buddhist tradition does not ascribe to an inherent value of Nature, neither in life as such, nor in any species or the eco-system. It does not deal with preserving, restricting, transforming or subjugating Nature but it works only for liberation (*vimutti*) for all constituents of the existence.[36] Even the soteriological orientation of early Buddhism cannot be constructed to have a positive ecological consequences in such a way that a person who has attained *nibbāna* or is motivated by *karuna* or *metta* is to act on behalf of other sentient beings.[37]

The 'eco-ethicists' perceive viable Buddhist environmental ethics to be evaluated in reference to it. The interest and concerns of religion and ecology should be closely interlinked. Shumacher says that the Buddha recommends a reverent and non-violent attitude to all sentient beings and plants. In his book *Small is Beautiful*, he advocates a non-exploitative Buddhist lifestyle of simplicity, and non-violent and moderate consumption.[38] The 'eco-contextualists' speak about Buddhist environmentalism in particular contexts and situations. The protests of Buddhist monks and civilians against deforestation and installation of cable cars on the revered southern mountains of Chiang Mai province of Thailand could be good examples of this. Donald K. Swearer says that ongoing narratives connect myth and history, past and present, humans and Nature, facilitating in environmental ethics a multidimensional inclusiveness which is otherwise lacking.[39]

Seth Devere Clippard in his essay 'The Lorax Wears Saffron: Towards a Buddhist Environmentalism' argues for the re-orientation of Buddhist ecological studies. His argument is based on suggestions given by Swearer with some modifications and adjustments in thought and methodology dealing with such studies. He says that eco-Buddhist ethics needs focus on establishing textual justification of what its environmental ethics says towards a discourse in which Buddhist rhetoric and environmental practices are intimately linked through specific communal encounters.[40] Harris, in his paper 'Causation and Telos: The Problem of Buddhist Environmental Ethics', says that early Buddhist literature possess elements that may harmonize with ecological consciousness but their outlook towards the causal process minimizes the chances of developing an authentic Buddhist environmental ethics. He categorizes the scholars engaging in ecological studies in Buddhism into the following four groups:

1. The representative Buddhist environmental ethics by Buddhist preachers and monks. His Holiness the Dalai Lama is the most suitable representative of this school.[41]
2. The Japanese and North American scholars who believe that Buddhism has the resources to address the current environmental issues.[42]

3. Scholars who accept difficulties involved in reconciling traditional modes of thought with scientific ecology. They are still optimistic about the possibility of framing an authentic Buddhist response to environmental problems.[43]
4. Scholars who outrightly reject possibility of Buddhist environmental ethics on the ground that the other-worldliness of Buddhism implies a negation of the *saṁsāra* for all practical purposes.[44]

Pragati Sahni following Ian Harris classifies the following four categories in Buddhist ecological studies: (a) Those scholars who ardently believe that Buddhism is environmental and are known as 'partisan', (b) those scholars who believe that claims of Buddhist environmentalism can be validated by Buddhist texts and are known as 'positivists', (c) those scholars who are judgemental in their approache to determine the extent of Buddhism as ecological and who are known as 'sanguine', (d) those who are sceptical about environmental ethics and are known as 'sceptics'.[45] Though the intention is not to divide Buddhist ecological studies into particular approaches and dialectical debates, but to facilitate these studies in a homogenous and holistic direction, the following taxonomical classification has been evolved:

1. Buddhism as Environmental Religion
2. Antithesis and Counter-arguments
3. Towards Engaged Buddhism

Buddhism as Environmental Religion

The followers of this hypothesis seek seeds of environmentalism in Buddhist canonical texts and traditions. They consider Nature to be an entity from which everything has originated and from which human beings can not be alienated. Nature is not a mere physical world external to man. One of the earliest exponents who supported this view is Lily de Silva who discovers a close relationship between human morality and Nature. In her essay *The Hill Wherein my Soul Delights*, she explores ecological aspects found in early Buddhist texts and says:

Modern humanity has exploited nature without any moral restraint to such an extent that nature has been rendered almost incapable of sustaining healthy life. Invaluable gifts of nature, such as air and water, have been polluted with disastrous consequences. Humanity is now search for ways and means of overcoming the pollution problem as our health is also alarmingly threatened.[46]

She points out the moral degeneration in the society by citing examples from Buddhist canonical literature and introspects on various dimensions of life. de Silva divides her essays into following sections—'Nature as Dynamic', 'Morality and Nature', 'Human Use of Natural Resources', 'Attitudes Towards Animal and Plant Life', and 'Attitudes Towards Pollution'. In 'Nature as Dynamic', de Silva addresses *anicca* as one of the important elements of Nature and the world is dynamic and deteriorating (*lujjati ti loko*).[47] While discussing the 'Morality and Nature' she reiterates Buddhist doctrines and how the natural process is affected by the human morality as exemplified in the *Aggañña* and the *Cakkavati Sīhanāda Sutta* of the *Dīgha Nikāya*. Both *suttas* narrate that *lobha* is the main cause for the decline of human civilization.[48] With references of the *Sigalovada Sutta*, *Kasaniyametta Sutta*, and *Nandivisāla Jātaka*, de Silva feels that humans survive on natural resources but their consumption must be accompanied by moral restraints and that true *kamma* and rebirth help people to adopt a sympathetic attitude towards Nature.[49]

Stephen Batchelor, in his essay 'The Sand of the Ganges—Notes towards a Buddhist Ecological Philosophy', relates human existence as one of the many forms of life existing in the universe, and among them birth as a human being is seen as an exceptional opportunity. The unwanted and unwarranted greed lead to deterioration of the universe and only the teachings of the Buddha can revive the lost vision of wholeness of universe to save it. The healing process starts by putting one's own life in order by avoiding *lobha* and *moha*.[50] In another essay 'The Buddhist Economics Reconsidered', Batchelor states that economic terms and values depend on non-duality in such a way that the separation between agent, act, and object became conceptual on the basis of the *śunyata*. The resultant economics here is to consider the Buddhist acceptance of reality as 'acentric' which means no one can monopolize in comparison to other.[51] Martine Batchelor asserts that ecological gleaning is possible from Buddhist texts and that Buddhism throughout the ages has been indifferent of any attempt to bestow human life with a flamboyance and a high standard of material life. The aim of the Buddha was to expound the true way of living in this mundane world.[52]

Padmasri de Silva is another prominent name who supports the view that ecological facets can be found in Buddhist canonical texts and traces Buddhist doctrines which are ecologically meaningful.[53] He says that Buddhism is able to look into the mirror of Nature without attachment, and with a mind of equanimity. One can discover the most profound truth in this mirror and can be blessed to feel the Nature of transience in the very rhythm of Nature.[54] Buddhism takes *lobha, dosa,* and *moha* as the roots of acquisitive, destructive, and confused lifestyle. The wanton greed finds expression in diffused life orientation bound to sensuality and hedonism in reference of *kama-taṇha.* The *lobha* also manifests in limitless demand and desire bound to *bhava-taṇha,* a destructive and violent attitude to oneself, others, and the natural world. It finds expression in the form of hatred and exhibits sometimes in an annihilative instinct or *vibhava-taṇha.* The unimaginative pattern of consumption leads to a cycle of desires and disasters. The psychological root of such disasters and recovery are very much imbibed in the tenets of Buddhism.[55] Scientific and technological progress has not only driven material progress but it has also accelerated and spread consumerism, competition, and conflict resulting in a high quality of life only for a few elite in society who enjoy affluence while the majority population is reeling under poverty and subsistence economy. Personal human progress has not been addressed at the global level; instead, politics, and religion have been used to creating strife, wars, and bloodshed.[56] But Buddhism has been engaged with human liberation and strengthening of a just social order. The *dhamma* and politics have been designed as two intertwined wheels of *dhammacakka* and *anacakka.* The aim is to spread the Buddha's messages without any ritual and ceremony.[57] The Buddha talks about three poisons—*lobha, moha,* and *dosa*—as manifestations of unhappiness. Capitalism and consumerism have been supported by these poisions conflict, aggression, and wars. It is hand-in-glove with the modern system which promotes knowledge without wisdom. It is actually delusion in the frame of knowledge.[58]

The *paticcasamuppada* is the most cherished metaphysical doctrine of the Buddha, discussed among scholars in support of or against environmentalism. Alan Sponberg mentions that environmentalism is conditioned in the Buddhist doctrine of *annata*. In this the individual identity is perceived as a dynamic and growing stream of *kammic* conditioning that goes to many life and lifeforms. The self is a form of dynamic stream which leads to consequential environment-sustaining altruism.[59] Sulak Sivaraksa uses the word 'interdependent' for *paticcasamuppada* in place of 'dependent origination' and propounds that the doctrine of interdependence, co-arising thus, is the *sui-generis* of the Buddhist understanding of Nature. The anthropocentric ideas are the major causes for environmental degradation and *paticcasamuppada* re-orients human vision towards a more eco-friendly world view.[60] Chatsumarn Kabilsingh also argues that *paticcasamuppada* can be exemplified for environmentalism and the human culture as a part of Nature can be identified as an individual or collectively as a nation and will be responsible for utilizing or violating the natural laws.[61]

Rita M. Gross uses Buddhist texts to solve issues such as population, consumption, and environment. She argues that Buddhism does not encourage reproduction and does not accept slavery and child abuse. She praised the Buddha for preaching *majjhima magga* as it moderates the level of consumption.[62] She applies Buddhist teachings to fertility and population control, mortality, birth rate, etc., and acts as a 'constructive theologian' explaining Buddhist tenets in such a way that involves Buddhism with contemporary issues. One can not increase the size of the earth but one can control the population. Buddhism does not encourage reproduction as a religious duty nor does it see sexuality negatively to be restrained with some ethical prohibitions. Therefore, population control through contraceptives and abstinence were acceptable. The rules regarding fertility and reproduction regulated by Buddhist tradition favour reproduction as an intentional choice rather than as a religious duty.[63] In all societies, usually pro-natalism acts as an ideology and people desires birth of child auspicious. The people who have less children are considered as less adequate and faceing socio-economic constraints. Pro-natalists consider reproduction to be a private affair, not open to public inquiry.[64] Rita Gross further explains that when sex could not be separated from fertility and women had no other authentic and valued identity or cultural role except motherhood, all women became mother. It has been perceived that every female deity was seen as a mother goddess, but the mythology and symbolism of different female forms reveal that they play different roles other than mothers. They are protector, consorts, teachers, goddess of wealth, etc., and they do not promote pro-natalism.[65] Gross believes that environmental ethics must discourage excessive consumption and reproduction even if demographic and cultural settings permit it. A rhetoric of worshipping and veneration of Nature is not optimum when it is combined with technologies of simple societies which has limited ability to damage the environment. But when such societies became acquainted with modern technologies, they likewise damage the environment in the name of progress. Because of sophisticated technologies their population also increases. If it is not restricted then it may damage the ecological balance of the society. It is prudent that the human population must be restricted to maintain the balance of Nature and its resources.[66] Gross says that human encroachment of ecosystem in the name of development could not be justified. The effect of growth and technology are interconnected with resources and population. Buddhist environmentalism has no such awareness programme and its ecological literature ignores the truth that the population growth is due to patriarchal values.[67]

Ken Jones in 'The Social Face of Buddhism', says that Buddhist virtues are a matter of character and its importance is on the cultivation of a personality which cannot but be moral, rather than focusing upon the morality of particular acts and choices.[68] Alan's idea is that Western environmentalism has conceived the notion of the individual as an autonomous entity while Buddhist virtues reflect a notion of the self in dynamic and developmental mode. Buddhist ethics and soteriology requires a significant integrity or coherence of personal identity, yet that identity or individuality of the self is seen as a dynamic *kammic* continuity rather than as an essential ontological substantiality. The environmentalism in Buddhism is based on its relationship with other species and is framed by the understanding of personal identity which is fundamentally trans-human. Buddhism has traditionally molded the problems of the relationship in different manner and as a result the traditional Buddhist environmentalism should be judged in a different manner from its counterpart in the West. Buddhism locates the humans in profound inter-relationship with other existing beings and ultimately with the ecosphere. It has been imbedded in the doctrine of *ahiṁsa* or *śunyavāda* which could be learnt as an example of non-dualism that entails compassionate activity towards all other beings.[69] All these scholars firmly believe that Buddhist traditions could directly be instrumental in the cultivation of eco-ethics in Buddhist texts and that the tenets of the Buddha envisage the formation of such ethics to actualize the goodwill for Nature and society.

Antithesis and Counter-arguments

The main exponents of this thought is Ian Harris who questions the presence of environmentalism in Buddhism and says that methodologically Buddhism lacks the power to sustain an environmental ethics. He believes that Buddhism might be sympathetic to animals but its chief motive could be different. For Harris Buddhism has no defined environmental ethics and is more or less concerned with *dukkha* which overwhelms every aspect of human life, and that the ultimate zeal of Buddhist doctrines is to attain *nibbāna*. In Buddhism there is no conformity between Nature and man and it has no doctrinal or historical basis for environmental ethics. In Buddhist metaphysical assumptions, life is a reality of conditioned existence, suffering, and constant rebirth which differs radically from the contemporary metaphysical assumptions of ecology and this makes it difficult to evolve an environmental ethics based on a Buddhist world view.[70] Harris is extremely critical of Joanna Macy and other scholars with a similar approach and he blames them for super imposing the teleological principles from process theology on eco-Buddhism. He says that Macy's conclusion leads to an anachronism in her treatment of early Buddhist-Indic sources.[71] He also criticizes David Kalupahana for his understanding of Nature that implies all conditioned things as subject to *paticcasamuppada* that form a prelude to human life as a segment of world process.[72] Harris says that the Buddha expressed *metta* towards animals—a method

to calm down the dangerous animals.[73] Harris believes that
Buddhist concern for the welfare of the animals is not a specific
domain of Buddhism but more an issue of the ethics of civility.
The sympathetic attitude towards animals is compatible with
Buddhism but it does not arise from its core ethics. The wilds
are praised in Buddhist texts and traditions not for the intrinsic
value they hold but more for the role they play in facilitating
the monastic life. Contemporary eco-ethics does easily fit in with
the Buddhist world view of *nibbānic* metaphysics. The absence
of concern for the future of *saṁsāra* due to over-emphasis on
liberation from it and impermanence renders the world a domain
devoid of such attributes and obviate the need to justify concerns
for the natural world.[74] Clippard accepts this because Harris
argues that Buddhism does not possess teleology that makes it
difficult by justifying particular entities which does not participate
in the process of *nibbāna*. Clippard finds this interpretation of
nibbāna problematic and thinks that his view is a compromise
between him and Harris.[75] Lambert Schmithausen also argues
that it is difficult to find an indisputable environmentalism in
early Buddhism due to contradictory view regarding Nature.
He interprets dimensions of Nature which is not directly linked
to human population or in direct relation with human beings
including plants and animals. He investigates these dimensions in
early Buddhist-Indic sources with special reference to sentiency
of plants in early Buddhist texts.[76] In his monumental work *The
Problem of Sentience of Plants in Earliest Buddhism* he finds that the
Vedic literature shows some sort of sentiency towards plants and
seeds, and indicates that everything in the universe has some
level of consciousness; the early Pāli texts, however, do not show
such tradition. Only positive induction which supplements such
views is *paticcasamuppada*. He contemplates that certain verses of
the Buddhist texts include plants in the group of animate being
though they are very few in number.[77]

Peter Harvey in his analysis of environmentalism in Buddhist
countries notes that Buddhist texts may not be always conducive to
modern ecological studies but may be seen as ecological because
human beings are not all set against Nature and have potential
to act in a compassionate manner towards all other beings.[78] Paul
Waldau harbours almost the same opinion. The treatment of

animal in early Buddhism is based on two different features: (a) sympathy based on *karuna* and *metta*, and (b) neglect.[79] The root of negligence is Buddhism's preoccupation with human being.[80] Florin Deleanu says that the unfair treatment towards animals depicted in literary sources is mainly because of the contemporary literary conventions and that they deserve sympathy.[81] Malcolm David Eckel has also been critical of environmental ethics in Buddhism and says that Buddhism is not subjective with regard to acting for the sake of Nature.[82] However, the opinion floated by Harris does not seems to be appropriate because in early Buddhist texts, especially in the *gātha* literature, many sources are found which praise wildlife and forests, because of their attributes and not for their role in monastic development. In Buddhism, the relationship between the human and animal population is symbiotic rather than competitive, and the use of cattle resources proceeds in such a way so as not to impair the survival and well being of animal population. The principles of *tikotiparisuddha* and the condemnation of the Vedic *yajnas* clearly give the sustainable approach of the Buddha and under new technoenvironmental conditions such ideas should be considered to diffuse the modern ecological crisis. The concept of *ahiṁsa* in its traditional context accounts for a reluctance to kill and eat meat. The Buddha's view of the eco-system provides, in principle and in fact, for adaptive and efficient utilization of cattle resources and products. The concept of *ahiṁsa* and protection of animal in its traditional context accounts for an abandonment of killing and eating of meat, and it is functionally interrelated with the traditional ecological system; its parts are certainly interwoven into a complex texture. The exponents of ecological studies are concerned with present-day world because the modern ecological crisis emerged in recent decades, but this eco-system reflects a millennium or more of massive culture contact, including conquest and the forcible imposition of alien principles of socio-political and economic organizations as well as the more subtle infiltration of alien values and alternatives. The most pragmatic relationships within the Buddhist ecology are unrecognized, frequently evaded or rejected by those who propounds the non-viability of Buddhist environmentalism.

Towards Engaged Buddhism

A socially-engaged Buddhism is a methodological tool to construct and analyse emerging socio-economic dimensions with special reference to Buddhism. It allows scholars to engage Buddhist traditions with current socio-economic issues.[83] It encourages widespread social movement that is prelude to the establishment of an ecumenical world of Buddhism.[84] Engaged Buddhism has all the essential features of traditional Buddhism but it also has substantive differences in that it accommodates ideas relevant to the modern age. The term 'engaged Buddhism' was coined by the Vietnamese monk, Thich Nhat Hanh, in 1963 and was recoined as 'socially engaged Buddhism' in the 1980s.[85] 'Engaged Buddhism' was inspired by traditional Buddhist virtues with the earnest intention to lessen the suffering of the world. The aim is to inculcate and engage Buddhist teaching to transform the socio-economic and political values for a sustainable and vibrant society.[86] Christopher S. Queen says that 'engaged Buddhism' in Asia is led by a charismatic Buddhist leader or leaders who usually came from the affluent and educated class. Some even face exile and imprisonment from their respective governments. His Holiness the Dalai Lama was exiled from Tibet, Sulak Sivaraksa was imprisoned by the Thai government for protesting in support of the environmental cause while Thich Nhat Hanh was exiled from Vietnam and had to finally settle in France.[87] Gananath Obeyesekere also says that modern engage Buddhism has a spatial shift symbolizing relevance of the teachings of the Buddha to the modern world. The key elements here are: (a) emergence of a leader who conceives and implements a charter as symbol of new order, (b) a paradigm shift in ideology in coherence with global ideas and for political action and social goals, and (c) a rationalization of the monastic and religious life through reforms to make Buddhism more practical, and moderate.[88] These leaders interpreted *dhamma*, especially *lobha, moha, dosa, paticcasamuppada*, and *brāhma vihāra*, in a different manner and integrated these elements with current socio-economic problems. These interpretations provide a new understanding and learning to the Buddha's teachings to end suffering. They not only provide solutions but also suggest innovative methodologies to remove suffering through training on mindfulness, awareness programmes, etc. These movements against global warming and environmental deterioration were not inclusive but very much part of socially engage movements which covers all socio-economic dimensions starting from poverty alleviation and deforestation to consumerism and materialism. For example, in Vietnam, Thich Quang Duc immolated in protest against war in 1963 while Thich Nhat Hanh spread awareness through his writings and meditation camps, and was later nominated by Martin Luther King Jr. for the Noble Peace Prize. Dalai Lama Tenzin Gyatso started human right activism and environmental awareness and was consequently awarded Noble Peace Prize. Aung San Suu Kyi began a socio-political movement in Myanmar while A.T. Ariyaratne and Sulak Sivaraksa launched sustainable development programmes in Sri Lanka and Thailand, respectively.[89] In the West too, Joanna Macy, John Seed, etc., started environmental awareness programmes.

It has been argued that Buddhist environmentalism is influenced by Western thought and the Judaeo-Christian tradition.[90] Robert N. Bellah and Donald K. Swearer examined effect of Modernization and Westernization on Buddhism in Asia. Bellah observes that when confronted with values of modern Western thought Buddhism consequently transformed in two ways. First, Buddhism embraced the challenges by reforming themselves in tune with Western thoughts and ideologies and accommodated Western views but also kept intact traditional Buddhist values at the spiritual, social, behavioural, and ideological level. This group may be called the 'neo-traditionalists'. The second group has been termed the 'reformists' the one who accepted that Buddhist tenets could be refined in view of modern circumstances and problems. Their view is that the interpretation of the old in a new form could start socio-economic reform and national regeneration.[91] Donald K. Swearer says that Buddhism in South-East Asia responded to the challenges of modernity through two contradictory group. The first one constitutes 'fundamentalists or Fundamental likes' and the other one constitutes 'liberals or reformists'. The fundamentalists emphasize traditional Buddhist virtues with simple and educative principles. They generally misunderstand the nature of the ongoing socio-economic crisis. The reformists, on the other hand, contemplate contemporary

problems and apply new interpretation to Buddhist tenets to
resolve these problems and issues.[92] Thich Nhat Hanh, Sulak
Sivaraksa, Walpola Rahula, Khemadhammo, A.T. Ariyaratne,
and Dhammaghosha belong to the first category while Patricia
Hunt Perry, Paula Green, Joanna Macy, Stephen Batchelor,
Bernard Glassman Roshi, and Robert Thurman are pioneers of
the second group.[93] S.J. Tambiah says that a reinterpretation of
Buddhism was not new because Buddhism was not a static religion
rather it represents historical cumulative movement whose virtues
have been continuously reinterpreted and reconstituted.[94] Many
scholars have criticized Buddhism as an 'other worldly religion'
prompting its followers to choose monkhood to end suffering. Early
Buddhism was totally ignorant about social suffering contrary to
the popular belief that the Buddha was a crusader against socio-
economic disabilities. There is no direct evidence that he fought
against the deteriorating system and engaged himself in any sort
of social revolution.[95] It has been further argued that the Buddha's
dhamma was more *nibbānic* in content which was always aloof
from socio-economic ethics. Some scholars consider Buddhist
socio-economic and political ideas are naive or even harmful
in modern context. While strong socio-economic values have
evolved in the West, and Buddhism has to learn from the West.
Thus, it is an ample opportunity to forge an alliance between two
great traditions.[96] Early Buddhism did not face such precarious
condition. If their teachers were born in such conditions, it was
a bit difficult for them how to respond to cope with the nuclear
age.[97] Aitken Roshi observes that the Buddha did not live in such
difficult situations like today when cut-throat competition and
jealousy among nations threatened to wipe out the world. He was
not aware of the complications developed due to technological-
biological dangers and holocausts.[98] The argument is also on
nature of Buddhism, i.e. as *nibbānic* religion or having enough
content for worldly affairs. One can not debate that Buddhist
teachings cannot provide adequate answers in modern context
and that the Buddha was basically an escapist who wandered in
the forest to end his suffering. Before his *mahābhnishkramana* and
after his *nibbāna*, however, he was very much part of the existing
society and world. The point here is that Buddha is considered
great primarily because he lived in *samsāra* but was not attached

to it. A.T. Ariyaratne thus accepts that 'engaged Buddhism' is not a new phenomenon but reinterpretation of Buddhist virtues in modern perspective.[99] It is consistent with traditional ethics but have eventual attributes of modern thoughts that make it a relatively new form of Buddhism. Rita Gross too argues in support of it, saying:

Buddhism in particular, with its emphasis on silent, motionless meditation practices, is accused of being other-worldly. But this widespread evaluation is, in my view, based on serious misunderstanding of Buddhist ethics regarding social action. Buddhism generally teaches that the first moral agenda is to develop clarity and equanimity one's self, before trying to intervene in or influence society at large. Thus Buddhist emphasis on practices promoting individual transformation is not anti-social or other worldly in any way but instead is aimed at avoiding the self righteous excesses so common inreligions promote activism for all.[100]

Western scholars who have examined Buddhism have learnt it exclusively from manuscripts and texts, especially of philosophy and metaphysics, which have been restricted to the monastic community. But, it would be wiser and more comprehensive to learn the wider spectrum of Buddhism also by other means.[101] The ideas, traditions, and learning could be substantiated with archaeological evidences, living traditions, and cultures which vary from region to region because their socio-economic and spatial conditions were different. It is beyond doubt that the Western education and institutions helped a lot to mould Buddhist engaged movements, but their methodology and practice seems to be truly Asian. The 'ecology monk' movement of Thailand could be compared to the *Chipko Andolan* (Chipko movement) of India that started in the 1970s in Garhwal Himalayas of India with growing awareness towards rapid deforestation. It was the Gandhian style of *satyagraha* and non-violent resistance through hugging of trees to protect them from being cut. The movement was pioneered by Sundar Lal Bahuguna and by the 1980s it spread throughout India which led to people-oriented policy regarding forest and environment. Sarvodaya Shramadana of Sri Lanka had a wide impact of Gandhian *sarvodaya* and *satyagraha*. Gandhi used the term *satyagraha* for the universal upliftment of people or for progress for all. Samdech Preah Mahaghoshananda of Cambodia combined this Gandhian ideology with the iconic *dhammayatra* of

Aśoka. His stay for a research degree in Nālandā in India led to some learning about the techniques and methodology of anti-colonial movements in India. Ghosananda did not acknowledge the difference between traditional Buddhist practice and social action. He started *dhammayatra* to transform Cambodia from a war ravaged nation to a developed nation through rehabilitation, socio-economic planning, forestation programmes, and removal of landmines.[102]

Environmentalism received another fillip when ideas of a deep and shallow ecology stormed academics in the 1970s. In 1973, the Norwegian philosopher Arne Naess described the notion of deep ecology in his article 'The Shallow and the Deep: Long Range Ecology Movement' as a wider process to rethink modern approaches to science, technology, and economics. Deep Ecology transforms us from an individual to an integral constituent of the earth along with other sentient.[103] Naess has given the following outlines for the practice of deep ecology: (a) overrule anthropocentric individualism, (b) biospheric egalitarianism, (c) diversity and symbiosis, (d) anti-class posture, (e) combat against pollution and resource depletion, (f) complexity but avoid complication, and (g) autonomy and decentralization.[104] He seeks biocentric equality with a firm belief in egalitarianism in which all communities, biotic and abiotic, have the right to live and flourish. He also accepts the pragmatism that necessitates some killing and suppression for survival of humankind. This gives rise to biocentrism that looks beyond traditional anthropocentrism. The System Theory and Gaia Theory are two main domains of deep ecology. The first considers a system where each segment is a whole that is more than the sum of its parts and is also itself a part of a larger system.[105] The Gaia Theory is an extension of the System Theory, covering the whole planet; it treats all animates on the Earth as a whole. It is also a part of a larger system with the whole being like a super life form known as Gaia, from the name of Greek goddess of the Earth.[106] Aldo Leopold extended this ethics to land and its relation to man, animals, and plants, christening it 'land ethic' with an intension to enlarge the community by including soil, water, plants and animals collectively known as land.[107] It reforms the role of *Homo sapiens* from the conqueror of the land to the protector with an action to preserve integrity, stability, and beauty of the biotic community.[108] It is said that humans are so prejudiced about their own species that they do not care about the needs and interests of others. Human ethical concern is so limited that it is difficult to bring in animates and inanimates into their moral framework. Animals are not capable of consciously showing their pleasure and pain but their feelings as visible when courting and mating. It is thus anthropocentric to view the value of different lives in a hierarchical manner.[109] The deep ecology movement has been criticized on the basis that if all sentient being are considered equal then dreadful insects will be equal to humans and this will adversely threaten the whole civilization. Parker says that unwanted anthropocentrism has deplorable consequences for the non-human world but a blind misanthropic ecocentrism is also no less deplorable.[110] Total egalitarianism to which every being has an absolutely equal right is not possible. Human chauvinism is incorrigible and some logical means in the form of environmentalism is necessary. Though there is asymmetry between humans and non-humans, the treatment to non-humans should not be based on chauvinist prejudice.

The engaged Buddhists prefer and popularize their traditions to get some positive response for environmentalism. The seed was sown by Joanna Macy and Deane Curtin who used Buddhist texts and traditions to counter the anthropocentric world view. Macy says that the conventional notion of the 'self' should be the ecological self or the eco-self, co-extensive with other beings, and the life of our planet. She terms it as 'the greening of the self' and further argues that the ecological self is arising

... because of three converging developments. First, the conventional small self, or ego-self is being impinged upon by the psychological and spiritual effects we are suffering from facing the dangers of mass annihilation. The second thing working to dismantle the ego-self is a way of seeing that has arisen out of science itself. It is called the systems view, cybernetics, or a new paradigm science. From this perspective, life is seen as dynamically composed of self-organizing systems, patterns that are sustained in and by their relationships. The third force is the resurgence in our time of non dualistic spiritualities. Here I am speaking from my experience with Buddhism.[111]

Macy admits that "the abstraction of a separate 'I' is an epistemological fallacy of the Western civilization", as proved by scientific inquiry, and cites:

Contemporary science and system science in particular, goes farther in challenging old assumptions about a distinct, separate, continuous self, by showing that there is no logical or scientific basis for construing one part of experienced world as 'me' and the rest as 'other'. That is so because as open, self-organizing systems, our breathing, acting and thinking arise in interaction with our shared world through the currents of matter, energy and information that move through us and sustain us. In the web of relationships that sustain these activities there is no clear line demarcating a separate, continuous self.[112]

To popularize their idea, John Seed and Joanna Macy developed the 'Council of All Beings' as a way to introduce people to the concept of deep ecology. The council facilitates rituals for expressing our grief over the loss of many species and imparts lessons to people to speak for other beings with compassion.[113] John Seed says that humanity became highly insensitive to Nature because of the Judaeo-Christian tradition that believes in human supremacy and treat others as a resource for human utilization. The primitive rituals and traditions are considered as redundant and superstitious but these were evolved to co-exist with Nature.[114] Macy uses rituals, visual programmes, and *vipassana* meditation to help people remove narrow anthropocentric ideas and to connect with Nature. She started 'Nuclear Guardianship Project' that flourished between 1991 and 1994 to preach about nuclear hazards and disasters and also the ill-effects of nuclear wastes and radioactivity.[115] It was a network of people grouped together to draft nuclear policies and practices. Macy filed a petition against Virginia Electric Power Company in 1978 but unfortunately lost the legal battle. In this protest, the slogan—'Not In My Backyard (NIMBY) Syndrome'—became rather popular.[116] In 1974, Gary Snyder too criticized the nuclear policies and techniques of nuclear waste management and Kenneth Kraft followed suit with his talks about nuclear ecology for safe disposal of nuclear wastes.[117] By then it had become evident that its mismanagement could lead to disaster and thus proper management heads like radiation ecology and industrial ecology were required.[118] Thich Nhat Hanh too opined that it is the most destructive kind of garbage to grapple with since it percolates in our daily life and if no remedy is provided then it will be impossible for the Earth to future generation.[119] In solving nuclear wastes problem, Kraft talked of researches in locally available energy sources to suggest sustainable alternative.[120] His Holiness the Dalai Lama also protested and advised to abandon altogether the nuclear policy for manufacturing atomic weapon.[121]

In Thailand, environmentalism began like a national uprising in response to the Thai Government's aggressive development agenda. Early industrial development of Thailand was planned on forest-based industries and excessive logging by the companies that led to massive deforestation. Its repercussion could be seen in the Thai society in the form of floods, droughts, and famines. The forest cover in Thailand dwindled from 72 per cent of total land in 1938 to 53 per cent in 1961, and further down to 29 per cent in 1985. In 2003, it was discovered that forest cover does not exceed beyond 15 per cent of the total area of Thailand.[122] Local people living in forests and peripheral areas were blamed for the flood due to their primitive shifting cultivation. It was recommended that these people should be rehabilitated and engaged in more productive and environment-friendly pursuits.[123] However, people have been living in forests since thousands of years and their livelihood and habitation were strictly on nature-man-spirit complex which endures sustainable life and mutual respect. Scholars and Philosophers soon realized that it was not crude tribalism but ill-conceived industrialization that was responsible for the damage. This can be understood as the seed of environmentalism in Thailand. In the nineteenth century, consequently, King Mongkut or Rama IV (1851–68) globalized Thai economy and accentuated Buddhist *saṃgha* to legitimize his plans for development. Thai plans for development are based on: (a) *thammathud* in which monks were sent as missionaries to politically fragile and economically backward border provinces, and (b) *thammacarik* through which monks were assigned function of public welfare to work among minority hill people for transforming them from animism to Buddhism and integrate them into national main stream. When National Economic and Social Development Board of Thailand conceived the first National Economic Development Plan in 1961, the government banned Buddhist monks propagating *santtuthi* as a virtue of life because they believed that it would hurt the rising market demand, consumerism, and consequently industrialization. Some monks argued against the government's plea and asserted that the teachings of the Buddha could contribute to real human progress based on *prajna* rather than material accumulation.[124] Some of the monks who were working in the rural areas realized that various development programmes of the Thai government was not oriented to the real development and they therefore resented these plans. Their heightened consciousness for the nation caused widespread protests in Thailand, first in the 1970s as the 'development monks' (*phranak phatthana*) and then in the 1980s as the 'ecology monks' (*phranak anuraksa*).[125] The 'Development Monks' contemplated the adverse impact of growing consumerism and advocated the dependence of agricultural community on market forces. They envisaged new policies and programmes for rural community conducive to their local requirements and demands. Phra Dhammadilok founded a non-government organization, called 'Foundation for Education and Development of Rural Areas', in 1974 in Chiang Mai for exploring possibilities of sustainable development without endangering forest and economic resources.[126] The first incident happened in 1985 when Thai monks protested against the government's proposal to build a cable car in the Doi Suthep Hills to connect Doi Suthep, an important pilgrimage centre with relics of the Buddha, and Pui National Park in Chiang Mai. Phra Phothirangsi, head of *saṃgha* of Chiang Mai protested against installation of cable car by articulating link between preservation of the forest and Buddhism.[127] Environmentalism received a major boost in 1988 when the Thai government decided to shelve the project of Nam Choen in the Kanchanaburi province after a strong protest from the Thai monks, local groups, farmers, and foreign environmentalists.[128] When logging companies did not stop cutting of forests, Phrakhru Manas Natheepitak, abbot of Wat Bodharma in northern Thailand, organized a passive resistance programme in 1988 but that did not yield any result. Subsequently Natheepitak came up with the idea of a tree ordination to protect the forest.[129] The *saṃgha* authorities reprimanded Manas for deviating Theravāda practices but he argued that people must have the privilege of managing their local resources and the teachings of the Buddha was subsequently drawn upon here to protect forests and the interest of the people.[130]

Seth Devere Clippard locates two different strategies applied by the protagonists of Buddhist environmentalists in Thailand, one being textual and the other applied.[131] The Thai environmental activist, Ajahn Pongsak Techathamamoo, started engaging the monks in the 1980s in rural areas to restore the forest surroundings after decades of ill-conceived deforestation. Such engaged Buddhism in Thailand started the ordination of trees which was wrapped in saffron robes to signify their status as that of a monk. The first tree ordination was performed by Natheepitak in 1988 in a response to a drought caused by excessive logging that adversely affected the rivers and the indigenous eco-system. His effort was fruitful and the Thai government subsequently imposed ban on logging.[132] Phrakhru Pitak Nanthakhun, a prominent ecology monk, started forest preservation programme in Nan province of Thailand in 1975. He initiated mass awareness schemes by educating people in his village Kew Muang and began development works like construction of roads, reservoirs, opening of cooperative shops, and reforestation programmes. When he learnt about Natheepitak's programme, he gave it a new form by combining *khaa paa* (kathina-like ceremony in Thailand) with tree ordination (*buat ton mai*). In 1991, he performed his first ordination ceremony in Kew Muang and in the following year at the Pong watershed area.[133] Susan Darligton who attended the ceremony wrote that the aim of ceremony was to make the people aware of environment degradation and revival of forest with the help of the Buddha's teachings, emphasizing upon the relationship between the Buddha and Nature and the interdependence between forest and human with this kindred saying—*Tham Laay paa khee tham laay chaat* (To destroy the forest is to destroy the nation).[134] She explained extensively about 'ecology monks' who actively engaged in conservation activities and responded to suffering that environmental degradation causes. The preferences of these monks were to preserve the resources of vanishing forests, water sources, and wildlife to mitigate the negative consequences of their disappearance from people's lives. She studied the life of Nanthakhun who adopted the practice of tree ordination and applied in different manner by citing the examples of basic tenets of the Buddha such as *paticcasamuppada* that highlights a close relationship of man with the forest.[135]

These environmental movements have many dimensions imbedded into material and ideological virtues. The focus is on multifaceted ideas coherent with certain socio-economic issues covering legitimization of resources.[136] The 'ecology monks' protect forests by performing rituals and ordinations on the trees with an ecological interpretation. In spite of their small numbers and restricted approach, their efforts paved the way for a broader based environmentalism in Thailand. Sulak Sivaraksa uses the term 'interdependent' in place of 'dependent origination' and propounds that the doctrine of interdependent co-arising is the beginning of Buddhist understanding of Nature.[137] Ideologically, Thai environmentalism is more Theravāda-oriented but modified, adjusted, and transformed for proper engagement of Buddhist virtues with modern problems like environmentalism, deforestation, and global warming. The practice of 'ordination of tree', the most popular ritual adopted by the monks, itself was not coherent with the Theravāda practices because trees cannot be given *pabajja*. But for mass appeal and fast propaganda of Buddhist environmentalism, certain Buddhist monks adopted this mechanism even against the wishes of the Thai Buddhist *saṃgha*. Some monks were punished for breaking the rules of the *saṃgha*. The Thai government and supporting *saṃgha* was initially adamant to support industrialization which was heavily based on logging companies. When Phra Prajak Kuttajitto, a monk of Dong-yai Forest in north-east Thailand, performed tree ordination in 1989, he was threatened with imprisonment and was forced to disrobe.[138] In 1991, Nanthakhun organised tree ordination ceremony in Nan province. In May 1993 again, a ceremony was performed by the monks to rejuvenate the life of Nan River. They organized a conference to highlight the problems of global warming and pollution. A fish sanctuary was established at the site of the ceremony and by 1999, over 39 community forests and 100 fish sanctuaries have been established by Nanthakun's non-government organization 'Love Nan Province Foundation'.[139] Phrakhru, in his effort to resist eucalyptus plantation, also started 'Love for Nan River Project'.[140] Phra Somkit, another monk innovated a new method to restrict deforestation around his village. In 1990, he adopted *bindbat* practice for forest regeneration which is traditionally practice of alms giving by laities to earn merit. His intention was to demonstrate to fellow villagers the benefits of traditional agriculture without endangering any natural resources.[141] These non-violent *satyagraha* technique adopted by the Thai monks remind us of the pan-Asian impact of *satyagraha* and 'boycott movement' adopted by Mahatma Gandhi during the anti-colonial non-cooperation movement (*Asahayog Andolana*) in India against the British government in the 1920s.

Swearer examined the activities of the monks, Buddhadasa and Phrayudha,who were related to the *bodhirukkha* movement in Thailand. Buddhadasa's ecological view identifies *dhamma* with Nature while Phrayudha focuses on the life of the Buddha and the traditional *samgha* as an exemplification of the Buddhist attitude towards Nature.[142] Sulak Sivaraksa encouraged environmentalism founded on fundamental Buddhist principles. The aim of such movements was to initiate Buddhist economics with pragmatic programmes to regenerate depleting forests. The Thai monk, Pongsak Tejadhamma, started ordination of tree with strict the *Vinaya* rules in Chiang Mai province of Thailand with a number of monks.[143] They were, however, criticized from within and outside the *samgha* that such ordination is not conducive to Buddhist tenets.[144] Tree ordination was considered inappropriate because the symbolic ritual was performed to make people aware of forest conservation and monks were doing it symbolically, and not claiming the full ordination.[145] Clippard states that 'linguistic analogy' was used by the 'ecology monks' for practical purpose.

The monk is the signifier, the tree is signified, and the ordination is the signification. On the one hand, the meaning of ordination is roughly same regardless of signified. On the other hand, the statement in which the tree is signified produces radically different effect on the listener for whom the signification (ordination) is meaningful. The signified, having been modified by signification, challenges the listener to adjust his/her relationship to the signified in the light of new semantic values attached to the signified. That is, the members of the Buddhist community are challenged to understand what an ordained tree means.[146]

Regardless of debate on the 'ecology monks' in Thailand, they managed to create awareness on environmentalism and also offer methods and tools to implement to ideas of saving the environment, best exemplified by Phrakhru Manas.

If a tree is wrapped in saffron robes, no one would dare cut it down. So I thought that perhaps this idea could be used to discourage logging, and I began performing ceremonies on trees in the forest near the temple. I called the ritual an 'ordination' to give it more weight. The term 'tree ordination' sounds weird to Thai people since an ordination is a ritual applied only to men. This weirdness has helped spread the news by word of mouth.[147]

In 1958, A.T. Ariyaratne started, *Sarvodaya*, in Sri Lanka with a small band of young followers based on the Buddhist ideas of loving-kindness, compassion, sympathetic joy, and equanimity, and their self-help groups were active in 4,000 towns and villages. It began with an intention to rediscover Buddhist heritage, and act with compassion towards socio-economic causes.[148] It was influenced by two great idols, Gandhi and Anagarika Dhammapala. Led by Mahatma Gandhi, the movement gave the Sri Lankan society a fundamental orientation about selfless service for humanity as the highest form of religious practice, a non-violent socio-economic order covering ordinary activities of common people, and the zeal to concentrate work in rural areas to establish a new socio-economic and religious order.[149] Anagarika Dhammapala accepts Buddhism as a 'gospel of activity' and the Buddha as an engaged Buddhist deeply involved in human welfare.[150] He denounced all monastic interpretations that impelled monks to be aloof from the society, and criticized traditional Theravāda path for laity to bank on rituals for acquaintance of merit of rebirth.[151] Sarvodaya's vision is sustainable development without eroding the socio-cultural fabric of the society and so it has been involved in health, sanitation, education, agriculture and rural economy. Ariyaratne was highly critical of development model adopted by both socialist and capitalist forms of the governments because development programmes will not be effective without cultural and spiritual values.[152] The philosophy of *Sarvodaya* is based on compassionate action, altruistic joy, equanimity as well as pleasant speech and friendly treatment with people of different origin and ethnicity.[153] The *Sarvodaya* movement revitalized the rural life and folk culture of Sri Lanka by initiating not only the development projects but also working as conflict resolution model to resolve conflicts among various warring groups for progress and peace.

In the war-ravaged society of Vietnam, Thich Nhat Hanh encouraged the Buddhist community to practice harmony and awareness in the society and offered meditation retreats for environmentalists. He founded the *Tiep Hien* order (Order of Inter Being) in Vietnam to preach 14 guiding principles of social justice, peace and ecological issues. The word *Tiep* means 'to be in touch with' and *Hien* means immediate realization. Thich Nhat Hanh belongs to the 42nd generation of the Lam Te (Lin Chi) School of Zen and the eight generation of the Lieu Quan School of Zen. He initiated engaged mission in two way: first by adopting psychological approach with the help of *Abhidhamma* to solve the problems of internal strife and to restore peace by reliving the suffering from inside and second, through regulation of the Buddhist approach to harmony and peace and Buddhist spirit of reverence of life.[154] He recommends that ecology in Buddhism should be deep ecology and also universal because there is also pollution in our consciousness.[155] Hanh suggests a coping mechanism by recitation of the *gāthās* and his poetry is praise of Nature.

I entrust myself to Buddha
Buddha entrust himself to me
I entrust myself to earth:
Earth entrusts himself to me.[156]

When one's mind concentrate on the *gāthās*, it becomes more aware about one's action and when the *gāthā* ends, the action continues with much awareness and promptness. The *gāthās* of Hanh reminds us about their responsibilities towards environmentalism.

Water flows from high in the mountains.
Water runs deep in the earth.
Miraculously, water comes to us,
and sustains all life.[157]

W.S. Yokoyama in his essay 'Circling the Mountain' studied the engaged Buddhist tradition in Japan. He argues that the Buddhist meditation can be instrumental for preservation and development of an environment-friendly society. He rejects the idea of meditation as a mindless mystical trance and calls it a profound technique that develops mental calmness and reduces mental dullness and anxiety. To substantiate his points he takes three examples of Buddhist life in Japan: (a) the Tendai Monastery, (b) the Zen Temple, and (c) the Shin Home.[158] The Tendai Monastery, situated on Mt. Hiei, is a ritualistic institution where pilgrims come for a thousand-day pilgrimage. The pilgrims take ardous walks to the monastery despite hostile climatic conditions to reach at a point where one enters in a realm of oneness with Nature. This continues for thousand days and as the practice deepens, one enters into communion with the benign beauty of the universe, its forests, rocks, and flowers.[159] He cites his second example from the gathering of lay followers on every Sunday morning in a Zen temple. They not only listen to religious discourses but also discuss the general problems of the society. The environmental concern was a major issue for them.[160] The Zen masters use *koan* (puzzle) to examine the intellectual depth of the students in order to make them aware about current environmentalism. Yokoyama's third example is from the Shin Temple family who have strong feeling for their religion and belong to the agricultural community of Japan. Their Buddha is a dynamic force working for their salvation and is engaged in helping others. The Shin emphasizes on the individual to consider their action in an appropriate manner because in the environmentally-compromised world the human action is an important tool to bear that they needed to maintain harmony with Nature.[161]

Gary Sherman Snyder has been acknowledged as a poet laureate of deep ecology. He was influenced by Buddhism, especially Mahāyāna Buddhism. With his innovative style, he composed eco-poetries dealing with modern environmental problems and eco-ethics, and permeated by the spirit of Japanese *Haiku* poetry.[162] His poem 'Mother Earth' speaks for a radical change in our conventional way of thinking and living to save the Earth. His monumental work *Mountain and Rivers without End* was a combination of lyrical and epic, celebrating virtues and piousness of the planet Earth.[163] His poems like *Reprop* and *The Cold Mountain Poems* show his interconnectedness with Nature. He relies on consciousness of Nature and endures Hua-yen philosophy, viz., 'all is one and the same time all is many'.[164] Snyder says that Dogen's attitude towards environment has been found not only in a literary context but also in Vajrayāna iconography which personifies:

Mountain and Water is the rupas–images of Fudo Myoo (Immovable Wisdom King) and kannon Bosatsu (The Bodhisattva who watches the waves), Fudo is almost comically ferocious looking with a blind eye and a fang, seated or standing on a slab of rock and enveloped in flames. He is known as an ally of Mountain ascetics. Kannon (Kuan-yin, Avalokitesvara) gracefully leans forward with her lotus and vase of water, a figure of compassion. The two are seen as 'Buddha–work partners: ascetic, discipline, and relentless spirituality balanced by compassionate tolerance and detached forgiveness. Mountains and waters are dyad that together make wholeness possible.[165]

John Daido Loori says that Dogen was a great inspirator of Nature who established his monastery in the deep mountains on the banks of the nine-headed Dragon River. Dogen accepts mountains and rivers as *dhammadhatu* and *saṁsāric* cycle, and composed majority of his work on the cliff of a mountain. Taking inspiration from Dogen's environmental views, Loori founded *Mountain and River Order* near a mountain with a cross section of two rivers, the Esopus and the Beaverkill.[166] Snyder also cultivates the bridge between the East and the West, and his poetic identification with Nature was influenced by *Hua-yen* School. His view on Nature represents the transition of idea from anthropocentricism to consideration for all living beings including non-humans.[167] He argues that intense and aggressive technological progress and scientific inquiry have nurtured anthropogenic activities that are harmful to Nature.[168] His poetry too was influenced by the *Haiku* poetry of Zen Buddhism and he preaches environmental deterioration. *Smokey the Bear Sutra* is among his famous poems reflecting serious environmental concerns. The first stanza of the poem shows his attachment with Nature and the planet.

Once in the Jurassic, about 150 million years ago
The great Sun Buddha in this corner of the Infinite
Void gave a great Discourse to all the assembled elements
And energies; to the standing beings, the walking beings,
The flying beings, and the setting beings-even grasses,
To the number of thirteen billion, each one born from a
Seed, assembled there: a discourse concerning
Enlightenment on the planet earth.

Towards the last, he says, *Namah samanta vajranam chanda maharoshana, sphataya hum traka ham mam* (I dedicated myself to the universal diamond be this raging fury destroyed to protect those who love woods and rivers, gods and animals, hoboes and madmen, prisoners and sick, people, musians, playful women, and hopeful children).[169] Another engaged Buddhist, Robert Aitken, believes in togetherness and working of the Buddhist communities to establish an alternative society. He founded the Diamond Saṃgha of Hawaii and started the Buddhist Peace fellowship in 1978, to encourage awareness programmes for ecology-based on social and economic development.

The Buddhist ecological movements and programmes suggest that there is no uniform and coherent ecological movement worldwide. Each of these movements emerges in a particular historical context when industrialization and development are confronted with the traditional socio-economic structure which erodes the natural resources. They intend to confront with the system by suggesting alternative models and policies. Each of these movements has the willingness to confront the system by suggesting alternative models and policies. The method could be best summarized by the three 'Ps'—preaching, petition, and protest. The monks and laities engaged in environmentalism speak of deforestation, and global warming at conferences, and meditation camps. Through petition, they attract the attention of government, media, and affected parties. Finally, they protest against harmful policies and practices adopted by government and industries. The important aspect of these ecological movements is the analytical construction of the problems with their proper solutions that permits to preserve common but different socio-religious stirrings throughout Buddhist Asia and in some parts of the West. These movements may share some essential features with traditional Buddhism, and contain enough substantive differences unique to the modern era. Such movements offer a unique interpretation of traditional Buddhism. Their most distinct innovation is the tendency to interpret Buddhist teachings in *saṁsāric* terms which suggests a kind of mundane awakening that has moral, cultural, economic, and political dimensions. These movements comprise a wide range of individuals from diverse political background who are inspired by Buddhist values and the common cause of environmentalism and global warming.[170] These movements demonstrate scientific progress and is meant to serve the real needs of the people, not the demands of markets or any economic system. It establishes a new type of relationship between people and Nature that is based on cooperation, not of exploitation. It encourages one to replace mutual antagonism with solidarity and cooperation.

Notes

1. G.P. Marsh, *Man and Nature*, New York: Scribner, repr., 1965, p. 9.
2. Charles Birch and John B. Cobb, Jr., *The Liberation of Life: From the Cell to the Community*, Denton, TX: Environmental Ethics Books, 1990, pp. 1–3.
3. John Passamore, *Man's Responsibility for Nature: Ecological Problems and Western Traditions*, London: Duckworth and Co., 1974, pp. 27–9.
4. Peter Timmerman, 'Western Buddhism and the Global Crisis', in *Dharma Rain: Sources of Buddhist Environmentalism*, ed. Stephanie Kaza and Kenneth Kraft, Boston: Shambhala, 2000, pp. 357–68.
5. Thomas S. Kuhn, *The Copernican Revolution: Planetary Astronomy in the Development of Western Thought*, New York: Random House, 1959, p. 2.
6. Bijoy H. Boruah, 'Environmental Wisdom', in *Readings in Environmental Ethics: Multidisciplinary Perspective*, ed. D.C. Srivastava, Delhi: Rawat Publications, 2005, pp. 22–8.
7. Timmerman, 'Western Buddhism and the Global Crisis', pp. 361–2.
8. Frank Thilly, *A History of Philosophy*, Allahabad: Central Publication House, 2007, pp. 56–7.
9. S.A. Shaida, 'Environmental Ethics: A Historical-Intellectual Background', in *Readings in Environmental Ethics: Multidisciplinary Perspectives*, ed. D.C. Srivastava, Delhi: Rawat Publications, 2005, pp. 3–13.
10. Jonathan Howard, *Darwin: A Very Short Introduction*, Delhi: Oxford University Press, 1982, pp. 25–6.
11. Thilly, *A History of Philosophy*, pp. 216–27.
12. Ibid., pp. 256–8.
13. Ibid., pp. 274–5.
14. Ibid., pp. 346–8.
15. Ibid., pp. 356–8.
16. John Rawls, *A Theory of Justice*, London: OUP, 1973, p. 60.
17. William Ophuls, 'Notes for a Buddhist Politics', in *Dharma Rain: Sources of Buddhist Environmentalism*, ed. Stephanie Kaza and Kenneth Kraft, Boston: Shambhala, 2000, pp. 369–78.
18. Padmasiri de Silva, *Buddhism, Ethics and Society: The Conflict and Dilemmas of Our Time*, Clayton: Monash Asia Institute, 2002, p. 26.

19. Andrew Goudie, *The Human Impact: On the Natural Environment*, Oxford: Basic Blackwell Ltd., 1990, pp. 4–8.
20. Dhruvasen Singh and Ajai Mishra, 'Gangotri Glacier Characteristics, Retreat and Processes of Sedimentation in the Bhagirathi Valley', *Natural Symposium on the Role of Earth Science in Integrated Development and Related Societal Issues*, Geological Survey of India Spl, no. 65, 2001, pp. 17–20.
21. Oswald Spenglar, *The Decline of the West*, New York: Oxford University Press, 1991, p. x.
22. Timmerman, 'Western Buddhism and the Global Crisis', pp. 359–62.
23. Ibid., pp. 363–4.
24. James E. Lovelock, *Gaiya: A New Look at Life on Earth*, New York: Oxford University Press, 1979, pp. 152–3. (The Gaia hypothesis proposes that organisms interact with their inorganic surroundings on Earth to form a self-regulating complex system that contributes to maintaining the conditions for life on the planet.)
25. Elizabeth Roberts, 'Gaian Buddhism', in *Dharma Gaia: A Harvest of Essays in Buddhism and Ecology*, ed. Allan Hunt Badiner, Berkeley: Parallax Press, 1990, pp. 147–54.
26. J. Baird Callicott, 'Conceptual Resources for Environmental Ethics in Asian Traditions of Thought: A Propaedeutic', *Philosophy East West*, 1987, vol. 37, no. 2, pp. 115–30.
27. Ibid., p. 117.
28. Ian L. McHarg, *Design with Nature*, New York: Doubleday and Co., 1969, p. 26.
29. Callicott, 'Conceptual Resources for Environmental Ethics in Asian Traditions of Thought', pp. 118, 128 [J. Baired Callicott has mentioned that after the writings of Ian McHarg and Lynn White, Jr., a flood of apologetic literature was written to support Judaeo-Christian views such as Francis A. Shaeffer's *Pollution and the Death of Man: The Christian View of Ecology* (Wheaton, IL: Tyndale House, 1971), Albert J. Fritsch's *Environmental Ethics: Choices for Concerned Citizen* (Garden City, New York: Anchor Books, 1980), and John Passmore's *Man's Responsibility for Nature: Ecological Problem and Western Tradition* (London: Duckworth and Co., 1974].
30. Lynn White Jr., 'The Historical Roots of Our Ecological Crisis', *Science*, n.s., 1967, pp. 1203–7.
31. Ibid., p. 1206.
32. James M. Gustafson, *A Sense of Divine: The Natural Environment From a Theocentric Perspective*, Cleveland: Pilgrim Press, 1994.
33. Donald K. Swearer, 'An Assessment of Buddhist Eco Philosophy', *Harvard Theological Review*, vol. 99, no. 2, 2006, pp. 123–37.
34. Ibid., pp. 125–8.
35. Ian Harris, 'Buddhism and Ecology', in *Contemporary Buddhist Ethics*, ed. Damien Keown, Surrey: Curzon Press, 2000, pp. 113–37.
36. Lambert Schmithausen, *Buddhism and Nature*, Tokyo: The International Institute of Buddhist Studies, 1991, p. 11.

37. Swearer, 'An Assessment of Buddhist Eco Philosophy', pp. 129–30.

38. E.F. Shumacher, *Small is Beautiful: A Study of Economics as if People Mattered*, New York: Harper and Row, 1973, p. 56.

39. Donald K. Swearer, 'Principles and Poetry, Places and Stories: The Resources of Buddhist Ecology', *Daedalus*, vol. 30, no. 4, 2001, pp. 225–41.

40. Seth Devere Clippard, 'The Lorax Wears Saffron: Towards a Buddhist Environmentalism', *Journal of Buddhist Ethics*, 2011, pp. 12, 211–45.

41. Ian Harris, 'Causation and Telos: The Problem of Buddhist Environmental Ethics', *Journal of Buddhist Ethics*, vol. 1, 1994, pp. 46–59. (Ian Harris develops his idea on Buddhist ecology on basis of Laurel Kearns assumption of tripartite typology on Christian ecological studies, i.e. 'eco-spirituality', 'eco-justice', and 'eco-traditionalism'. Ian Harris, 'Getting the Grip with Buddhist Environmentalism: A Provisional Typology', *Journal of Buddhist Ethics*, vol. 2, 1995, pp. 173–90. Tenzin Gyatso, His Holiness, the 14th Dalai Lama, 'A Tibetan Buddhist Perspective on Spirit in Nature', in *Spirit and Nature-Why the Environment is a Religious Issue*, ed. Steven C. Rockefeller and John C. Elder, Boston: Becon Press, 1992, pp. 109–23.)

42. Ibid., pp. 46–7. (According to Harris, the main exponents of this school are Noritoshi Aramaki, *Shizen-hakai kara-sasei e-Rekeshi no tenkai ni tsuiti (From Destruction of Nature to Revival of Nature: On a Historical Conversion)*, ed. Desai, vols. I–II, 1992, pp. 3–22; Joanna Macy, 'The Greening of Self', in *Dharma Gaia: A Harvest of Essays in Buddhism and Ecology*, ed. Allan Hunt Badiner, Berkely: Parallex Press, 1990, pp. 53–63; Brian Brown, 'Towards a Buddhist Ecological Cosmology', *Bucknell Review*, vol. 37, no. 2, 1993, pp. 124–37.)

43. Lambert Schmithausen, *Buddhism and Nature* and *The Problems of the Sentience of Plants in Early Buddhism*, Studia Philologica Studia, VI, Tokyo: The International Institute of Buddhist Studies, 1991.

44. Noriaki Hakamaya, *Shizen-hihan to-shite no Bukkyo (Buddhism as a criticism of Physis/Natura)*, *Komazaw-daigaku Bukk Yoogakabu Romshooo*, vol. 21, 1990, pp. 280–4.

45. Pragati Sahni, *Environmental Ethics in Buddhism: A Virtue Approach*, London: Routledge, 2012, p. 12.

46. Lily de Silva, 'The Hill Wherein My Soul Delights', in *Buddhism and Ecology*, ed. Martin Batchelor and Kerry Brown, Delhi: MLBD, 1994, pp. 17–30.

47. Ibid., pp. 25–30.

48. Ibid., pp. 19–21. (Lily de Silva cites *Anguttara Nikāya* which mentions Mt. Sineru with a depth of 1,84,000 leagues and emerges above the sea level up to 84,000 leagues. It was a classic symbol of stability and steadfastness but which was destroyed by heat without leaving even ashes at a time when multiple suns shone. *Anguttara Nikāya*, vol. IV, p. 100.)

49. Ibid., pp. 22–3.

50. Stephen Batchelor, 'The Sands of the Ganges: Notes Towards a Buddhist Ecological Philosophy', in *Buddhism and Ecology*, ed. Martine Batchelor and Kerry Brown, Delhi: MLBD, 1994, pp. 31–40.

51. Stephen Batchelor, 'Buddhist Economics Reconsidered', in *Dharma Gaia: A Harvest of Essays in Buddhism and Ecology*, ed. Allan Hunt Badiner, Berkeley: Parallax Press, 1990, pp. 178–82.
52. Martine Batchelor, 'Even the Stones Smile', in *Buddhism and Ecology*, ed. Martine Batchelor and Kerry Brown, Delhi: MLBD, 1994, pp. 1–17.
53. Padmasiri de Silva, *Environmental Philosophy and Ethics in Buddhism*, London: Macmillan, 1998, pp. 23–5.
54. Ibid., p. 24.
55. Ibid., p. 26.
56. Prayudh Payutto, 'Buddhist Solutions for Twenty-first Century', in *Dharma Rain: Sources of Buddhist Environmentalism*, ed. Stephanie Kaza and Kenneth Kraft, Boston: Shambhala, 2000, pp. 171–5.
57. Sulak Sivaraksa, 'Buddhism with a Small b', in *Dharma Rain: Sources of Buddhist Environmentalism*, ed. Stephanie Kaza and Kenneth Kraft, Boston: Shambhala, 2000, pp. 117–24.
58. Sulak Sivaraksa, 'Development as If People Mattered', in *Dharma Rain: Sources of Buddhist Environmentalism*, ed. Stephanie Kaza and Kenneth Kraft, Boston: Shambhala, 2000, pp. 181–90.
59. Alan Sponberg, 'The Buddhist Conception of Ecological Self', in *The Sounds of Liberating Truth: Buddhist Christian Dialogues in Honour of Fredrick J. Streng*, ed. Sallie B. King and Paul O. Ingram, Richmond Surrey: Curzon Press, 1999, pp. 107–27.
60. Sulak Sivaraksa, *Conflict, Culture and Change: Engaged Buddhism in a Globalized World*, Somerville: Wisdom Publications, 2005, pp. 71–5.
61. Chatsumarn Kabilsingh, 'Buddhist Monks and Forest Conservation', in *Radical Conservatism: Buddhism in the Contemporary World; Essays in Honour of Bhikkhu Buddhadasa's 84th Birthday*, ed. Sulak Sivaraksa, Bangkok: Sathirakoses–Nagapradipa Foundation, 1990, pp. 301–10.
62. Rita M. Gross, 'Buddhist Resources for Issues of Population, Consumption and the Environment', in *Population Consumption and the Environment*, ed. Harold Coward, Albany: State University of New York, 1995, pp. 291–312.
63. Gross, 'Population, Consumption and Environment', in *Dharma Rain: Sources of Buddhist Environment*, ed. Stephanie Kaza and Kenneth Kraft, Boston: Shambhala, 2000, pp. 409–22.
64. Ibid., pp. 410–11.
65. Ibid., p. 420.
66. Rita M. Gross, 'Toward a Buddhist Environmental Ethic', *Journal of the American Academy of Religion*, vol. 65, no. 2, 1997, pp. 333–53.
67. Ibid., pp. 338–40.
68. Ken Jones, *The Social Face of Buddhism: An Approach to Political and Social Activism*, London: Wisdom, 1992, p. 157.
69. Sponberg, 'The Buddhist Conception of an Ecological Self', pp. 107–27.
70. Harris, 'Causation and Telos', pp. 54–5.
71. Ian Harris, 'Buddhist Environmental Ethics and Detraditionalization: The Case of Eco-Buddhism', *Religion*, vol. 25, no. 3, 1995, pp. 199–211.

72. Sahni, *Environmental Ethics in Buddhism*, p. 27.

73. Ian Harris, 'How Environmental is Buddhism?', *Religion*, vol. 21, 1991, p. 107.

74. Ian Harris, 'Ecological Buddhism?', in *Worldviews, Religion, and the Environment: A Global Anthology*, ed. Richard S. Foltz, Belmont, CA: Wadsworth, 2003, pp. 171–81.

75. Clippard, 'The Lorax Wears Saffron', pp. 13–14.

76. Schmithausen, *Buddhism and Nature*, p. 1.

77. Schmithausen, *The Problem of Sentience of Plants in Earliest Buddhism*, pp. 2–6.

78. Peter Harvey, *An Introduction to Buddhist Ethics*, New York: Cambridge University Press, 2000, pp. 11–30.

79. Paul Waldau, 'Buddhism and Animal Right', in *Contemporary Buddhist Ethics*, ed. Damien Keown, Richmond Surrey: Curzon Press, 2000, pp. 81–112.

80. Paul Waldau, *The Specter of Speciesism: Buddhist and Christian Views of Animals*, Oxford: Oxford University Press, 2001, pp. 35–6.

81. Florin Deleanu, 'Buddhist "Ethology", in Pāli Canon between Symbol and Observation', *The Eastern Buddhist*, vol. 32, no. 2, 2000, pp. 79–127.

82. Malcom David Eckel, 'Is There Buddhist Philosohy of Nature?', in *Buddhism and Ecology: The Interconnection of Dharma and Deeds*, ed. M.E. Tucker and D.R. Williams, Cambridge MA: Harvard University Press, 1997, pp. 327–49.

83. James E. Deitrick, 'Engaged Buddhist Ethics: Mistaking the Boat for Shore', in *Action Dharma: New Studies in Engaged Buddhism*, ed. Christopher Queen, Charles Prebish and Damien Keown, London: Routledge, 2003, pp. 252–69.

84. Christopher S. Queen, 'Introduction: The Shapes and Sources of Engaged Buddhism', in *Engaged Buddhism: Buddhist Liberation Movement in Asia*, ed. Christopher S. Queen and Sallie B. King, Albany: State University of New York, 1996, pp. 23, 30.

85. Kenneth Kraft, *Inner Peace, World Peace: Essays on Buddhism and Non Violence*, Albany: State University of New York, 1992, p. 18.

86. Thomas Freeman Yarnall, 'Engaged Buddhism New and Improved? Made in the USA of Asian Material', in *Action Dharama: New Studies in Engaged Buddhism*, ed. Christopher Queen, Charles Prebish and Damien Keown, London: Routledge, 2003, pp. 286–7.

87. Queen, 'Introduction: The Shapes and Sources of Engaged Buddhism', pp. 7–8.

88. Gananath Obeyesekere, 'Religious Symbolism and Political Change in Ceylon', in *The Two Wheels of Dhamma: Essays on the Theravāda Tradition in India and Ceylon*, ed. Gananath Obeyesekere, Frank Renoyld, and Bardwell L. Smith, Chamberberg: American Academy of Religion, 1972, pp. 63–5.

89. Queen, 'Introduction: The Shapes and Sources of Engaged Buddhism', p. 23.

90. Deitrick, 'Engaged Buddhist Ethics', pp. 253–4.

91. Robert N. Bellah, 'Epilogue: Religion and Progress in Modern Asia', in *Religion and Progress in Modern Asia*, ed. Robert N. Bellah, New York: Free Press, 1965, pp. 201, 210, <http://www.jstor.org/stable/40860347>, accessed on 28 March 2012.

92. Donald K. Swearer, 'Sulak Sivaraksa's Buddhist Vision for Renewing Society', *Crossroads: An Interdisciplinary Journal of Southeast Asian Studies*, vol. 6, no. 2, 1991, pp. 17–57.

93. Yarnall, 'Engaged Buddhism New and Improved?', p. 289.

94. S.J. Tambiah, *World Conqueror and World Renouncer: A Study of Buddhism and Polity in Thailand against a Historical Background*, New York: Cambridge University Press, 1976, p. 217.

95. Joseph M. Kitagawa, 'Buddhism and Social Change: An Historical Perspective', in *Buddhist Studies in Honour of Rahula Walapola*, ed. Somaratna Balasooriya et al., London: Gorden Frazer, 1980, pp. 87–8.

96. Jones, *The Social Face of Buddhism*, pp. 37–8.

97. Fred Eppsteiner, ed., *The Path of Compassion: Writings on Socially Engaged Buddhism*, Berkeley: Parallax Press, 1988, p. 51.

98. Helen Tworkow, *Zen in America: Five Teachers and the Search for an American Buddhism*, New York: Kondansha International, 1994, p. 52.

99. George D. Bond, 'A.T. Ariyaratne and the Sarvodaya Shramadana Movement in Sri Lanka', in *Engaged Buddhism: Buddhist Liberation Movements in Asia*, ed. Christopher S. Queen and Sallie B. King, Albany: State University of New York Press, 1996, pp. 121–46.

100. Gross, 'Toward a Buddhist Environmental Ethics', p. 347.

101. Donald S. Lopez, Jr., *Curators of the Buddha: The Study of Buddhism under Colonialism*, Chicago: University of Chicago Press, 1996, pp. 7–9.

102. Mathew Weiner, 'Mahaghoshananda as a Contemplative Social Activists', in *Action Dharma: New Studies in Engaged Buddhism*, ed. Christopher S. Queen, Charles Prebish and Damien Kewon, London: Routledge, 2003, pp. 110–12.

103. Peter Singer, *Practical Ethics*, Cambridge: Cambridge University Press, 1979, p. 280. (In 1984 Arne Naess and George Session resolved several principles for deep ecology. (a) The well being and flourishing of human and the non-human lives on Earth have value in themselves. These values are independent of the usefulness of non-human world for human purpose. (b) Richness and diversity of life form contribute to the realization of these values and are also values in themselves. (c) Human have no right to reduce this richness and diversity except to satisfy vital needs. Ibid., p. 281.)

104. Arne Naess, 'Deep Ecology', in *Ecology*, ed. Carolyn Merchant, Delhi: Rawat Publications, 1996, p. 120. (John Seed says that 'our technological culture has co-opted and absorbed all other criticism, so that parts may be questioned but not the whole, while deep ecology as foundation of revolutionary thought subjects the care of our social existence and our thinking to piercing scrutiny. Deep ecology recognizes that nothing short

of a total revolution in consciousness will be of lasting use in presence of life support system of our planet.' See John Seed, Joanna Macy, Pat Fleming and Arne Naess, *Think Like a Mountain: Towards a Council of All Beings*, Philadelphia: New Society Publication, 1988, p. 9.)

105. Ibid., pp. 28, 69. (Deep ecology is different from shallow ecology or reformed environmentalism. It recognizes the possibility to carry on usual activities with more careful and rightful attitude while increasing human resources. It takes up environmental problems such as resource depletion and resultant problems from technocratic worldview. Ibid., p. 66.)

106. Ibid., p. 29.

107. Aldo Leopold, 'The Land Ethics', in *Ethics in Practice: An Anthology*, ed. Hugh La Follette, Oxford: Blackwell Publication, 1997, pp. 635–7.

108. Aldo Leopold, *A Sand County Almanac*, Oxford: Oxford University Press, 1949, pp. 224–6.

109. Singer, *Practical Ethics*, pp. 88–9.

110. Kelly A. Parker, 'Pragmatism and Environmental Thought', in *Environmental Pragmatism*, ed. Andrew Light and Eric Katz, London: Routledge, 1996, pp. 33–4.

111. Macy, 'The Greening of the Self', pp. 53, 56.

112. Ibid., p. 58.

113. Bill Devall, 'Deep Ecology and Political Activism', in *Dharma Rain: Sources of Buddhist Environmentalism*, ed. Stephanie Kaza and Kenneth Kraft, Boston: Shambhala, 2000, p. 390.

114. John Seed, 'The Rainforest as Teacher', *Dharma Rain: Sources of Buddhist Environmentalism*, ed. Stephanie Kaza and Kenneth Kraft, Boston: Shambhala, 2000, p. 290.

115. Devall, 'Deep Ecology and Political Activism', p. 387.

116. Joanna Macy, 'Guarding the Earth', in *Dharma Rain: Sources of Buddhist Environmentalism*, ed. Stephanie Kaza and Kenneth Kraft, Boston: Shambhala, 2000, pp. 297–301.

117. Kenneth Kraft, 'Nuclear Ecology and Engaged Buddhism', in *Dharma Rain: Sources of Buddhist Environmentalism*, ed. Stephanie Kaza and Kenneth Kraft, Boston: Shambhala, 2000, pp. 393–5.

118. Ibid., p. 393.

119. Thich Nhat Hanh, 'The Last Tree', in *Dharma Gaia: A Harvest of Essays in Buddhism and Ecology*, ed. Allan Hunt Badiner, Berkeley: Parallex Press, 1990, p. 220.

120. Kraft, 'Nuclear Ecology and Engaged Buddhism', p. 396.

121. Dalai Lama, 'Make Tibet a Zone of Peace', in *Dharma Gaia: A Harvest of Essays in Buddhism and Ecology*, ed. Allan Hunt Badiner, Berkely: Parallex Press, 1990, p. 233.

122. Philippa England, 'UNCED and the Implementation of Forest Policy in Thailand', in *Seeing Forest for Trees: Environment and Environmentalism in Thailand* ed. Philip Hirsch, Chiang Mai: Silkworm Books, 1996, pp. 53–71.

123. Susan M. Darlington, 'Buddhism and Development: The Ecology Monks of Thailand', in *Action Dharma: New Studies in Engaged Buddhism*, ed. Christopher S. Queen, Charles Prebish and Damien Keown, London: Routledge, 2003, pp. 101–2.

124. Pipob Udomittipong, 'Thailand's Ecology Monks', in *Dharma Rain: Sources of Buddhist Environmentalism*, ed. Stephanie Kaza and Kenneth Kraft, Boston: Shambhala, 2000, p. 191.

125. Ibid., pp. 97–9.

126. Rigg Jonathan, 'Counting the Costs: Economic Growth and Environmental Change in Thailand', in *Counting the Costs: Economic Growth and Environmental Change in Thailand*, ed. Rigg Jonathan, Singapore: Institute of Southeast Asian Studies, 1995, pp. 8-9.

127. Suksamran Somboon, 'A Buddhist Approach to Development: The Case of "Development Monks" in Thailand', in *Reflections on Development in Southeast Asia*, ed. Lim Tech Ghee, Singapore: ASEAN Economic Research Unit, Institute of Southeast Asian Studies, 1988, pp. 26–48.

128. Chayant Pholpoke, 'The Chiang Mai Cable Car Project: Local Controversy over Cultural and Eco-Tourism', in *The Politics of Environment in Southeast Asia: Resource and Resistance*, ed. Philip Hirsch and Carol Warren, London: Routledge, 1998, pp. 262–77.

129. Susan M. Darlington, 'The Ordination of a Tree: The Buddhist Ecology Movement in Thailand', *Ethnology*, vol. 37, no. I, 1998, pp. 1–15.

130. Udomittipong, 'Thailand's Ecology Monk', pp. 193–5.

131. Clippard, 'The Lorax Wears Saffron', p. 12.

132. Susan M. Darlington, 'The Good Buddha and the Fierce Spirit Protecting the Northern Thai Forest', *Contemporary Buddhism*, vol. 8, no. 2, 2007, pp. 169–85.

133. Darlington, 'Buddhism and Development: The Ecology Monks of Thailand', pp. 96–8, ed. Christpher S. Quuen, Charles Prebish and Damien Keown, in *Action Dharma: New Studies in Engaged Buddhism*, ed. Christpher S. Queen, Charles Prebish and Damien Keown, London: Routledge, pp. 96–109, and 'The Ordination of Tree'.

134. Darlington, 'Tree Ordination in Thailand', pp. 198, 202.

135. Darlington, 'The Ordination of Tree'.

136. Philip, Hirsch, 'Environment and Environmentalism in Thailand: Material and Ideological Bases', in *Seeing Forest for Trees: Environment and Environmentalism in Thailand*, ed. Philip Hirsch, Chiang Mai: Silkworm Books, 1996, pp. 15–36.

137. Sulak Sivaraksa, 'The Religion of Consumerism', in *Dharma Rain: Sources of Buddhist Environmentalism*, ed. Stephanie Kaza and Kenneth Kraft, Boston: Shambhala, 2000, pp. 181–2.

138. Ibid., pp. 199–200.

139. Susan M. Darlington, 'Not Only Preaching—The Work of the Ecology Monk Phrakhru Pitak Nanthakhun of Thailand', *Forest, Trees and People*, newsletter, vol. 34, September 1997, pp. 17–20.

140. Udomittipong, 'Thailand's Ecology Monk', pp. 193–4.

141. Darlington, 'Buddhism and Development', p. 106.
142. Donald K. Swearer, 'The Hermeneutics of Buddhist Ecology in Contemporaray Thailand: Buddhadasa and Dhammapitaka', in *Buddhism and Ecology: The Interconnection of Dharma and Deeds*, ed. Mary Evelyn Tucker and Duncan Ryūken Williams, Cambridge, MA: Harvard University Press, 1997, pp. 21–44. (Buddhadasa Bhikshu condemned Thai government's attempt to prohibit the teaching of *santutthi*).
143. Harris, 'Buddhism and Ecology', p. 118.
144. Darlington, 'The Good Buddha and the Fierce Spirit', pp. 170, 178.
145. Darlington, 'Tree Ordination in Thailand', p. 200.
146. Clippard, 'The Lorax Wears Saffron', pp. 228–9.
147. Udomittipong, 'Thailand's Ecology Monk', p. 193.
148. Bond, 'A.T. Ariyaratne and the Sarvodaya Shramadana Movement in Sri Lanka', p. 121.
149. Ibid., pp. 122–3.
150. Anand P. Gurge, *Return to Righteousness: A Collection of Speeches, Essays and Letters of Anagarika Dhammapala*, Colombo: Government Press, 1965, p. 137.
151. A.T. Ariyaratne, *Collected Works*, vols. I–IV, Moratuwa: Sri Lanka Sarvodaya Research Institute, 1978–91, vol. I, p. 124.
152. A.T. Ariyaratne and Joanna Macy, *The Island of Temple and Tank, Sarvodaya—Self-Help in Sri Lanka*, pp. 78–9.
153. Ibid., p. 82.
154. Thich Nhat Hanh, 'Look Deep and Smile: The Thoughts and Experiences of a Vietnamese Monk', *Buddhism and Ecology*, ed. Martine Batchelor and Kerry Brown, p. 101.
155. Thich Nhat Hanh, *Present Moment, Wonderful Moment*, Shambhala: Parallax Press, 1990, p. 102.
156. Thich Nhat Hanh, 'Earth Verses', p. 441, ed. Stephanie Kaza and Kenneth Kraft, *Dharma Rain: Sources of Buddhist Environmentalism*, Boston: Shambhala, 2000, pp. 446–7.
157. Thich Nhat Hanh, *Present Moment, Wonderful Moment*, Shambhala: Parallax Press, 1990, p. 105.
158. W.S. Yokayama, 'Circling the Mountain', *Buddhism and Ecology*, ed. Martine Batchelor and Kerry Brown, London: Cassel, 1992, pp. 55–6.
159. Ibid., pp. 59–60.
160. Ibid., p. 60.
161. Ibid., p. 64.
162. Hwa Yol Jung and Peter Jung, 'Gary Snyder's Ecopiety', *Environmental History Review*, vol. 14, no. 3, 1990, pp. 74–87. (*Haiku* is form of Japanese poetry developed under Mahāyāna influence. It is a way of life, thinking and visualization of Nature which recognizes interdependence of all things and harmonious co-existence of Nature.)
163. Hwa Yol Jung and Peter Jung, 'Gary Snyder's Ecopiety', *Environmental History Review*, vol. 14, 1990, pp. 76–7. (Some of Gary Snyder's important work are: 'Good, Wild, Sacred', *The Co-Evolution Quarterly*, vol. 39, 1983,

pp. 8–17; *Axe Handle*, San Francisco: North Point Press, 1983; *Earth House Hold*, New York: New Directions Book, 1969; *Myths and Texts, Hold*, New York: New Directions Book, 1978; *The Old Ways*, San Fancisco: City Light Books, 1977; *The Real Work: Interviews and Talks*, 1964–79, ed. Acott Mclean, New York: New Directions Book, 1980; *Regarding Wave, Reprop and Gold Mountain Poems*, Berkeley: Four Seasons Foundation, 1977; *Turtle Island*, New York: New Directions Book, 1974).

164. Ayako Takahashi, 'The Shaping of Gary Snyder's Ecological Concsciousness', *Comparative Literature Studies*, vol. 39, no. 4, 2002, pp. 314–17.

165. Gary Snyder, 'Blue Mountain Constantly Walking', in *Dharma Rain: Sources of Buddhist Environmentalism*, ed. Stephanie Kaza and Kenneth Kraft, Boston: Shambhala, 2000, p. 128.

166. John Daido Loori, 'River Seeing the River', in *Dharma Rain: Sources of Buddhist Environmentalism*, ed. Stephanie Kaza and Kenneth Kraft, Boston: Shambhala, 2000, pp. 142–4.

167. Jung and Jung, 'Gary Snyder's Ecopiety'.

168. J. Baird Callicott, 'The New New (Buddhist?) Ecology', *Journal for the Study of Religion, Nature and Culture*, vol. 2, no. 2, 2008, pp. 1–3.

169. Gary Snyder, 'Smokey the Bear Sutra', in *Dharma Rain: Sources of Buddhist Environmentalism*, ed. Stephanie Kaza and Kenneth Kraft, Boston: Shambhala, 2000, pp. 474–6.

170. Anand Singh, 'Buddhist Response to Global Warming and Environmental Protection: Ideology, Methodology and Dissemination', *Buddhist Response to Global Protection*, Vietnam: Vietnam Buddhist University, 2015, pp. 1–17.

1

Animals, Yajnas, and Population Dynamics

Animals in Early Buddhism

Human proximity and dependence on animals is one of the most wonderful phenomena of Nature. Both impact on human beings deliberately and inadvertently, and such a relationship has been channelized through miscellaneous efforts. The relationship humans share with animals has been pondered over since the beginning of the time. Buddhism has widely discussed, explored, and examined human-animal relationship and introspected the range of impact that humans have on animals, mainly on domains of economic dependency, sense perception, knowledge (*prajna*), and rebirth of humans as animals. It explores the status of living beings not only for who they domesticate but also as who co-exist with humans in the form of clouds of microorganisms that surround land, food, shelter, and water.

Non-violence is considered an intrinsic part of Buddhism and the Buddha's views on moderate and rational doctrine of *ahiṁsa* formulate unique and pragmatic approach of co-existence with Nature. The Buddha says that addiction to injury and killing must be abandoned as it leads to suffering and is an obstacle in attaining liberation (*paṇātipā tissa purisa puggalassa pāṇātipata veramani hoti parinivva nāya*).[1] It is harmful to deprive vitalities and beneficial to be aloof from injury and violence (*pāṇāti pāto akusalam paṇāti pāte veramani kusalam*).[2] All living beings are afraid of life. So one should neither inflict injury on others nor should one cause to kill.[3] Buddhist literature suggest that the Buddha's view on non-violence was evolved slowly with an intention to respect life of all living beings and also to adjust with practical difficulties in formation of such non-violent ethics. He strictly adhered to the policy of non-violence for monks and nuns but allowed the lay followers to be preventive, restrictive, and pragmatic while abstaining from inflicting injury on animal and plants. The Buddha says that killing a creature is neither of great value nor it satisfies personal whims. This conduct is very similar to activities of a peasant who enters in a field without a plough and seeds. He sowed the seeds in an unfertile tract, among uprooted stumps and the seeds were intended to be broken, rotten, and spoilt by wind and heat.[4] The monks should abstain from destroying life, live with modesty and pity. He should be compassionate and kind to all creatures and refrain from injuring any plant and creature.[5] The people should not destroy life of any creature, how small it may be.[6] It is forbidden to throw remains of food on grass or into water because the tiny creatures living on grass or water might be harmed.[7] However, contrary view also exists saying that leftover food should be thrown into the pond where tiny living beings can feed on it.[8] Such contradictions are accepted by the Buddha because the people were advised to respect even the minutest living beings on the one hand, while understanding the value of leftover food and the requirements of other living beings. The Buddha even promulgated rules against travelling during rainy season because of possible injury to insects and worms coming to surface in the bad weather.[9] The *Vinaya Pitaka* says that once upon a time a monk, who was a potter before his ordination, built himself a hut of burnt clay. The Buddha strongly objected to the monk's action as so many living creatures could be burnt in the process and the hut was subsequently broken down on the Buddha's instruction to prevent a bad precedent from being set.[10] The Buddha exhorts mutual respect between humans and animals and says that mutual respect between monks and the wild accrue merit to humans and welfare to countless sentient beings.[11] Even reptiles like snakes and other dangerous animals do not harm people who show compassion.[12] The *Pacittiya* rule prescribes that monks should not deprive any human being of life or encourage anyone to commit suicide or instigate anyone to kill.[13] The monks and the nuns were prohibited from participating in professional fights although they were advised to adopt war-like qualities. The Buddha says that a monk should not be like an elephant who falters in a battle or like a fatigued soldier who lost his courage before the battle begins. It to show that they are still not free from the affliction of five senses.[14] Again, they were supposed to wipe out all sensual desires and adopt physical discomfort to lead an austere life.[15] The moderate life of a monk is a prelude to the better understanding of getting acquainted with the path of enlightenment.

Sometimes, animals were praised better than humans.[16] The Buddha says that if animals can be cooperative, generous, and courteous to each other then can be the monks.[17] He admonished a discourteous monk by citing example of a jackal who was howling as a gratitude before sunrise.[18] On other occasion, he says that it is easy to decipher the yelp of the jackals rather than knowing the true intention of human beings.[19] Usually, the Buddha and the elephant are likened to wanderers in the forest, away from all *saṁsāric* activities.[20] He has also been compared to a fearless lion.[21] He instructed the monks that they should be like a thorough-bred horse and respond quickly to their aim, i.e. meditation and mindfulness.[22] He tamed many wild and ferocious animals with his kind words. After achieving *nibbāna*, when the Buddha was sitting in incessant rain, he was saved by nāga Mucalinda.[23] When Devadutta sent the infuriated elephant Nālagiri to kill the Buddha, he was tamed with the power of love and affection. And when Nālagiri beheld the Buddha, all his fury abated and he submitted to him with full calm and peace. The Buddha replied to him that if he had not been a four-legged creature, he might have led into the path of *nibbāna*.[24] It can be said that Nālagiri was denied opportunity of enlightenment because he was an animal. Again, when the Buddha left Kośambī in disgust, annoyed by quarrelsome monks, and resided in Parilliya forest, Parilliya, an elephant, served him food and fruits.[25] In Vaiśali, monkeys offered him honey.[26] When Moggallana needed lotus stark to treat Sariputta's fever; he visited a lotus lake where he was helped by an elephant who uprooted a number of lotus stalks and bundled it for Moggallana.[27] The monks were shown example that how a partridge, a monkey, and an elephant have been lived together with the support of each other. The Buddha narrated the story to the *bhikkhus* once there was a great banyan tree on the slopes of the Himalayas. Three friends lived there dependent on the tree: a partridge, a monkey, and an elephant. They were disrespectful, discourteous, and impolite with one another. Then the thought occurred to the three friends to find out who among them was most senior by birth. The partridge and the monkey asked the elephant about his past and the elephant replied that during his youth he would walk over the banyan tree between his thighs, and that the topmost buds brushed against his belly. The partridge and the elephant asked the monkey about his life. The monkey replied that during his youth he would sit on the ground and chew the topmost buds from the banyan tree. This, friends, is an ancient incident that I remember. Then the monkey and the elephant asked the partridge, 'What ancient thing do you remember? The partridge replies saying that that spot was once a great banyan tree. Having eaten one of its fruits, I relieved myself at this spot and from there, this banyan tree was born. Thus, I am the most senior among us by birth, said the partridge. So the monkey and elephant accepted the partridge's seniority. Then the partridge, monkey, and elephant undertook. They started living respectful, courteous, and polite toward one another.[28] Similar story is found showing friendship among an elephant, a monkey, a rabbit and a partridge (Plate 1). The stories and examples of friendly and compassionate relation between monks and animals are numerous in the Buddhist literature. The *Harshacarita* gives wonderful similes of animals that follow Buddhist practices. For example:

Even some monkeys who had fled to the 'three Refuges' were gravely busy performing the ritual of the caitya, while some devout parrots, skilled in the Shakya shastras, were explaining the Kosha, and some mainas, who had obtained calm by expositions of the duties of the monastery life, were giving lectures on the law, and some owls, who had gained insight by listening to the ceaseless round of instruction, were muttering the various births of the Bodhisattva, and even some tigers waited in attendance who had given up eating flesh under the calming influence of Buddhist teaching, while the fact that some young lions sat undisturbed near his seat shewed at once what a great sage he was, as he thus sat as it were on a natural lion-throne. His feet were licked by some deer who seemed to drink in ascetic calmness; he propitiated universal charity by means of a young dove which sat on his left hand like a lotus dropped from his ear and ate wild rice, while he dazzled the spectators by the rays which streamed from the nails of his other hand, as he poured water on a peacock, which stood near with

PLATE 1. Interdependence

its neck uplifted, like an emerald water-jar, or strewed grains of panic and rice for ants. He was clad in a very soft red cloth, as if he were the Eastern quarter of the sky, bathed in morning sunshine, teaching the other quarters to assume the red Buddhist attire, while they were flushed with the pure red glow of his body like a ruby freshly cut; with his gently bright eye bent down in humility, before which the lotuses in the lake closed their buds, he seemed to rain ambrosia to revive the little insects which the crowd has unwillingly crushed.[29]

The Buddha's world view on animals has been criticized since animals have been treated as inferior because humans have been considered to exercise spiritual superiority over other beings. Animals are also considered inferior because thay lack *prajna* (insight).[30] They cannot understand Buddhist *suttas* and were unable to attain *nibbāna*. But like humans, animals too are also subject to suffering and are treated as wicked and inferior because of some promiscuous and incestuous characteristics.[31] Paul Waldau says that 'Buddhism is speciest' because humans, in Buddhism, are treated with greater moral values than other animals.[32] Herbert Hartel says that Buddhism treats the killing of animals and the killing of a man differently. The killing of man is considered unethical because it is treated as a criminal offence by society and it leads to condemnation and punitive action. In the case a monk kills an animal, the killing is not considered a crime because the animal belongs to an inferior species.[33] The Buddhist views on killing and non-violence have also been embedded in the early tenets. It was evolved in such a way that it remained practical and pragmatic. For the lay followers, extreme non-violence towards animals, plants, soils, and water will only create obstacle in their day to day life because humans can not survive without these entities. But for the monks, however this way of life can be strictly regulated because they can survive without breaking the vow of non-violence because of their dependence on alms given by the *upāsakas*.[34] The principle of *ahiṃsa* in the context of animal-human relationship thus shows abstinence of conscious destruction of any sentient beings from human to the smallest animalcule.[35] Animals are treated at the theoretical and *kammic* level by ethical principles of speech and action. The tenet of right action in the context of human-animal relationship meant abstinence from destruction of any sentient being. The Buddha questions on the moral ground the cruel occupations (*kururakammanta*) of, say, butcher, fowler, fisherman, and executioner, and even considers them inferior and wicked.[36] He says that *kamma* like inflicting injury to life is an unpleasant state which leads to pain and depriving living being of life. Even if a person is born, he may be infirm, ugly, unpopular, coward, dejected, and mournful.[37] A cattle-butcher suffers as many as hundreds of thousands years of purgatory.[38] The human can be reborn in the animal world (*tiracchanayoni*).[39] As animals they cannot attain *nibbāna* because they lack discriminative intelligence (*prajna*). But they are not entirely excluded from the *nibbānic* state inorder to be able to attain *nibbāna* they have to be reborn as human.[40] The Buddha never denies that humans have very complex relationships with each other, but he always tries to rationalize the discriminative mindset of humans against animals.

Meat Eating in Early Buddhism

The Buddha allowed meat eating at a moderate level because it was rather prevalent at that time, especially in the Ganga-Yamuna doab. Meat was in fact a major source of food for the people who were living in the forest or near it. Meat eating might also have been necessary for the expansion of Buddhism in remote areas where the agrarian economy was not well-developed and people were still relying on hunting and food gathering. Meat, fish, and cereals were allowed for monks and nuns.[41] Once the Buddha told Jivaka, the great physician of Magadha, that he forbade eating of meat only if someone has seen or heard that an animal was intentionally slaughtered for him (*na ca bhikkhave appativkkhatvā masaṃ pari bhuṇitabbaṃ*). Fish and meat eating is considred blameless by the Buddha in three ways—unseen (*adittham*), unheard (*asutam*), and unsuspected (*aparusamkitam*). It is known as the rule of *tikotiparisuddha* which prevents the monks from being instrumental in killing of animals for meat.[42] Meat cravings may lead to experiences pain and distress and such monks earn demerit.[43] The *Puttamaṁsa Sutta* mentions four kinds of food—material food, contact, will and consciousness, and their importance. The Buddha says that material gift including food (*kabalavkara āhāra*) should not be received for pleasure (*davaya*), for indulgence (*madaya*), for personal instinct (*mandanaya*), or for comeliness (*vibhusanaya*) but for appropriateness of the life of the monks and *samgha*.[44] Even the monks were allowed to receive the flesh of certain wild animals.[45] The Buddha's view on meat eating can be traced from references of Devadutta who with the help of fellow monks Kokalika, Katamoraka-tissa, Khandadivyaputta, and Samuddadatta tried to bring about schism in the *samgha*. They asked for the exposition of the five rules on all members of the *samgha*. These are:

1. The monk should reside all his life in forest.
2. He should not accept any invitation for meals but live entirely on alms.
3. He should have robes made from discarded cloths from laity.
4. He should dwell at the foot of the tree and not under the roof.
5. He should abstain completely from eating fish and meat.

The Buddha rejected the demands of Devadutta but allowed those who were inclined to accept all these conditions, except that of sleeping under a tree in the rainy season.[46] In case of illness, the monks were allowed to take flesh and blood.[47] He permitted monks to partake of the raw flesh and blood of bear, fish, alligator, swine, and ass during illness.[48] At the border, southern states, and the Avanti region, monks were allowed to use skin of goat and deer as coverlet.[49] Once, the Buddha heard that some monks had eaten the flesh of elephant, horse, dog, snake, lion, leopard, and hyena during famine. The Buddha declared that the flesh of such animals was inedible and they could not be killed for food.[50] He also imposed ban on eating of human flesh after hearing that Suppiya, a nun had offered flesh of her thigh to a sick monk who ate it, perhaps unknowingly.[51] I.B. Horner says that ban on these animals do not indicate that monks and laities were not allowed to eat meat. Elephant and horse were royal insignia and eating of snake was considered disgusting while killing and eating of wild animals would be dangerous as they might injure them.[52] It is also true that elephant and horse are not readily available to people to consume and it was not practical to consume meat of animals considered precious and sacred. However, in the *Soma yajnas* (*Aśvamedha*) the horse was sacrificed and consumed although the Buddha criticized such endeavours. Eating of reptiles was also known in some of the Buddhist traditions but it was not universally applicable, especially in the Ganga-Yamuna doab.

The reference to meat eating is a common in the Buddhist literature. For example Uppalavana, a nun once procured some meat from a robber in Andhavana and prepared it for the Buddha.[53] The *Aṅguttara Nikāya* also mentions that a person bought meat from the market to prepare it for the Buddha.[54] A group of people prepared porridge and rice soup and mixed it with pieces of meat to serve it to the Buddha and his associates.[55] Siha, the Lichhavi commander, served a variety of food including meat to the Buddha in Vaiśalī.[56] Even a monk could not set free an animal trapped in a cage or net on the ground of compassion because the animal was considered to be property of the hunter who set the trap.[57] It was a conscious decision of the Buddha to allow monks and nuns to accept what was given by lay followers. It was a necessity of the time to accept food in alms because the monk cannot demand or deny particular type of food. The *saṃgha* was still in developing stage and community-cooking or arrangement of food for the monks in the monasteries was still a distant dream. The demand for a particular food showed preference. Peter Harvey argues that if the monks were given non-vegetarian food and they denied to accept it, then they became responsible of depriving the *kammic* fruits accrued by the donor due to this *dāna*. This was a sin since food for the monks was supposed to be just a source of sustenance and not an indulgence and privilege. In fact, it will also encourage the monks to demand the preferable food and refuse the food what is not to be edible for them.[58] The *Aṅguttara Nikāya* mentions that the monks should be contend with what is given by the *upāsakas*.[59] It is also said that as an almsman, the *bhikkhu* could not depend on any particular offering but as a *dakkhineyya* (respected one) and *punnakhetta*, they are responsible to receive alms in good faith by any benevolent donor. If the *bhikkhu* does not fulfil such responsibility, then he would intentionally deny the *kammic* fruit to be accrued to that donor.[60] On the other hand, preference of vegetarian food could encourage conscious cravings among the monks and such actions have always been criticized by the Buddha.[61] The Buddha allowed *dāna* to the *saṃgha* (*kappakata*), if it was with good intention and under the prescribe rules of the *saṃgha*. The monks were to accept such *dāna* because denial of it might be treated as an offence.[62] Even in times of scarcity, they had no right to demand food and if they were not offered, it was considered an offence.[63] The intention of the Buddha was to avoid the unintentional killings and to facilitate the *saṃgha* to get enough food for survival, presumably not seeking preferences but to accept what is given.

The principle of *ahiṃsa* was encouraged not only by the religious thinkers of the age but it also became an administrative ethic, especially for animals. Non-slaughter day was observed to control the killing of animals. The *Vinaya Pitaka* mentions that Suppiya cut a piece of flesh from her thigh to prepare meat broth for a sick monk. She sent her servant to buy the meat from market but was informed that the meat was not available in the market because of that being a non-slaughter day (*māghāta ajja*).[64] The *Arthaśāstra* issues prolonged list of 'do's and don'ts' for killing and non-killing of certain groups of animals. Kautilya instructs *sunadhyaksha* (superintendent of slaughter house), to monitor the hunting, fishing and slaughtering of animals. He prohibits killing of animals like:

Elephant, horses, or animals having the form of a man, bull or an ass living in oceans, as well as fish in tanks, lakes, channels and rivers; and such game birds as *krauncha* (a kind of heron), *utkrosaka* (osprey), *datyuha* (a sort of cuckoo), *hamsa* (swan), *chakravaka* (a brahamany duck), *jivanjivaka* (a kind of pheasant), *bhrangaraja* (lanius malabaricus), *chakora* (partridge), *mattakokila* (cuckoo), peacock, parrot, and *mandanasarika* (maina) as well as other auspicious animals, whether birds or beasts, shall be protected from all kinds of molestations.[65]

Kautilya might have issued such instructions to restrain and protect animals under the influence of Upanishadic thoughts which opposed futile killings of animals in *Soma yajnas*. Kautilya and influence of Jainism encouged Chandragupta Maurya to make the policy of non-violence for animals and birds. Aśoka also followed the same dictum with more pronounced concerns for animals. He tried to minimize killings of animals in his palace. His Rock Edict I says that:

purā mahānasamhi Devānampriyasa Priyadasino rāño anudivasam bahūni prāna-sata-sahasrāni ārabhisu sūpāthāya, se aja yadā ayaṃ dhammalipī likhitā ti eva prāṇā ārabhare sūpāthāya dvo morā eko mago so pi mago na dhruvo, ete pi trī prāṇā pachhā na ārabhisare.

Aśoka says that before writing the *dhamma*, thousands of animals were killed for food in the royal kitchen. Later only two peacocks and one deer were killed but this was not a regular affair. Even in future such killings were to be abandoned.[66] His concern for welfare of animals has been reiterated in his Rock Edict II where gave instructions for setting up of hospitals for human beings and animals: *Osudhāni cha yāni manusa chikīchhā cha pasu-chikīchhā cha.*[67] His Pillar Edict V is exhaustive in this regard. His greatness lies in the fact that he follows ideals and concurrent thoughts on *ahiṃsa*, especially from Buddhism, but never mentions any sort of religious inclination because the edicts were issued over public concerns. His list includes in addition to the prohibition of killings of various animals and birds, observation of non-slaughter day on various occasions. The inscription says:

The following animals were declared by me inviolable, viz., parrots, mainas, the aruna, ruddy geese, wild geese, the nandimukha, the gelata, bats, queen-ants, terrapins, boneless fish, the vedaveyaka, the Ganga-puputaka, skate-fish, tortoise, and porcupines, squirrels, the srimara, bulls, set at liberty, iguanas, the rhinoceros, white doves, domestic doves, (and) all the quadrupeds which are neither useful nor edible. Those (she-goats), ewes, and sows (which are) either with young or in milk. Are inviolable, and also those (of their) of young ones (which are) less than six months old. Cocks must not be caponed. Husks containing living animals must not be burnt. Forests must not be burnt either uselessly or in order to destroy (living beings). Living animals must not be fed with (other) living animals. Fish are inviolable, and must not be sold, on the three Chaturmasis (and) in the Tishya full moon during three days, (viz.), the fourteenth, the fifteenth), and the first (*tithi*) and invariably on every fast day. And during these same these days also no other classes of animals which are in the elephant park (and) in the preserves of the fishermen, must be killed. On the eight (*tithi*) of (every) fortnight, on the fourteenth, on the fifteenth on Tishya, on Punarvasu, on the three Chaturmasis, (and) on festivals, bull must not be castrated, (and) he-goats, rams, boars, and whatever other (animals) are castrated (otherwise), must not be castrated (then). On Tishya, on Punarvasu, on the Chaturmasis, (and) during the fortnight of (every) Chaturmasis, horses and bullocks must not be branded.[68]

Non-killing of animals as a state regulation has also been found in later records. Faxian says that in the Madhyadesa, the king inflicts no corporal punishment and the inhabitants of the region do not kill animal for food. Even the people of this region do not eat garlic and onion. Xuanzang says that Harsha issued proclamation prohibiting the slaughter of any living being and banning sale of meat in his empire.[69] Only Candalas practice hunting and deal in flesh.[70] It might be a possibility that due to emerging influence of Vaishnavism and Mahāyāna Buddhism, the meat eating practice became less frequent in the Gupta Age but pure vegetarianism was far from the truth.

Debate on *Sukaramaddava*

At Cabala cetiya, Vaiśalī, the Buddha declared his intention to take *mahāparinibbāna* within three months. The next day he left Vaiśalī for Bhandagāma after eyeing the city in circumambulating gesture like an elephant (*nāgāpalokitam apalokitvā*).[71] On his way to Kuśināra, he reached Pāvā and stayed at Ambavana of Cunda Kammaraputta. Cunda visited the Buddha and invited him and other monks to a meal the next day.[72] The meal consisted of sweet rice, cakes, and *Sukaramaddava*. The *Mahāparinibbāna Sutta* mentions that the Buddha advising Cunda to serve him the *Sukaramaddava*. The other food that Cunda had prepared could be served to the rest of the monks. After the meals were served, the Buddha taught him *dhamma* and asked Cunda to bury the remaining *Sukaramaddava* in a hole. He also praised Cunda for the meal. But soon after, the Buddha suffered from an attack of the dysentery. Being strong willed, the Buddha was able to bear pain. Though extremely weak he decided to continue his journey to Kuśināra.[73] The Buddha gave special instructions to Ananda to visit Cunda to let him know that he was not being blamed for the Buddha's sickness.[74] The *Sumangalavilāsinī* says that *Sukaramaddava* was the flesh of single first born pig, neither too young nor too old, and was available in the market (*sukara maddavanti natituranassa natijinassa eka jetthaka sukarassa pavatta mamsam*). It might also be a preparation of soft boiled rice cooked with five cow products or even a kind of alchemistic medicine.[75] Dhammapala in the *Paramārthadīpanī*, a commentary on the *Udāna*, says that apart from Buddhaghosa's assumption on *Sukaramaddava*, it might also mean young bamboo shoots trampled by pigs (*sukerehi maddita vamsa kaliro*).[76] In case of sickness and diseases, the monks were allowed to take raw flesh and blood.[77] The term *sukaramaddava* was interpreted in many ways, both by Theravāda and Mahāyāna scholars. Theravāda scholars were inclined towards non-vegetarianism (pork) with a few exceptions while the Mahāyāna towards vegetarianism (mushroom/bulbous roots).

Modern scholars have accepted it as pork or a variety of mushroom, or *sakarkanda*, *putika*, *soma* or ginseng plant. K.E. Neumann in his German translation of the *Majjhima Nikāya* cites Narhari Rajanigantu's Indian compendium for medical plants to identify the real meaning of *Sukaramaddava*. He considers it a kind of truffle (pig's delight) and says that there are many names of medical plants with compound word having pig as prefix like *sakarkanda*, *sukarapadika*, etc.[78] T.W. Rhys Davids, on reference of Dr William Hoey, also identifies *Sukaramaddava* as a kind of truffle while Dr Hoey believes it to be a type of bulbous root which is a very popular edible item in the Middle-Ganga Valley.[79] R. Gordon Wasson says that this truffle is actually a kind of underground fungus named *Scleroderma*. There are many types of such fungi and it is one of them.[80] Stella Kramrisch argues that the term *Sukaramaddava* can be identified as *putika*, a plant that is mentioned in the *Brāhmana* and other Vedic literature. It is type of mushroom which is the mythically and ritually authenticated substitute of the divine plant, *soma*.[81] Ananda Coomaraswamy says that *Sukaramaddava* may be identified as the pork but there is a possibility that it can be a kind of truffle.[82] Andre Bareau says this food (*Sukaramaddava*), the last that the Buddha consumes before his *mahāparinibbāna*, is a food somehow sacred, whose rich qualities, the essential power, will enable him to accomplish this great cause, the supreme extinction. This wealth, this power, is too big to be borne by other beings, men or gods, who never, by far, have executed a comparable action.[83] E.J. Thomas on records of Buddhaghosa and Dhammapala, accepts that *Sukaramaddava* was the boar's flesh.[84] Fa Chow has opposite view of Thomas. He says that *Sukaramaddava* was a stew of ears of the sandal wood tree. In China fungus grows on the tree is known as 'tree ear' (*shu-er*) or 'wood ear' (*mu-er*) while that grown on the ground known as 'chun'. He says that Buddhaghosa's pleading for non-vegetarianism was due to the fact that he himself was non-vegetarian. The account of Buddhayasa can be considered as more accountable who says that *Sukaramaddava* was a kind of fungus. So it is plant or fungus liable to poison the body.[85]

Substantial arguments have been made proving that early Buddhism did not give much importance to interpreting what *Sukaramaddava* means. Theravāda literature does not explain even the last meal of the Buddha. Meat eating was common. Arthur Waley says that Theravāda did not condemn eating of meat and if they did so, they could not have accepted the eating of *Sukaramaddava*. It may be possibile that when abhorrence for meat eating emerged in India, the Theravāda as well as Mahāyāna theologians found it difficult to explain how the Buddha died because of eating pork and developed the idea that *Sukaramaddava* was a kind of mushroom.[86] Arthur says that the notion that the Buddha died of eating pork is wholly absent in Chinese and far-Eastern Buddhism and became known only by the end of the nineteenth century when Pāli scriptures were translated and studied.

The account of Buddha's Decease occurs in the second book of the 'Diirghaagama'. This version was translated in 412–413 and is therefore contemporary with Buddhaghosha. It supports the 'vegetarian' theory. Cunda makes 'a separate stew of ears of the sandalwood tree, which the world esteems as a great dainty'. Tree ear is still the current Chinese for a fungus growing on a tree. Fragments of the Sanskrit 'Diirghaagama' exists, but unfortunately not this passage. Presumbly the Sanskrit phrase in front of the Chinese translator was Candana ahicchatraka, candanachattra or the like.[87]

Chinese literature was taken and translated after the Common Era when vegetarian ethics was fully developed in India. The Mahāyāna treatises well conceived the idea that the Buddha did not die by eating pork but that it was a certain form of mushroom or vegetable that caused his death. It was out of question to think that the Buddha died after eating the pork. The *Laṅkavatāra Sutra*, a great Mahāyāna treatise is considered to be the first literature which vigorously recommended vegetarianism. The Buddha preached the *Bodhisattva* Mahamati which says that food for the Sravakas, Pratyekabuddhas, and the *Bodhisattvas* is *dhamma* and not meat. It says:

It is not true, Mahamati, that meat is proper food and permissible for the Sravaka when (the victim) was not killed by himself, when he did not order others to kill it, when it was not specially meant for him. Again Mahamati, there may be some unwitted people in the future time who, beginning to lead the homeless life according to my teaching, are acknowledged as son of Sakya, and carry the Kashaya robe about them as a badge, but who are in thought evilly affected by erroneous reasonings. They may talk about various discriminations which they make in their moral discipline, being abdicted to the view of a personal soul. Being under the influence of the thirst for (meat) taste, they will string together in various ways some sophistic arguments to defend meat eating. They think they are giving me unprecedented calumny when they discriminate and talk about the facts that are capable of various interpretations. Imagining that this fact allows this interpretation, (they conclude that) the Blessed one permits meat as proper food, and it is mentioned among permitted foods and that probably the Tathagata himself partook of it. But Mahamati, nowhere in the Sutras is meat permitted as something enjoyable, nor it is referred to as proper among the foods prescribed (for the Buddha's followers).[88]

The *Laṅkavatāra Sutra* endorses vegetarianism through various examples of positive and negative *kamma* formation. It issues recommendations and advisories that people follow. One of its recommendations is that one should avoid meat, onion, various kinds of liquor, alliums, and garlic since they are contemptuous, have a stinking smell, and the person eating was condemned to be reborn among the families of the Candala, the Pukkasa, and the Domba. In fact, flesh eating was not allowed even as a medicine.[89] The change in the Buddhist attitude towards meat eating shaped at a far later date when Mahāyāna treatises theoretically evolved that flesh eating is not only prohibited but that also attracted negative *kamma* cycle. It is to be examined how successful such ethical impositions were.

This has been argued that *Sukaramaddava* was a kind of mushroom or bulbous root. It has been linked to *soma* and *putika* plants which had some ritual significance in the Vedic literature. Stella Kramrisch identifies *Sukaramaddava* as putika. The plant *putika* was used in the *Pravargya* sacrifice, devoted to the Sun. In this, a type of vessel, Mahāvira, was made to which four other elements were added and *putika* was one them. It was considered very auspicious because it was performed just before or at the beginning of every *Soma* sacrifice. Kramrisch says that *putika* still survives and is significant amongst the Santhals of Chotanagpur.[90] Two types of assumptions have been developed, the first is that *Sukaramaddava* was a mushroom, and the other, that there was some linkage between the Vedic and the Santhal *putika*. It is also said if *soma* and *putika* have been identified as the same then *soma* is also a kind of mushroom. W.W. Malandra says that the hymn 2.27 of the *Atharvaveda* mentions a plant in a magic ceremony to emerge victorious in disputation. It is named *pata*; it was worn as an amulet and its leaves were also eaten for auspicious reasons. It also says that *suparna* (eagle) discovers the *pata* and *sukara* (boar) dug it with its snout.[91] This means that it is the root of tuber. Boar's fondness for truffle suggest that *pata* was a truffle.[92] Malandra also found a number of parallels between *pata* and *soma*. The eagle searched both, Indra ate both to overcome the *asuras*, and both are invoked to counter falsehood.[93] Margaret Stutley also argues in favour of truffle and says that *pata* in the *Atharvaveda* is *soma*. *Pata* (*clypea hernandifolia*) has bitter root. It was discovered by an eagle and dug up by a Sukara.[94] Wasson says that *Sukaramaddava* might be a type of mushroom fly agaric (*amanita muscaria*) and can be identified with *putika* (*stropharia cubensis*) of the Santhal *pargana*. It is an underground fungus that is collected for eating as it appears on surface. It had to be consumed within hours of plucking and gathering as it starts stinking.[95] Wasson argues that the Buddha knew about this character of *putika* and that is why he instructed Cunda to serve *Sukaramaddava* to him only and to bury the rest. The Buddha says that no one on the earth nor the gods can digest it except the Tathāgata. As Buddhaghosa says that Cunda thought that the meal prepared with *putika* would extend the Tathagata's life. The *putika* enjoyed esteemed position as exalted surrogate for *soma* since it was taken by the Buddha for longivity of life.[96] Wasson's idea about *putika/soma* was not acceptable on the ground that Indra ties an amulet of *pata* root and wears a wreath of its seven leaves which contradicts the identification of *pata* as truffle.[97] G.L. Windfuhr says that any attempt to identify *soma* as a mushroom will prelude to the risk of emphasizing its physical identification over its spiritual motives. The fly-agaric is hallucinogenic but *soma/haoma* (*Jend Avesta*) leads to exhilaration not intoxication. The fly-agaric is red, whereas *haoma/soma* is identified as *zairi/hari*, a colour that may be golden, yellow, or green but which never includes red. The fly-agaric does not have leaves or branches, whereas *haoma* has leaves.[98] Wendy Doniger O'Flaherty in epilogue to Wasson's paper contradicts that *soma* can be a kind of mushroom. He says:

I was, however, not yet convinced that soma was a mushroom. I felt that the arguments rested primarily on the interpretation of adjectives, many of them words of colours and mythological traits, many of them applied to other gods as well, permitting other interpretations as well as their interpretations that identified soma with fly-agaric. As an Indologist, rather than a botanist, I still feel that the broader hypothesis—that soma was an entheogen–is more significant than the narrower one—that it was a mushroom.[99]

Wasson's idea can be contradictory at many stages. He accepts *putika* as animate while the rest of the plants and grasses fall in the inanimate category. The Vedic religion and Jainism categorically describe plants and grasses in the animate group. In Buddhism, they are considered 'borderline' beings. Jainism vastly examine life in every single being and categorizes them in different life cycle based on different levels of sense-perception. So, not only *putika* but all other plants can be treated as animate beings. His other idea was that rituals pertaining to *putika* were parochialized among the Santhals of Chota Nagpur from later Vedic people. These Santhals were isolated tribes scattered in hilly areas of Chota Nagpur and they strictly maintained the 'Nature-Man-Spirit Complex' based on the local environment. It was only in the late nineteenth and the early twentieth century that they came into contact with the larger Hindu communities of the neighbouring areas when the British people started making roads and developed transport facilities to exploit the natural resources of the Chota Nagpur region. Subsequently the Sanskritization and assimilation of the Santhals with the larger Hindu communities started. The question is how can the Santhals imbibe the *putika* rituals which were lost by the Brāhmanical society in the later Vedic age.

Wasson also says that the Buddha and his *saṃgha* mainly come from the Hindus of the upper castes who had left the traditional customs. The Buddha modified infinite complexities of habits, practices, subtle ways of thinking, pertaining to Brāhmanical religion. It also includes the tradition of *soma*, the Vedic rituals, and also the significance of *putika*. When Cunda served *Sukaramaddava* to the Buddha, he recognized it immediately and could not intend to serve it to the rest of the Aryan community. Wasson says:

Cunda, as we said before, was a Sudra, a man of the lowest caste. On the other hand, as the metal worker of the region he was technician, comfortably off, extending hospitability on a moment's notice to the Buddha and his numerous followers, one accustomed to meeting and mixing with travellers including individuals of what today called the 'scheduled caste' aboriginal tribesmen who were not Hindus and therefore not part of the dominant Hindu society.[100]

Again, Wasson's idea is too hypothetical that the Buddha wanted to maintain a racial superiority for himself and his *saṃgha*, so he instructed Cunda to serve *Sukaramaddava* to him and bury the rest. It is well known that Buddhism arose in the Ganga valley to oppose the counter racial discrimination and socio-economic rigidities. Uma Chakravarti cites T.W. Rhys Davids who says that for the Buddha, birth, occupation, and social status were irrelevant. He says that Upāli, a barber; Sunita, a pukkusa; Sati, a fisherman; Punna and Punnika, slave girls; and Subha, daughter of a Smith; can be among several examples found in the Buddhist literature where these individuals held respected position in the *saṃgha*. Rhys Davids say that the Buddha was antagonistic to the caste system and that he exhorted regularly that defilements did not come from inter-dining and food prepared by one or other, but from evil deeds and words.[101] Cunda may have belonged to the *nīcakula* (Śudra).[102] But, Cunda was one of his favourite disciples. The Buddha visited several times and stayed at *ambavana* of Cunda *kammantakara*. Had the Buddha any feeling of superiority, he could not have stayed there in his earlier visits.

The following assumptions can be made regarding *Sukaramaddava*. It can be a meal made of pork. Cunda requested the Buddha for a meal and he served *Sukaramaddava*. Had this meal been prepared with pork then it would have violated the rules of *tikotiparisuddha*. The Buddha did not see and heard but the pig was intentionally killed for him and this act was a violation of the rule of *aparusamkitam* (unsuspected). Because the Buddha could not deny the food served by an *upāsaka*, he ate the food himself but denied it to the rest of his fellow monks. Buddhaghosa might have been aware of this problem and because of that he says that the food could be pork mixed with some medicine (*rasayana*) to remove the Buddha's sickness. Again if *sukara* was not killed for the Buddha, it means it was killed before the Buddha's visit to Cunda's place. In such circumstances, the pork may get spoilt because of the high temperature of summer. The possibility that it was a kind of mushroom is dim because in summer there is very little growth of mushrooms in the middle Ganga valley. Also the Kuśināra region being forested area had plenty of vegetables and so the people even today do not necessarily eat mushroom much. The other possibility may be of *kanda* or *jimikanda* (*amorphophallus paeonnifolius*), the 'elephant foot' a tuber crop found in the states of Uttar Pradesh and Bihar in India. This is a common edible item and is also used to make medicine in Ayurveda to treat abdomen pain and dysentery. It may also be 'aravi' (*colocasia esculenta*), 'elephant year', a tuber crop commonly grown in Uttar Pradesh. Being a heavily irrigated, it may be trampled by boars (*maddita*) or dug up by their snouts.

Yajnas and Animal Sacrifice

In the later Vedic age, the cult of the *yajnas*, especially the Soma *yajnas*, became highly ritualistic and expensive. For Śrauta (*Soma*) *yajnas*, a cumbersome science of sacrifices was evolved with the help of the *Yajurveda* and the *Sāmaveda*. In these sacrifices, three sacred fires were essential and the *chitis* or altars were made on a vast sacrificial place set up according to the rules with the accompaniment of elaborate rituals, oblations and animal sacrifices. Some *Soma yajnas* lasted for months and sometimes even a year. These sacrifices required a large number of priests to perform extremely complicated and elaborate sacrifices. In *Śrauta Sūtras*, a long list of priests are mentioned, like the Hotri, Potri, Neshtri, Agnidh, Adhvaryu, Brāhmana, Praśāstries, Upavakri, etc.[103] The priests became the custodian of the *yajnas* and claimed that they could not only force the gods to do what they desired, but could also ruin even the patron for whom they officiated by deliberately committing errors. These sacrifices increased the arrogance of the priestly class and encouraged the futile and brutal killing of animals not meant for consumption.

The Buddha was highly critical of such gruesome *yajnas* because it was not only hampering the growth of the cattle economy of the Ganga valley but was also deteriorating the social ecology of the region. The *Suttanipāta*[104] says that the king performed a number of sacrifices and thus doomed thousands of cows to be sacrificed.

Na pādā na visāṇena nāssu hiṃsanti kenaci
Gāvo elasamānā soratā kumbhadūhanā
Tā visāṇe gahetvāna rājā satthena ghātayī.

(Cows do not harm with horn and hoof. They are mellow like lambs and give plenty of milk. The kings seized them by the horn and sacrificed.)

The others narrate the same sentiment:

Tato ca devā pitaro indo asurarakkhasā
Adhammo iti pakkanduṃ yaṃ satthaṃ nipatī gave.[105]

(The Brahmas, *devas*, *asuras*, Indra, and the *rakshasas* wailed as cows were butchered for sacrifices.)

Tayo rogā pure āsuṃ icchā anasanaṃ jarā
Pasūnañca samārambhā aṭṭhānavutimāgamuṃ.[106]

(In the ancient days, there were three diseases—desire, hunger and old age; but after the beginning of sacrifices (cows), now there are 98 diseases.)

The degeneracy of the brāhmanas is shown in the next verse of the *Suttanipāta*.

Eso adhammo daṇḍānamokkanno purāṇo ahu
Adūsikāyo haññanti dhammā dhaṃsanti yājakā.[107]

(The injustice of killing in sacrifices have come from the past and innocent animals were killed in sacrifices and it was gruesome.)

In the *Kūtadanta Sutta* of the *Dīgha Nikāya*, the Buddha ridiculed these *yajnas* and recommended an alternative mechanism.[108] Kūtadanta, dwelling at Khanumata in Magadha, organized a *yajna* in which hundred of bulls, steers, heifers, goats, and rams were brought to the *yupa* for sacrifice. The Buddha, by giving the reference of King Mahavijita, told Kūtadanta that killing of animal was futile and painful. The construction of *vihāras*, abstinences from destroying life, from taking what is not given, from evil conduct, from lying, etc., are better ways of sacrifices than killing of innocent animals. So, people should desist from animal-killing and follow the virtuous way of *dhammayajna*. The *Saṃyutta Nikāya*[109] says that once during the visit of the Buddha, Prasenjit, the king of Kośala, planned a great sacrifice of 500 oxen, 500 male calves, 500 female calves, and 500 sheep. When the Buddha came to know about it, he condemned the sacrifice and advised the king to abandon such salacious exercise. The *Suttanipata* says that:

Evameso aṇudhammo porāṇo viññūgarahīto
Yattha edisakaṃ passati yājakaṃ garahatī jano.

Many wise men condemn this ancient guilt of sacrifice and the people blame the sacrificer for such futile killing.[110] The time was conducive for abolition of killing of animals in sacrifices and the Buddha entered the arena with much vigour to counter such practice.[111] He instructed his followers that attainment of *jhāna* in the company of intellectuals is a better way to lead a virtuous life.

The *Dhammapada* says that one must pay homage to a man who has a sound knowledge and thought since he is better than the person who has indulged in sacrifices for over hundred years.[112] Only the company of the righteous persons, therefore, can lead to a good life. In this way, the Buddha not only denounced the *yajnas* and animal sacrifices performed by the kings and laymen but also questioned the *yajnas* performed by the Vedic *rishis* in the forest.[113] The *Suttanipāta* says:

Yathā mātā pitā bhātā aññe vipi ca ñātakā
Gāvo no paramā mittā yāsu jāyanti osadhā.

Like a mother, father, and brother, cows too are our best friends since they are the source of all healthy things.[114] Thus, in the case of wasteful sacrifices, it was possible to address without contradiction that such human action led to waste of cattle economy and environmental pollution. The socio-religious environment of the Ganga valley in the Northern Black Polished Ware age was complex and priestly class was but one component of it. Many human actions could lead to results which are intrinsically similar to those that may be produced by the natural forces. It may be a case of equi-probability whereby different processes can lead to similar results. The Buddha might have this idea in his mind when he gave the ideas of *karuna* and *mudita*. It may be *yajna* violence that led to the killing of animals in the Ganga valley or may it was the hunting economy of the bordering states. The frequency and complexity of the problems vary from region to region. It may be applied to some extent to changes which have been brought about deliberately and knowingly or where people may have initiated changes inadvertently and unintentionally. So, the Buddha has a vision not only on the cause and effect but also on spatial and temporal discontinuities.

The Ganga-Yamuna doab is supposed to be the most densely populated area of the Indian subcontinent. Among the priestly groups, only some of them, and especially the kings of the Ganga-Yamuna doab, were instrumental in the performance of Soma *yajnas* and sacrifices of the animals. The rest of the population did not show any inclination for it. These elite priets and kings were in minority compared to rest of the population. Futile animal sacrifices definitely devastated the cattle resources. But during this period the cattle resource was in abundance and their population could not be diminished because of these animal sacrifices. The Buddha's idea of non-violence was based on a pragmatic approach that devastation of animal wealth always brings about, not just a catastrophe, but a series of catastrophes because in Nature there is interdependence. Therefore, he propounded a restriction on animal slaughter rather than prohibition. The *Bhūridatta Jātaka*[115] also condemns the *yajnas* saying:

> *The Vedas have no hidden power to save*
> *The Traitor or the Coward or the knave,*
> *The fire though tended well for long years past,*
> *Leaves his base master without hope at last.*

The *Brāhmandhammika Sutta*[116] says that brāhmanas became degraded by accumulating wealth through sacrifices. The Buddha describes that earlier brāhmanas as self-restrained and penitent. They had no cattle, gold, nor corn. The riches and corn of meditation were their best treasure. However, slowly the brāhmanas changed and they induced the kings to commit the sin of killing living creatures in wasteful sacrifices. The degeneration among the priests led to them amassing public wealth by charging the sacrificial fees. The conflict of interest and denouncement of the *yajnas* perhaps reinforced the hostility between Brāhmanism and Buddhism. Therefore, priest like Aggikabharadvaja were contemptuous towards the Buddha.[117] Though the Buddha might not have expressly prohibited meat eating, yet he openly condemned complicated and elaborate sacrifices and inordinate killings. His aim was to meet the human needs while preserving the cattle economy and to encourage sustainable use of infrastructure while protecting and replenishing it for the indefinite future.

The vitality of iron technology and the 'Bull Economy' in the Ganga-Yamuna doab in the age of the Buddha cannot be ignored. These were instrumental in the growth of agrarian activities and surplus economy. However, the expansion of agriculture, nature, and pattern of cattle resources can be scrutinized in ecological perspectives with the support of teachings of the Buddha and archaeological explorations. A close examination of the population dynamics and the vegetation structure of the Ganga Valley suggest that the Buddha recommended the sustainable use of the existing resources. I.B. Horner believes that large scale sacrifice was both spiritually and economically unsound and Buddhism played a decisive role in wiping it out. She says:

The people were sympathetic, broadminded and not completely dominated by the priestly superstition. They provided excellent material on which to work in the matter of suppressing the destruction of animals for quasi religious purposes, and the growing realization that large scale sacrifice was both spiritually and economically unsound, will have played a deceive role in stamping it out.[118]

D.D. Kosambi supports Horner and argues that Vedic sacrifices became very complicated and expensive and Buddhism countered this practice for economic reasons.

Buddhism and Jainism preach ahiṃsa successfully because it was an economic necessity. The killing of animals in 'yajna' sacrifice had become intolerable burdon upon the subjects whose cattle were taken away without compensation; the fruits of the 'yajna' were success in battle, and the constant warfare implied thereby meant heavy losses to the traders and general distress. The whole basis had to be denied and non killing, which is what ahiṃsa means literally cuts at the roots of both sacrifice and war.[119]

R.S. Sharma echoes the same view that the emerging agrarian economy was one of the potent factors for the rise of Buddhism in the Ganga valley. The new agricultural economy requires bullocks and could not flourish without animal husbandry. But large scale sacrifice decimated large cattle wealth.[120] He says that the rise of new forces of production in the sixth century BC demanded promotion of agriculture. The existing animal sacrifice among the Vedic people and prevalence of hunting-gathering economy on the fringes of the southern and eastern parts of Magadha hindered the preservation of cattle for agriculture. Buddhist texts vigorously denounced sacrifice because they wished to promote agriculture. The same stand was adopted by the *Zend Avesta* for the preservation of cattle wealth.[121] Romila Thapar says that the performance of sacrifice demands a lot of wealth. It also drains cattle resources, dairy products, and agricultural produce.[122] She says that a *yajna* requires mobilization of resources and attention of numerous social problems. The estimated material used in a *yajna* seems to be enormous and a substantial drain on the economic resources of *yajmana* who had used his best livestocks for the sacrifice and also gift material wealth and cattle. Sometimes a *yajna* has left *yajmāna* impoverished. Generally animals were not killed indiscriminately for food; animals were slaughtered for special occasions like when a guest came or for a ritual.[123] It is undeniable that cattle was an important source of the emerging economy of the Ganga valley and that the stopping merciless slaughtrer of cattle in large scale sacrifices supported this. The Shramanic religion's adaptation of the general prohibition against the killing of animals was to support and sustain harmonious co-existence among all living beings.

Population Dynamics, Forests, and Animals

The interaction between humans and Nature has often been examined mechanically and altruistically. Human beings have learnt to understand the relationship between population dynamics, cattle resources, and forest. It is accepted that the human population tends to grow exponentially when food production grows. In the sixth century BC, iron technology and technical improvements in agrarian practices helped to produce substantial food for consumption and trade. Such large scale agricultural activities also changed the demographic and natural landscape of the Ganga valley. It seems that the Buddha tried to learn the peculiarities of this relationship. The contemporary Buddhist and Jain literature show that it was well-perceived how cultural adaptation, technological development, and institutional arrangements facilitated food production and consequent population growth. The conversion of natural land to farmlands, pastures, urban areas, reservoir, and other anthropogenic landscapes accentuated demographic and geographical changes in the age of the second urbanization. It represented the most pervasive and visible form of human impact on the environment. It elucidates the complexities and contextual specificities of the population-environment relationship in the domain of cattle resources, forests, and human beings. It expresses the way to understand the relationship among population, animals, and environment change.

It is interesting that a closer examination of archaeological and literary data suggest that in the sixth century BC the cattle population was massive and land use was only limited to the riverside and adjoining regions. The *Śatapatha Brāhmana* says that the area between the Saraswatī and Sadānirā (Gandak) rivers was dense forest and Aryanization of this area was done by King Videgh Mathava and his priest after he burnt down the forest.[124] The excavation of Atranjikhera of the upper Gangetic doab at NBPW level suggests that trees and plants like *Pinus roxburghii, Dalbergia sissoo, Tectona grandis, Boehmeria platipyla, Cedrus deodara, Cupressus torulosa, Terminalai tomentosa, Tamarix articulata, Dendrocalamus strictus, Acacia nilotica, Acacia Arabica,* etc., were flourishing in the sixth century BC.[125] The *Rāmayana* mentions the dense forest of the Gangetic valley and its troubled life.[126]

> *To live a forest life, resign*
> *The names of troubles and distress*
> *Suit well the tangled wilderness*
> *In the wild wood no joy I know,*
> *A forest life is naught but woe*
> *The lion in his mountain cave*
> *Answers the torrents as they rave,*
> *And forth his voice of terror throws*
> *The wood, my love, is full of woes.*

The *Arthaśastra* mentions four types of *vana—pasuvana* (forest of wild animals), *mrgavana* (forest of domesticated animals), *dravyavana* (forest of economic importance), and *hastivana* (elephant forest).[127] He places due importance to *hastivana* and advised to plant them at the border of the empire for strategic and military requirements. He instruct the officials to maintain the records of every elephant and to keep register for it.[128] His order to record the numbers might be for state owned elephants, otherwise it was very difficult as elephant were unaccountable in numbers those days and it was not possible to maintain record of each one. The *Arthaśastra* gives elaborate account and safety of forests where the elephants live.[129]

Makkhan Lal[130] explored 150 sites in Kanpur district, the core area of the Ganga-Yamuna doab (Ganga-Rind and Yamuna-Rind doab), and stratified their cultural sequence on the basis of their ceramic type. The number of settlements of each cultural phase are as follows:

1. Black and Red Ware or BRW (1400 BC–1200 BC): 9 sites.
2. Painted Grey Ware or PGW (1300 BC–600 BC): 46 sites.
3. Northern Black Polished Ware or NBPW (700 BC–100 BC): 99 sites.
4. Early Historic Age or Red Slipped Ware (200 BC–300 BC): 141 sites.

The excavation results show that in the PGW period, 26 sites had a population below 250 while 12 sites had a population between 251 and 500. The villages of higher status were further less in number. There were only 4 sites between 501 and 750, 3 between 751 and 1,000, and only 1 above 1,000.[131] During the PGW period the total population on these sites was 14,509 of which 10,155 (70 per cent) was distributed in 31 sites in the Ganga-Rind doab and 4,354 (30 per cent) was scattered in 15 sites in the Yamuna-Rind doab. The findings suggest that a substantial chunk of population was residing in small villages (38) with the population of less than 500 people. In the group of above 500 persons, there were only 8 settlements of which 6 were in the Ganga-Yamuna doab and 2 were in the Yamuna-Rind doab. The mean population per settlement during this period was 315 and the average population per square kilometre was 2.35 persons.[132] During NBPW period in the same area of Kanpur district, 99 settlements were discovered. Of these sites 65 were situated on the riverside and 34 sites were away from the river. The population of the NBPW period moved beyond the range of that of the PGW period and land settlement started in the forest area. This may have been because of the widespread use of iron technology. The iron axes were helpful in clearing the dense forest. The increasing population along the lake shores and the river bank were also an important factor for the drift of population away from rivers. The larger settlements were located on the bank of river Ganga along with its agricultural land and other habitation facilities that were supposed to be attractive and profitable.[133] This region is flanked by the Ganga and the Yamuna forming the famous Ganga-Yamuna doab. The topography here is same to the rest of the doab. Because of that, it is possible to understand the impact of these two rivers and the micro-level ecological conditions on the distribution pattern of the human population.[134] The settlement pattern of the doab shows that for a settlement of 1,000 people, the land requirement would be between 800 and 1,200 acres (1.3–1.6 km. radius), for that of 3,000 people it would be 2,400 and 3,600 acres (2.2–2.7 km. radius) and for a smaller settlement of 200 to 500 people the land requirement would be 250 to 1,000 acres (less than 1 km. radius).[135] The settlement of the Aryans in the Ganga-Yamuna doab probably could not substantially change the ecology of the area. It has been found that it was densely forested during the second and first millennium BC.[136] During the NBPW period, the total area under settlement was 6,167 sq. km. and the maximum population in 99 settlements was nearly 37,909.[137] The settlements on the banks of the Ganga had a remarkable increase in size. The total increase in size was sometimes more than 250 per cent. The mean population here per settlement in NBPW period was 383 persons and that in the district was 6.15 persons per sq. km. [138] To support this population the land requirement was 122 to 184 sq. km., covering the plains, the land along the rivers, the lakes, and other open areas in the forests.[139] During the Early Historic period, majority of the population was still living in small villages in the Ganga plain, probably because of better resources and economic growth. Social factors like economy, family, and kinship seem to be the same across the Indian subcontinent throughout the Early Historic age and so was the technological support available to exploit the environment. Therefore, the environmental impact and resource management have been the main factors in stabilizing the population. On the basis of the estimated population of Kanpur district, the average growth rate of population in the subcontinent may have been 0.21 per cent from 1350 BC to 250 BC and 0.17 per cent from 250 BC to 150 CE.[140] The finding shows minor decline in population growth since 250 BC onwards. After decline of the Mauryans, frequent wars, drought and femine may be the cause for decrease in population. In the Indian subcontinent, the Ganga valley has been the most populated and population of this region could be assumed as the average population density of the Indian subcontinent. An exact count may not be available because the maximum density of people has been accepted as the base unit but some parts of the Indian subcontinent is substantially hilly and arid with forest regions where population is very scarce and scattered. It has also been argued that without any exact data, history of population within restricted area could not be predictor of demographic change and population density of whole subcontinent. Josiah C. Russel, on the basis of the accounts of Megasthenes, Xuanzang, and the *Skanda Purana*, count the Indian population to be approximately 14 million in the Mauryan Age (fourth century BC) and 22–37 million in the Gupta and the Harshavardhana Age (third to seventh centuries CE).[141] The geographical references found in the religious texts and supporting archaeological evidences suggest whole of the India was well-inhabited but not over populated.

George Erdosy accepts the relevance of iron in the expansion of agriculture and settlements in the Ganga valley but he raised doubt regarding the catalytic role of iron for such a revolutionary change. He emphasized the identification of agrarian activities by the use of existing tools and introduction of double cropping.[142] It has been argued that acceptance of any causal link between iron technology, the spread of agriculture, and the expansion of a settlement would be a fallacy.[143] R.S. Sharma says that the growing agrarian activities, rising production, and unprecedented proliferation of settlements and crafts were possible due to the introduction of iron technology in the Ganga valley.[144] K.M. Srimali says that intensive use of existing tools in agriculture was quite imaginary and iron played a pivotal role in colonizing the Ganga plain.[145] Despite vast agrarian expansion and population growth, the dearth of cattle is not recorded in the contemporary literature. However, as mentioned earlier, the killings of animals for rituals was checked by the Buddha and other heterodox saints because cattle do have right to live and they should not have been killed for rituals. Cattle were also utilized in socio-economic activities and their futile decimation would have jeopardized the newly-emerging agrarian structure. So, the intention of the Buddha may have been to sustain the cattle population for their right to life, as also to avoid futile killing. The Buddha is also not considered a pro-natalist and he never emphasized having children as a religious obligation. He always encouged a virtuous life. With this, Buddhism was able to check population explosion which eventually restricted deforestation and the decimation of plants and animals.

This trend presumably continued up to the historical age. The dense forest in the area continued even upto the medieval age. Barani says that during the Delhi Sultanate, the doab was full of forests and Balban had taken a great interest in hunting. It was pursued with utmost zest during winter. In fact he ordered the preservation of an area of 20 *kosa* (about 40 miles) around Delhi for his hunt where no one was allowed to visit. A thousand horsemen of the palace guard would accompany Balban, in addition to 1,000 old and trustworthy footmen and archers for such hunting excursions.[146] The Mughals were fond of hunting (*shikar*) and they built special kind of large scale enclosed hunting grounds known as *qamargah* and *shikargaha.* Some of these were situated at Bari, Hisar, Sunnam, Bhatinda, Bhatner, Nagaur, Narwar, Sheikhupura, and Palam.[147] The *Ain-i-Akbari* says that Akbar was very fond of hunting lions, tigers, elephants, cheetah, deer, waterfowl, dogs, wild asses, etc., and he has also devised new methods for that purpose.[148] Irfan Habib in *The Atlas of the Mughal Empire* (Map 1) shows that in the Upper Ganga valley there was vast forest cover and hunting grounds.[149] In the South, Portugese travellers Domingo Paes and Fernao Nuniz reported Mahānavami festival celebrated for nine days in the Vijaynagar Empire. In this festival on each of nine nights many buffaloes and sheep were sacrificed. Paes says that on the first day, 24 buffaloes and 150 sheep were sacrificed to the deity. Fifty buffaloes and 4,500 sheep were sacrificed on the last day of the festival. Nuniz says that on the first day nine buffaloes, nine sheep, and nine goats were sacrificed and each day this number was doubled.[150] The ritual was performed not only by the king but also by the ministers and feudatories of the empire. Despite such large slaughters of the cattle wealth, no deterioration in cattle wealth has been reported by these court historians and foreign travellers. The vast alluvial plains of northern India have been continuously deforestated for thousands of years. On large scales, the man-made deforestation started in the nineteenth and twentieth centuries with commercialization of forest by the introduction of the railways.[151] Due to this not only forests but animal population also started dwindling and some of them even became extinct or seen only in biodiversity parks and zoos. The annexation of Oudh in 1856 by the East India Company ushered in the new economic era. With the introduction of the new land revenue policy, by the British, land became a 'commodity' which could be sold, purchased, or mortgaged. All such activities placed heavy pressure on the land and resulted in deforestation. Slowly, the whole upper Ganga valley was converted into an agrarian or pastoral land. *The Imperial Gazetteer Atlas of India* (Map 2) shows that in the twentieth century the entire upper Ganga valley was devoid of any substantial forest cover. The dense forests were replaced by growing human population, their habitations, agrarian fields, and industries.[152]

The Buddha was born in an age when the Indian subcontinent was reeling under tremendous pressure of superstitious, wasteful, and brutal sacrifices and ceremonies. He was an earnest social reformer who denounced the two extreme paths—self-indulgence and self-mortification—and preached the middle path. The simple principle of cause and effect that governed the whole universe was applied by him to the events of the human life. Because of the complex interactions between the different components of the multiple environment systems and sub-systems it was difficult to scale the intensity of human activities in the universe. The primary cause may produce a myriad of successive repercussions throughout the ecosystem. At this juncture, it is pertinent to ponder whether the world is entering in a spam of unparalleled humanly induced modifications. Our scientific inquiry and predictions endorse substantial change in the eco-system. It may be advantageous or disadvantageous for a particular environment. The wisdom, perspicacity, and prescience of the Buddha must be capitalized to minimize the evil impact of natural degradation and maximize the advantages of natural resources and co-existence for animal planet. Lastly, the religious view of the Buddha should not be considered as the intervening factor in the progressive material world but as a positive mandamus to guide and enlighten the path of development.

Notes

1. *Majjhima Nikāya*, I.43.
2. Ibid., I.47.
3. *Dhammapada*, V.129.
4. *Dīgha Nikāya*, II.307.
5. T.W. Rhys Davids, *Buddhist Suttas* (*Tevigga Sutta*), vol. XI, SBE, Delhi: LPP, 2007, repr., p. 189.
6. *Mahāvagga*, V.10.9.
7. *Majjhima Nikāya*, I.13.
8. *Aṅguttara Nikāya*, I.161.
9. *Vinaya Pitaka*, III.1.
10. Ibid., III.42.
11. Ibid., IV.246.
12. Ibid., II.72.
13. Ibid., IV.33, 35, 49.
14. *Aṅguttara Nikāya*, III.151.
15. *Vinaya Pitaka*, II.162.
16. *Majjhima Nikāya*, I.341.
17. *Vinaya Pitaka*, II.162.
18. *Saṃyutta Nikāya*, II.272.
19. *Jātaka*, no. 217.
20. *Aṅguttara Nikāya*, IV.435–7.
21. Ibid., II.33, V.35.
22. Ibid., II.114; *Majjhima Nikāya*, I.446.
23. Anand Singh, *Buddhism at Sārnāth*, Delhi: Primus, 2014, p. 16
24. *Vinaya Pitaka*, II.194ff.
25. *Dhammapadaaṭṭhakathā*, I.58ff.
26. Singh, *Buddhism at Sārnāth*, p. 89.
27. *Vinaya Pitaka*, I.214–15.
28. *Cullavagga*, VI.6.
29. *Harshacarita* (Banabhatta), VIII.266–7, tr. E.B. Cowell and F.W Thomas, London: Royal Asiatic Society, 1897.
30. Harris, 'How Environmental is Buddhism', pp. 101–14.
31. Schmithausen, *Buddhism and Nature*, VII, pp. 14–15.
32. Waldau, *The Specter of Speciesism*, pp. 154–5.
33. Schmithausen, *Buddhism and Nature*, p. 18.
34. Ibid., p. 29.
35. J.P. McDermott, 'Animals and Humans in Early Buddhism', *Indo-Iranian Journal*, vol. 32, 1989, pp. 269–80.
36. *Aṅguttara Nikāya*, III.383.
37. *Saṃyutta Nikāya*, IV.314; *Aṅguttara Nikāya*, II.210.
38. Ibid., II.170; *Saṃyutta Nikāya*, II.170.
39. *Aṅguttara Nikāya*, I.35.
40. *Milindapañho*, 32.25–7.

41. *Vinaya Pitaka*, IV.83.
42. *Majjhima Nikāya*, V.12; *Vinaya Pitaka*, IV.80.
43. Ibid., II.55.
44. *Saṃyutta Nikāya*, II.98–100.
45. *Vinaya Pitaka*, III.58.
46. Ibid., IV.66, 335; *Dhammapadatthakatha*, I.122.
47. *Vinaya Pitaka*, I.21–2.
48. *Mahāvagga*, VI.2.
49. Ibid., V.13.
50. Ibid., III.58.
51. Ibid., VI.4.
52. I.B. Horner, *Early Buddhism and the Taking of Life*, no. 104, Kandy: BPS and Wheel Publications, 2008, repr., p. 10.
53. *Vinaya Pitaka*, III.208.
54. *Aṅguttara Nikāya*, IV.187.
55. *Vinaya Pitaka*, I.239.
56. *Aṅguttara Nikāya*, IV.187.
57. *Vinaya Pitaka*, III.62.
58. Harvey, *An Introduction to Buddhist Ethics*, p. 160.
59. *Aṅguttara Nikāya*, XIII.13, 31.
60. D. Seyfrot Ruegg, 'Ahiṃsa and Vegetarianism in *Buddhist Studies in Honour of Walapola Rahula*', ed. Somaratna Balasooriya, London: Gordon Frazer, 1980, p. 229.
61. James J. Steward, 'The Question of Vegetarianism and Diet in Pāli Buddhism', *Journal of Buddhist Ethics*, vol. 17, 2010, p. 111.
62. *Parājika*, no. 2.
63. *Vinaya Pitaka*, III.58.
64. Ibid., I.217.
65. Kautilya, *Arthaśāstra*, tr. R Shamasastri, Delhi: LPP, 2012, repr., p. 135.
66. E. Hultzsch, *Inscriptions of Aśoka (Corpus Inscriptionum Indicarum)*, MRE.1 (Girnar), Delhi: Indological Books, 1969, vol. 1, pp. 2–3.
67. Ibid., MRE.II (Girnar), pp. 3–4.
68. Ibid., Pillar Edict V (Delhi-Topra), pp. 127–8.
69. Samuel Beal, *The Life of Hiuen-Tsiang by Shaman Hwui Li*, Delhi: LPP, 2008, repr., p. 83.
70. Samuel Beal, *Travels of Fah-Hian and Sung-Yun from China to India*, Delhi: LPP, 2005, repr., pp. 54–5.
71. *Dīgha Nikāya*, II.122.
72. G.P. Malalasekera, *Dictionary of Pāli Proper Names*, Delhi: MLBD, vol. 1, 2007, p. 876.
73. *Dīgha Nikāya*, II.126; *Udana*, VIII.5.
74. Ibid., II.135.
75. *Sumangalavilāsinī*, II.568.
76. Dhammapala, *Udāna Commentary*, tr. Peter Masefield, vol. 2, London: PTS, 1995, p. 125.
77. *Vinaya Pitaka*, I.21–2.

78. Kar Eugen Neumann, *Die Reden Gotamo Buddho's aus des Mittleren Sammlung Majjhimanikayo des Pālī Kanons,* Leipzig, 1896, pp. xiv–xxii.
79. T.W. Rhys Davids, *Dialogues of the Buddha,* vol. 2, p. 137.
80. R. Gordon Wasson, 'The Last Meal of the Buddha', *Journal of American Oriental Society,* vol. 12, no. 4, 1982, p. 591.
81. Stella Kramrisch, 'The Mahavira Vessel and the Plant Putika', *Journal of the American Oriental Society,* vol. 95, no. 2, 1975, pp. 222–35.
82. Ananda K. Coomaraswamy, *Buddha and the Gospel of Buddhism,* Delhi: Asia Publishing House, 1956, p. 76.
83. Andre Bareau, *Recherches sur la biographie du Buddha (Research on the Biography of the Buddha),* vol. 1, Paris, 1970, p. 271.
84. E.J. Thomas, 'Buddha's Last Meal', *Indian Culture,* vol. XV, nos. 1–4, 1948–9, pp. 1–3.
85. Fa Chow, 'Sukara-Maddava and the Buddha's Death', *Annals of Bhandarkar Orientlal Research Institute,* vol. XXIII, 1942, pp. 127–33.
86. Arthur Waley, 'Did Buddha Died of Eating Pork? With a Note on Buddha's Image', *Melanges Chinois et Bounddhiques,* vol. 1931–2, 1932, pp. 343–54, see p. 350.
87. Ibid., p. 346.
88. *Laṅkavatāra Sutra,* vol. IV, pp. 253–5.
89. Ibid., IV.258–9.
90. Kramrisch, 'The Mahavira Vessel and the Plant Putika', p. 225.
91. W.W. Malandra, 'Atharvaveda 2.27: Evidence for a Soma-Amulet', *Journal of American Oriental Society,* vol. 99, 1979, p. 220.
92. Ibid., pp. 222–3.
93. David Stophlet Flattery and Martin Schwartz, *Haoma and Haomaline: The Botanical Identity of the Leagacy in Religion, Language and Middle Eastern Folklore,* Berkeley: University of California Press, 1989, p. 134. (W.W. Malandra cites verses VII.104–12 to substantiate his point.)
94. Margaret Stutley, *Ancient Indian Magic and Folklore: An Introduction,* London: Routledge & Kegan Paul, 1980, p. 130–1.
95. Wasson, 'The Last Meal of the Buddha', pp. 594–5.
96. Ibid., p. 594.
97. Flattery and Schwartz, *Haoma and Haomaline,* p. 137.
98. Gernot L. Windfuhr, 'Haoma/Soma: The Plant', *Acta Iranica,* vol. XI, no. 25, 1985, pp. 699–726, see p. 700.
99. W.D. O'Flaherty, 'Epilogue: The Last Meal of The Buddha', p. 603, *Journal of the American Oriental Society,* vol. 102, no. 4, 1982, pp. 591–603.
100. Wasson, 'The Last Meal of the Buddha', p. 593.
101. Uma Chakravarti, *The Social Dimensions of Early Buddhism,* Delhi: Munshiram Manoharlal, 1996, p. 95.
102. Ibid., p. 217.
103. *Kātyāyana Śrauta Sūtra,* IX.8.8ff.
104. *Suttanipāta,* V.309, tr. K.R. Norman, London: PTS, 2001.
105. Ibid., V.310.
106. Ibid., V.311.

107. Ibid., V.312.
108. *Dīgha Nikāya*, I.127–45.
109. *Saṃyutta Nikāya*, I.74.
110. *Suttanipāta*, V.313.
111. *Saṃyutta Nikāya*. I.76; *Aṅguttara Nikāya*, II.42, IV.151.
112. *Suttanipāta*, V.106.
113. Ibid., VV.107–8.
114. Ibid., V.296.
115. *Jātaka*, no. 543.
116. *Suttanipāta*, VV.265–313.
117. Ibid., VV.115–23.
118. I.B. Horner, *Early Buddhism and the Taking of Life*, p. 5.
119. B.D. Chattopadhyaya, *D.D. Kosambi: Combined Methods in Indology and Other Writings*, Delhi: OUP, 2003, p. 233.
120. R.S. Sharma, *India's Ancient Past*, Delhi: Oxford University Press, 2005, p. 131.
121. Sharma, *Material Culture and Social Formation in Ancient India*, New Delhi: Macmillan, 2001, p. 109.
122. Romila Thapar, 'The Evolution of State in Ganga Valley in the Mid First Millennium BC', in *Cultrual Past: Essay in Early Indian History*, ed. Romila Thapar, Delhi: Oxford University Press, 2004, pp. 377–95, see p. 385.
123. Thapar, 'Sacrifice, Surplus and Soul', in *Cultrual Past: Essay in Early Indian History*, ed. Romila Thapar, Delhi: Oxford University Press, 2004, pp. 809–31, see pp. 816–18.
124. *Śatpatha Brāhmana*, 14.1.4.14–16.
125. K.A. Chaudhary, K.S. Saraswat and G.M. Buth, *Ancient Agriculture and Forestry in Northern India*, New Delhi: Asia Publishing House, 1977.
126. *Rāmayana*, XXVIII, 148–9.
127. Kautilya, *Arthaśastra*, tr. R. Shamasastry, II.6.
128. Ibid. II.20.
129. Ibid. II.2.
130. Makkhan Lal, 'Summary of Four Season Explorations in Kanpur District, Uttar Pradesh', *Man and Environment*, 1984, pp. 61–80.
131. Lal, *Archaeology of Population*, Varanasi: Banaras Hindu University, 1984, p. 23.
132. Ibid., pp. 21–4.
133. Lal, *Iron Tools, Forest Clearance, Urbanization in the Gangetic Plains*, pp. 145–6.
134. Lal, *Archaeology of Population*, p. 3.
135. Lal, 'Iron Tools, Forest Clearance, and Urbanization in the Gangetic Plains', pp. 145–6; B.P. Sahu, *Iron and Social Change in Early India*, Delhi: Oxford University Press, 2006, pp. 137–49.
136. D.P. Agarwal, *Steps Towards Urban Revolution in Doab: Archaeological & Ecological Data*, p. 130.
137. Lal, *Archaeology of Population*, p. 29.
138. Ibid., pp. 23–46.

139. Lal, *Settlement History and the Rise of Civilization in the Ganga-Yamuna Doab*, pp. 240–2.

140. Lal, *Archaeology of Population*, p.40.

141. Josiah C. Russell, 'The Population of Ancient India: A Tentative Pattern', *Journal of Indian History* (Golden Jublee Volume), 1973, pp. 267–81; 'The Population of Hiuen Tsang's India', *Journal of Indian History*, vol. XLVII, no. 1, 1969, pp. 367–83.

142. George Erdosy, 'The Origin of Cities in the Ganges Valley', *Journal of the Economic and Social History of Orient*, vol. 28, no. 1, 1985, pp. 85–109.

143. D.K. Chakravarti and Nayajot Lahiri, 'The Iron Age in India, the Beginning and Consequences', *Puratattva*, vol. 24, 1994, pp. 12–32.

144. K.K. Mandal, 'Agricultual Technology in the Jātakas', *Proceedings of Indian History Congress*, 59th Session, 1998, pp. 97–107.

145. K.M. Srimali, *The Age of Iron and the Religious Revolution (700-350 BC)*, New Delhi: Tulika Books, 2010, pp. 18–19.

146. H.M. Elliot, and John Dowson, *The History of India as Told by Its Own Historians*, vol. III, pp. 102–3.

147. M.A. Ansari, 'The Hunt of the Great Mughals', *Islamic Culture*, vol. XXXIV, no. 1, Hyderabad, 1959, pp. 1–5.

148. Abul Fazl, *Ain-I Akbari*, tr. H. Biochmann, vol. I, New Delhi, 1977, pp. 292–3.

149. Irfan Habib, *The Atlas of the Mughal Empire; Political and Economic Maps with Detailed Notes, Bibliography and Index*, Delhi: Oxford University Press, 1982, p. 8B. (Irfan Habib on basis of James Renell, *Bengal Atlas*, 1781, sheet no. X, informs that 26°, i.e. the area of Ganga-Yamuna doab in the Indian Subcontinent was full of forests and hunting grounds. In the same source Bernier informs that Agra to Mathura zone was full of tigers indicating the rich flora and fauna.)

150. T.V. Mahalingam, *Administration and Social Life Under Vijaynagar*, Madras: University of Madras, 1969, pp. 398–9.

151. Madhav Gadgil and Ramchandra Guha, *This Fissured Land: An Ecological History of India*, Delhi: Oxford University Press, 1994, pp. 120–1.

152. *The Imperial Gazetteer Atlas of India*, Delhi: LPP, (edn. 1931), 2007, repr., Plate 5.

2

Plants in Early Buddhism

Plants which play a very distinctive role in the universe, forms an important aspect amongst the animate or inanimate beings of the Earth. The general perception in Buddhism is that grasses and plants (*tinarukkha*) are *ekandriyajīva* and *sparśa* (touch) with their *kāyā* (body) and *tvac* (skin) are their main sense organs. Religious doctrines affirm that plants are to be understood in terms of life, evolution, and decay. The ecological models understand plants and their experiences in a continuous natural process. The life of a plant is not in the hands of chance and necessity. In Buddhism human decisions are extremely important to maintain the healthy human-plant relationship. These relations can be exemplified by human thoughts and purposive actions. In religious literature, plants have been divided into seven categories: medical herbs (*osadhi*), forest vegetation (*vanaspati*), trees with fruits and flowers (*vrksa*), shrubs (*gumba*), grasses (*tina*), and plants with tendrils (*patāna*) and vines (*valli*).[1] In Buddhism, plants are identified on the basis of their roots (*mula*), stems (*khandha*), joints (*phulla*), head or upper most pores (*agga*), or seeds (*bija*).[2] The *Anguttara Nikāya* says that plants can be classified as herbs (*osadhi*), grasses (*tina*), and forests (*vanaspatyo*).[3] It also describes different birth categories (*yonio*): egg-born (*andaja*), womb-born (*jalabuja*), moisture-born or arising from rotten things like fish (*samsedaja*), and spontaneously-born or *devas* (*opapatika yoni*).[4] The plants may be put in *samsedaja* category as seeds need both moisture and water.

The earliest literary reference of reverence and protection of plants are found in the *Rigveda* where plants are requested not to injure a person who is digging the plant for medicines.[5] The *Gobila Grihyasutra* relates trees with gods, like Asvattha is related to the Sun, Palaksa to the Yama, Nyagrodha to God Varuna, and Udumbara to Prajapati.[6] The *kalpavrksa* (wishing tree) was a charming tree which is said to fulfil all the wishes of human beings. In Vedic literature, *kalpavrksa* has been depicted as bestowing boons and material wealth to human beings.[7] The *Anguttara Nikāya* mentions the banyan (wishing) tree in the courtyard of King Koravya of Vārānasī. It bore sweet fruits sufficient for all people of the kingdom. But a person broke a branch of the tree and such an action invited the wrath of the tree spirit, which bore no fruit after the incident.[8] The *Mahāvanija Jātaka* praises a banyan tree (*kalpavrksa*) which provides cool and pleasant shade, pure water, and varieties of food to eat to the merchants.[9] The *Vinaya Pitaka* prohibits destruction and injury to plants which are treated as the *pacittiya* offence.[10] The monks and nuns are also instructed not to dig the earth as that will harm the living beings.[11] Buddhaghosa describes the quality of a tree and the ill-effects of harming it:

When a great tree is growing on the earth's surface supported by the essence of humus and water and, with that as condition, increases its roots, trunks, branches, twigs, shoots, foliage, flowers, and fruit, till it fills the sky, and continues the tree's lineage through the succession of the speed up till the end of thereon, it cannot be said that the essence of humus, etc., are found only in its root and not in trunk, etc., that they are not only in fruit and not in the root, etc., Why? Because they spread indiscriminately through the whole of it from the roots onwards. But some man who felt revulsion for that same tree's flowers, fruits, etc., might puncture it on four sides with the poison thorn called 'mandūka thorn' and then the tree, being poisoned, would be no more able to prolong its continuity since it would have become with the contamination of the essences of humus and water.[12]

The early Buddhist literature vividly describes plant protection and that can be adopted and practiced by monks, nuns, and lay followers. The Buddha says that intentional good or bad action functions like a seed and the *kammic* results of that action lead to fruition of merit, i.e. seeds of good action are always rewarding (*anuttaram punna khettam*). It is like agriculture where a good harvest always depends on the quality of the soil, appropriate water supply, etc.[13] It has been emphasized that good quality of seed produces good crops just as good action always reaps good *kamma* and evil always produces evil.[14] The Buddha says that faith is the seed, austerity the rain, wisdom the yoke and plough, modesty the plough pole, mind the strap, and mindfulness the ploughshare and goad.[15] The *Dīgha Nikāya* mentions that monks and nuns are prohibited from injuring plants and seeds. They should be compassionate towards them.[16] The precept of *śila* consists of abstention from killing or injuring seeds and plants (*bijagama bhutagama samarambho*).[17] The *Vinaya Pitaka* mentions that the Buddha was annoyed with some monks because they plucked young palmyra leaves or bamboo to wear them as sandals.[18] The people of Magadha were once angry with the monks because they wandered around in the rainy season and crushed the green grasses underfoot.[19] A monk was also admonished by the Buddha for cutting trees for his hut.[20] They were also prohibited from eating garlic and any transgression was a *dukkhata* offence[21] and for nuns this was a *pacittiya* offence.[22] Lambert Schmithausen says that garlic was prohibited because it was considered as sentient.[23] The Jain literature corroborates this view where it is prohibited to eat bulbs, bulbous roots, and parts of plants capable of sprouting because they are considered to be sentient.[24] The rule for monks and nuns prohibiting them from destroying trees, plants, and digging the earth was a reminder of the warning that even minute living beings should not be harmed.[25] There were two types of land, *jāta* and *ajāta*. The *jāta* land was full of living beings and *ajāta* was the barren land. It was a *pacittiya* offence to dig *jāta* land.[26] The *Ghatakāra Sutta* says that a lay follower not only practices five precepts but he also does not dig the earth to get clay for making pottery.[27] It was also a *pacittiya* offence for monks and nuns to kindle fire for warmth although it was allowed in dire conditions and illness.[28] The monks were also prohibited to set fire in the forest as it would destroy plants and animals.[29] The Buddha was even critical of cutting of trees for *yajnas* and for sacrificial posts and also strewing of *darba* grass for sacrificial grounds.[30]

In Buddhism, two types of living beings have been defined, mobile (*tasa*) and stationary (*thavara*). The plants and trees were categorized as *thavara* and, thus, monks, nuns, and lay followers have been advised to show friendliness and compassion towards them.[31] The *upāsakas* thus sometimes felt anxious that they might injure grass and herbs, i.e. *ekandriyajiva*.[32] The Buddha was told that some of the monks trample down crops and grains during summer, rainy, and winter seasons causing injury to tiny living beings.[33] The Buddha says that even *sāla* tree can attain liberation and happiness if they are stimulated by his teaching to abandon unwholesomeness and imbibe wholesome action.[34] When Channa severed the tree which was considered auspicious by the villagers, they complained to the Buddha. The Buddha admonished Channa and treated it as a *saṃghadesesa* offence which might suspend or temporarily expel monks from the *saṃgha*.[35] Buddhaghosa has extreme views on injury caused to plants and trees, and believed that a monk should not harm a tree even for saving his own life. So far example, even if it falls over a monk but he should not cut the tree.[36] The other monks are, however, allowed to cut the tree or dig the Earth to rescue their fellow monk because motive is not self interest but rather compassion for a fellow being.[37] A contrary view is found when the *Visuddhimagga*[38] says that grasses and trees along with minerals, jewels, soil, and stones are not treated as sense faculties. The process of sprouting, growth, withering, and dropping of leaves by trees is not described in the context of compassion but to set an example for the monks to meditate on impermanence.[39] In Eastern Buddhism like Zen, plants possess Buddha Nature and may attain Buddhahood. Some however believe that if plants have Buddha Nature, this does not mean that they can attain Buddhahood. Some sects like Tendai accept that 32 *lakkhanas* are not necessary to depict the Buddha. The trees can attain *nibbāna* through their leaves, branches, and stems.[40] The plants having Buddha Nature show reverence towards other plants and other forms of nature. Their observance, like shedding leaves, withering, and decaying, exhibit impermanence and give positive direction to society.[41] Hajime Nakamura says that the idea of non-violence for plants and tress in Buddhism is not as extreme as is in Jainism. It is more pragmatic and accommodating.[42] Early Buddhism did not clearly define plants and trees as sentient like that in Jainism and the Vedic religion where *tinarukkha* (grass and tree) are accepted as sentient. However, plants have a revered position in Buddhism. Prohibitions, restrictions, and advisories have been issued from time to time for the protection of plants and trees.

Sentience of Plants in Buddhism

Lambert Schmithausen[43] has critically examined sentiency among the plants in early Buddhism. In his two short monographs and one voluminous reference work, he widely discussed sentient characteristics of plants with special reference to Theravāda and Eastern Buddhism. Ellison Banks Findly[44] is another scholar who vividly describes this subject. Schmithausen argues that the canonical passages in the early Buddhist texts do not expressively corroborate sentiency of plants or that injury to plants and trees or digging of the earth will yield bad *kamma*. However, this was kind of a 'borderline' case. Though the monks and nuns are instructed to follow a path of non-injury to plants, for those who roamed from place to place for alms and preaching *dhamma*, complete abstention from non-injury was not possible. In order to overcome such problem the Buddha ignored to discuss the sentient characteristics of plants.[45] The seeds and plants have not been recognized as living beings in the early Buddhist literature since the killing of living beings was a *pacittiya* offence (no. 61), if the seeds and plants have to be accepted as sentient, this will entail providing a separate rule of prohibition in the *pacittiyas* or somewhere else.[46] The seeds and plants too are 'borderline' beings and therefore the monks and nuns are instructed not to harm them; for the lay followers the Buddha took a liberal view.[47] It is also believed that non-injury to crops and cultivated plants was regulated because it might harm a potential donor.[48] Schmithausen says that abstention from killing of animals and plants was prevalent among the heterodox sects because they borrowed it from the early cultural stratum. In such cultures, killing of animals, plants, earth, and water was considered equal to the killing of man because these animals were said to take revenge in their next birth.[49] The non-killing and non-injury were vigorously propounded by the *Upanishads*, Jainism, and other contemporary sects and it was was firmly established in India before advent of Buddhism. The *Rigveda*, later Vedic literature, and Jain literature accept both animals and plants as sentient.[50] The Buddha adopted a moderate view with regard to sentience of plants in comparison to other contemporary religions and sects. When non-violence became an established belief in the society, the lay followers also became conscious that agriculture, housing, and food demanded the killing of animals and cutting of plants and forests. Buddhism thus adopted a judicious approach by propounding non injury to animals but took a liberal view on seeds and plants because the laity could freely exercise their consciousness to fulfil their daily necessities.

From other perspectives, Buddhist view on the sentience of plant extends to the idea that grasses and plants possess some faculty that make their living significant although their ability to develop useful insights into the *saṁsāric* world is limited.[51] Peter Harvey says that the practical notion of dualism about sentience of plants in early Buddhism was adopted to avoid hurting popular sentiment of the sixth century BC population.

The Buddha is described as having avoided harm to seed and plant life, and there are monastic rules against harming trees and plants. It is an offence requiring expiation (by acknowledgement) for a monks to fell a tree or to ask someone else to do so. Here the occasion for making the rule is that a god who lived in a felled tree complained to the Buddha. In addition, lay people complained that Buddhist monks, in felling trees, were 'harming life that is one facultied' (ekendriya jiva): i.e. only possessing the sense of touch, an idea found in Jainism. The Buddha thus ban the destruction of 'vegetable growth' by monks. One might speculate that the 'one facultied life' could refer to many small insects living on trees and plants. However the explanation of above rules only refers to various kinds of plants and trees, not to insects that live on them.[52]

Schmithausen says that the different views adopted by early and later Buddhism regarding sentience of plants and seeds are due to different prevailing conditions in the society at different time rather than the ideological differences among the different sects of Buddhism.[53] It may be true that the Buddha did not take a strong view on the sentience of seeds and plants. Jainism tried to establish living attributes in seeds and plants both scientifically and ethically. They propounded sentience character among plants, water, trees, and earth. The Buddha adopted a pragmatic approach because the foundation of Buddhism was laid on eradication of prevailing rituals and violence in *yajnas*. The Buddha took a stronger view on those matters directly relevant to society. The animals, plants, water, and earth are parts of the universe and human respect for them was necessary for survival and growth of all species. Early Buddhism tried to sustain pragmatic and revered view on all animate and inanimate beings with a rider not to injure grasses, plants, and trees (*tinarukkha*).

Ellison Banks Findly begins her discussion on the sentience of plants by examining Schmithausen's propositions about sentience characters among the plants in early Buddhism. She considers those Pāli texts referring to plants as sentient beings as the real belief of the earliest Buddhism and also ponders over the ambiguities of religious texts that refer to plants as living beings as something vague. Since it was difficult to accept one clear proposition, Schmithausen calls it the 'borderline' being.[54] She says,

If plants and seeds including grasses and trees, creepers, bushes, and trees are, as one of the objects of the ethic of the non-violence, not to be injured then it would make sense that they would be included among those designated as living, sentient beings, then they should concomitantly, be a part of samsaric world and in some way subject to the laws of kamma.[55]

Findly argues that in early Buddhism plants were counted among living beings. In Pāli literature, *bhuto, jiva, satta*, and *pana* denotes sentient beings. The term *bhūtagāma* indicates vegetation and within it plants could be included as objects of non-violence. The Pāli texts represent plants as *ekandriyajīva* that are not to be injured.[56] The term *satta* in these texts refers to sentient beings and includes living beings like plants and it also came occasionally with other terms such as *sabbe satta, sabbe pana, sabbe bhūta,* and *sabbe jīva* that include all creatures.[57] Early Buddhism defines *pana* as living beings comprising seeds and plants. It means that Buddhism considered plants as living or animate beings.[58]

Findly also says that scientific properties, sap (fluid), birth, maturity, decay, and death, breath or respiration can be traced in plants and Indian traditions mention such qualities in plants.[59] Sap in plants may be in the form of water because plant requires water for growth and survival which they circulate inside their body through various channels.[60] Such example is found in the *Dīgha Nikāya* saying that in conditions seed will grow large and after maturity it will wither, decay, and die.[61] The general term for vegetation, i.e. *bhūtagāma*, suggests continuous process of arising and decay. The term *bhuta* in Pāli normally denotes animate being such as animals including plants.[62] The texts mention plant growth (*bhūtagāma*) through five processes: roots (*mulabija*), stems (*khandabija*), joints (*phalabija*), cuttings (*aggabija*), and seeds (*bijabija*).[63] Bidwell says that growth of plant is distinguished from animals and humans because animals can roam from place to place to acquire food while plants can seek food resources, water, and other nutrients from restricted geography throughout their life by adding leaves, stems, and shedding their decaying organs.[64] Despite being stationary they are subject to environmental change. The *Majjhima Nikāya* tells that trees can grow by expanding their stems, branches, leaves, roots, and that they are responsive to resources of earth, water, and air.[65] Plants respond vigorously with plenty of water but lack growth in its absence.[66] The canonical literature also suggests that if the right environment is not provided to seeds and plants, they wither, decay and die. The *Aṅguttara Nikāya* says that if the field is rocky, pebbly or salty, the plant will not get the proper environment to grow.[67]

It is also argued that sensory characteristic is an important element for the growth of plants and the sense of touch also leads to other sense faculties since it acts as a foundation for reception for all sense data. The sense of the touch in plant is all pervasive to make contact (*phassa*) between sensory organs and the objects involving consciousness (*vinnana*). It leads to expression of feeling like pleasure and pain. In the cycle of *paticcasamuppada*, plants may be included as subject to ignorance, desire, and attachment. Because of this attribute, trees also participate in *kamma*-oriented rebirth in the *saṁsāric* cycle. Findly says that *kāyā* denotes both for the faculty of touch and body as one of the three mediums through which *kamma* is produced. Since such dualism does not seem to be coincidental, it simply means plants were endowed with *kāyā* (body) which was a *kamma*-producing feature. They also maintain succession like humans through their lineage in the form of seeds-plants-seed.[68] Schmithausen, however, counters Findly's proposition that plants can be sentient because they are endowed with touch. Her hypothesis has been mainly taken from Pāli sources exhibiting observable characteristics of plants showing sense of touch. She mentions that growing, withering, and dying of plants are all attributed to the sense of touch. The plants grow in the warmth of the sun and wither in the cold. They prosper with water and decay in its absence. They grow towards the light and their roots respond to water beneath the earth's surface. So they are endowed with a sense of touch and express pleasure and pain. Schmithausen says that such ideas of Findly are based on observable properties only and are not properly corroborated by doctrinal evidences.[69] She says that the sentience of plants can be supported by the term *satta* (sentient). The *Sondanda Sutta* and *Kūtadanta Sutta* include plants in *satta*, i.e. grass, timber, water, and corn.[70] Schmithausen's argument is that that Pāli texts do not explicitly mention plants as sentient beings and the reference of *satta* in the *Dīgha Nikāya* simply shows donations given by King Bimbisāra to the brāhmana Sonadanda and Kūtadanta. So the term *satta* should not be qualified as sentient being. It does not only comprise living beings but also timber (*kattha*) and water (*udaka*); both considered insentient in Buddhism.[71]

The *Mangandiya Sutta* has examined the case of sentiency of grasses and plants and it narrates an incident that occured when Mangandiya visited the house of a Bharadwaja brāhmana and saw that the brāhmana had put grass as seat (*tina-santharaka*) for the Buddha. Mangandiya's reaction to the Buddha sitting in the grass was that the Buddha is a killer of plants (*bhūnahuno*).[72] Findly says that it shows that plants are sentient but Schmithausen says that her argument is inappropriate as Mangandiya was a wanderer ascetic and was not a disciple of the Buddha. He may believe that plants are sentient. But the term *bhūnahuno* represents killer of embryos not killer of plants. Mangandiya reacted against the Buddha's view on discarding sensual pleasures and control of senses.[73] Vetter says that *bhūnahuno* can be a synonym of *bhrutahan* which literally means killer of embryos. In the context of *Mangandiya Sutta*, the embryo killer means prevention of having children and sexual intercourse.[74] The Brāhmanical sources accepts that preventing procreation during the time of a women's fertile period is considered *bhrunahatyā*.[75] Schmithausen may be true that Mangandiya was not a follower of the Buddha when he met brāhmana of Bharadwaja *gotra* but his reaction against the seat of grass shows that he had knowledge and belief that plants are sentient. He instantly reacted against the spread of the grass. Later, when he came to know that it was meant for the Buddha, he called him *bhūnohuno*. He may be a Jain ascetic or from a contemporary sect that believed plants to be living beings. The discussion between Mangandiya and Bharadwaja brāhmana also indicates that sentiency among seeds and plants was well discussed among the ascetic groups and the wanderers of the time. The Buddha also seems to be aware of this and may have intentionally avoided a discussion on such issues as it would create problems for the monks and nuns and also for lay followers in their day to day activities. Regarding the ban on the killing of embryos, the monks and nuns were in a minority during the age of the Buddha and even in the later age. The celibate life was necessary for them. The lay followers were never instructed to be celibate, however, they were always advised to not indulge in sexual pleasure.

Mamiko Okada has also examined sentience among plants in Buddhism by analysing Buddhist narrative literature, especially *Jātakas*. Okada highlights close connection between tree spirits and trees in the *Bhaddasala Jātaka* and how the trees are saved by the spirit's intervention.[76] Okada says that in the Northern and Mahāyāna forms of Buddhism plants are not fully treated as sentient but in the earliest and Theravāda Buddhism, they were regarded as living beings and accepted as *ekandriyajiva*. She substantiates her argument with the help of the Pāli *Jātakas*.[77] Schmithausen opines about the soul-body relationship of trees saying:

It seems that Okada considers this relationship to be genuine and that she takes it as additional support for her assumption that in earlier and Theravāda Buddhism plants were considered sentient. In this way, the potential for becoming a Buddha attributed to tree or plant deities by virtue of their identification with the Bodhisattva would practically accrue to the trees or plants themselves. It is all the more remarkable in this connection that Okada herself observes that in narrative literature of the Northern Tradition stories in which a tree deity, not to consider a tree, is equated with the Bodhisattva sees to be entirely missing.[78]

The symbolic relationship between plants and spirit in the *Jātaka* stories showed that spirits were dependent upon the grasses or trees for their existence. Schmithausen's view is more relevant here that tree deities were more concerned about their life and existence, but during this process they did everything to save that plant. In this connection tree deities jointly made an effort.[79] However, it can not be established that the tree and spirit relationship directly indicates any sentient characteristics in plants but, thus, their mutual dependence on each other definitely showed environmental concerns.

Akira Fujimoto explores the attributes of life among plants and found that in Theravāda Buddhism plants were regarded as insentient. They were not part of *kamma*-conditioned *saṃsāra*. The canonical passages do not subscribe to the belief that plants and seeds were living beings. Theravāda Abhidharma says that plants lack *kamma*-oriented rebirth but were endowed with material life faculty (*rūpajivitindriya*). For plants, what is ethically precious is life rather than their sentience character. Instead of indulging in a precarious 'borderline' status between sentient and insentient, plants have a specific status of being living beings.[80] His hypothesis that plants in the Theravāda do not have *kamma* conditioned rebirth but have a *kamma* conditioned material life faculty is difficult to accept. If plants and their material life faculty are conditioned by common *kamma* of sentient beings then the whole world can be affected by such *kamma* of sentient beings. His view that plant consists of material life faculty has not been given in the Theravāda doctrines.[81] The sentience among the plants is highly debatable topic in Buddhism. Two contrary views are found in the early Buddhism and Mahāyāna tradition. Schmithausen and Findly have critically examined the various possible strands of sentience of plants in Buddhism. The possibilities suggest that the early Buddhism did not emphasize on putting clear view on sentience of seeds and plants because it was not pragmatic for nascent religion like Buddhism to engage in philosophical arguments and debates but to concentrate on principles that could help its growth.

Forests Associated with the Buddha (Map 3)

Sacred forests and groves may be seen as a bridge between the nature and the religion. In sacred geography of the Ganga valley, forests continue to connect the present with the past, the material with the symbolic. Sacred forests are integral part of lived tradition of Buddhism and it has a deep and long-standing association with Buddhism, figuring prominently in the religion's tradition. It was

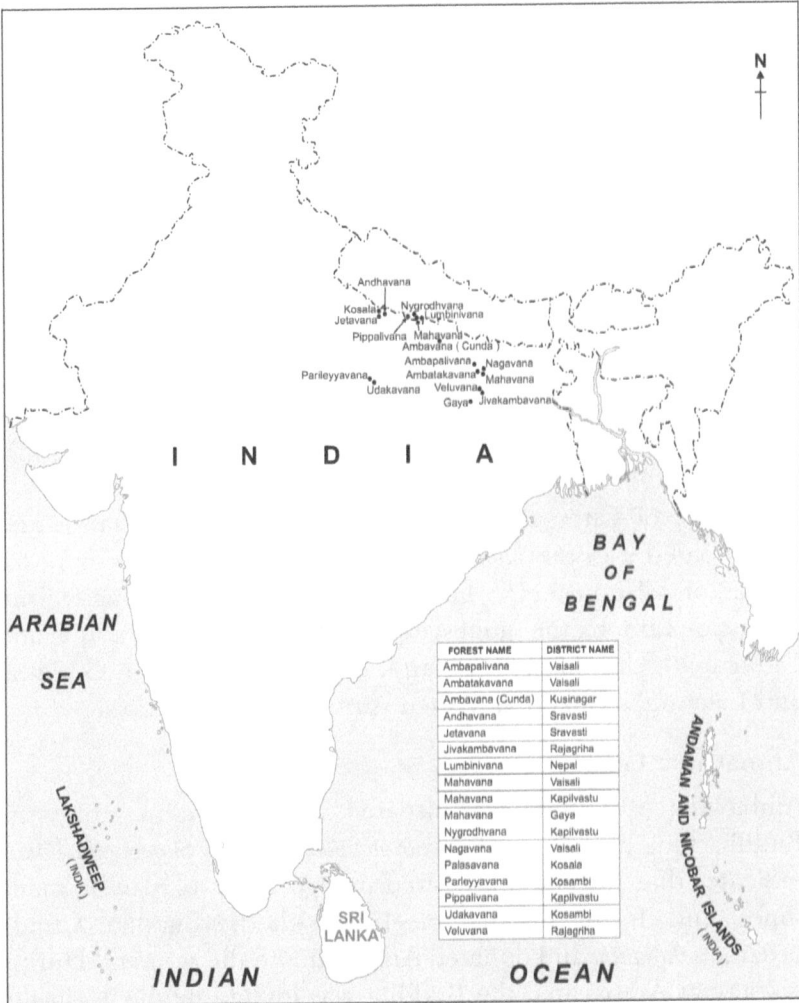

1. The International boundaries and territorial waters of India as shown in this map are neither authentic nor correct. 2. Sketch map not to scale.

MAP 3: India Forests

FOREST NAME	DISTRICT NAME
Ambapalivana	Vaisali
Ambatakavana	Vaisali
Ambavana (Cunda)	Kusinagar
Andhavana	Sravasti
Jetavana	Sravasti
Jivakambavana	Rajagriha
Lumbinivana	Nepal
Mahavana	Vaisali
Mahavana	Kapilvastu
Mahavana	Gaya
Nygrodhvana	Kapilvastu
Nagavana	Vaisali
Palasavana	Kosala
Parleyyavana	Kosambi
Pippalivana	Kapilvastu
Udakavana	Kosambi
Veluvana	Rajagriha

under the *sālavana* Siddhārtha was born in Lumbinī. Under Bodhi tree at Bodhgayā, he attained enlightenment and in grove of *sāla* trees at Kuśināra, he took *mahāparinibbāna*. The Buddha frequently dwelt in forests during his spiritual quest and wanderings. In the Pāli texts, the Buddha often instructed the monks to seek the seclusion of forest dwellings and it will be conducive to purify the mind from all sort of defilements. Many of his disciples were strict forest dwellers. Some of the important forests mentioned in the Pāli texts are:

Ambapalīvana

The Ambapalīvana was a mango grove owned by Ambapalī the famous courtesan of Vaiśalī.[82] She invited the Buddha for a meal and donated him the grove during his last visit to Vaiśalī.[83] The Buddha resided in this grove in his previous visits to Vaiśalī and delivered many important *suttas*.[84] He preached here impermanence of the world and emphasized on good *kamma*.[85] Anuruddha and Sariputta also stayed here and held fruitful discussions.[86]

Ambatakavana

This grove of Cittagahapati was situated at Macchikasanda and he donoated it to the *samgha*. He built Ambatkarama Vihāra for monks of all quarters.[87] The *Samyutta Nikāya* mentions fruitful discussions among the monks, especially between the Buddha and Cittagapati.[88] Monks like Isidatta, Mahaka, Kamabhu, Godatta, and Lakuntaka Bhaddiya visited Ambatakavana and resided.[89]

Ambavana (Cunda)

Ambavana of Cunda was situated near Kuśināra. Here the Buddha took his last meal, *Sukaramaddava*.[90] The *Sumaṅgalavilāsinī* indicates that the Buddha visited mango grove of Cunda many times, and during his first meeting with the Buddha, Cunda became *sotapaṅna* and donated Ambavana to the *samgha*.[91] During his stay at Ambavana, the Buddha was invited by the Mallas to inaugurate their assembly hall (*Ubbhataka*), which he accepted. At this occasion Sariputta preached the *Sangiti Sutta*.[92] The *Aṅguttara Nikāya* says that during his early stay at Ambavana, the Buddha preached Cunda, the threefold defilements and the purification of body and mind, and the fourfold defilement and the purification of speech.[93]

Andhavana

Andhavana was situated near Sāvatthī.[94] The Buddha preached Rahula in Andhavana and he became *arahanta*.[95] *Bhikkhunis* like Alavika, Soma, Kisagotami, Vijaya, Uppalavana, Kala, Upacala,

Sisupacala, Sela, and Vajira lived here to attain knowledge.[96] Sariputta also resided here for sometime.[97] King Prasenjit met the Buddha in Andhavana.[98] After a nun, Uppalavana, was raped here by a brāhmana, the Buddha made a rule that nuns would not live in the forests and that monks will not enter in village in their waist cloth.[99] In Andhavana, Uppalavana got the piece of flesh from Udayi to offer it to the Buddha.[100] The Buddha made a rule in Andhavana that monks will not enter in village in their waist cloth. The rule was made by the Buddha when robe of a monk was stolen by thieves in Andhavana.[101] The number of *parajika* rules were also framed here by the Buddha.[102]

Jetavana

The Jetavana garden at Sāvatthī was built by great *upāsaka* and *setthi* of Saketa, Anathapindika (Sudatta). He purchased the garden from prince Jeta by covering the land with pieces of gold and only the space for a gateway was left on request of the prince.[103] Anathapindika purchased Jetavana for 18 crores and all the money was spent by Prince Jeta for construction of the ornamented gateway.[104] King Prasenjit also built *sālagraha* at Jetavana.[105] In front of the gateway, a mango orchard and a branch of bodhi tree was planted by Ananda on advice of Anathapindika, which was later on popularly known as Ananda Bodhi. At this ceremony large congregation of people including the king and Visakha participated. The Buddha spent nineteen *vassavāsa* at Jetavana.[106] Other *setthis* like Punabbasumita, Sirivaddha, Sothiya, Accuta, Ugga, and Sumangala also built monasteries and other buildings for the *samgha* from time to time.[107]

Jivakambavana

This mango grove was situated in Rājagaha and belonged to the great physician Jīvaka of Magadha. He donated it to the Buddha and built a *vihāra*. The Buddha visited this mango grove several times.[108] Ajatshatru, the king of Magadha, visited the Buddha at this grove and he preached him the *Samannaphala Sutta*.[109] The Buddha also preached here the *Jīvaka Sutta*.[110] When Devadatta conspired to hurl rock on the Buddha and he was injured by a splinter, the Buddha was carried to Jivakambavana.[111] Culapanthaka[112] became *arahanta* at this grove.

Lumbinīvana

Lumbinī was situated between Kapilvatthu and Devadaha in the *tarai* region of eastern India. Siddhartha was born in this forest when his mother Mahāmāyā was visiting her parents at Devadaha.[113] Aśoka marked this spot by raising a pillar. The Rumendei pllar inscription informs that in the twentieth year of his coronation, Aśoka visited this place and exempted the religious tax (*bali*) because it was the birth place of the Buddha.[114] The Buddha visited Lumbinivana while going to Devadaha. He preached here the *Devadaha Sutta*.[115]

Mahāvana

There are three Mahāvanas at Vaiśali, Kapilvatthu, and Uruvela respectively. The Mahāvana of Vaiśali was very famous for its Kutagarasala and it extended to the Himalayas.[116] The Buddha stayed here many times. Some eminent persons like Siha, Mahali, Otthatthaddha, Nandaka, Sunakkhata, Bhaddiya, Salha, and Abhaya met the Buddha at Kūtagāraśala of Mahāvana of Vaiśali.[117] The Buddha at Mahāvana finally granted permission to Prajapati Gotami to be a nun with certain restrictions.[118] At Kūtagāraśala of Mahāvana, the Buddha declared his prophecy for the downfall of the Licchavis.[119] He used to go for meditation in the Mahāvana during his stay at Kūtagāraśala of Vaiśali.[120] At Kūtagāraśala, Mahāvana, he declared that he will die in three months.[121] Eighteen thousand *bhikkhus* from Mahāvana, visited Sri Lanka under the leadership of Maha-Buddharakkhita for the foundation ceremony of Mahāthūpa.[122]

The Mahāvana of Kapilavatthu was extended from Kapilvatthu to the Himalayas.[123] The Buddha preached the *Mahāsamaya Sutta* and the *Madhupindika Sutta* in Mahāvana of Kapilavatthu.[124] He used to go for meditation at Mahāvana during his stay at Nigrodhavana.[125]

The third Mahāvana was situated at Uruvela on the banks of Niranjana.[126] The Buddha also meditated here. Here Tappassu journeyed accompanied by Ananda to meet the Buddha.[127]

Nāgavana

Nāgavana was situated at Hatthigama, near Vaiśali. It belonged to *Uggagahapati* where he first met the Buddha and became his follower.[128] The Buddha praised him as one of the *upāsaka* who had great respect for the *saṃgha*.[129]

Nygrodhavana

Nygrodhavana was situated near Kapilvatthu and the Buddha resided here when he visited Kapilvatthu.[130] Here the Buddha performed a miracle *yamakapatihariya* and showered rain.[131] The Buddha's aunt, Prajapati Gotami, asked the permission of the Buddha to join the order at Nygrodhavana but was denied permission.[132] Several *Vinaya* rules were evolved by the Buddha during his stay at Nygrodhavana.[133] Once during his stay the Śakyans invited him to inaugurate their newly-built *sabhāgara*.[134] Several Śakyans like Mahānāma, Godha, Sarakani, Vappa, and Anuruddha visited and stayed here.[135] Once the Buddha stayed here when dispute between the Śakyan and the Koliyas emerged for sharing of the water of Rohini. The dispute was resolved on mediation of the Buddha.[136] It is said that the *Cariya Pitaka* and the *Buddhavaṃśa* was preached by the Buddha to Sariputta during his first stay at Nygrodhavana.[137] There was another Nygrodhavana at Rājagaha where the Buddha gave opportunity to Ananda to live for a whole year but he missed it.[138]

Palāśavana

Palāśavana was situated near Nalakapana, in Kośala. The Buddha resided here.[139] He preached the *Nalakapana Sutta* here.[140]

Parileyyavana

It was situated near Kośambi and when dissident occurred among the Kośambi monks and the Buddha failed to solve the dispute, he left the place and resided in Parileyyavana at the outskirts of Kośambi.[141] When the Buddha was staying in the forest, some monks visited him and here the Buddha preached the *Parileyyaka Sutta*, discoursing on the destruction of the *asavas* by realizing the impermanence and *anatta*.[142] At this forest, an elephant Parileyya served the Buddha and other monks with fruits and meals. When the Buddha left the forest for Savatthī, Parileyya died in grief and was born in Tavatimsa heaven.[143] A monkey also offerd honeycomb to the Buddha. After his death he was born in Tavatimsa heaven.[144]

Pippalivana

The Pippalivana was situated in the *tarai* region of the Uttar Pradesh–Nepal. The Moriyas of Pippalivana were a branch of the Śakyas of Kapilvatthu. Because of abundance of *pipala* trees, it was known as Pippalivana. When Vidudbha, the king of Kośala, massacred the Śakyas of Kapilvatthi, some of them migrated and settled at Pippalivana.[145] They got the share of the Buddha's relic but requested for their share very late; so they had to be contend only with ashes.[146] Faxian[147] and Xuanzang[148] have given references of it.

Udakavana

Udakavana was pleasure garden of King Udayana at Kośambī.[149] Pindola Bharadwaja used to practice meditation here. Once, King Udyana visited the garden when Pindola was meditating. When women accompanied by the king visited Pindola for listening to his discourse, it annoyed Udayana. He became enraged and tried to harm Pindola but the latter was saved by miraculous powers.[150]

Veluvana

Veluvana, a bamboo grove, was situated near Rājagaha. It was *arama*, built by King Bimbisāra. When the Buddha visited Rājagaha for the first time after his *nibbāna*, he was invited by King Bimbisara. Later on, he donated Veluvana to the Buddha. It was the first *dana* of *arama* in Buddhism.[151] During the Buddha's first visit at *saṃgharama* of Veluvana, Sariputta and Moggalana joined the *saṃgha*.[152] The Buddha spent his second, third, and fourth *vassavāsa* at Veluvana.[153] A number of monastic rules were framed by the Buddha during his stay here. Some of the rules are— keeping of *vassavāsa*,[154] use of food cooked in the monastery,[155] use of kinds of residence, etc.[156] Prominent persons like Mahakappina, Annakondanna, Sonagahapatiputta, Samiddhi, Moliya, Sivaka, Talaputta, Visakha, Prince Abhaya, Gulissani, Vacchagotta, Bhumija, Vassakara, Suppabuddha, Pilindavaccha, and Queen Khema visited the Buddha at Veluvana.[157] The *stūpas* of Annakondanna[158] and Mogallana[159] were built at Veluvana. Two other Veluvanas were that of Kajangala[160] and Kimbila.[161]

Trees and Flowers Associated with the Buddha

Many trees, plants, flowers, and fruits appear as metaphors in the discourses and texts of Buddhism. Due to the strong tradition of herbal medicine in *saṃgha* various trees and plants are dicussed and protected. The trees and flowers also figure in the life story of the Buddha and the *bodhisattva*. Some trees are acknowledged as divine that bear fruits in abundance. In Buddhism, nature, plants, trees, and flowers are always revered and several rituals are connected to them.

Āmalaka (*Emblica officinalis*)

As mentioned in *Vinaya Pitaka*,[162] Āmalaka or Indian Gooseberry has curative properties and is used in India for both domestic and therapeutic use. It is rich in gallic acid and vitamin C. It is a medicine and is a common edible item in every household in India. Phussa Buddha attained enlightenment under *āmalaka* tree.[163] In his last days emperor Aśoka gifted only half *āmalaka* fruit to Kukkutārāma vihāra.[164]

Amba (*Mangifera indica*)

Amba/mango is considered as a divine fruit in India. The wood of Amba (Amra) tree is also considered auspicious while the fruit is relished and is also used as shake.[165] It is also taken as an ayurvedic medicine.[166] *Ambatthi*,[167] the kernel of mango fruit, *kanjika*,[168] the mango gruel and the *ambapanaka*[169] is a drink made from mango. Mango peel is used put in curries and other edible items.[170] Sometimes the colour of the *civara* of the monks and the nuns was compared to mango.[171] The texts mention a number of mango groves where the Buddha delivered sermons, like Pāvārika's mango grove at Nālandā, Cunda's mango grove at Pāvā, and Jivaka's mango grove at Rājagaha. The Amba tree was the *bodhi* tree for the earlier Buddhas and Sikkhi attained enlightenment under Amba tree.[172]

Arjuna (*Terminalia arjuna*)

Arjuna tree is found in moist climate and grows around the rivers.[173] In Pāli literature, it is known as *kakudha* or *kakubha*. It was grown in abundance in the Uruvela region and the Buddha took the support of the branches of *kakudha* tree while bathing in river Niranjanā.[174] The *Mahāvastu* coins it as *kakubha*.[175] The tree was *bodhi* tree of the earlier Buddhas and Anomadassī attained *nibbāna* under an *ajjuna* tree.[176]

Asvattha (*Ficus religiosa*)

The *asvattha* tree (Plate 2) is also known as *pipala* tree and is considered as sacred in all religious traditions of India. The *pipala* was worshipped in the Indus Valley Civilization and depictions of *pipala* motifs have been found from various cities of the Indus Valley Civilization.[177] The *Rigveda*[178] praises *asvattha* tree. It is a type of fig with large spreading boughs and leaves. The *asvattha* is considered to be semi-parasitic, sometimes growing up against other trees or against the wall of the houses. If proper care is not taken, they can harm other trees or structures.[179] The *Dīgha Nikāya* calls it the tree of awakening because the Buddha attained *nibbāna* under it.[180] The *Vinaya Pitaka* also mentions it as the tree of enlightenment.[181] The *Mahāvastu* calls it 'The Great Tree' (*Mahādruma*).[182] A branch of *the bodhi* tree was brought to Sri Lanka by Mahendra and Saṃghamittā, the son and the daughter of King Aśoka, and it was planted in Anuradhapura (Plate 3). The original *bodhi* tree at Bodh Gayā was harmed many times. Such a reference was first found during Aśoka's time when one of his wives, Tisyarakkha, tried to harm it but the king discovered the plot and tree was saved.[183] Xuanzang[184] informs that Śaśānka, the King of Gauda (Bengal), destroyed the tree and threw it in Ganga. But it was again revived and replanted by Alexander Cunningham in 1881 when he took a branch of bodhi tree from Anuradhapura.[185] The depiction of *bodhi* tree has also been found in Sānchi (Plate 4), Bharhut, Sārnāth, Amarāvatī, and other places.

Badara (*Zizyphus jujube*)

Badara is an egg-shaped, green and red fruit of the Jujube and is also known as *badarapandu* or *bhadarapandu*.[186] Ānanda aesthetically compares the Buddha's complexion to the beautiful jujube fruit.[187] It was edible fruit in India and consumed as a fruit or sauces.[188] On number of occasions the Buddha was offered meal with jujube sauce.[189] Sometimes during the time of his wandering, Siddhārtha used to partake jujube fruit.[190]

PLATE 2. *Asvattha* (Pipala)

PLATE 3. Anuradhapura Bodhi Tree

PLATE 4. Sānchi Bodhi Tree

Beluva (*Aegle marmelos*)

Beluva or *vilva* (wood apple) is a round shaped, popular fruit in India. While raw, its colour is green but turns yellow after ripening and has a yellowish, tasty pulp which is used for its medicinal properties like curing stomach ailments.[191] Its hard cover is used to make various types of musical instruments.[192] Pandu, a yellow flute made of Beluva wood, first belonged to Māra and then Sakka gave it to the divine musian, Pancasikha.[193]

Bhaṅga (*Cannabis sativa*)

Cannabis is a herbal plant commonly found in India. It has been mentioned in the *Atharavaveda*.[194] It is famous for its aromatic and hallucinogenic characteristics.[195] Cannabis is also used for medicinal purpose.[196] Its fibre is used for making ropes.[197]

Candana (*Santalum album/Pterocarpus santainus*)

Sandalwood is an endemic plant commonly grown in south India and parts of Deccan. It is white and red in colour and have scented stems.[198] Sandalwood is mainly applied as a coolant, and it also has a sedative effect. It has been used as a powerful and lasting aromatic substance and as a medicine. It is also useful as a disinfectant for bronchial tracts, diuretic, expectorant, and stimulant. The same is also used as a tonic for heart, stomach, and liver. It is also used as an anti-poison, and helps in fever, memory improvement, and as a blood purifier. Its references have been found in Pāli literature (*lohita candana* or *rattacandana*).[199] Sandalwood objects and oil were very famous in early India.[200] Siddhārtha as a prince used sandalwood articles brought from Vārāṇasī.[201] Sandalwood powder was said to have sprinkled from the sky just before the Buddha's *mahāparinibbāna* at Kusīnāra.[202] The *Milindapañho* compares *nibbāna* to the precious and rare red sandalwood since it is praised by good people just as *nibbāna* is praised by the noble ones.[203]

Dabba (*Eragnostis cynosuroides/Imperata cylendrica*)

Dabba/durva or *darba*, a type of grass, is mentioned in the *Rigveda*[204] and the *Atharvaveda*[205] as a divine grass used in the Vedic rituals. Buddhist canonical treatise also mention it.[206] The Buddha has cited many similes and examples of *dabba* grass in his discourses.[207]

Eraṇḍa (*Ricinus communi*)

Eraṇḍa is the castor oil tree.[208] The oil is used for medicinal purposes and as a lubricant.[209] The *Bodhisattva* is said to sometimes reside as a spirit in a castor oil tree.[210]

Godhūma (*Triticum aestivum/Triticum durum/
Triticum dicoccum*)

Wheat is one of the earliest crops grown in India primarily for food. Its remains have been found in the Indus Valley Civilization. The *Rigveda* also mentions it as a staple crop of the early Aryans. Its scientific name is *Gramineae* and it belongs to the genus *Triticum*. It is one of the most important crops of India and is used in many forms as a staple diet.[211] After rice, wheat constitutes the most important grain in northern India.[212]

Jambu (*Eugenia jambolana*)

Jambu, a rose apple tree, bears an oval, dark, purple fruit containing a single seed.[213] It is highly relished.[214] Because of abundance of this tree, Indian subcontinent is known as as Jambudvīpa.[215] The *Vinaya Pitaka* also mentions its edible qualities.[216] Siddhārtha, in his childhood, meditated at the foot of a *jambu* tree.[217] While at Uruvelā the Buddha ate *jambu* fruits.[218] *Jambu* has medicinal attributes and is used in diabetes. The Bodhisatta was once reborn as a spirit in a grove of *jambu* trees.[219]

Kadalī (*Musa paradisiaca*)

Banana or kadalī grows in all parts of Indian subcontinent and are edible in both raw and ripe conditions. The banana plant bear fruits only once and withers away after it.[220] The trunk of banana plant is porous.[221] The colour of its flower is compared with the colour of gums.[222] Banana leaves were earlier used as plates to eat from.[223] A banana plant is always compared to a man who destroyed fruits of his own karma.[224] Banana stems, leaves, and fruits are used in many auspicious occasions and rituals.

Kappāsa (*Gossypium arboreum*)

Kappāsa is cotton bush that is grown in different parts of India.[225] Kappāsika is a cloth made of cotton.[226] The round black seeds of cotton are embedded in a white fluffy fibre which can be weaved as thread.[227] Cotton cloth was the most common fabric used in ancient India and probably produced first time in the Indus Valley Civilization. After being harvested and separated from the seed, the fibre was spun into thread and then woven into cloth.[228] Nakulamātā, one of the Buddha's female disciples, was very accomplished at spinning cotton.[229] Brāhmana Velāma once made a gift of 84,000 lengths of cotton cloth to the Buddha.[230] Cotton was used for a variety of purposes right from dress fabric to padding sandals.[231] The Buddha's dead body was, in fact, wrapped in gentle cotton and silk from Kaśī.[232] *Sukhuma* is a variety of fine cotton.[233]

Kappūra (*Cinnamomum camphora*)

Kappūra or Camphor is a plant with aromatic properties and is used as a medicine and also in religious ceremonies.[234] It is made from the bark or wood of the tree through distilling process. People believe burning camphor before the God signifies the act of union with them. It is compared to fire scarifies to god for burning ego and arrogance like burning of camphor. Camphor light is known to drive away ghosts, evil forces, and negative energies.

Kapittha (*Feronia elephantum*)

It is a wood-apple tree.[235] The pulp of the fruit has an acidic taste and is used to make sauces and to acidify curd. Buddhist literature mention this fruit along with the *assattha, nigrodha, pilakkha, udumbara,* and the *kacchaka* as having tiny seeds but always grow as lofty trees and also have parasitic characteristic.[236]

Khadira (*Acacia catechu*)

It is known as *khaira/babula*.[237] The *Rigveda* mentions it.[238] Buddhist literature also mentions pillars of khadira tree (*khadiratthambha*).[239] The timber of this tree is used for making houses, plough and spade handles, and other domestic articles. It is sometimes used in medicine. The stakes for impaling robbers is made of *khadira* wood.[240] The *Jātaka* stories narrate that woodpeckers are known to live in a grove of *khadira* trees.[241]

Kiṃsuka (*Butea frondosa/monosperma*)

This plant is known as *palāsa/dhaka* in the *Rigveda*.[242] Because of its colour, *palaśavana* is popularly known as the forest of flame. The whole forest burst into red flame when these flowers are in full bloom. Some of its substances are used for medicinal purposes.[243] The *Jātaka* says that a *Bodhisattva* was born as a spirit in a *palaśavana*.[244]

Kuśa (*Desmostachya bipinnata*)

Kuśa is a type of perennial grass with sharp spiky leaves.[245] For performing rigorous practices, ascetics sometimes wore garments made of *kuśa* grass.[246] *Kuśa* grass is used for making huts during the age of the Buddha. Fishermen used *kuśa* string for catching fish.[247] Growth of *kuśa* grass shows presence of water in the area.[248] The Buddha says that if *kuśa* grass is injurious if not treated properly, in the same way unlawful monastic life leads to purgatory.[249] The

Buddha meditated at the foot of the *bodhi* tree sitting on matted *kuśa* grass. It was offered to him by Sotthika or Sotthiya.[250] The *Bodhisattva* was once born as a spirit in a clump of *kuśa* grass.[251]

Lākha (*Laccifer indicola*)

Lac/Lākha is one of the most valuable gifts of the Nature to man. It is a unique material as it is the only resin of animal origin, being actually the secretion of a tiny insect, *Laccifer lacca*; however, it is usually considered as a plant product.[252] The tiny red larvae of this insect reside on the young shoots of some variety of plants and secrete red-coloured lac to protect their bodies.[253] Lac is used to make seals,[254] paints,[255] and dye.[256]

Lasuṇa (*Allium sativum*)

Lasuṇa has been identified as garlic and the *Vinaya Pitaka* restricted its use except under specific circumstances.[257] The Buddha forbade monks to eat, although he allowed it to be taken for medicinal purposes.[258] Garlic was sometimes also known as *māgadhaka*, i.e. belonging to Magadha because of its high productivity in Bihar. Faxian says that onions and garlic were little grown and few people eat them; if anyone used them as food they were expelled beyond the walls of the town.[259]

Madhuka (*Bassia latifolia*)

A tree of *mahua*, also known as *Maduca latifolia*. Mahua, a native fruit and drink of India, has high economic value.[260] *Mahua* wine was very popular in ancient India. The Buddha forbade monks and nuns to consume *mahua* drink.[261]

Mandārava (*Erythrina sublobata*)

It is the Indian coral tree and is also known as *mandara*.[262] It was considered as divine tree that grows in heaven.[263] It is said that petals of flowers of mandārava tree were sprinkled from the sky just before the Buddha's *mahāparinibbāna* at Kuśinārā.[264]

Muñja (*Saccharum munja/bengalense*)

Munja is a spiky, tufted grass, and generally grows upto 6 m. It is found in arid areas and along river banks. It is used for making ropes, mats, and baskets.[265] The *Rigveda* mentions it with a variety of grasses, viz., *sāra, darbha, kuśa, sariya,* and *virana.*[266] The Buddha said that *samsāra* is tangled like a rope made of *muñja* grass.[267] Warriors wore wreaths made from *muñja* grass to avoid evil spirits and attin victory.[268] When Māra tried to discourage Siddhārtha in his efforts for achieving *nibbāna,* the latter replied that he was wearing *muñja* grass to remove obstacles created by Māra.[269]

Naḷa (*Phragmites australis/Calamagrostis*)

It is common term used for reeds grown moist and wet climate.[270] Numerous such types of reeds grow in northern India.[271] The people cut the stalks and use it for many purposes.[272] The Buddha says that worldly clinging fades away like a green reed turns dry and yellow after cutting from root.[273] Numerous household articles such as sandals, stools, baskets, and mats are made from reed.[274] Small huts were also thatched from it.[275] The *Jātaka* mentions a story of merchants who sailed to Nāḷamala sea looking like vast expanse of reeds.[276] *Isikā,*[277] *kaṭṭhaka,*[278] and *pabbaja*[279] were different types of reeds known in India. *Santha* was variety of reed which was used to make bow strings[280] and *saravana,* a type of reed with sharp leaves was used to make arrow shafts.[281]

Nimba (*Azadirachta indica*)

Azadirachta indica or neem, is a tree of mahogany family, *Meliaceae.*[282] This is variety of a large deciduous tree the leaves of which have bitter taste with medicinal and insecticidal properties. The extract from its stem, leaves and roots was used as medicine.[283] Neem provide rich variety of timber.[284] The Buddha encouraged using neem tooth-sticks because it cleans the eyes, purifies the sinuses, remove breath problems, cleans the taste buds, and prevents phlegm and mucus.[285] Sumedha Buddha attained enlightenment under a *nimba* tree.[286]

Nygrodha (*Ficus benghalensis*)

Nygrodha/banyan/*bargada,* a variety of fig is a plant native to the Indian subcontinent. Aerial roots hang down from the ever-spreading branches and these eventually become trunks. Their welcome shade is famous worldwide and they are known in the Hindu and Buddhist mythologies as 'wishing tree'. This large evergreen tree has a red fruit.[287] The *Jātaka* mentions a story of a bird eating banyan figs, later dropping its excrement a tree where the banyan seeds germinated, and eventually strangled the tree.[288] The Buddha told that craving is like the trunk of the banyan tree that clings and eventually wraps the sources.[289] He reminded the monks to be alert as passions come to one just as the aerial roots (*khandahaya*) of the banyan emerge from its branches.[290] The fruits of banyan may be as sweet as sugar.[291] After the enlightenment the Buddha spent seven days sitting at the foot of the goatherd's banyan tree.[292] He compared generous lay persons to a banyan tree standing at crossroad in a countryside.[293] Banyan tree is also known as 'vow tree' (*vararukkha*) because people pay reverencae to them by offering flowers, scent sticks, and water.[294] One of the thirty-two characteristics of the Mahāpurusa's *lakkhana* has the attributes of a banyan tree, i.e. the Buddha's length of his arm is equal to his height.[295] The Buddha Kassapa got enlightenment under a banyan tree.[296]

Paduma (*Nelumbo necifera*)

Paduma or *ambujā* is a lotus flower.[297] It is an aquatic plant with large circular pastel-green leaves floating on the surface of the water.[298] Many varieties of lotuses like *kokāsaka* or *kumuda*[299] and *kokanada* or *puṇḍarīka* are known according to their colours.[300] The Buddha tells *paduma* as being white, pink or blue.[301] In Campa, the Buddha resided at Gaggara Lotus Lake.[302] Siddhārtha lived in palaces surrounded by ponds of blue water lilies, pink and white lotuses.[303] The lotus has powerful fragrance.[304] In Pali texts young men or women are compared with lotus flower.[305] The Buddha comapres a devoted lay person as pious as lotus flower.[306] Lotus stems and roots are edible.[307] A variety of drinks was made from lotus flowers.[308] Moggallāna went to collect lotus roots and stalks to prepare medicine for fever and in his effort he was helped by an elephant.[309] People drink lotus juice[310] and its leaves were used to wrap food.[311] The Buddha drew analogies to the enlightened person's transcendence of *saṁsāra* just as the beautiful lotus is born in muddy water and yet remains undefiled.[312]

Pūga (*Areca catechu*)

Areca catechu is a species of palm and it is popularly known as betel palm.[313] It is an evergreen vine with heart-shaped leaves, and generally found in shady tropical conditions. The tree is dioecious and produce white flowers arranged in small spikes known as catkins. For chewing, a betel quid is prepared by wrapping a small piece of the areca palm seed in a leaf of the betel pepper, along with a pellet of slaked lime (calcium hydroxide). In early Buddhist tradition, chewing betel was prohibited but in some later traditions it got acceptance.

Rājāyatana (*Buchanania latifolia*)

It is *chiraunji* or *piyāla* tree.[314] Its fruit is edible and put in various types of dishes.[315] After enlightenment the Buddha spent seven days sitting at the foot of a *rājāyatana* tree. Here Tapassu and Bhallika met the Buddha and offered food to him.[316]

Sāka (*Tectona grandis*)

Sāka or *sagwan* is a large tree and the Buddha suggested that brāhmanas and teak wood are high in social order.[317] One legend says that the Śakyas derived their name from this tree. The Buddha once narrated to Ambaṭṭha the hoary legend of King Okkāka who loved his queen and wished to give his kingdom to her son. So he banished his earlier sons, Okkāmukha, Karaṇḍu, Hatthinīya, and Sīnipura, who settled at the foot of the Himalayas near a lotus pond surrounded by *sāka* forest. Not desiring to degenerate their lineage, they cohabited with their own sisters and sons were born to them. King Okkāka later knew about these princes and found them as strong as the *sākas* trees. They were later known as Śakyas.[318]

Sāla (*Shorea robusta*)

This tree is known as *sakhu* or *assakaṇṇa* because sepals enclosing the flower resemble ear of a horse.[319] The *sāla* and its flowers are often mentioned in the Buddhist texts.[320] The best quality sāla trees grows in the lower reaches of the Himalayas.[321] The *Aṅguttara Nikāya* says how a man can make a boat of *sāla* wood. After planning and shaping the exterior and making the empty space inside, the structure would be smoothened with a rock ball. Finally, a rudder, a pair of oars would be fixed to give it shape of a boat.[322] The Buddha informs that people go to a *sāla* forest near their villages to cut down the crooked *sāla* saplings so that healthy sāla trees would grow bigger and straighter.[323] These trees were sometimes destroyed by parasitic vines.[324] The *Rukkhadhamma Jātaka* uses similie of sāla forest to illustrate unity. It is said that during King Vessavana's time, one day a mighty storm swept over the region uprooting even the mightiest and the most deeply-rooted trees growing in the forest. But the *sāla* trees in the forest, supported by each other withstood the storm.[325] When the Buddha reached in Kuśināra for his *mahāparinibbāna*, he lays down between branches of two *sāla* trees, it is said that they burst into flower out of season and sprinkled their petals over him. The Buddha once told that *dhamma* preached by him was so convincing and articulate that if *sāla* trees had consciousness and ability to comprehend, even they would be imbibed by his teachings.[326] Sometimes dishes were made from or flavoured with *sāla* flowers or its resin.[327] The Vessabhū Buddha attained *nibbāna* under a *sāla* tree.[328] The Koṇḍañña Buddha also attained enlightenment under Sālakalyāṇī, a type of *sāla* tree.[329] The *Milindapañho* says that the roots of a *sāla* tree penetrate into the earth for 100 cubits and at maturity they shoot up into the air for 100 cubits in a single day.[330]

Śalmali (*Bombax Ceiba/heptaphyllum*)

Śalmali is also known as senwala/sembhala/semala. It bears flower which gives it a soft stuff usually used in pillows and quilts.[331] Pāli literature mentions it as sembali (silk cotton tree).[332] The *Rigveda* mentions it in two contexts—first, some kind of poison found in it, and second, its wood along with that of kiṃśuka was used for manufacturing chariots.[333] Its stout trunk is useful for timber but its wood is too soft to be very useful. It is not durable anywhere other than under water. Semal is very good and prized for manufacture of plywood, match boxes and sticks, scabbards, etc. Semal wood is also used for making canoes and light duty boats.

Sāsapa (*Brassica sarson*)

It is also known as *rai/sarson*.[334] The plant with a bright-yellow flowers is abundant in winter season. Its numerous tiny black seeds produce good quality of edible oil. It is one of the earliest oil crops in India and its evidences are found in the Indus Valley Civilization. It is also used for medicinal purposes.[335] The Buddha exhorts that like a mustard seed on the tip of awl, craving will not persist in a good monk.[336] *Sarson* is a common edible oil in north India especially in Uttar Pradesh and Bihar region.

Siṃsapā (*Dalbergia sissoo*)

Śiśam or *sissu* is a deciduous tree. The *Rigveda* mentions this tree.[337] The Buddha once stayed in the *siṃsapā* grove at Ālavī.[338] The *siṃsapā* grove of Setavya was also famous during the age of the Buddha.[339] While living in a *siṃsapā* forest near Kośambī, the Buddha gathered up a few leaves and asked the monks which were more numerous, leaves in his hands or those on the trees. The Buddha explained that the things he had discovered were numerous and subtle while the knowledge he taught were few as it depends upon grasping powers of concerned persons and its relavant to them.[340]

Sirīsa (*Acacia sirissa*)

Sirīsa is a tree blossom with crimson flowers.[341] It is often grown along the roads and provide ample shades to travellers and animals. It is most observed when it becomes leafless and covered with pods which are similar to the *kiṃsuka* pods.[342] The Buddha Kakusandha got enlightenment under a *sirīsa* tree.[343]

Sogandhika (*Nymphaea lotus*)

Sogandhika is a variety of white water lily or *kallahāra*.[344] The *Vinaya Pitaka* mentions a type of drink made of *sāluka* which contains the root of water lilies and lotuses.[345] Buddhist texts inform that one of the purgatories was named after this plant.[346]

Sumanā (*Oleaceae jasminum*)

A lot of varieties of *sumanā* or Jasmine is known in India. It produces small white star-shaped flowers with nice fragrance. The Pāli names, *jātisumanā*,[347] *mallikā*,[348] *sumanā*,[349] *vassika, vassikī,* and *yūthikā*, are all usually described as jasmine. The *mallikā* was considered its most popular variety and perfume is made from it.[350] There is a reference in a *jataka* to a dress with a *sumanā* and *mallikā* type of flower pattern printed on it. The Buddha asked the monks to imitate the *vassika* as flowers as it sheds its withered flowers, so as the monks should shed their desire and hatred.[351]

Tagara (*Tabernaemontana coronaria*)

It is a tree with small height, dark green leaves and white flower.[352] The fragrance of its flower seductive especially at night and scent sticks are made from *tagara* flowers.[353] The Buddha praises that among all the fragrances like, *candana*, *tagara*, and *vassika*, the fragrance of virtue is the best.[354]

Tāla (*Borassus flabellifer*)

It is also called palmyra, palm, or sometimes *tālataruṇa*. It has large fan-like torny leaves and yields fruit of yellow colour. The leaves of the Palmyra are used for making huts, fans, and other household articles.[355] The Buddha often compares the enlightened person's annihilation of the defilements to trunk of a Palmyra tree which will not grow again after it is cut down.[356] Hatred must be withered from the mind just as a palmyra fruit is separated from the stalk.[357] Sometimes the Buddha's radiant face was compared to the ripen fruit of the palmyra.[358] In early India, the height of the palmyra was used as a unit of measurement.[359]

Taṇḍula (*Oryza sativa*)

In Indian subcontinent a number of variety of paddy cultivation is known. Paddy cultivation started in India since the Neolithic age and the earliest of its evidences are traced from Koldiwaha and Mahadaha of Belan Valley near Allahabad. Several of its varieties are known in India. *Daddula*, an inferior one;[360] *nivāra*, a low quality wild rice;[361] *Pavīhi*, a common variety;[362] and *vīrhi*, a popular one;[363] were some of the varieties while *sāli* was considered the best variety.[364] *Sāli* and *mahāsāli* are often praised in the Pāli literature. Its another variety is *sūkarasāli*, i.e. trampled by pigs.[365] Paddy cultivation requires abundance of water supply.[366] Rice is considered as pious and divine.[367] Boiled rice is known as *odana* or *bhatta* and is usually partaken with various curries and condiments.[368] Bran (*kaṇa*, *kukkusa*, or *kuṇḍaka*), the brown husk of grains removed during polishing or milling, and it is also considered as a variet food.[369] Rice dishes are also prepared with sesame seeds.[370] *Kaṇājaka* was a type of porridge made from the broken rice grains.[371] Porridge of rice boiled in milk is known as *khīrodana* or *pāyāsa* and it is highly relished in India.[372] The Buddha told five attributes of rice gruel—it dispels hunger, quenches thirst, regulates wind, cleanses the bowels, and helps to digest.[373]

Tila *(Sesamum indicum)*

Tila or Sesame was considered as an essential food along with rice, butter, sugar, and salt during the age of the Buddha.[374] The tiny seeds of *tila* were grinded and mixed with cereals.[375] The gruel of sesame, rice, and green gram was considered as digestive food.[376] When a *Bodhisattva* was meditating, what he ate was *piññāka*, the pulp left after the pressing of oil from sesame seeds.[377] The *Saṃyutta Nikāya* informs that sesame fields could be struck with insects and because of that plants were dried.[378] Oil from sesame were pressed in oil mills consisting of a large stone wheels.[379] To extract the oil, sesame meal would be sprinkled with water and then pressed.[380] The Buddha mentioned that a border fortress would be supplied with fuel and food, including sesame, presumably to feed the inmates and to use when under siege.[381]

Tiṇa *(Cynodon dactylon)*

Tiṇa or *saddala* grasses belongs the family *Gramineae*. The Buddha told that the monks or the nun should not steal anything, not even a blade of *tiṇa*.[382] Various domestic items were made like grass mats and huts thatched with grass.[383] When developed in crops, it became a curse.[384] The Buddha instructed the monks and the nuns to reside in their abode during the rainy season so that they would not trample down crops and grass and injure the tiny creatures.[385] He says that during his wandering, he gathered grass and leaves to sit for meditation.[386] Māgandiya a brāhmana, however, disapproved of it since it destroys their growth.[387] Several species of grass are mentioned in Buddhist texts such as *jantu*, a yellow-coloured grass, *poṭakila*, a soft grass, and *kamala*, used to make sandals, *tiriyā* a common type of grass, and *eragu*.[388]

Tulsi *(Ocimum sanctum/Ocimum gratissimim/ Ocimum basilicum)*

Basil or *tulsi/sulas*, is a herbal plant with leaves reaching down.[389] It is an aromatic perennial plant native to the Indian subcontinent. It is revered as one of the most sacred herbs in India and it has medicinal qualities. It is also known as holy basil.

Uppala (*Nymphaea stellata*)

It is blue water lily, or *indīvara* and it grows in the muddy water of ponds and swamps. Its flowers have numerous spear-shaped petals and are beautiful deep blue in colour, although sometimes also crimson, white, or pink. Its fragrance is long lasting.[390] Sometimes eyes of a beautiful woman are compared to a water lily.[391] Water lily also has medicinal qualities and its perfume is considered the best.[392]

Vassikā (*Justicia adhatoda*)

This plant is also *vassikā* and is identified with jasmine.[393] Its plant grows up to 2.5 m. in height and it has elliptical leaves and large white fragrant flowers. The flower is known for its addictive fragrance and perfumes, scent sticks are made from it.[394]

Veḷu (*Bambusa arundinacea*)

Bamboo, *veṇu* or *vaṃsa*, is one of the most popular plants of India. Its number of varieties from tall to small are known across Asia.[395] Thirty varieties of it are found in north India. Bamboo are used for making baskets, thatching huts and are used in the making of various domestic goods.[396] Bamboo has rare flowers which blooms when it dies.[397] The earliest *ārāma* donated to the Buddha was the Veluvana. It was one of the Buddha's favourite resort in Rājagaha gifted to him by King Bimbisāra.[398] Nāgasena says that bamboo bends the way the wind blows. Likewise, the monk, having followed the nine teachings of the Buddha, will be a true ascetic and will be moulded similarly.[399] Bamboo, or *nāḷi*, was also used as a unit of measurement.[400]

Vibhītaka (*Terminalia bellirica*)

This plant is known as *bahera*. The *Rigveda* says that *bahera* is used for dice.[401] Together with *āmalaka* and *harītaka*, the mixture is known as *triphala*. It is long credited in Āyurveda with powerful medical properties especially for stomach ailment.[402]

Yava (*Hordeum vulgare*)

Yava or barley is an edible variety of cereal.[403] Barley was known in the Indus Valley Civilization and in the *Rigveda*. The barley or *yava* was a famous crop in the early Vedic age. The *Rigveda* mentions *yava* crops and its various dishes.[404] The Buddha's first meal after *nibbāna* was barley gruel and honey balls offered to him by Tapassu and Bhallika.[405] Monks used to put barley husk in their needle case to prevent it to become blut.[406] However, importance of barley got diminished during the age of the Buddha when paddy became dominant crops in the Ganga Valley.

Notes

1. S. Dhammika, *Nature and the Environment in Early Buddhism*, Singapore: Buddha Dhamma Mandala Society, 2015, p. 8.
2. *Dīgha Nikāya*, I.5.
3. *Aṅguttara Nikāya*, IV.100.
4. *Dīgha Nikāya*, III.230.
5. *Rigveda*, X.27.20.
6. *Gobila Grihyasutra*, IV.7.22–5.
7. V.S. Agrawal, *Studies in Indian Art*, Vārānasī: Vishwavidalaya Prakashan, 2003, p. 48.
8. *Aṅguttara Nikāya*, III.369–70.
9. *Jātaka*, no. 493.
10. *Pacittiya*, no. 11.
11. Ibid., no. 10.
12. *Viśuddhimagga*, V.688.
13. *Saṃyutta Nikāya*, I.134.
14. Ibid., I.227.
15. *Suttanipāta*, V.77.
16. *Dīgha Nikāya*, I.64.
17. Ibid., I.5, *Majjhima Nikāya*, I.180.
18. *Vinaya Pitaka*, I.189.
19. Ibid., IV.296.
20. Ibid., III.155.
21. Ibid., II.140.
22. *Pacittiya*, no. 1.
23. Schmithausen, *The Problem of the Sentience of Plants in Earliest Buddhism*, p. 44.
24. *Ācāraṅga Sūtra*, II.1.8.3.
25. de Silva, *Environmental Philosophy and Ethics in Buddhism*, p. 62.
26. *Vinaya Pitaka*, IV.32–3.
27. *Majjhima Nikāya*, II.51.
28. *Pacittiya*, no. 56.
29. *Vinaya Pitaka*, II.138.

30. *Dīgha Nikāya*, I.141.
31. *Saṃyutta Nikāya*, IV.351.
32. *Vinaya Pitaka*, I.137–8.
33. Ibid., IV.183.
34. *Aṅguttara Nikāya*, II.194.
35. *Vinaya Pitaka*, III.155–7.
36. *Sāmantapasādika*, VV.477, 768.
37. Ibid., V.769.
38. *Viśuddhimagga*, XX.73.
39. Ibid., XX.74.
40. Schmithausen, *Buddhism and Nature*, pp. 22–3.
41. William R. LaFleur, 'Saigyo and the Buddhist Value of Nature', *History of Religion*, vol. 13, no. 2, 1974, pp. 93–128.
42. Hujime Nakamura, 'The Idea of Nature: East and West', in *The Great Ideas Today, Encyclopaedia Britannica*, 1980, p. 282.
43. Schmithausen, *The Problem of the Sentience of Plants in Earliest Buddhism*; *Plants in Early Buddhism and the Far Eastern Idea of the Buddha Nature of Grasses and Trees*, Lumbini: Lumbini Research Institute, 2009; *Buddhism and Nature*.
44. Ellison Banks Findly, *Plant Lives: Borderline Beings in Indian Tradition*, Delhi: MLBD, 2008.
45. Schmithausen, *Buddhism and Nature*, pp. 6–8.
46. Schmithausen, *The Problem of the Sentience of the Plants in Earliest Buddhism*, p. 18.
47. Ibid., p. 21.
48. Albircht Wezler, 'Cattle Field and Barley: A Note on Mahābhāsya', *Brahmavidya: Adyar Library Bulletin*, vol. I, no. 337, 1986, pp. 24–7.
49. Schmithausen, *Buddhism and Nature*, p. 39.
50. Schmithausen, 'The Early Buddhist Tradition and Ecological Ethics', pp. 9–10, <dharmaflower.net>, accessed on 9 May 2018. (The *Rigveda* is concerned with plants, both *vanaspati* and *osadhi; Rigveda*. II.33.4, 33.13; VI.74. The *Satapatha Brāhmana* mentions that not only animals but plants, trees, water and earth are also sentient. Same thing is narrated in the Ācārāṅga *Sutra, Satapatha Brāhmana*, II.6.1, III.3.1, III.8.5.9, I.2.2.11; Ācārāṅga *Sutra*, II.5.1.14.)
51. Chatsumarn Kabilsingh, 'Early Buddhist View on Nature', in *Dharma Gaia: A Harvest of Essays in Buddhism and Ecology*, ed. Allan Hunt Badiner, Berkeley: Parallax Press, 1990, p. 9.
52. Harvey, *An Introduction to Buddhist Ethics*, p. 175. (He cites references of *Dīgha Nikāya*, I.5 and *Vinaya Pitaka*, IV.34–5 to substantiate his points.)
53. Schmithausen, *Buddhism and Nature*, pp. 5–6.
54. Findly, *Plant Lives*, p. 96.
55. Findly, 'Borderline Beings: Plant Possibilities in Early Buddhism',

Journal of the American Oriental Society, vol. 122, no. 2, April–June 2002, p. 52.

56. Ibid., pp. 43, 71.
57. Ibid., p. 43 (Findly explains it on interpretation of references based on *Aṅguttara* and *Dīgha Nikāya*; *Aṅguttara Nikāya*, I.35; *Dīgha Nikāya*, I.53.)
58. Ibid., p. 67.
59. Ibid., p. 83.
60. R.G. Bidwell, *Plant Physiology*, New York: Macmillan, 1979, p. 4.
61. *Dīgha Nikāya*, I.87; *Aṅguttara Nikāya*, III.19, 200.
62. Findly, *Plant Lives*, pp. 88–9.
63. *Vinaya Pitaka*, IV.34.
64. Bidwell, *Plant Physiology*, pp. 3–4.
65. *Majjhima Nikāya*, I.457; *Saṃyutta Nikāya*, III.137.
66. *Suttanipāta*, V.77; *Saṃyutta Nikāya*, I.134.
67. *Aṅguttara Nikāya*, IV.237.
68. Findly, *Plant Lives*, pp. 141–4, 161–5, 209.
69. Schmithausen, *Plants in Early Buddhism*, pp. 66–7.
70. *Dīgha Nikāya*, I.111, 114, 127.
71. Schmithausen, *Plants in Early Buddhism*, p. 59.
72. *Majjhima Nikāya*, I.502–5.
73. Schmithausen, *Plants in Early Buddhism*, pp. 64–5. (I.B. Horner has translated *bhūnahunu* as wreaker of embryo on basis of reference found in *Papancasudanī*, III.24, *bhūnahuno ti hata*.)
74. Tilmann Vetter, 'The Khandha Passage in the *Vinaya Pitaka* and Four Main *Nikāyas*', Wien: QAW, 2000, p. 132.
75. Albricht Wezler, 'A Notes on Sanskrit Bhruna and Bhrunahatya', in *Festschrft Klaces Bruhn*, ed. Nalni Balbir and Joalhem K. Boulze, Reenbek: Dr Inge Wezler, 1994, pp. 623–46.
76. *Jātaka*, no. 465.
77. Mamiko Okada, 'Eco-paradigm in Buddhist Narrative Literature: Plants, Trees and Eco-Ethics', *IBK*, vol. 93, no. 47–1, 1998, pp. 226–30. [Some other *Jātakas* also mention tree deity and tree relationship. The *Phandana Jātaka* (no. 475) says that a lion intended to cut down a tree but was outwitted by the tree spirit. The *Hatthipala Jātaka* (no. 509) tells of the gate of Vārāṇasī where a tree deity resided. The *Kotisimbali Jātaka* (no. 412) mentions a tree spirit that was frightened by a bird who lived on top of a cotton tree. The bird spread the seed of banyan tree among the branches of the cotton tree. The deity of the tree was terrified that her abode would be destroyed with the growth of the banyan tree but she was comforted by the rock king.]
78. Schmithausen, *Plants in Early Buddhism*, p. 32.
79. The *Kusanali Jātaka* (no. 121) says that a grass spirit and a tree spirit were friends and when the tree was about to cut down, the grass spirit assumed form of a chameleon and converted the tree full of holes.

80. Akira Fujimoto, 'Do Plants Have Lives? Two Kinds of Jivitendriyas by the Theravadins', *NBGK*, vol. 68, 2003, pp. 103–4,
81. Schmithausen, *Plants in Early Buddhism*, pp. 54–5.
82. *Sumangalavilāsinī*, II.545.
83. *Vinaya Pitaka*, I.231–3
84. *Dīgha Nikāya*, II.94; *Saṃyutta Nikāya*, V.141, 301.
85. *Aṅguttara Nikāya*, IV.100-106.
86. *Saṃyutta Nikāya*, V.310.
87. *Dhammapadatthakathā*, II.74.
88. *Saṃyutta Nikāya*, IV.281–8.
89. Ibid., IV.288–91; *Theragāthā*, V.466.
90. *Dīgha Nikāya*, II.126.
91. *Sumangalavilāsinī*, II.568.
92. *Dīgha Nikāya*, II.207–10.
93. *Aṅguttara Nikāya*, V.263.
94. G.P. Malalasekera, *Dictionary of Pāli Proper Names*, vol. 1, p. 111.
95. *Saṃyutta Nikāya*, IV.105–7.
96. *Therigātha Commentary*, 64, 66, 163.
97. *Aṅguttara Nikāya*, III.358.
98. *Sarathappakasinī*, I.131–2.
99. *Dhammapadaṭṭhakathā*, II.49, 52.
100. *Vinaya Pitaka*, III.208–9.
101. Ibid., III.28.
102. Ibid., III.64.
103. *Vinaya Pitaka*, II.158, *Papancasudani*, I.471.
104. *Manorathapuranī*, vol. I, pp. 208–9.
105. *Sumangalavilāsini*, II.407.
106. *Dhammapadaṭṭhakathā*, I.3; *Manorathapurani*, I.314.
107. Malalasekera, *Dictionary of Pāli Proper Names*, vol. I, p. 965.
108. Ibid., vol. I, p. 959.
109. *Dīgha Nikāya*, I.47.
110. *Majjhima Nikāya*, I.368ff.
111. *Dhammapadatthakatha*, II.164.
112. *Jātaka*, no. 114.
113. Alexander Cunningham, *The Ancient Geography of India*, Delhi: LPP, repr. 2006, pp. 350–1.
114. Hultzsch, *Corpus Inscriptionum Indicarum*, p. 164.
115. *Papancasudanī*, II.810.
116. Ibid., I.288.
117. Malalasekera, *Dictionary of Pāli Proper Names*, vol. I, pp. 66–1.
118. *Aṅguttara Nikāya*, IV.274.
119. *Saṃyutta Nikāya*, II.267.
120. *Dīgha Nikāya*, I.151.
121. Ibid., II.119.

122. *Mahāvaṃśa*, IV.12.

123. *Papancasudanī*, I.298.

124. Malalasekera, *Dictionary of Pāli Proper Names*, vol. II, p. 555.

125. *Saṃyutta Nikāya*, III.9.

126. *Dhammapadaṭṭhakathā*, I.88.

127. *Aṅguttara Nikāya*, IV.437.

128. Ibid., I.213.

129. Ibid., I.26.

130. *Papancasudanī*, I.289.

131. *Vinaya Pitaka*, I.82.

132. Ibid., II.253.

133. Ibid., III.235, 244; IV.55, 101, 167, 262, 314.

134. *Saṃyutta Nikāya*, IV.182.

135. Malalasekera, *Dictionary of Pāli Proper Names*, vol. II, pp. 70–1.

136. *Suttanipāta Commentary*, I.357.

137. *Buddhavaṃśa Commentary*, 3.

138. *Dīgha Nikāya*, II.116.

139. *Aṅguttara Nikāya*, V.122.

140. *Majjhima Nikāya*, I.482.

141. Malalasekera, *Dictionary of Pāli Proper Names*, vol. II, p. 192.

142. *Saṃyutta Nikāya*, III.95.

143. *Vinaya Pitaka*, I.352; *Majjhima Nikāya*, I.320. (*Bhisa Jātaka*, no. 314.)

144. Malalasekera, *Dictionary of Pāli Proper Names*, vol. II, p. 192.

145. Hemchandra Raychaudhuri, *Political History of Ancient India*, Calcutta: University of Calcutta, 1972, pp. 169, 172.

146. Cunningham, *The Ancient Geography of India*, p. 362, New Delhi: LPP, repr. 2006.

147. Samuel Beal, *Travels of Fah-Hian and Sung-Yun from China to India*, Delhi: LPP, repr. 2005, pp. 87–8.

148. Samuel Beal, *The Life of Hiuen Tsang*, Delhi: LPP, repr. 2008, pp. 97–8.

149. Malalasekera, *Dictionary of Pāli Proper Names*, vol. I, p. 369.

150. *Suttanipāta Commentary*, II.514.

151. *Vinaya Pitaka*, I.39.

152. Ibid., I.42.

153. *Buddhavaṃśa Commentary*, 3.

154. *Vinaya Pitaka*, I.137.

155. Ibid., I.212.

156. Ibid., I.146.

157. Malalasekera, *Dictionary of Pāli Proper Names*, vol. I, p. 938.

158. *Sarathapakasinī*, I.219.

159. *Suttanipāta Commentary*, II.419.

160. *Aṅguttara Nikāya*, V.54.

161. Ibid., III.247, 339.

162. *Vinaya Pitaka*, I.201; III.49.

163. *Buddhavaṃśa Commentary,* 192ff.

164. John S. Strong, *The Legend of King Aśoka: A Study and Translation of the Aśokāvadana,* Delhi: MLBD, 2008, p. 290.

165. *Vinaya Pitaka,* I.246.

166. *Dīgha Nikāya,* I.46, 53, 235; *Milindapanho,* V.46.

167. *Dhammapadaṭṭhakathā,* III.207.

168. *Vimānvatthu,* 33.

169. *Dhammapadatthakathā,* III.207.

170. *Vinaya Pitaka,* II.109.

171. *Theragātha,* V.197.

172. *Buddhavaṃśa,* 54–5.

173. *Dhammapadaṭṭhakathā,* I.105.

174. *Vinaya Pitaka,* I.28.

175. *Mahāvastu,* III.302.

176. *Buddhavaṃśa,* 8, 23.

177. B.B. Lal, *The Earliest Civilization of South Asia, Rise, Maturity and Decline,* Delhi: Aryan Books International, 1997, pp. 223–4.

178. *Rigveda,* I.135.8; X.97.5.

179. *Saṃyutta Nikāya,* V.96.

180. *Dīgha Nikāya,* II.4.

181. *Vinaya Pitaka,* I.1.

182. *Mahāvastu,* II.280.

183. Thomas Watters, *On Yuan Chwang's Travels in India,* vol. II, Delhi: LPP, repr. 2004, p. 14.

184. Ibid., pp. 14–15.

185. J. Gorden Milton, *The Encyclopaedia of Religious Phenomenon,* Canton: Visible Ink Press, 2008, p. 40.

186. *Aṅguttara Nikāya,* I.130.

187. Ibid., I.181.

188. *Vinaya Pitaka,* IV.76.

189. *Aṅguttara Nikāya,* III.49.

190. *Majjhima Nikāya,* I.80.

191. *Jātaka,* nos. 77, 363.

192. *Dīgha Nikāya,* II.265.

193. *Dhammapadatthakathā,* I.433.

194. *Atharavaveda,* XI.6.15.

195. *Vinaya Pitaka,* I.58.

196. Ibid., I.205.

197. *Dīgha Nikāya,* II.350.

198. *Dhammapada,* V.54.

199. *Aṅguttara Nikāya,* III.237; *Milindapanho,* 321.

200. *Aṅguttara Nikāya,* I.9; *Vinaya Pitaka,* I.110.

201. Ibid., I.145.

202. *Dīgha Nikāya,* II.137.

203. *Milindapañho*, 321.
204. *Rigveda*, I.191.3.
205. *Atharavaveda*, XIX.32.7.
206. *Aṅguttara Nikāya*, II.207; *Theragātha*, V.27.
207. *Dhammapada*, V.345.
208. *Majjhima Nikāya*, II,152.
209. *Vinaya Pitaka*, III.250.
210. *Jātaka.*, nos. 423, 440.
211. *Dīgha Nikāya*, III.71; *Vinaya Pitaka*, IV.264.
212. *Vinaya Pitaka*, I.248.
213. *Saṃyutta Nikāya*, V.237, *Vimānavatthu*, 6.
214. *Visuddhimagga*, 409.
215. *Aṅguttara Nikāya*, I.35; *Suttanipāta*, V.552; *Theragātha*, V.822; *Milindapanho*, 27.
216. *Vinaya Pitaka*, I.246.
217. *Milindapanho*, I.246.
218. *Vinaya Pitaka*, I.30.
219. *Jātaka*, no. 438.
220. *Aṅguttara Nikāya*, II.73; *Saṃyutta Nikāya*, I.154; II.241.
221. *Saṃyutta Nikāya*, III.141.
222. *Therīgātha*, V.260.
223. *Dhammapadaṭṭhakathā*, I.59.
224. *Saṃyutta Nikāya*, I.154; II.241; *Vinaya Pitaka*, II.188; *Aṅguttara Nikāya*, II.73; *Milindapanho*, 166.
225. *Dīgha Nikāya*, II.141; *Aṅguttara Nikāya*, III.295.
226. *Vinaya Pitaka*, I.50.
227. Ibid., 284; I.271.
228. *Dīgha Nikāya*, II.351.
229. *Aṅguttara Nikāya*, III.295.
230. Ibid., IV.394.
231. *Vinaya Pitaka*, I.196.
232. *Dīgha Nikāya*, II.141-2.
233. Ibid., II.188, *Milindapanho* 105.
234. *Dhammapadaṭṭhakathā*, III.475, *Milindapañho*, 382.
235. *Vinaya Pitaka*, IV.35; *Visuddhimagga*, 137.
236. *Saṃyutta Nikāya*, V.96.
237. B.B. Lal, *The Homeland of Aryans: Evidence of Rigvedic Flora and Fauna and Archaeology*, Delhi: Aryan Books, 2005, p. 114.
238. *Rigveda*, III.53.29.
239. *Dhammapadaṭṭhakathā*, III.206.
240. *Jātaka*, no. 29.
241. Ibid., no. 162.
242. *Rigveda*, X.85.20.
243. *Saṃyutta Nikāya*, IV.193.

244. *Jātaka*, no. 23.
245. *Saṃyutta Nikāya*, III.137; IV, 198.
246. *Aṅguttara Nikāya*, I.240; *Dīgha Nikāya*, I.67.
247. *Itivuttaka*, 68.
248. *Jātaka*, no. 108.
249. *Dhammapada*, V.31.
250. *Buddhavaṃśa*, 22, 25.
251. *Jātaka*, no. 441.
252. *Jātaka*, no. 55.
253. *Therigatha*, V.440.
254. *Vinaya Pitaka*, III.237.
255. *Saṃyutta Nikāya*, II.101; III.152.
256. *Jātaka*, no. 269.
257. *Vinaya Pitaka*. II.140–1.
258. Ibid., II.140.
259. Samuel Beal, *Travels of Fah-Hian and Sung-Yun from China to India*, p. 55.
260. *Jātaka*, nos. 434, 529.
261. *Vinaya Pitaka*, I.246.
262. *Jātaka*, no. 359.
263. Ibid., nos. 281, 392.
264. *Dīgha Nikāya*, II.137.
265. Ibid., I.77; *Majjhima Nikāya*, II.17.
266. *Rigveda*, I.161.8.
267. *Aṅguttara Nikāya*, II.21.
268. *Jātaka*, no. 202.
269. *Suttanipāta*, V.440.
270. *Dīgha Nikāya*, III.75.
271. Ibid., I.51.
272. *Saṃyutta Nikāya*, III.155.
273. Ibid., I.5.
274. *Vinaya Pitaka*, IV.39.
275. *Saṃyutta Nikāya*, I.156; IV.185.
276. Ibid., no. 140.
277. *Dīgha Nikāya*, I.77; *Majjhima Nikāya*, II.17.
278. *Dhammapada*, V.164.
279. *Vinaya Pitaka*, I.190; *Saṃyutta Nikāya*, I.77.
280. *Majjhima Nikāya*, I.429.
281. *Saṃyutta Nikāya*, IV.198.
282. *Aṅguttara Nikāya*, I.32.
283. *Vinaya Pitaka*, I.201.
284. *Jātaka*, no. 34.
285. *Aṅguttara Nikāya*, III.250.
286. *Buddhavaṃśa Commentary*, 163ff.
287. *Saṃyutta Nikāya*, I.207.

288. *Jātaka*, no. 208.
289. *Saṃyutta Nikāya*, I.207.
290. *Suttanipata*, V.272.
291. *Jātaka*, no. 110.
292. *Udāna*, 3.
293. *Aṅguttara Nikāya*, III.42-3.
294. *Jātaka*, no. 259.
295. *Dīgha Nikāya*, II.18.
296. Ibid., II.4.
297. *Dīgha Nikāya*, I.75; *Theragātha*, V.1089.
298. *Suttanipāta*, V.845.
299. *Dhammapada*, V.285; *Dīgha Nikāya*, II.179.
300. *Aṅguttara Nikāya*, III.239; *Saṃyutta Nikāya*, I.81.
301. Ibid., I.145.
302. *Dīgha Nikāya*, I.111.
303. *Aṅguttara Nikāya*, I.145.
304. *Saṃyutta Nikāya*, III.130.
305. *Aṅguttara Nikāya*, III.90.
306. Ibid., III.206.
307. *Jātaka*, no. 308.
308. *Vinaya Pitaka*, I.246.
309. Ibid., I.215.
310. *Jātaka*, no. 466.
311. *Saṃyutta Nikāya*, V.438.
312. *Aṅguttara Nikāya*, III.347; *Saṃyutta Nikāya*, III.140.
313. *Jātaka*, nos. 37, 323.
314. Ibid., no. 363.
315. Ibid., no. 324.
316. *Vinaya Pitaka*, I.3.
317. *Majjhima Nikāya*, II.129–30.
318. *Dīgha Nikāya*, I.92–3.
319. *Jātaka*, nos. 161, 528.
320. *Theragātha*, V.948.
321. *Aṅguttara Nikāya*, I.152.
322. Ibid., II.201.
323. *Majjhima Nikāya*, I.124.
324. *Dhammapada*, V.162.
325. *Jātaka*, no. 328.
326. *Aṅguttara Nikāya*, II.194.
327. Ibid., III.49.
328. *Dīgha Nikāya*, II.4.
329. *Buddhavaṃsa*, 3, 31; *Buddhavaṃsa Commentary*, 107ff.
330. *Milindapañho*, V.376.
331. Lal, *The Homeland of Aryans,* p. 17.

332. *Visuddhimagga*, V.206; *Dhammapadaṭṭhakathā*, I.279.
333. *Rigveda*, VII.50.3; X.85.20.
334. *Aṅguttara Nikāya*, V.170; *Saṃyutta Nikāya*, II.137.
335. *Vinaya Pitaka*, I.204.
336. *Dhammapada*, V.401; *Suttanipāta*, V.625.
337. *Rigveda*, III.53.19.
338. *Aṅguttara Nikāya*, I.136.
339. *Dīgha Nikāya*, II.316.
340. *Saṃyutta Nikāya*,V.437–8.
341. *Jātaka*, no. 535.
342. *Saṃyutta Nikāya*, IV.193.
343. *Dīgha Nikāya*, II.4.
344. *Buddhavaṃśa Commentary*, 209ff.
345. *Vinaya Pitaka*, I.246.
346. *Aṅguttara Nikāya*, V.173; *Saṃyutta Nikāya*, I.152.
347. *Jātaka*, no. 420.
348. *Dhammapada*, V.54.
349. *Jātaka*, no. 537.
350. *Saṃyutta Nikāya*, III.156.
351. *Dhammapada*, V.377.
352. Ibid., V.54.
353. *Vinaya Pitaka*, I.203.
354. *Dhammapada*, V.55.
355. *Dīgha Nikāya*, II.171, 182; *Majjhima Nikāya*, I.187; *Vinaya Pitaka*, I.189; *Theragātha*, V.127.
356. *Aṅguttara Nikāya*, I.137.
357. *Itivuttaka*, 84.
358. *Aṅguttara Nikāya*, I.181.
359. *Dīgha Nikāya*, III.27.
360. *Aṅguttara Nikāya*, I.241; *Dīgha Nikāya*, I.166; *Majjhima Nikāya*, I.78.
361. *Dīgha Nikāya*, I.166.
362. *Jātaka*, no. 405.
363. *Theragātha*, V.381.
364. *Aṅguttara Nikāya*, I.8; III.49; IV.231; *Dīgha Nikāya*, I.105.
365. *Jātaka*, no. 531.
366. *Aṅguttara Nikāya*, IV.237; *Vinaya Pitaka*, II.180.
367. Ibid., V.212–3.
368. *Aṅguttara Nikāya*, IV.231.
369. *Dīgha Nikāya*, I.166.
370. *Jātaka*, no. 425.
371. Ibid., no. 230.
372. *Vimānvatthu*, 33, 24; *Saṃyutta Nikāya*, I.166.
373. *Aṅguttara Nikāya*, III.250.
374. Ibid., I.130; IV.108; *Vinaya Pitaka*, I.212.

375. *Vinaya Pitaka*, I.205.
376. Ibid., I.210.
377. *Majjhima Nikāya*, I.78.
378. *Saṃyutta Nikāya*, I.170.
379. *Buddhavaṃsa*, 2, 168.
380. *Majjhima Nikāya*, III.142.
381. *Aṅguttara Nikāya*, IV.108.
382. Ibid., I.145; *Dīgha Nikāya*, II.19; *Vinaya Pitaka*, I.96.
383. *Aṅguttara Nikāya*, I.101; *Vinaya Pitaka*, I.286; II.148.
384. *Dhammapada*, V.358.
385. *Vinaya Pitaka*, I.137.
386. *Aṅguttara Nikāya*, I.182.
387. *Majjhima Nikāya*, I.502.
388. *Vinaya Pitaka*, I.192, 196; II.150; *Theragātha*, V.27.
389. *Jātaka*, no. 536; *Vinaya Pitaka*, IV.35.
390. *Jātaka*, no. 536; *Vimānvatthu*, 45, 5.
391. *Therīgātha*, V.382.
392. *Vinaya Pitaka*, I.279.
393. *Dhammapada*, V.377.
394. *Aṅguttara Niakya*, V.22; *Majjhima Nikāya*, I.32.
395. *Jātaka*, no. 38; *Suttanipāta*, no. 38.
396. *Vinaya Pitaka*, II.154; IV.6.
397. *Jātaka*, V.71; *Saṃyutta Nikāya*, II.241.
398. *Vinaya Pitaka*, I.39.
399. *Milindapanho*, V.372.
400. *Vinaya Pitaka*, I.249.
401. *Rigveda*, XII.86.6; X.34.1.
402. Ibid., I.201.
403. *Saṃyutta Nikāya*, IV.195; V.10; *Vinaya Pitaka*, III.15; IV.264.
404. *Rigveda*. I.16.2; IV.27.7.
405. *Vinaya Pitaka*, I.3.
406. Ibid., II.116.

3

Formation of Buddhist Environmental Ethics

Analysis of the early Buddhist doctrines for the formation of environmental ethics lead to a adaptation of new methodological approach to reinterpret the discourses. Doctrines like *Paticcasamuppada*, *Majjhimamagga*, *Brahmavihāras*, etc., are used to re-orient Buddhist teachings showing concerns for modern environmental problems and to provide solutions. By determining what can constitute Buddhist environmental ethics and keeping in mind the various circumstances that led to the rise of environmental concerns, a careful ethical tradition could be drafted to trace the petals of environmental ethics embedded in Buddhist thought.

Paticcasamuppada as an Ethical Tool

The doctrine of *paticcasamuppada* (dependent origination) reveals human's true place in the universe. It has been reinvented to cope with many problems engulfing the modern world, like environmental degeneration. Dependent origination is the beginning of Buddhist understanding of Nature. It ushers in the basic Buddhist insight to learn the attributes of Nature. It can be treated as the central teaching of Buddhism, not only on philosophical ground but also as an authenticated tool to understand the socio-economic and environmental perspectives.[1] In Indian philosophical traditions, the theory of causation has generally two types of interpretation and orientation. The philosophies believing in *satkaryavada* like the *Saṃkhya* and *Yoga* accept that the effect pre-exist in cause. The cause exposes the effect and is not really responsible to create it. Again, *Asatkaryavada* exponents like the *Nyāya-Vaisheśika* accept that effect does not pre-exist in material cause but is created with a new phenomenon known as *ārambhavāda*. According to them, the cause and the effect are two different things and can not be identical. But the Buddha adopted the middle path by avoiding both the schools and expounded impermanence of things. He learnt the nature of things which can be of great help to learn the causes of environmental degeneration and other anthropocentric activities. He discovered uniformity of the causal process (*dhammani yamata*) which ends sufferings and leads to *vimutti*.[2] The Buddha declared that he could succeed in vanishing all defilements and attain *vimutti* because he had understood the doctrine of *paticcasamuppada*. It can be elaborated with the reference of the *Paccaya Sutta*[3] which explains causality (*paticcasamuppada*) and causally-conditioned phenomenon (*pabccasamuppada dhamma*). These two factors are inseparably connected and are capable to explain every action of the world, individually and in relative terms. The understanding of social and physical processes can give a better insight into *saṁsāric* actions, their results, and future goals. The Buddha says that causal pattern could be recognized in physical, moral, and social spectrum, and causality was more or less a condition.[4] In the *Paccaya Sutta*, the Buddha comprehends four attributes of *paticcasamuppada*: objectivity (*tathatā*), necessity (*avitathatā*), invariability (*anaññathatā*), and conditionality (*idappaccayatā*). The first enumerates the objectivity of the causal relationship which is real. Factors like 'necessity' and 'invariability' emphasize the absence of any exceptions.[5] A determined set of conditions is prelude to a certain effect and cannot be different. If conditions are not properly recognized, then the eventual happening diagnosed in this phenomenal world cannot be analysed satisfactorily. The accidental occurrences or incidences without any causal pattern are just ignorance of the causal process.[6] The causal pattern for deterioration of environment could be examined by removing the ignorance of its cause and acting upon it to rectify. If one accepts that there is no accidental cause for such deterioration then it will be easy to discover the real cause. The conditionality (*idappaccayata*) determines the two extremes, the unconditional necessity accentuated by determinism and the unconditional arbitrariness encouraged by accidentalism. On these attributes of causation the Buddha discovered the formula of causation:

Imasmim sati idam hoti
Imassa uppādā idam uppajjati
Imamim asati idam na hoti
Imassa nirodhā idam nirujjhoti. [7]

(When it is present, that comes to be; on the arising of that, it arises. When that is absent, it does not come to be; on the ceasing of that, it ceases.)

The Buddha, after examining the conception of causality at various stages of causal happenings, discovers this truth about the world. It has a golden meaning which avoids two extremes of the contemporary religious thoughts, eternalists as well as annihilationists.[8] Individual occurrences of causality were examined on the basis of sensory and extrasensory experiences and the uniformity of the causal law was obtained through inductive inference based on such experiences. The causation was considered as a phenomenal experience and the causal uniformity was considered as an inductive inference. The existence of experiences of causal happening determined the past and future occurrences of inductive inferences.[9] The experiences (*dhammeñāna*) consisted of knowledge of causality-conditioned phenomenon (*paticcasamuppanna-dhamma*) and the causal relation (*paticcasamuppada*) of the present and partly of the past. Again, inferential knowledge (*anvaye jañanā*) was mainly manifestation of the future and partly of the past. The uniformity of the causal principle which comprised prediction of the future was an inductive generalization.[10] *Paticcasamuppada* was used to explain every phenomenon. The universal applicability of the causal law was used to explain the causal principles and functioning of inorganic and organic phenomenon. The Buddha explains with help of this causal law the evolution, dissolution of the world, and causes and conditions of various natural phenomenon like drought and earthquake.[11] In the *Aṅguttara Nikāya*, the Buddha gives five reasons for draught—when heat in upper sky became condensed, when atmospheric pressure was disturbed because of air pressure, when Rahu who discarded water into the ocean, the heedless actions of the *devas* and humans.[12] The Buddha explains causes of earthquake—because of depression, when an ascetic or brāhmana or a deity developed a limited knowledge of the earth and and his senseless action makes this Earth tremble, when a *Bodhisattva* who passed from Tusita heaven to enter his mother's womb, when a *Bodhisattva* was born, when the Buddha gets awakening to attain *nibbāna* and during turning the wheel of law (*dhammacakkapabattana*) by the Buddha. The seventh cause was letting go of the vital force by the Buddha and the eighth and the final cause was *mahāparinibbāna* of the Buddha.[13]

Causal relationship has been defined especially with reference to human personality. The Buddhist view is that causality functions in five main sphere: physical or inorganic order (*utu-niyāma*), physical or organic order (*bija niyāma*), psychological order (*citta niyāma*), moral order (*kamma niyāma*), and spiritual order (*dhamma niyāma*).[14] These five groups are inclusive and nothing could be excluded from them. Everything which exists in the universe comes under the circumference of causality and it exhibits the truth. These *niyamas* refer to the nature of things or natural principles. The *utu niyāma* comprises the inorganic as part of Nature and accepts inherant changes in Nature. The *bija niyāma* indicates the organic aspect of Nature as plant life. The *citta niyāma* is the sphere of mind while the *kamma niyāma* deals with moral or immoral actions. The Buddha says that Nature with all its dimensions including human being is considered as a phenomenon governed by one universal principle called *paticcasamuppada*. The environmental deterioration could be compared with sufferings faced by the human world. The Buddha says that worldly pleasures appear as such only to those who are short-sighted and conceited. Its true cause has not been recognized and thus human life is full of misery. The Buddha says that nothing is unconditional and every happening depends on some conditions. As the existence of every eventuality depends on some reason, there must be something from which human misery comes into existence. The ignorance (*avijja*) leads to evil or unwholesome behaviour and when it is completely wiped out, it culminates into enlightenment. The Buddha says that *samma ditthi* can eliminate *avijja* (ignorance) and *tanha* (craving). David J. Kalupahana says:

Ignorance is said to condition the dispositions (saṅkhāra) which play a significant role in determining the nature of man's behaviour (kamma). The nature of one's consciousness (viññāna) also depends on nature of dispositions. Consciousness being the factor that determines the nature of the new psychological personality (nāmarūpa), the part played by the dispositions in determining the life after death is emphasized. Dispositions therefore account for the nature of one's behaviour (kamma) as well as one's future birth or rebirth (punnbhava). The process of rebirth is explained as combining of two factors consciousness (viññāna) and the psychological personality (nāmrūpa). The psychological personality referred to here is the foetus formed in mother's womb (gabba) and which represents beginning of new life span.[15]

The *Mahāhatthipadopama Sutta* informs that the Buddha accepts that one who visualizes the *paticcasamuppada* sees the *dhamma* and the one who sees the *dhamma* also knows *paticcasamuppada*. It thus makes *paticcasamuppada* and *dhamma* same and coterminous.[16] The *Nalakalapa Sutta* mentions that two bunches of reeds can stand only with the other's support, showing relative dependence of phenomenon and not a sequential relationship between cause and effect. It endorses conditionality (*idappaccayata*).[17] The *dvadasanidāna* deals with human suffering. It expresses a non-linear enumeration of factors of causality as a circular process commencing at any point. Among the factors, *avijja* may be the most potent element. The causality dependent phenomenon could be applied and explained in various ways and could be used as a fully potent method to counter environmental degradation. The *Bīja Sutta* explains co-relations among various elements of Nature and exhibits how co-existence and interdependence of five elements lead to develop a seed into plant. In the sprouting of seed, soil, water, and moisture also play pivotal roles.[18] The ecological interdependence could also be traced from the *Accayika Sutta* which explains the causal connection of conditions that lead to production of a good harvest.[19]

The *paticcasamuppada* as a tool to counter environmental problems could be used to curtail harmful pursuits with regard to the environment. Desires always lead to *tanha* (craving). It is obvious that craving for material affluence leads to follow such pursuits. Such actions lead to possessions that cause avarice which further cause strife, anxiety, conflict, and complication. The *paticcasamuppada* not only explains the arising of *dukkha* but also provides remedies. It motivates to understand the individuality and *samsāra*. It also awakes to realize the phenomenon that arise from conditions. It shows the co-relation between action (*kamma*) and consequences (*vipāka*) just as human being is dependent on plants, animals, and water. Even mind works dependently because the existence of thoughts is dependent on same spectrum which are derived from the external world of objects and persons.[20] The *Kosambiya Sutta* explains the way problems of the modern world can be resolved. It says that it is not obligatory to become enlightened or to get acquainted with the doctrine of *paticcasamuppada* but it is pertinent to grasp the true nature of the problems that lead to removal of the obstacles.[21] If one fails to realize the true nature of problems in its totality then the real cause and effect relation would not be known. It will lead to adaptation of fragmented methodology that may prelude to disastrous result or failure. The *paticcasamuppada* has not been used to explain arising and ceasing of suffering which could be applied to modern problems too. The Buddhist texts mention suffering as individual suffering but in the larger context it is accepted that an individual is a unit of society. So, the suffering of an individual might be the suffering of the whole society. The Buddha rejected the metaphysical and absolutist nature of suffering saying that it is created by individuals. Both reality and humans are subject to some attributes of extremes. These attributes are *tilakkhana*, i.e. *anicca* (impermanence), *dukkha* (dissatisfaction), and *anatta* (non-substantiality). Buddhism accepts that *sabbe sankhāra anicca* (all conditioned phenomenon are impermanent).[22] Here *sankhāra* comprises reality indicating that everything animate and inanimate share certain fundamental attributes and dependence.

The Buddha gives many examples on how suffering arises due to wrong perceptions. The *Madhupindika Sutta* explains the process of perception:

Dependent on the ear and sounds . . . dependent on the nose and odours . . . dependent on the tongue and flavours . . . dependent on the body and tangibles . . . dependent on the mind and mind objects, mind consciousness arises. The meeting of the three is contact. With contact as condition there is feeling. What one feels, that one perceives. What one perceives, that one thinks about. What one thinks about, that one mentally proliferates. With what one has mentally proliferated as the source, perceptions and notions (born of) mental proliferations beset a man with respect to past, future, and present mind objects cognizable through the mind.[23]

The *Cakkavati Sihnada Sutta* explains social manifestation of human suffering in a causally conditioned manner. It says that because of false opinion, excessive greed, and deviant practices, the life span of human being will degenerate until the average human lifespan is reduced to 10 years and the marriageable age to 5 years. There will be fierce enmity for one another, fierce hatred, fierce anger, and thoughts of killing, just as the hunter feels hatred for the beast he stalks.[24] The *Rathapala Sutta* describes reasons for Siddhārtha renouncing his house. He feels that life is impermanent and world is not a shelter. It is incomplete, insatiate, and full of cravings.[25] These are considered to be natural results of reality attributed by dependent existence.

The *paticcasamuppada* is the most cherished metaphysical doctrine of the Buddha discussed among scholars in support or against environmentalism. In a soteriological explanation, Alan Sponberg says that environmentalism is conditioned in the Buddhist doctrine of *annata*. Here individual identity is perceived as a dynamic and growing stream of *kammic* conditioning that goes to many lives and life forms. The self is a form of dynamic stream which leads to consequential environment sustaining altruism.[26] Sulak Sivaraksa uses the word 'interdependent' for *paticcasamuppada* in place of 'dependent origination' and propounds that the doctrine of interdependence co-arising is the sui generis of Buddhist understanding of Nature. The anthropocentric ideas are the major causes for environmental degradation and *paticcasamuppada* re-orients human vision towards a more eco-friendly world view.[27] David Kalupahana says that Buddhism considers humans as a part of Nature and dependently arisen like everything existed. The learning of such distinctions will reveal significant relationship between Nature and humanity.[28] Chatsumarn Kabil-singh also argues that *paticcasamuppada* can be exemplified for environmentalism and the human culture as a part of Nature can be identified as an individual or collectively as a nation, and will be responsible for utilizing or violating the natural laws.[29] Andrew Olendzki accepts that the doctrine of *paticcasamuppada* has not been properly utilized for environmentalism in Buddhism. If human beings are more interconnected, then there is more attachment in the conditioned phenomenon; but the inherent core of idea of Buddhism lies beyond it, viz., more efforts to get less connected, less entangled, and less attached.[30] Clippard agreed with Olendzki's observation but contradicted on the application of *paticcasamuppada* in the development of eco-ethics. The zeal and aim may be to become unconnected but *paticcasamuppada*, in the context of eco-Buddhism, emphasizes how to survive and live in this world while still living in the realm of *saṁsāra*.[31] Joanna Macy applies the idea of *kamma, annata*, and *paticcasamuppada* with Nature. In her book *World as Lover, World as Self,* she takes inspiration from dependent origination from which she moves to the nature of the self. The self co-exists with the people and an act for the sake of self means doing it for the sake of others which may be termed as 'giving the self'.[32]

P.A. Payutto connects the root of environmentalism to *lobha* and *dosa* which led to ill-conceived consumerism and consumption, the main cause of pollution, poverty, and other social evils. He refers to environment-friendly *suttas* from Buddhist texts without sacrificing its very essentials of tradition.[33] The potential for promoting a positive and optimistic attitude towards environment in kindred in the sayings of the Buddha, like *katvekitā* (gratitude), *mudita* (altruistic joy), *metta*, and *sukkha*. Bhikkhu Buddhadasa defines human-Nature relationship by applying the *dhamma* as a Nature and compared the degeneration of environment to disregard and harm *dhamma*.[34] He argues that *Dhamma* represents Nature in the sense of natural law and so, *dhamma* as a law of Nature can be equated with *paticcasamuppada*.[35] Donald K. Swearer says that the difference between Payutto and Buddhadasa could be surmised by differentiating Buddhadasa's spiritual bio-centrism based on identification of Nature and *dhamma* with Payutto's textual strategy in which teachings are more systematic and more carefully grounded in the Pālī texts and the Theravāda historical traditions. Payutto says that Buddhist world view of mutual trust and cooperation can be an alternative to the Western dualism and materialism which he feels responsible for many forms of global imperils.[36] Christopher Ives tries to solve the controversy over the use of *paticcasamuppada* by Buddhist environmentalists. Ives illustrates that when a common environmental concern is explained in terms of *paticcasamuppada*, one succumbs to certain 'rhetorical pitfalls' and these might be avoided by translating *paticcasamuppada* as 'conditional arising'.[37]

Kamma (Karma) Theory

Kamma is one of the most precious aspects of Indian religions. It has been defined as a deed or action and also connotes the motivation behind such actions. Buddhism accepts that the essence of *kamma* is a voluntary mental act which originates and destroys through will.[38] The greatest emphasis is laid on one's just action and non-dependence on miraculous powers, rituals, and ceremonies. The Buddha says that human beings have *kamma* as their own, as their source, as their kin, as their refuge. He propounded ownership of *kamma* without the possession of metaphysical self (*atta*). It divides humanity into states of superiority and inferiority.[39] The *Nibbdikapariyaya Sutta* says that *kamma* is volition and all volitional act performed through body, speech, and mind can be identified as *kamma*.[40] The *Kammanidana Sutta* says that there are six mental states that form the root causes of *kamma-lobha* (craving), *dosa* (hatred), *moha* (attachment), and their anti-thesis, *alobha* (non-craving), *adosa* (non-hatred), and *amoha* (non-attachment). The *sutta* emphasizes upon the notion that *kammic* process is not controlled by any external potency but by human beings' own action.[41] Any *kamma* that creates ill-will towards other is a result of ignorance. *Kamma* determines moral or immoral character. The categories and differences among human beings are primarily due to their *kamma*.[42]

The Buddha visualizes the psychological aspects of *kamma* and also accounts for the moral nature of *kamma*. He says that *kamma* is one of the causal processes. This view is in contrast to Jainism which recommends that *kamma* and resulted action is directly associated to the person who has done it. When one acts, the resultant positive or negative consequences are to be with that person. The *Mahāmangala Sutta* says that there are three factors that could be considered auspicious in the life of a person—merit acquired in the past, to reside in appropriate surrounding, and self-resolution. All such factors result in the *kammic* action of man and its consequences.[43] The *Mahākammavibhanga Sutta* says that it is possible for an evil doer to be reborn in a happy state, albeit if he endeavours to change his intention and act. This contradicts the deterministic theory of *kamma* which says that everything experienced in this life is due to one's past *kamma*. The Buddha accept action is a field, consciousness and craving lead to the rebirth.[44] The Buddha incorporates two moral paths for *kamma*— the *śilas* which consist of higher moral life and the virtues of *ariya atthanikamagga* (eightfold path) that provide direction for higher moral life. The *Brahmajāla Sutta* categorizes virtues into three categories as small, middle, and great. The virtues have two aspects—refraining from the bad (*akuśala*) or abstinence (*varitta*) from wrong doings and practicing good (*kuśala*) or the cultivation of good deeds (*cāritta*). The *sutta* emphasizes on not harming seeds and plants by destroying their roots, cutting them from stems and joints, and also advises to refrain from addictions and enjoying stored-up goods such as food, drink, clothing, carriages, beds, perfumes, and meat.[45] The Buddha encouraged moral attitude by promoting middle way (*majjhima patipāda*). It avoids extremes in personal as well public life and gives up what is before and what is behind.[46] The middle path acknowledges that knowledge of the past is necessary for the learning of the present and the future expectations play a vital role in human understanding and endeavour.[47] The Buddha told his disciples not to pursue fixed views about the past (*pubbantānuditthi*) or about the future (*aparantānuditthi*).[48] The middle path is not one between two extremes, but also that is grounded in concrete experiences. It does not corroborate to aloofness and disillusion from *samsāric* activities but responds to emphatic attempt to carefully examine the existing situation or evidence before taking a decision.[49] Buddhists accepts that good *kamma* frees man from the bane of determinism and fatalism and its moral consequences. The accumulation of *kamma* should not be misunderstood as a hindrance to liberation because all *samsāric* actions are not deterrent to *nibbāna*. The *Dhammapada* says that while repeated indulgence in doing evil lead to accumulation of bad *kamma*.[50] The moral consequences of bad *kamma* are repeatedly mentioned in Buddhist literature. The *Dhammapada*[51] further says that one cannot escape consequences of one's bad *kamma* even if one is hiding in sky, in the mid-ocean or in the cliff of the mountain. One must always act like a judicious merchant who avoids dangerous trade routes.[52] Such trivial tendencies should not be followed only in action but prevention starts in mind.[53]

Some scholars have their own explanation about *kamma*.
Melford Spiro says that Buddhism refutes everything within the
spatio-temporal world, i.e. *saṁsāra*. It encourages renunciation
of *lokiya*. Only physical retreat from the world is not enough; a
normal condition is to severe all ties from the *saṁsāra*. The *nibbāna*
could be attained only by a total and radical abandonment of all
saṁsāric actions.[54] Max Weber argues about world renunciation
saying that the Buddha encouraged total *saṁsāric* negation.[55]
But, in the larger context, no such practice was known in
Buddhism. The accumulation of merit was also not condemned
in Buddhism. The *Dhammapada* says that person engaged in good
deeds should do it again and again (*puññañ ce puriso kayirā kayirāth
enam punappunam*) to gain pleasure.[56] It also says that good action
awaits one when he goes from one world to the next just as kins
and friends welcome a dear friend on his return from a journey.[57]
The *Piya Sutta*[58] mentions lengthy admonitions by the Buddha
praising good deeds. During his stay in Mynamar, Spiro even
found that Budddhists are more *saṁsāric* than the rest. He writes:

Contrary, then to the ideology of nibbanic Buddhism, Buddhism for most
Buddhists is a mean not so much for the extinction of desire as for its
satisfaction; not so much for the cessation of rebirth as far a better rebirth;
not so much for one kind of absolute Deliverance –whether this be conceived
as the extinction of being or less extremely, of an individualized ego-as far
the persistence of the individualized ego in a state of sensate happiness.
Hence, even when the soteriological aim is expressed innibbanic rhetoric—
'May I attain nirvana'—the content of the aspiration is samsāric rather
than nibbanic. What is desired in kammatic Buddhism is the extinction of
samsāric suffering, but not samsāric pleasure.[59]

In reality, it is a contradiction in Buddhism that at one end
it preached to bring about the cessation of *saṁsāra* and on the
other, offers advice to accumulate merit for its continuity. The
Buddha's approach was more realistic that *kamma* should be
oriented towards realism rather than deterministic or fatalistic.
The *Vajji Sutta* shows that knowledge is a precursor of wholesome
things and is followed by moral consequences and fear. Punna
has no potential to avail *nibbāna* but is capable of creating
happy consequences in *saṁsāra* while *kusala* have the power to
produce both happy consequences in *saṁsara* as well as to attain
nibbāna.[60] The Buddha accepts diversity of views but recommends

graduated path to harmony. *The Ariyapariyesana Sutta*[61] elucidate a graphic account of diversity in the population. He compares the people like a lotus pond where some lotuses remained subdued in the water, some remained at surface level, and some blossom above the water surface. Like that some are of diverse character, some being ignorant, and some being wise.[62]

Buddhism not only provides dimensions about good or bad *kamma* but also discusses various stages and procedure to get acquainted with good *kamma*. The environmental ethics can get its inspiration for rectification even in adverse situations. The *Kitagiri Sutta*[63] says that full realization of knowledge can not be attained at the beginning but through a gradual process of training, action, and practice. The *Upanissa Sutta*[64] systematically explains such gradual process of internal change that starts in an individual till he realizes the final emancipation caused by his initial confidence kindled by *dukkha*. The Buddha says that good *kamma* is endowed with the strength of bringing happiness in *saṁsāric* action as well as destroying defilements. The unrighteousness conduct causes deterioration and good action prelude to positive consequences.[65] If such actions could be applied in the larger context of society, it could be altruistic to deal with ideal economic growth and the protection of natural resources for sustainable future.

Eightfold Path and Environmental Ethics

While forming the environmental ethics, the noble eightfold path constitutes an important element. The Buddha tried to dispel doubts and propitiate moral values in *saṁsāric* and *alukika* sphere through his noble eightfold path. It ascertains a sustained way of living which is the core of modern environmental ethics. It also suggests correction of wrong doings, method of rectification, and socio-economic morals to live and let live. The moral conception of right leads to epistemological notion of truth (*sacca*). The noble eightfold path—right view (*sammā diṭṭhi*), right conception (*sammā sankappa*), right speech (*sammā vāca*), right activity (*sammā kammanta*), right livelihood (*sammāājīva*), right effort (*sammā vayāma*), right mindfulness (*sammā sati*), and right concentration (*sammā samādhi*)—correspond the comprehensiveness of the path of moral perfection.[66] This noble eightfold path is both descriptive and narrative highlighting factors for lessening conflict, discrimination, and violence in the society. The first factor *samma ditthi* avoids eternalism and nihilism by propounding that anyone who perceives arising of phenomenon will not subscribe to the view of non-existence (nihilism). Similarly, anyone who perceives the ceasing of phenomenon will not substantiate to the view of existence (eternalism).[67] The Right View is dependent upon the arising *(uppāda)* and ceasing *(nirodha)*, and on the *majjhimamagga* of perceiving the world, the human beings, and others. *Samma ditthī* is the perception of four noble truth *(cattāri ariyasaccāri)* and its foundation is *paticcasamuppada*.[68] Right Conception *(samma sankappa)* is the right view of perceiving or viewing the world. It is a pragmatic way of putting things together and expressing in right direction. These may be of positive or negative values. The negative conceptions are those of pleasure associated with lust and greed *(kāma-sankappa),*—ill-will *(byāpāda sankappa)*, and harm *(vihimsa sankappa)*.[69] The conception of positive moral quality are the values of renunciation *(nekkhamma sankappa)*, conceptions of goodwill *(abyāpāda sankappa)*, and compassion *(avihimsa sankappa)*.[70]

Right Speech explains aloofness from wrong speech, falsehood, slander, and frivolous talks.[71] The avoidance of harsh language prevents self-infliction and humiliation of others. People who speak well *(svakkhata)* are highly praised and good speech always leads to cessation of suffering. Right *Kammanta* can be interpreted as a pattern of action or behaviour. It includes abstinence from taking life *(pānatipāta)*, from stealing *(adinnadāna)* and from other ignoble behaviour *(abrahamacariya)*.[72] The *Brahamajāla Sutta* gives a list of various forms of wrong livelihood *(micchajīva)* which are hindrances in the development of a just society.[73] The Buddha endorsed that the noblest form of life is one of attaining *nibbāna*, although he never discourage lay life.

The moral characteristics of virtuous life of a common people is fourfold: (i) happiness relating to resources *(atthisukkha)* that says that livelihood should be obtained without indulging in any fraudulent means, (ii) happiness relating to economic well-being *(bhogasukha)* that resulted from lawfully-acquired wealth, and (iii) happiness to be free from debt *(anana sukha)* and blame *(anavajja sukha)*.[74] The dyad of Right *Kammanta* and Right *Ditthi* can be a nice combination to develop environmental ethics. If society functions in a right direction with optimum and just utilization of resources, the harmonious co-existence between animate and inanimate will automatically develop. Right Effort (*sammā vāyāma*) advocates efficacy of human efforts. It persuades effectiveness of physical and mental welfare (*attha*) of oneself and others.[75] Right Mindfulness is understood as a way of clearing the mind of all discrimination and defilements. The *Satipatthana Sutta* emphasizes on retrospection (*anupassanā*) of the functioning of physical personality (*kāyā*), feeling or sensations (*vedana*), thought (*citta*), and the ideas (*dhamma*).[76] Right Concentration encourages in making the right decision regarding behaviour pattern. One's past experience could supplement knowledge or an event, status or process. It is envisioned to focus on the understanding of right perception and use it for appropriate action. It focuses upon *kuśala* and avoids *akuśala*. It endorses theory of momentariness (*kshanikavāda*) which says that there is no absolutely true event. In the absence of absolute knowledge, constant revision of understanding and behaviour are possible.[77] The Buddha always argues for the revision of ideas for welfare of all beings.[78] The *Mahacattarisaka Sutta* says that noble eightfold path could be followed at two level—one with defilements (*sasava*), partaking merit (*puññabhagiya*) and producing rebirth (*upadhi vipāka*) and the other is a noble path without defilements (*anasava*) and super mundane (*lokuttara*). This twofold mode can be applied to environmentalism as well. If one seeks living through deceit, conflict, and antagonism, it will damage the socio-economic fabric of the world. The abstention from wrong intention and following the right pursuit will lead to Right Mindfulness. The *Dhammacakkapabattana Sutta* discards practices involving indulgence in sensual pleasures (*kamasukhallekanuyoga*) considering them as being low, vulgar, and prelude to harm. It also discards the practice of self-mortification (*attakilamathanuyoga*) as being suffering, ignoble, and conducive to harm. After discarding those two extreme paths, the noble eightfold path leads to the *majjhima patipada*. Ignobleness and harmfulness are two facets that are common to these two extremes and form a contrast to noble deeds. The eightfold path when embraced by the commoners (*gahattha*) is considered to bear fruit for their happiness. There is nothing wrong in such actions so long as it is not derived from *lobha* and *moha*. But the wealth one enjoys will be the fruit of one's own effort and earned through just means. The *Saccavibhanga Sutta* says that Right *Ditthi* is the understanding of fourfold truth as it makes clear distinction between the right and wrong livelihood.[79] The cause and path have to be analysed in relation to the occasion. The middle path visualizes a way to the present consumer-oriented society which indulges in unwarranted destruction of resources as well as unlimited consumption under the influence of a new globalized economy. It presents the most needed tool to correct such mindset that are under the influence of modern economic system flourishing with benefits of technology at the cost of intensive destruction of natural resources. The noble eightfold path is thus a mean and not an end. The economic system here is the mean that has to be moralized in a way that can create friendliness and harmony towards Nature. It can be instrumental to draft an ethical code to solve a multitude of problems arising due to post-renaissance economic system. The present economic arrangement has advocated development sans morality. Buddhism considers the arena of business as an integral component of life which is associated to holistic ethical values seeking to control defilements and evils. The main aim of such ethics is to remove craving and consumerism which are detrimental to environment.

Pancaśila: Source of Environmental Ethics

In a consideration of ongoing environmentalism, Buddhist ethics may be re-arranged in a direction to make adjustments between moral teaching and human cause which continues and rises above the common limitations of time and space. The *Pancaśilas* are important medium to visualize eco-friendly policies and practices. These are: (i) *panatopataveramani sikkhapadam samadiyami* (to abstain from taking life), (ii) *adinnadanaveramani sikkhapadam samadiyami* (not to take what is not given), (iii) *kamesumicchacara vermani sikkhapadam samadiyami* (to abstain from indulging in sensual activities), (iv) *musavada vermani sikkhapadam samadiyami* (to abstain from false speech), and (iv) *sura-meraya majja pamadatthana vermani sikhapadam samadiyami* (to abstain from intoxication and indolence).[80] The *Pancaśilas* describe the moral principles derived essentially on the idea of mutual existence and progress. The first precept recognizes mutual respect for all living beings by not harming any living creature. The Buddha says that everyone fears violence and everyone loves life. So one should not cause to kill.[81] Certain societies living in different parts of world, however, survives only on animal economy because of shortage of cereals. Questions have been raised whether total relinquishing of killing of animals is a pragmatic approach. The Buddha himself takes moderate view here on killing of animals trying to minimize the damage and drawing a distinction between being culpable to a lesser degree (*appasavajja*) and to a greater degree (*mahāsavajja*). Either way, the Buddha was strictly against using force against the strong or the weak.[82] Buddhism bans killing by various means like, (i) killing by self (*sahatthika*), (ii) giving order to kill (*anattika*), (iii) killing by shooting, pelting stone, stics (*nissaggaiya*), etc., (iv) killing by digging ditches and entrapping (*thāvara*), (v) killing by using *iddhi* or occult means (*iddhimāyā*), and (vi) killing by *mantras* or occult sciences (*vijjamaya*).[83] The Buddha says that the person who kills a sentient being commits deed of *panatipata-kama-patha*.[84]

The person committing the killings earns bad *kammic* result. Therefore, he should develop *metta* to cultivate understanding with fellow beings and other sentients. It avoids conflict and promotes happiness—*aham avero homi abbyapajjho homi*, i.e. free from enimity and ill will.[85] Buddhist idea of non killing is not without debate but it gives ray of hope to invisage a policy for protection and respect of Nature.

The second precept advices people to abstain from taking the things that are not given. It restricts the person's desire to acquire more even if he/she is not capable to do so and such intentions lead to acquiring things not followed by the established procedure. The modern society is facing grave crisis when the market is creating fictitious demands through advertisements and other means and people are succumbing to these offers even if they are not capable to buy. The *Brahamajala Sutta* advises the *bhikkhus* to be patience and calm while taking gifts. They should receive their requisite (*paccaya*) that were offered and the *upāsakas* should lead their economic activities according to the principles of *sammā-ajīva*.[86] Acquiring things and earning profit by illicit means, by fraud or force are prohibited and outlawed. [87] The *adiññadāna verāmani* is an instrument to avoid fraudlent possessions and prohibit to possess what is not given.[88] The *Dhammapada* says that one who destroys life and speaks falsehood, takes what is not given, or indulges in sexual pleasure and intoxication, actually destroys his own being in this group.[89] This precept encourages to cultivate the state of mind which gives rise to freedom from clinging to mortal and changeable things. It purges dwindling and perturbed minds, and purifies it from lust and longing of material things. The *adiññadāna* gives five factors for the immoral volition to take other's possession. These are: (i) possessing other's property, (ii) awareness of the fact that other's property is possessed, (iii) immoral volition of stealing, (iv) taking the property by illegal means, and (v) removal of evidences of illegal possession.[90] The Buddha says that such *kammic* action leads to suffering and unhappy state of mind. The second precept is conducive to advice people who indulge in extreme consumerism and materialism. Such person is unstable to enjoy good life and such desires create discontent and suffering in their mind.[91]

The third precept deals with abstaining from lustful attachments. It controls the sensual desires of a person for the opposite sex. The Buddha says that a wise man should avoid unchastity as it is considered as pit of burning cinders. One who is not able to live in a state of celibacy should atleast not break the purity of another man's wife.[92] Sex is considered the strongest instinct of living beings. In other beings this phenomenon is periodical and seasonal while in humans it is a continuous process. The sex is still the strongest instinct and the mental development of human being is always challenged by the physical world.[93] It is a universal desire to continue human civilization by producing more children. It represents the aspiration of mankind to constitute a mean to develop community for future. But misuse and misconduct of sexual relationship deteriorates the respectable and honourable state of life and promotes promiscuity. Presently materialization of sexual activities because of legalization of brothels and sex workers and such phenomenon is now associated with market demand and economy. Even desire to make demand brings illegal trafficking and a great loss to dignity of women. This precept signifies abstinence from all sorts of indulgences and from all sensuous objects.

The fourth precept *mūsavāda verāmani* deals with abstention from falsehood. It covers domain like speaking lie, concealments of truth, exaggeration, or boasting trivial issues. It prohibits deviation from truth or hiding of truth or reality. It avoids deceitful and frivolous talks hurting the sentiments of others, volition setting up the bodily and vocal effort to deceive or intention to deceive.[94] The precept says that truth spoken to a person should be full of feeling and kind expression and lying or foul language is of no good.[95]

The fifth precept *surā-meraya magga pamadatthana verāmani* recommends abstaining from taking any intoxicating drink. Alcoholic drink has been a regular feature of many societies. In such society it acts as a value embedded and in some it is prohibited. In extreme cold weather areas such drinks are allowed for limited consumption. However, excessive drinking is not only harmful but disgustful. It leads to unwholesome situation. The basic objection to intoxication and alcoholic drink lies in the fact that it distorts mental balance and develops fragility. It is maddening, deluding, and a delight for fools.[96] Deriving pleasure from drinking alcohol is temporary indulgence. Such addiction is harmful and grave. The intoxication effects the nervous system producing both the visionary and auditory hallucination which embolden aggression and distortion. It also produces fear, over excitement, connect with temporary and false happiness, and a sense of grief. The perturbed alcoholic state encourages high-handedness, conflict, and strife.

Bodhisattva and Environmentalism

In the Theravāda, the term *Bodhisattva* is applied to the Buddha to signify his pre-awakening experiences. This term is mainly related to various aspects of the *Bodhisattva* Gautama's meditative development and it is coterminous with three main attributes the *Bodhisattva*'s overcoming of unwholesome state of mind, his development of mental tranquility, and growth of his insight.[97] The *Bodhisattva*'s struggle with unwholesome mental qualities shows how he developed a clear distinction between unwholesome thoughts and wholesome thoughts.[98] The *Bodhisattva*'s development of mental tranquility has been in close relationship with the development of psychic power and that can be achieved by the practice of mindfulness.[99] The *Ariyapariyesana Sutta* says that an average person's quest is for worldly things that are subject to decay and death. In contrast to it Gautama as a *Bodhisattva* went for a noble quest that is not subject to decay and death.[100] The *Sutta* indicates that the Buddha was disinclined to preach his knowledge to others and decided to remain content by attaining the liberation. But the Pāli commentary on *Ariyapariyesana Sutta* says that the Buddha only hesitated to give discourses because he realized that teaching is very subtle and people are under the influence of defilements. It further says that the Buddha also wanted God Brahma to invite since this would encourage regards for the Buddha's teaching among the people in the world.[101] The early phase of the Buddha's quest for knowledge indicates that his main concern was to find liberation for himself. However, his view was transformed after his attainment of *nibbāna*. His compassionate concern for others developed as a consequence of his awakening and realizing the true cause and nature of *dukkha*.

The emergence of Mahāyāna absolutized and deified the Buddha as the incarnation of *karunā*. The Buddha as a *Bodhisattva* faces suffering for the welfare of human being. It is acknowledged that the Buddha never visited this world personally but instead his illusory form appeared on the Earth for propagating compassion and remove suffering.[102] It has been accepted that the *Bodhisattva* is free from greed (*kāmasamjña*), anger (*vyāpādasamjña*), and harming others (*vihimsāsamjña*).[103] It is said that the *Bodhisattva* has a self governed destiny and he takes difficulties and suffering as a destined phenomena.[104] The *Bodhisattva* sacrifice himself for the benefit of sentient beings (*sattva*), and takes birth at will into bad states (*durgati*) for the welfare of people.[105]

Three types of the *Bodhisattvas* have been mentioned in Buddhist literature—forest, city, and monastic. The forest *Bodhisattvas* are likely to be more friendly, compassionate, and self giving. He meditates in dense forests.[106] The *Mahāprajnapāramita Śāstra* says that the forest *Bodhisattva* secludes himself in the forest and find solitude in hills. In his lonely retreat he practices meditation and earns wisdom for welfare of others. It is like attaining rejuvenation to engage himself for human cause.[107] He thus attains a status where all suffering is forever transcended and the knowledge of ultimate reality is achieved with his altruistic propositions used to remove the suffering. In the modern perspective, environmental problem is one of the biggest forms of suffering which is taking the world on the brink of destruction and devastation and the *Bodhisattva* ideals can be exemplified here to show the world the path of emancipation.

Notes

1. David J. Kalupahana, *Buddhist Philosophy: A Historical Analysis*, Hawaii: The University Press of Hawaii, 1976, pp. 63–5.
2. *Udāna*, 1ff.
3. *Saṃyutta Nikāya*, III.25ff.
4. Kalupahana, *Buddhist Philosophy*, p. 27.
5. Ibid., p. 28.
6. George Grimm, *The Doctrine of the Buddha: The Religion of Reason and Meditation*, Leipzig: W. Drugulin, 1926, pp. 165–8.
7. *Saṃyutta Nikāya*, II.20; *Majjhima Nikāya*, I.226ff.
8. *Udāna*, 1ff.
9. *Saṃyutta Nikāya*, II.58.
10. Kalupahana, *Buddhist Philosophy*, pp. 29–30.
11. *Dīgha Nikāya*, III.80ff; *Aṅguttara Nikāya*, IV.100–3.
12. *Aṅguttara Nikāya*, III.244.
13. Ibid., IV.312.
14. *Sumangalvilāsinī*, II.432.
15. Kalupahana, *Buddhist Philosophy*, p. 30.
16. *Majjhima Nikāya*, I.184.
17. *Saṃyutta Nikāya*, II.114.
18. Ibid., III.54.
19. *Aṅguttara Nikāya*, I.239.
20. Gunapala Dharmasiri, *Fundamentals of Buddhist Ethics*, Singapore: The Buddhist Research Society, 1986, pp. 18–20.
21. *Saṃyutta Nikāya*, II.115.
22. *Dhammapada*, V.
23. *Majjhima Nikāya*, I.112.
24. *Dīgha Nikāya*, III.71.
25. *Majjhima Nikāya*, II.72–4.
26. Alan Sponberg, 'The Buddhist Conception of Ecological Self', pp. 107–27.
27. Sivaraksa, *Conflict, Culture and Change*, pp. 71–5.

28. David J. Kalupahana, 'Man and Nature: Towards a Middle Path of Survival', *Environmental Ethics*, vol. 8, no. 4, 1986, pp. 371–80.
29. Kabilsingh, 'Buddhist Monks and Forest Conservation', pp. 301–9.
30. David L. McMahan, *The Making of Buddhist Modernism*, New York: Oxford University Press, 2008, pp. 181–2.
31. Clippard, 'The Lorax Wears Saffron', p. 220.
32. Joanna Macy, *World as Lover ,World as Self*, California: Parallax Press, 1991, pp. 182–92.
33. Payutto, 'Buddhist Solution for the Twenty-first Century', pp. 170–1.
34. Swearer, 'The Hermeuneutics of Buddhist Ecology in Contemporary Thailand', pp. 21–44.
35. Santikaro Bhikkhu, 'Buddhadasa Bhikkhu: Life and Society Through the Natural Eyes of Voidness', *in Engaged Buddhism: Buddhist Libration Movements in Asia*, ed. Christopherv S. Queen and Sallie B. King, Albany: State University of New York, 1996, pp. 158–61
36. Swearer, 'The Hermeuneutics of Buddhist Ecology in Contemporary Thailand', pp. 30–7.
37. Christofer Ives, 'In Search of a Green Dharma: Philosophical Issues in Buddhist Environmental Ethics', in *Destroying Mara Forever: Buddhist Ethics Essays in Honor of Damien Keown*, ed. John Powers and Charles S. Prebish, Ithaca, NY: Snow Lion Publications, 2009, pp. 165–85.
38. G.C. Pandey, *Studies in the Origin of Buddhism*, Delhi: Orient Books, 1974, p. 430.
39. *Majjhima Nikāya*, III.203.
40. *Aṅguttara Nikāya*, III.410–17.
41. *Dhammapada*, V.165.
42. *Aṅguttara Nikāya*, III.288.
43. *Suttanipāta*, V.260.
44. *Aṅguttara Nikāya*, I.223ff.
45. *Dīgha Nikāya*, I.7–10.
46. *Dhammapada*, VV.348–9.
47. *Dīgha Nikāya*, III.275.
48. *Majjhima Nikāya*, II.233.
49. David J. Kalupahana, *Karma and Rebirth: Foundations of The Buddha's Moral Philosophy*, Colombo: Buddhist Cultural Centre, 2009, p. 58.
50. *Dhammapada*, V.126.
51. Ibid., V.127.
52. Ibid., V.123.
53. Ibid., V.116.
54. Melford Spiro, *Buddhism and Society: A Great Tradition and its Burmese Vicissitudes*, Berkeley: University of California Press, 1982, pp. 65–6.
55. Max Weber, *The Religion of India: The Sociology of Hinduism and Buddhism*, New York: The Free Press, 1958, p. 200.
56. *Dhammapada*, V.118.

57. Ibid., VV.219–20.
58. *Saṃyutta Nikāya*, I.72.
59. Spiro, *Buddhism and Society*, p. 67.
60. *Aṅguttara Nikāya*, IV.16ff.
61. *Majjhima Nikāya*, I.169.
62. *Dhammapada*, V.64.
63. *Majjhima Nikāya*, I.473.
64. *Saṃyutta Nikāya*, II.29.
65. *Majjhima Nikāya*, I.285.
66. Kaluphana, *Karma and Rebirth*, p. 60.
67. *Saṃyutta Nikāya*, II.17.
68. Kalupahana, *Karma and Rebirth*, pp. 61–2.
69. *Majjhima Nikāya*, II.27.
70. Ibid., II.28.
71. *Saṃyutta Nikāya*, V.9.
72. Ibid., V.94.
73. *Dīgha Nikāya*, I.9–12.
74. *Aṅguttara Nikāya*, II.69–70.
75. Kalupahana, *Karma and Rebirth*, pp. 65–6.
76. *Dīgha Nikāya*, II.290–315.
77. Kalupahana, *Karma and Rebirth*, p. 67.
78. *Majjhima Nikāya*, I.395.
79. Ibid., III.71.
80. *Aṅguttara Nikāya*, VIII.39.
81. *Dhammapada*, V.130.
82. *Suttanipāta*, V.394.
83. *Atthasālini*, ed. E. Muller, London: PTS, 1897, p. 129.
84. H. Saddhatissa, *Buddhist Ethics: Essence of Buddhism*, London: George Allen and Unwin Ltd., 1970, p. 89.
85. *Vibhanga*, V.272.
86. *Dīgha Nikāya*, I.4.
87. *Atthasālini*, 130.
88. *Suttanipāta*, V.395.
89. *Dhammapada*, V.146, 147.
90. *Atthasālini*, 130.
91. Saddhatissa, *Buddhist Ethics*, pp. 101–2.
92. *Suttanipāta*, V.396.
93. Saddhatissa, *Buddhist Ethics*, p. 103.
94. *Atthasālini*, 130–1.
95. *Vinaya Pitaka*, I.349.
96. *Suttanipāta*, VV.393, 399.
97. Bhikkhu Analayo, *The Genesis of the Bodhisattva Ideal*, Hamburg: Hamburg University Press, 2010, pp. 15–16.
98. *Majjhima Nikāya*, I.114.

99. *Saṃyutta Nikāya*, II.10.
100. *Majjhima Nikāya*, I.163.
101. *Papañcasūdanī*, 176–7.
102. S.N. Dube, *Cross Currents in Early Buddhism*, New Delhi: Manohar, 1980, p. 151.
103. Jiryo Masuda, 'Origin and Doctrine of Early Indian Buddhist Schools', *Asia Major*, vol. II, 1925, pp. 1–78, see p. 21.
104. *Kathāvatthu*, XXIII.3.
105. K. Venkata Ramonan, *Nagarjuna Philosophy*, Tokyo: 1966, pp. 315–16.
106. Reginald A. Ray, *Buddhist Saints in India: A Study in Buddhist Values and Orientations*, Oxford: Oxford University Press, 1994, p. 251.
107. Etienne Lamotte, tr., *Mahaprajnaparamita Sastra*, 1984, 5 vols., Louvain, 1944–80.

4

Animals, Trees and Spirits in Jātakas

The *Jātakas* are considered as sources of the *Bodhisattva's* experience and learning through his gradual inculcations of *pārmitas*.[1] Fausboll says that the *Jātakas* contribute to preach about the social life of early India especially of the age of the Buddha, its relevance in the history of world literature, especially fables and tales, vivid discussion on transmigration of soul, and the study of Pāli language.[2] In this Buddhist litrary genre the human-non-human (animals, tree, and spirits) relations are truly enlightening. The animals, spirits, trees, etc., have been depicted in benevolent moods and their sacrifices are eulogized in painstaking details. In the *Jātakas* cosmological pattern is discussed again and again; however, exploration of environmentalism in the *Jātakas* is not without debate. Scholars like Christopher Key Chapple,[3] Mamiko Okada,[4] Rafe Martin,[5] Paul Waldau,[6] Pragati Sahni[7] and others who are working on the subject have their own theses and anti-theses. It can be candidly accepted that it is difficult to directly co-relate modern environmentalism with *Jātaka* stories but overwhelming environmental concerns shown in that could be a source of environmental ethics. The *Jātakas*, a part of the *Khuddaka Nikāya* of the *Sutta Pitaka*, narrate 550 stories of the Buddha. The *Jātakas* has been organized in 22 *nipātas* containing *gāthās* (verses/verse) quoted in each story which is usually narrated by the *Bodhisattva* while its part and commentaries are known as *Jātakatthavaññanā*. It has been further elaborated in commentaries (*multikas* and *atthakathā*). Sometimes, the *gāthā* was told by the Buddha to the *Bodhisattva*. Such *gāthās* are known as the *Abhisambuddha Gāthās*. Each story begins with *paccuppannavatthu* or 'story of the present' starting with a particular situation in the life of the Buddha that propelled him to tell a story. The *atītavatthu* contains real birth stories having verses told by the *Bodhisattva*. At the end of the tale *samodhana* was summarized by the Buddha.[8] Because of different factors, diverse genres has been incorporated to write down and portray the *Jātaka* stories. The original text of the *Jātakas* in Pāli canons and the different narrative forms it differs in content style, language, and tradition. In the *Cāriyapitaka* and the *Jātakasmālā* more stress are given on the Buddha's past virtues while in the Pāli *Jātakas* the episodes are narrated by the first person in the voice of the Buddha. The *Cāriyapitaka* and the *Jātakasmālā* are poetic compositions by named authors and both exhibit absence of narrative framework in which these stories were originally told by the historical Buddha. In the *Jātakakathāvannana* and *Mahāvadāna*, the Buddha himself narrate the stories and such narrations are in the voice of the Buddha. He is considered to be revealer of these stories.[9] These narrative styles influenced regional writings and aesthetic attributes. Haribhatta's *Jātakasmālā* had emphatic impact and contribution on literary and art genre in Kashmir, Afghanistan, and Central Asia. The Tibetan literature mention that Haribhatta was well acquainted with hilly terrain of north-west part of Indian subcontinent and he died in Kashmir. A long passage of his work has been quoted in a Chinese work written in 445 CE when a group of Chinese monks visited Central Asia and studied it. His *Jātakasmālā* must have been compiled in the first decade of the fifth century. A complete manuscript of Sanskrit-Uigur bilingual legend No. 32 (*Simha*), legend No. 25 (*Kinnarisudhana*), have become the basis of the Khotanese stories, legend No. 6 (*Rupyāvati*) has been copied in Tocharian; two fragments of legend No. 32 are traced in Afghanistan; Kshemendra modelled his *Sudhanakinnaryavadāna* (No. 64) on Haribhatta's version of same story No. 25 and a Gilgit manuscript could be identified as belonging to legend No. 32. Total 90 folios are in the *Jātakasmālā* in which 27 are missing. In Nepal some more folios are known and in Tibet complete manuscript of the work is available.[10] In the middle of the eleventh-century Kshemendra of Kashmir wrote a monumental compendium of Buddhist legends in verse (*sargabandh*), the *Bodhisattvavadānakalpalata*. It has 107 legends. Later on his son Somendra added a story of Jimutavahana to give the auspicious number 108. Kshemendra's style of writing had substantial impact on writings of Tibet and

Nepal. Michael Hanh says that during such course of writings, *Campu* (mixed form of prose and poetry) is the most important contribution of Buddhism to classical Sanskrit literature. This genre was invented within the Buddhist literature and its early visibility could be identified in the writings of the *Vinayavastu* of the Mūlsarvāstivāda; the intermediate stages could be in writing of Kumarlata's *Kalpanāmaṇḍitika*, *Drstāntapanktih* and Sanghasena's *Jātakasmālā* and the final development in works of Aryasura, Haribhatta and Gopaldatta.[11]

There is a debate among scholars whether the *Jātakas* should be treated as a part of canonical literature or not. The contention is that the *Jātakas* overwhelmingly absorbed little traditions scattered in the Indian society, so they lost their originality. Though the *Jātakas* are Buddhist in nature and could be distinguished from other folklore traditions found in India, the amalgamation of Buddhist canonical thought with little tradition of hoary past cannot be denied altogether.[12] One interpretation is that the *Jātakas* should not be interpreted as 'narrative because it will diminish its Buddhist vision and should not be treated as Buddhist because of its absorption of early folk traditions.[13] Ian Harris, not imbibing this idea, accepts it as highly anthropocentric with pre-Buddhist folk tradition thus negating the idea of those who propose them as evidence for true Buddhist environmental ethics.[14] Pragati Sahni says that its ethical credentials were transmitted to lay followers in which few of them showed environmental concerns. As majority of the *Pali* sources are for the monks and nuns, the *Jātakas* and the *Avadānas* are meant for lay persons. However, the *Jātakas* show that these were preached to the monks at their general assembly. The Buddha by narrating his previous birth as the *Bodhisattva* tried to comprehend problems concerned to laities.[15] The *Jātaka* stories can be accepted as dominantly canonical to shower virtues to lay people but preaching to monks could not be denied. In some stories even monks are admonished or praised. These stories are not only narrated but also visualized by the art and architecture to spread the virtue of *Jātakas* far and wide. Many *stūpas* were raised in memories of the *Bodhisattvas* showing compassion and sacrifices for society.[16] Various ancient fables, anecdotes, and parable were incorporated in it. In many such *stūpas* and art reliefs depicting various *Jātakas*, seed of environmentalism could be traced.

Animals as Source of Environmental Virtues

The animal representation in the *Jātakas* means animal other than human. It is said that various deliberations with metaphysical, religious, and socio-political concerns for other animals began to involve since the end of eighteenth century only and especially in reference to 'animal rights'. In Buddhism, Theravāda has sympathetic and benevolent view for other living beings. The Mahāyāna further extends it when the *Bodhisattva* spread the message of *karuna* to all living beings.[17] Martin says that animals are frequently shown compassion and exhibiting self-sacrifice in the *Jātakas*.[18] The *Jātaka* stories postulates continuation of life with notion of *maitree* and *karunā* for co-existence and survival. There are 70 different characters of animal that are narrated in different stories. Numerically, monkeys are the most found with 27 references described in the *Pāli Jātaka* followed by elephants (24), jackals (20), lions (19), crows (17), etc.[19] Waldau contends that the *Jātaka* stories lack real information about animals and some animals are described in negative character like monkeys lack wisdom although those with positive traits also find mention.[20] He says that the real character of animals have not been explored and anthropomorphic portraits of animals have been painted to describe the welfare of humans such as elephants who are always depicted in the *Jātakas* as male although they are governed by matriarchal rules.[21] Sometimes, the *Jātakas* even narrate torture and depravation of animals. Waldau has opines that 'Buddhist reference to elephants are not very appropriate in understanding the truth of real-world animals. The same kind of arguments could be made about other animals which are socially complex, large-brained, and intelligent animals. He informs that elephants are very complex individuals who grow and develop slowly and richly individualistic social system which are essential part of their lives, having very distinctive personalities, keeping large brain with a capacity to interact with one another. The keeping such large, powerful and complex creature as a captive involves a great deal of hardship on the part of human. The captivity of elephants lends to at least two ethically significant problems: 'intentional curtailment of another being captured for the purpose of advancing one's own interest and intentional infliction of harm for the some self-interested reasons'.[22]

The prime argument is that breaking down of elephants is prone to torture and pain. In the *Jātakas*, infact, predisposition to understand a complex system of domestication of elephant was not a motive. Yet the *Bodhisattva* constantly adhered to belief that such wondrous creature has some right in an orderly world and ageless folk tradition. In the *Saṃgamavācara Jātaka*,[23] the *Bodhisattva* himself was a *mahaout* of the elephant and constantly encouraged him to fight the war while in the *Dubbalakattha Jātaka*,[24] the *Bodhisattva* was a tree spirit living in the Himalaya. An elephant who was unable to bear pain during the breaking down, broke the training post and fled to the Himalayas. The *Bodhisattvas* a tree spirit shows compassion for him and after his advice he feared no more. The domestication of elephants was practical necessity of the time but the *Bodhisattva* concerned that elephants should be trained and tamed with compassion.

It has, however, been counter-argued that killing of the animals was supported by Buddhism since its foundation. The meagre account of sympathetic attitude towards other animals does not mean that the Buddha supported environmentalism.[25] Waldau says that,

attempt by a contemporary individual to ask ancient traditions for answers to contemporary problems entails risk, perhaps it is inevitable that some anachronistic thinking will take place by virtue of very effort to use the wisdom of older views to address concern which (i) have emerged in our culturally distinct circumstances and (ii) are framed in our culturally distinct discourses.[26]

Florin Deleanu echoes the same opinion by citing example of jackal who is often overwhelmingly treated as cunning and vile in the *Jātakas* showing man's apathy and disgust towards them.[27] But, at the same time, it was not him who was badly represented but his act of cunningness and violent action. Here animals like jackal is not a central theme of disrespect and maltreatment but his misdeeds. If the jackal involves in good conduct, he will become a subject of appreciation. The *Sigāla Jātaka*[28] tells that a jackal lures a brāhmana by promising him to reward a hidden treasure and in lieu of it he will help him get out of city. Here the brāhmana has been depicted as greedier than the jackal and the moral of the story also indicates that overindulgence in food may lead to life-threat. In another *Jātaka*, the jackal was a *Bodhisattva* who lived in a charnel grove with his fellow species. He saved himself and other jackals when a wicked person came to hunt them and pretended to be lying dead in the burial ground. Here the moral was to treat jackal as a symbol of mercy and kindness and man as wicked and rogue.[29] The *Guna Jātaka* narrates friendship between lion and a jackal; he saved the former's life who reciprocated by cementing their friendship lasting for seven generations.[30] The jackal has been depicted as animal of good character showing sympathy to others, even after knowing that strong always manage his way. The *Pañc Upostha Jātaka*[31] shows how a wood-pigeon, a snake, a jackal, and a bear subdued their desire and passion and repented their past actions which aggravated their lust while in the *Virocana Jātaka*, a jackal has been depicted as a foolish animal, quite in contrast to his usual cunning character. He was friends with a lion. Soon he considered himself as powerful as lion and dared to kill an elephant but was trampled to death.[32] Thus, jackals have not been depicted in the same manner in every *Jātaka*. Sometimes they are very happy and kind while sometimes vile and cunning too. The *Jātakas* primarily emphasize character and situation rather than animal.

Again, Rafe Martin counters the ideas floated by Waldau and Deleanu and says that the Buddha of the *Jātakas* is not withdrawing from *saṁsāra* but acts as savour of the world with his compassion and generosity. The *Bodhisattva* in the form of animal or human, usually in a leadership position, finds joy in solving the mundane problems.[33] Pragati Sahni deplores that the *Jātakas* have substantial resources pertaining to *karuna*, *mudita*, *maitree*, and appropriate environmental ethics could be drawn from it.[34] The *Jātakas* were not meant to preach children but were moral tools to spread Buddhist ideology among noices, monks, and folklore traditions. These stories were used to exemplify particular event and draw consequent moral from it.

Early Buddhism also favoured aniconism to interpret and depict the life event of the Buddha. The figures of elephant, bull, horse, lion, serpent, *bodhi* tree, footprint, etc., have been depicted to signify that Buddhism has respect for them. The elephant signifies a dream seen by Mahāmāyā indicating her conception and the birth of Siddhartha. The male elephant was depicted everywhere as the Buddha, the bull as presiding over the nativity, the horse as a great departure, and lion as Śakyasimha.[35] When animal depiction was imparted in the *Jātaka* and the *Avadānas*, the same idea was imbibed though not generalized everywhere. Lisa Kremmer opines that:

> Jātaka focuses on animal as an individual with personality volition, flaws, and moral excellence. Buddhist are often introduced to Jātaka tales at a young age and children began to learn that a rabbit is not just as an alien character but an individual, a member of rabbit community and also a member of larger community that includes all life. It helps reminding us of significance of other species.[36]

The animal depiction and symbolism started in Buddhism simultaneously at two level—one at philosophical and ritualistic, and the other at the level of laity and folk tradition. It was well conceived and planned aniconic representation of animals, not in anthropocentric form but real. It was a conscious volition of the Buddha to judge the intellect of person then to give them sermons. Even all monks are not categorized at par and the lay followers were intentionally avoided to entangle with subtle teachings. The laities were advised on the merits of giving *dāna* (*dānakatham*), moral precepts (*śilakatham*), and the consequential rewards of heavenly existence (*saggakatham*). If they could easily imbibe these then the higher lessons of *dukkha, dukkha samudaya, dukkha nirodha,* and *ariyamagga* should be prescribed to them (*yam kiñci samudayadhammam sabbantam niroghadhammanti*).[37] The lay followers like Cittagahapati and Anāthapindika were able to learn the subtleties of the Buddha's teachings.[38] The same tradition continued after *mahāparinibbāna* of the Buddha and with orthodox teaching of the *Vinaya* and the *Suttas*, worshipping of symbols also ushered in. Aśoka might be the first emperor who used these art symbols to disseminate Buddhism in both lay and monk communities.

On the other end, altruistic as well as depraved character of animals were embraced to frame the stories which could preach and popularize the teachings of the Buddha in prevalent folk tradition. The *Jātakas*, potential to construct an environmental

ethics due to abundance of compassion and generosity, have also
been disseminated in art forms. Such visual remains are scattered
throughout the Buddhist archaeological sites. Foucher says that
at least 25 depictions of animals representing the *Jātakas* have
been inscribed at Bharhut. It expresses biographical sequence of
successive lives and hierarchical order of biological evolutions
into which the *Bodhisattva* was to take birth. It is evolutionary
with first as animal, then women, and finally men.[39] The story of
the *Chaddanta Jātaka* (Plate 5) has been depicted at many sites.[40]
Foucher informs that at least 12 versions of these depictions,
6 in art and 6 in literature, have been depicted in these respective
traditions.[41] At Bharhut (Plate 6), the six tusk elephant is shown
standing leaning against the banyan tree. Beside him stood his
first consort with her left temple decorated with a lotus, depicted
full face in the background is his second wife looking angry and
jealous.[42] In a sculptured frieze from Gandhāra the *Bodhisattva* as
a noble elephant has been carved out who allowed a hunter to
cut off his tusk.[43] The same legend has been depicted in Ajanta's
cave no. 17. Here the *Bodhisattva* himself performs the arduous
task of wrapping his enormous trunk around one of his tusks
and reeling under excruciating pain as he wrenches the tusk. The
hunter kneels besides him in awful manner.[44] The same story is
represented with a little variation at Amarāvatī[45] and Sanchī.[46]
The cave no. 10 of Ajanta exhibits the *Chaddanta Jātaka* with a
minor variation.[47] The depiction of *Kakkata Jātaka*[48] has been found
at Bharhut where the *Bodhisattva* as an elephant was entrapped

PLATE 5. Chadanta Jātaka, Sanchi

PLATE 6. Chadanta Jātaka, Bharhut

by a big crab residing in a lake and could kill and devour the elephants. Foucher gives list of many such depictions at Bharhut *stūpa*.[49] Cunningham also discovered depiction of *Latukika Jātakas* on the wall of Bharhut *stūpa* depicting story of a quail and an arrogant elephant as Devadutta who killed spring of the quail.[50] Foucher's list includes the following depictions:

1. The depiction of *Nacca Jātaka* that shows a royal swan who refuses to marry his daughter to a peacock because he did not show modesty and decency in his outward behaviour.[51] The story exemplifies that decency and modesty is necessary in life.

2. In *Kapota Jātaka*, the *Bodhisattva* is a pigeon in Vārānasī who reprimanded the greedy crow for stealing food from a kitchen. The *Lola Jātaka* (no. 272) and *Kapota Jātaka* (no. 375) have similar stories with slight variations.[52]

3. The *Kukkuta Jātaka* describes a cock perched on tree and drive she-cat away who was enticing to eat him.[53] The story talks about moral relationship among animals by showing how cunningness could be avoided by clever skills.

4. The depiction of *Kuruṅga-miga Jātaka* that shows how a woodpecker and a tortoise rescued their friend, the antelope, from a trap. It has been found from a medallion at Bharhut.[54]

5. The story of a rich man who was saved by a deer, and he repaid the service by betraying the deer to capture. But the deer saved himself and his herd by foiling his attempt. This depiction too has been found on a medallion from Bharhut.[55]

6. The representation of the *Mahākapi Jātaka* showing how a peasant searching for his strayed oxen, was lost in a forest and fell in a deep ditch. He was rescued by a monkey. Later on, he made an attempt upon the life of his rescuer, and for his ingratitude he suffered from leprosy.[56]

7. The *Mahākapi Jātaka* shows how a monkey saved his followers at the cost of his own life. It was also found on a medallion from Bharhut.[57]

8. The depiction of the *Kacchapa Jātaka* showing how a tortoise is addicted to his home and died. This has been found on a rail coping stone.[58] The moral of the story is that obsession of any kind may prove to be disastrous.

9. The *Ārāmadusaka Jātaka* showing monkeys engaged to water a garden pull up the plants in order to judge the size of the roots to know how much water to sprinkle. There is a similar story in *Ārāmadusa Jātaka* (no. 268). The depiction too has been found on rail coping.[59]

10. The depiction of the *Cammasātaka Jātaka* showing a foolish mendicant who died by mistaking the butting of a ram for respectful salutation.[60] The story shows that a person must realize the real situation and should act accordingly.

11. The *Dabbhaapuppha Jātaka* showing two otters who caught a fish but were cheated by a jackal. It has been found on a rail coping too.[61] The story speaks of contentment and greed, the key components used in modern environmentalism.

12. The *Dasaratha Jātaka* depicting Rama and Sita with an an elephant and a monkey.[62] It describes the doctrine of impermanence by exemplifying discourses on human

relationship. The moral of the story suggests that one must perform his duty even in adverse conditions.

13. The depiction of the *Nalinikā Jātaka* shows the Sakka, jealous of a Rishisranga (antelope born), appears as king of the country and pronounce that the drought from which land was suffering was due to king's action.[63] The story ended with messages of charity, pity, sympathy and equanimity as key attribute.

14. The *Sujāta Jātaka* showing a father cursed of inordinate grief due to loss of his son. The grief was removed by the *Bodhisattva* by giving fodder and water to a dead ox.[64] It shows the way to get real wisdom and exhibits impermanence of all existence things.

15. The depiction of the *Latukika Jātaka* that shows a quail that brought about the destruction of an elephant that killed her offspring.[65] It shows that co-existence is the ideal way of living and one should not consider others weak merely on basis of physical appearance.

16. The *Dūbhiya-Makkata Jātaka* showing that the *Bodhisattva* drew water for a monkey, and for which he was insulted.[66]

17. The *Kakkata Jātaka* depicting an elephant who with the help of his spouse killed a mighty crab who intended to devour him.[67] It shows that *metta* could play better living and strength.

18. The *Bhallātiya Jātaka* depicted two fairies who could not tolerate separation from each other even for one night.[68] It exemplifies obsession as a bad character.

19. The *Chaddanta Jātaka* was one of the most depicted *Jātaka* in the history of Buddhist art. It shows elephant gifting his tusk to a wicked hunter.[69]

20. The *Vidhurapandita Jātaka* depicted four kings, a *nāga*, and a *yakkha*.[70] The story shows how people of different attitude could live harmoniously.

However, it is not easy to subscribe that in the *Jātakas* animals are always represented in good faith. They are recognized the best when they were born as the *Bodhisattva*. Their characteristics show that compassion, generosity, gratitude, foolishness, aggressive instinct, etc., are not only privileges of human beings but other animals have same experience and feelings. The *Jātakas* have some exceptional cases when a particular animal shows generosity to a man who is wicked and cruel. The aim of visual art of these stories was to attract little tradition to learn the teachings of the Buddha. The visual traditions in Buddhism are excellently rich but not always acknowledged as a source of knowledge as Foucher says:

The close relation which exists between the written and figured form of Buddhist tradition has no longer to be proved. It is known by experience. Rare indeed are those narratives of Buddha's miracle where of no illustration has yet been discovered; still more rare are the images which do not at once find their commentary in the texts already published. And thus we have naturally come to speak of the help, which on numerous details of exegesis, the texts and monuments reciprocally lend. All the same, it is to be observed that until now we have principally made use of the first to explain the second. In fact the two sorts of documents seem to be unequally matched and the muteness of the stones will never, in the estimation of philologists be able to equal (as regards the extent and variety of information which can be derived from them) the verbosity of writings. However, this is one point in which the sculptures have an advantage over the manuscripts, namely the permanent fixity of their testimony.[71]

The *Jātakas* maintain that wild species have right to co-exist with human on this planet and the humans have no right to exterminate them. The transformation and modification of flora and fauna may damage the equilibrium of co-existence. Any profligate and unwise action may lead to side effects and consequences that can be disadvantageous. They demonstrate that greed (*lobha*) and resultant precarious action can harm environment and complexity, frequency, and magnitude of impact may be emphatic. The *Silavanaga Jātaka*[72] also mentions the *Bodhisattva* born as an elephant in the Himalayas. Once a wood-cutter of Vārānasī lost his way and reached to abode of the *Bodhisattva* who provided him shelter and food for few days. he was doomed to be killed because of his greed and ungratefulness. The *Alinacitta Jātaka* tells story of an elephant, a guild of carpenters, and a king of Vārānasī. Once the carpenter saved the life of an elephant who was suffering with excruciating pain because of splinter of acacia wood pierced in his foot. The carpenters removed the splinters and healed his wound. The elephant reciprocated their gratefulness by offering himself to their services.[73] Here great friendship has been shown between elephant and human beings and the elephant served the human on their own not by being captive or any sort of training. In the story the Buddha was himself the elder elephant and Sariputta was his son.

The stories of the *Vanarinda Jātaka*[74] and the *Vanara Jātaka*[75] have been developed on the same canvass but with different results at the end. In the *Vanara Jātaka*, the *Bodhisattva* was born as a monkey living on the banks of river Ganga. A female crocodile became fascinated with him and decided to kill him for his heart. The plot explains not to indulge in greed and how to escape in precarious situations. The *Tenduka Jātaka* informs how greed and indulgence can trouble anyone. Here, the *Bodhisattva* was born as a monkey king heading a troop of 80,000 in the great Himalayas. At the adjacent village there was *tenduka* tree full of fruits. The monkeys requested the king to permit them to get ripen fruits. They requested him to visit at night. The villagers hurriedly chased them and the monkeys escaped.[76] The *Jātakas* suggest that greed has dramatic consequences on a person/animal. A deterioration in system and inadequate planning may create sudden and specific changes.

The deliberate fatal attraction and undesirable obsession are one of the most long-standing and significant features discussed in the *Jātakas*. The stories exhibit a marked deterioration in the social structure and provide the ultimate solutions. Sometimes norms have been broken insidiously just as an obsession like eating lizard by a monk attachment to a particular habitats, etc. The *Godha Jātaka* says that an ascetic was addicted to eating lizards. One day he tried to kill the *Bodhisattva* who was born as a lizard but he was admonished by the *Bodhisattva* for his precarious lust.[77] The *Kacchapa Jātaka* tells that how a tortoise lost his life due to obsession for not leaving the lake which was drying up due to drought. The *Bodhisattva* lamented on his death and also gave admonished not to be possessive and obsessed.[78] Sometimes fierce loyalty has also been rewarded. The *Mahaśuka Jātaka* shows that many myriads of parrots living in a grove of fig trees on the banks of river Ganga near the Himalayas had to fly away when Sakka decided to test their loyalty for fig tree by drying it up. All but the king parrot decided not to leave and was later rewarded by the Sakka.[79] The *Vatamiga Jātaka* mentions how an antelope was lured by a royal gardner to the palace with an offering of grass with honey. On him the *Bodhisattva* remarked that 'nothing is vile in this world than this lust of taste'.[80]

Tree and Tree Spirits

The tree and tree spirits formed an integral part of the *Jātakas* to depict compassion and co-existence. Some stories directly relate how sustainable use can prolong the fruits and how indulgence leads to destruction. In some stories, *kalpavriksha* (wish tree) fulfils all desires right from giving water, food, and fruits to even treasures. In others, the *Bodhisattva* occasionally became spirit to deliver some important message but sometimes spirits themselves became harmful and got admonition or punishment from the *Bodhisattva*. The dyad of spirits and tree persistently reflects questions concerning the habitable Earth and their relationship with man and other animals. It influences moral and social values of the society and moulds the character and nature of human culture. They also exemplify the diminishing natural environment and human ubiquity which require systematic attention. The *Mahavanija Jātaka*[81] informs about a banyan wish tree which gave pleasant shade, clean water, food, porridge, lentil soup, and many other things to merchants who lost their route. The merchants became greedy except their chief and tried to cut the tree. The tree spirit got annoyed and got killed all the merchants except the chief who was rewarded for his benevolence. In the *Kalingabodhi Jātaka*[82] the *Bodhisattva* worships the great banyan tree showing compassion towards tree. The *Kusalija Jātaka*[83] informs that the *Bodhisattva* was a deity dwelling in clump *kuśa* grass in a royal garden who gave message how to avoid precarious situations. The *Palāsa Jātaka* informs that the *Bodhisattva* was a golden goose in the Himalayas and used to eat wild paddy grown in a nearby natural lake. Near it there was a *judas* tree, an abode of a deity with whom goose developed friendship. A fowl after eating ripe banyan fruit on *judas* dropped excrement into its fork. Subsequently a young banyan tree sprang from it. The goose advised tree deity to exterminate banyan tree but he did not listen. Consequently the banyan tree broken down *judas* tree to

reduce it to a mere stump.[84] The *Pasimanda Jātaka* mentions the
Bodhisattva as nimba tree spirit.[85] The *Phandana Jātaka*[86] depicts how
a black lion and a tree spirit were destroyed by mutual jealously
and mistrust. The *Vyaggha Jātaka*[87] says that the *Bodhisattva* was a
tree spirit residing a dense forest and her immediate neighbour
was another spirit. Their neighbourhood was also inhabited by a
lion and a tiger. Both used to go for hunting and left the decaying
carcass in the forest creating bad smell. The spirit was annoyed
with their presence and asked the *Bodhisattva* to frightened and
derive them out. The *Bodhisattva* warned her not to do so as it gave
chance to the humans to encroach. But she did not heed advice
and frightened them to leave. The absence of both the deadly
creatures facilitated the humans to encroach the forest and cutting
the trees for agrarian purposes. The *Rajovada Jātaka* mentions the
Bodhisattva as a brāhmana residing in the Himalayas. Once the
king Brahamadatta of Vārānasī wanted to know his merits and
demerits, he met the *Bodhisattva* in the forest. The *Bodhisattva* gave
him exposition on just and unjust with the example of ripen fig
which became sweet when the king was just, and bitter when the
king was unjust.[88] The *Rukkhadhamma Jātaka* says that the king of
Vārānasī requested tree fairies to choose their abodes on trees,
shrubs, and plants. The *Bodhisattva,* as a tree fairy, advised all the
fairies to select their abode in the dense forest.[89] The *Bhaddasala
Jātaka*[90] informs how a spirit saved a *sāla* tree. These evidences show
how mutual understanding refrained devastating action or vice
versa. It can be learnt from thes examples that depletion of land,
wild plants, and animals will disappear quickly if the traditional
culture is substituted without planning and understanding. Such
substitutions will bring an extreme use of natural resources which
aims at complacent attitude towards Nature and animals.

Sacrifices and Environmental Virtues

Buddhism deals with sacrifices in two opposite directions. At
one end, it denounced Vedic sacrifices in which thousands of
animals were killed in expensive Soma *yajnas*, and at the other, the
Bodhisattva as a human, dear, serpent, etc., sacrificed his body out
of compassion. The first directly disseminate the environmental
virtues. In the later Vedic age (1,000–600 BC) *Yajurveda* sacrifices

started decimating thousands of animals without any productive purpose. The Buddha condemned such brutal *yajnas* because such killings could not be justified on pretext of religious merits and rituals. The thousands of decaying carcass scattered around the *yajna* pole could also cause bad smells, pollution, and diseases. Opposite to it the *Bodhisattva* sacrificed his body, eyes, and organs to save human beings and animals. This reflection has also been found in the *Jātakas*. Reiko Ohnuma writes that:

most of the north-western sites (Indian subcontinent), however, were associated with the Buddha's previous lifetimes and commemorated the various heroic deeds he had performed while still a Bodhisattva. Since north-west India could not be clearly associated with the Buddha's last life, it made sense to localize and acclimatize Buddhism within the region by identifying various north-western sites as the locales of his previous lives, as recorded in Buddhist Jātakas.[91]

The *Jātaka* story of King Sibi has been depicted at many places. A frieze of Gandhāra shows him with a piece of flesh cut from his thigh and put on a scale in order to match the exact weight of the a dove whose life is being ransomed.[92] In cave no. 1 of Ajanta, Sibi is shown giving his entire body on scale but the weight of the dove could not be compensated. Similar depictions have been found at Amarāvatī, Nagarjunakonda, and Mathurā.[93] Faxian observes that a number of Buddhist pilgrimages have been associated with the *Jātakas* eulogizing heroics of the *Bodhisattva*. He came across a beautiful *stūpa* near Suvastu which was decorated with gold and silver, and was devoted to Sibi.[94] In Gandhāra, he spotted an adorned *stūpa* devoted to Sibi who gifted his eyes as alms.[95] Faxian says there was another *stūpa* devoted to the *Bodhisattva* Mahāsattva who gifted his body to feed a starving tigress.[96] Xuanzang mentions many such *stūpas* related to the *Bodhisattva* performing body sacrifice and showing compassion.[97] At Rahitak, a *stūpa* was built where the *Bodhisattva* as King Maitribala gave his own blood to feed five *yakkhas*.[98] John S. Strong has given long list of such spots where *stūpas* were raised to commemorate the *Bodhisattvas* showing compassion.[99] The most depicted one is the *Sibi Jātaka*.[100] In the *Nigrodhamiga Jātaka*,[101] the *Bodhisattva* has been depicted as deer king. Again, the *Sasa Jātaka*[102] talks about the *Bodhisattva* as a young hare who with his friends, a monkey, jackal, and a otter decided to distribute alms on the day of fast. Sakka tested hare's virtue and disguised himself as a wanderer and requested for help. The otter offered his fish, the jackal gave his dead lizard, and the monkey offered his mangoes. The hare could not offer grass, so he jumped into fire to offer his body but was saved by Sakka.

The *Ayakūta Jātaka*[103] says that once the *Bodhisattva* was a prince of Vārānasī where the people used to sacrifice goats, rams, and other living creature to appease the gods and *yakkhas*. The prince stopped such exercises and the *yakkhas* became enraged. They planned to kill the *Bodhisattva* but he was saved by Sakka.[104] The *Dumeddha Jātaka* informs that once the people of Vārānasī were involved in wanton sacrifice of living creatures like sheep, goat, etc. The *Bodhisattva*, as a prince, was determined to stop such killings and proclaimed the futility of sacrifice by exposing what is sin or unrighteousness.[105] The *Lohakubhi Jātaka* refers the *Bodhisattva's* effort to stop sacrifice.[106]

Various arguments have been marshalled to support or disown environmental virtues in the *Jātakas*. The great diversity and complexity of stories related to animal, birds, and humans offered greater ability to minimize the magnitude and irreversibility of changes brought about by some external perturbation. The *Jātakas* demonstrate that wild species, forests, trees, etc. have right to co-exist with human being. The knowledge, perceptiveness, and prudence as mentioned in the *Jātakas* should be given due importance and attention they deserve in formation of environmental ethics. Despite limitations it can provide solutions to many of our serious environmental problems which are causing the most widespread changes in the landscape. It has become apparent that the *Jātakas* argue the role and relevance of human agency in environmental change. It is worth noting that the concerns expressed in the *Jātakas* can be instrumental to remove undesirable effects created by anthropogenic activities.

Notes

1. Bhikkhu Analayo, 'Canonical Jātaka Tales in Comparative Perspective: The Evolution of Tales of the Buddha's Past Life', *Fuyan Buddhist Studies*, no. 7, 2012, pp. 75–100.
2. Elisabeth Strandberg, 'Fausboll and Pāli Jātaka', *The Journal of the*

International Association of Buddhist Studies, vol. 3, no. 2, 1980, pp. 95–101.

3. Christopher Key Chapple, 'Animals and Environment in Buddhist Birth Stories', in *Buddhism and Ecology: The Interconnection of Dharma and Deed*, ed. Mary Evelyn Tucker and Duncan Ryuken Williams, Cambridge, MA: Harvard University Press, 1997, pp. 131–48.

4. Mamiko Okada, 'Eco-paradigm in Buddhist Narrative Literature: Plants, Trees and Ecoethics', *IBK*, 93[47.1]: 226-30 (rL 285-291), 1998, doi: https://doi.org/10.4259/ibk.47.285.

5. Rafe Martin, 'Thoughts on Jātakas', in *Dharma Rain: Sources of Buddhist Environmentalism*, ed. Stephannie Kaza and Kenneth Kraft, Boston: Shambhala, 2000, pp. 104–8.

6. Waldau, 'Buddhism and Animal Rights', pp. 81–112.

7. Sahni, *Environmental Ethics in Buddhism*.

8. E.B. Cowell, ed., *The Jātaka or Stories of Buddha's Former Birth*, New Delhi: LPP, repr., pp. ix, 200.

9. Naomi Appleton, *Jātakas' Oxford Research Encyclopedia of Religion*, August 2016, pp. 5–6.

10. Michael Hanh, 'Buddhist Contribution to Indian Belles Letters', *Acta Orientalia Acadiamiae Scientiarum Hungaricae*, vol. 63, no. 4, December 2010, p. 467.

11. Ibid., pp. 61, 66.

12. Nirmala Salgado, 'The Structure of Evil and Ethical Action in the Jātakatthavaṅṅanā', unpublished thesis, Northwestern University, 1992, pp. 310–12.

13. James Whittal, 'Buddhism and Virtues', *Contemporary Buddhist Ethics*, ed. Damien Keown, Richmond: Curzon Press, 2000, p. 27.

14. Harris, 'Buddhism and Ecology', pp. 113–35.

15. Sahni, *Environmental Ethics in Buddhism*, p. 146.

16. Reiko Ohnuma, *Bodily Sacrifice in Indian Buddhist Literature*, Delhi: Motilal Banarsidass, 2009, pp. 2–6.

17. Waldau, 'Buddhism and Animal Rights', pp. 81–3.

18. Martin, 'Thoughts on Jātakas', p. 97.

19. Chapple, 'Animals and Environment in Buddhist Birth Stories', pp. 134–46.

20. Paul Waldau, 'Speciesism in Christianity and Buddhism', unpublished thesis, University of Oxford, 1998, pp. 174–5.

21. Waldau, 'Buddhism and Animal Rights', p. 99.

22. Ibid., pp. 101–2.

23. *Jātaka*, no. 182.

24. Ibid., no. 105.

25. Waldau, 'Buddhism and Animal Rights', pp. 83–4.

26. Ibid., p. 84.

27. Deleanu, 'Buddhist "Ethology" in the Pāli Canon', p. 115.

28. *Jātaka*, no. 113.
29. Ibid., no. 142.
30. Ibid., no. 157.
31. Ibid., no. 490.
32. Ibid., no. 143.
33. Martin, 'Thoughts on Jātakas', pp. 104–5.
34. Pragati Sahni, 'Environmental Ethics in *Jātakas*: Further Reflections', UNDV Conference Volume, Bangkok, 2009, p. 129.
35. R.K. Mookerjee, *Aśoka*, Delhi: Motilal Banarsidass, 2007, p. 62.
36. Lisa Kemmerer, 'Buddhist Ethics and Nonhuman Animals', *Peace Study Journal*, vol. I, no. 1, Fall 2008, p. 20.
37. *Majjhima Nikāya*, I.379; II.145.
38. N. Dutt, 'Place of Laity In Early Buddhism', *Indian Historical Quarterly*, vol. 21, nos. 1–4, 1945, p. 239.
39. A. Foucher, *The Beginning of Buddhist Art and Other Essay in India and Central Asian Archaeology*, Delhi: Asean Educational Services, repr. 1994, p. 35.
40. *Jātaka*, no. 514.
41. Foucher, *The Beginning of Buddhist Art*, pp. 189, 196.
42. Ibid., pl. XXIX, 1.
43. Ibid., pl. XXX (i).
44. John. Griffith, *The Paintings in the Buddhist Cave Temples of Ajanta*, London: The Author, 1896, pl. 63; fig. 73.
45. James Burgress, *Buddhist Stūpas of Amaravati and Jaggayyapeta*, London: ASI, 1887, pl. XIVI.
46. J. Fergusson, *Tree and Serpent Worship*, Delhi: Asean Educational Services, repr. 2004, pl. VIII.
47. Griffith, *Buddhist Stūpas of Amaravati and Jaggayyapeta*, p. 5.
48. *Jātaka*, no. 267.
49. Alexander Cunningham, *The Stūpa of Bharhut*, London, 1879, pl. XXV, 2.
50. *Jātaka*, no. 357; Cunningham, *The Stūpa of Bharhut*, pl. V, I.
51. *Jātaka*, no. 32; Cunningham, *The Stūpa of Bharhut*, pl. XXVII, 2.
52. *Jātaka*, no. 42, 274, 375; Cunningham, *The Stūpa of Bharhut*, pl. XLV, 7.
53. *Jātaka*, no. 383; Cunningham, *The Stūpa of Bharhut*, pl. XLVII, 5.
54. *Jātaka*, no. 206; Foucher, *The Beginning of Buddhist Art*, pl. V, 2.
55. *Jātaka*, no. 482; Foucher, *The Beginning of Buddhist Arts*, pl. V, 3.
56. *Jātaka*, no. 516; Cunningham, *The Stūpa of Bharhut*, pl. XXXIII.
57. *Jātaka*, no. 407; Foucher, *The Beginning of Buddhist Art*, pl. V, 4.
58. *Jātaka*, no. 178; Foucher, *The Beginning of Buddhist Art*, pl. V, 1.
59. *Jātaka*, no. 46, 268; Foucher, *The Beginning of Buddhist Art*, pl. VI, 2.
60. *Jātaka*, no. 324; Cunningham, *The Stūpa of Bharhut*, pls. XLI, 1–3.
61. *Jātaka*, no. 400: Foucher, *The Beginning of Buddhist Art*, pl. VI, 3.

62. *Jātaka*, no. 488: Foucher, *The Beginning of Buddhist Art*, pl. VI, 4.
63. *Jātaka*, no. 526; Cunningham, *The Stūpa of Bharhut*, pl. XXVI, 7.
64. *Jātaka*, no. 352; Cunningham, *The Stūpa of Bharhut*, pl. XXVII, 3.
65. *Jātaka*, no. 357; Foucher, *The Beginning of Buddhist Art*, pl. V, 1.
66. *Jātaka*, no. 174; Foucher, *The Beginning of Buddhist Art*, pl. VI, 1.
67. *Jātaka*, no. 267; Cunningham, *The Stūpa of Bharhut*, pl. XXV, 2.
68. *Jātaka*, no. 504; Cunningham, *The Stūpa of Bharhut*, pl. XXVII, 12.
69. *Jātaka*, no. 514; Foucher, *The Beginning of Buddhist Art*, pl. XXIV, 1.
70. *Jātaka*, no. 545; Cunningham, *The Stūpa of Bharhut*, pl. XXVII, 12.
71. Foucher, *The Beginning of Buddhist Art*, p. 185.
72. *Jātaka*, no. 72.
73. Ibid., no. 156.
74. Ibid., no. 57.
75. Ibid., no. 342.
76. Ibid., no. 177.
77. Ibid., no. 138.
78. Ibid., no. 178.
79. Ibid., no. 429.
80. Ibid., no. 14.
81. Ibid., no. 493.
82. Ibid., no. 479.
83. Ibid., no. 121.
84. Ibid., no. 370.
85. Ibid., no. 311.
86. Ibid., no. 475.
87. Ibid., no. 272.
88. Ibid., no. 334.
89. Ibid., no. 74.
90. Ibid., no. 465.
91. Ohnuma, *Bodily Sacrifice in Indian Buddhist Literature*, p. 2.
92. Ibid., p. 5.
93. Mary Cumming, 'The Lives of the Buddha in Art and Literature of Asia', Michigan papers on South and Southeast Asia, 20, Ann Arbor: Centre for South and Southeast Asian Studies, Michigan, 1982, pp. 74–83.
94. Beal, *Travels of Fah-hian and Sung-Yun from China to India*, p. 29.
95. Ibid., p. 31.
96. Ibid., p. 32. (This story has not been found in Pāli *Jātaka* but described in *Jātakamalā*, by Aryasura as *Vyaghrajātaka*, no. 1; J.S. Sepeyer, tr., *The Gātakamala or Garland of Birth Stories*, Aryasura, Sacred Book of Buddhist, London: Oxford University Press, 1895.)
97. Thomas Watters, *On Yuan Chwang's Travels in India* (AD 629–645), Delhi: LPP, repr. 2004, p. 234.
98. Ibid., p. 237 (*Jātakamala*, Aryasura as *Maitribalajātaka*, no. 8).

99. John S. Strong, *Relics of the Buddha*, Delhi: Motilal Banarsidass, 2007, p. 52.
100. Ibid., no. 499.
101. Ibid., no. 359.
102. Ibid., no. 316.
103. Ibid., no. 347.
104. Ibid., no. 19.
105. Ibid., no. 50.
106. Ibid., no. 314.

5

Ecological Consciousness in Jainism and Comparisons with Buddhism

Jainism is embedded with mutual sensitivity towards all animate and inanimate beings and envisages interconnectedness of life forms. It ponders that human is not a privileged species but a constituent of a cosmos consisting of millions of lives. A person with deluded vision is considered as insane who follows arbitrary whims and sycophancies and cannot differentiate between the good and the bad.[1] *Anekāntavāda* can be antidote to modern conception of machine based industrialization that deteriorated and polluted the environment. It understands the problems from many dimensions.[2] *Anekāntavāda* can act as an instrument which deducts truth by judiciously analysing the facts with *Saptbhanginaya* of *Syādvvda*. The *Nayavāda* can be used as a sophisticated tool to accept the partial view of others while at the same time realizing the other dimensions. It is a method of reconciliation that can be used as an ecological tool. John M. Koller says:

Jain metaphysics of non-absolutism (*anekāntavāda*) supported by the epistemological theory of viewpoints (*nayavāda*) and the sevenfold scheme (*saptabhangi*) of qualified prediction (*syādvāda*), as providing a basis for the central moral principle of ahiṃsa. Because violence proceeds from intolerance rooted in ideological absolutism, ahiṃsa requires a firm foundation provided by philosophy of anekānta. The *anekāntavāda* philosophy can be seen as providing an ontological basis for the principle of non-violence. It also grounds an epistemological basis for the respects of others that ahiṃsa incorporates. The perspectivalism embodied in the theory of epistemic standpoints (*nayavāda*) recognizes the ordinary, nonomniscient knowledge claims are always limited by the particular standpoint on which they are based. Consequently, claim from one perspective must always be balanced and complimented by claim from other perspectives. This has important ecological implications.[3]

The teachings of *Tīrthānkaras* can be translated into action to investigate and solve the dichotomy between the real life and fiction. When differences within two fundamental standpoints of similarities and differences are considered, the seven *nayas*, namely, *naigma* (undifferentiated), *samgraha* (general), *vyavahāra* (practical), *rjusutra* (manifested), *sabda* (verbal), *samabhirudha* (subtle), and *evambhuta* (happened) are applied. The first three are considered as a way to judge the standpoints as a substance while the rest four are instrumental to examine the changes that substance undergoes. It is one of the core constituents of Jainism and re-interpretation of some of the teachings will inculcate values, and support an ecologically positive way of living. The interrogation of such teachings will also enquire where they promote values and practices that are harmful to the environment.

The antiquity of Jain traditions has been sought by the scholars since the inception of the Indus Valley Civilization. It has been suggested that the first *Tīrthānkara* Rishabhanātha may have belonged to the Indus Valley Civilization and the yogic posture depicted on the Indus seals can be a Jain *Tīrthānkara*. McEvilley argues about a possible relation between the yogic worship in the Indus Valley Civilization and the meditative posture of Jain *Tīrthānkaras*. He thinks that representation of *yogi* on seal no. 420 of Mohenjodaro has close resemblance with Jain *Tīrthānkaras* as Jain iconography depicts them with four faces, symbolizing propagation of their teachings in all the four directions of universe. Such iconographic details have been mentioned in *Ācārānga Sūtra* and *Kalpa Sūtra*.[4] The *Ācārānga Sūtra* depicts Mahāvīra in cross-legged position sitting under śāla tree.[5] It also says that when Mahāvīra left his royal palace in search of *kaivalya*, animals and gods were represented in his palanquin. Sakra worshipped him and anointed him for his decision to leave in search of *kaivalya*. He clads Mahāvīra in beautiful robes:

interwoven with gold and ornamented with design of flamingoes, adorned him with necklace, a turban, wreaths of precious stones, ribbons and more. He then creates a giant palanquin adorned with pictures of wolves, bulls, horses, men, dolphins, birds, monkeys, elephants, antelopes, sarabhas (fantastic animals with eight legs), yaks, tigers, lions [and], creeping plants.[6]

Such depictions give indications of Jain orientation of harmonious co-existence with other beings of the cosmos. However, there is a debate over ascetic depiction found from Mohenjodaro. John Marshall identifies it with proto-Siva who is seated cross-legged in *padmasanamudra*. He had three visible faces with a headgear consisting of the horns of buffalo. He is surrounded from the right and in anti-clock direction, by a buffalo, a rhinoceros, a man, five signs of Indus script, an elephant, a man again, and a tiger. Below his seat two deers are seated.[7] D. Srinivasan holds the view that the deity seems to be not three-faced and—not resembling Śiva of the later period. She contends that the depiction of Rudra in Vedic literature with respect to all animals is wrath, rather than protection while John Marshall says that Śiva is the lord and protector of animals.[8] McEvilley also suggests that a depiction found in a seal from Mohenjodaro showing seven deities in an upright posture with their arms hanging in *kyotsargamudra* is a representation of *Tīrthānkara* Rishabhanātha.[9] Richard Lannoy also supports this view and says that a naked man has been depicted as a repeat motif in an upright posture. His legs slightly put parallel with sides of his body which frequently occurs later as Jain *Tīrthānkara*. However, he also associates it with the proto-goddess worship.[10]

Allchin and Allchin record that the seven figures could be identified with the seven rishis or seven mothers worshipped in contemporary India.[11] Katherine says that it is associated with the worshipping of mother goddess tradition in India[12] while B.B. Lal accepts that seven seers or seven mothers are associated with some form of rituals.[13] Again, W.A. Fairservis associates it with wedding rituals in which women are depicted with peacock feather headdresses, a sacrificial animal, and the bride adorned with floral crown.[14] The prevalence of *muni* or *yogic* tradition in the Indus Valley Civilization cannot be denied. It is a possibility that the first *Tīrthānkara* may not be associated to it but the Jains and other sects borrowed *yogic* tradition from the Indus Valley Civilization. The evidence of *śramanic* or *muni* tradition could be traced from *Keśi Sukta* of the *Rigveda* where they were identified as long-haired (*keśi*), clad in rough garment (*piśangavasatemala*), and ecstasic in mood (*unmaditamaunayena*).[15]

Padmanath Jaini relates worshipping of bull in the Indus Valley Civilization as worshipping of the first *Tīrthānkara* Rishabhanātha.[16] It is difficult to accept his view that prevalence representation of humped bull in the Indus Valley Civilization is associated to the first Tirthankara Adinātha/Rishabhanātha but it is very conspicuous that 16 out of 24 *Tīrthānkaras* have symbols as animals or birds. Two of the rests are associated with flowers (lotus). Ādinātha or Rishabhanātha (Bull), Adinātha (elephant), Sambhavanātha (horse), Abhinandanātha (monkey), Sumatinātha (krauncha), Suvidhanātha (makara), Sreyaṃsanātha (rhinoceros), Vasupujya (buffalo), Vimalanātha (boar), Anantanātha (falcon), Santinātha (deer), Kunthanātha (goat), Munisuvrata (tortoise), Aristanemi/Neminātha (conch shell), Parśvanātha (snake), and Mahāvīra (lion) have been symbolized with animals and birds while the sixth *Tīrthānkara* Padmaprabha and the twenty-first *Tīrthānkara* Naminātha have been symbolized with lotus and blue lotus respectively.[17] The Jain *Tīrthānkaras* always maintain cordial relations with animals and birds. Such interdependence is well exhibited in their symbols and teachings.

In Buddhism, association of the Buddha with animals and plants is vividly represented. In the Buddhist iconography the Buddha is depicted with elephant, bull, horse, and lion symbolizing dream of his mother Mahāmāyā, birth, *mahābhinishkramana*, and the Buddhahood, respectively.[18] In Buddhism, with the emergence of Vajrayāna, interconnectedness, and interdependence among humans, plants, animals, and gods increased and its horizon was further expanded to planets, *yakṣas, kinnaras, gandharvas,* and *vidyadharas*.[19]

Evolution of Universe: Cosmological Interdependence

The origin, interdependence, and interconnectedness among the various elements of the universe were first discussed and elaborated in the *Rigveda* which says that *Hiraṇyagarbha* arose from great waters pervading the whole universe and then led to creation of the world out of pre-existing matters.[20] The *purushasukta* of the *Rigveda* tells the mythical legend of the sacrifice of primeval being called *purusha* who created four *varnas* and other beings.[21] The *Rigvedic* model of creation was the first theoretical assumption to understand and learn about various elements of universe in which human beings were living. The Aryans evolved various rituals and prayers to perpetuate, sustain, and even confront the different elements of Nature. The prayers and sacrifices were developed not only to propitiate the Nature but also to remove hurdles which were considered harmful and hostile to the Aryans.

Jainism and Buddhism might have taken some influence from *purusha* model of origin of the universe but their theories of origin seem to be more realistic and pragmatic in the sense that *śramanic* religions tried to remove the problem encountered in the *purusha* model. The horrific sacrificial cult was replaced by more pragmatic approach towards Nature including humans and non-humans. The animal sacrifices were replaced by more harmonious approaches by propagating non-violence and mutual respect.

Jain cosmology enumerates universe in shape of a female body. The Earth is considered as an intermediate sphere (*manushyaloka*) and consists of three continents and two oceans where all animal world including humans reside. Below the Earth, seven hells are situated occupied by the wicked people. The top was the *siddhaloka* occupied by *kevalins* and other librated people. They are free from all sorts of bondages and this status can be attained by humans through practices thought by the *Tīrthānkaras*.[22] Jainism accepts four main destinies or *gatis* souls as human beings (*manushyas*), heavenly beings (*devas*), hell beings (*narkis*), and animals and plants (*tiryanca*). The animals and plants are put into hierarchy as per their senses. The *vanaspati* and *nigodas* (microorganism) are categorized as one sensed souls.[23] The *nigoda* is formed by a common body producing *karma* and is known as 'group souls'. It consists of infinite souls occupying the same body, sharing common food, and respiration. Though souls in such structure have short life but *nigoda* body continues to survive for a very long life as infinite souls continuously died and new souls used to take births simultaneously.[24] The *nigodas* or one-sensed beings feel four vitalities of energies, respiration, life span, and touch but they could not be examined through sense perception.[25] One-sensed beings feel four instincts (*samjnas*). They have cravings for food (*āhārasamjna*), fear (*bhayasamjna*), feel for reproduction (*maithunasamjna*), and sense to accumulate for future (*parigrahasamjna*).[26] Beings can not be treated as primitive and archaic whose souls are in linear progressive evolution for higher senses. The *nigodas* are tiny souls living in *lokakāyā* (universe) since evolution of the earth and their sense-perception have linear progression. Even it can achieve the status of human being and attain *moksa*.[27]

Two-sensed beings have senses of touch and taste. These include worms, leeches, mollusks, weevils, etc. Three-sensed beings, on the other hand, bear senses of touch, taste, and smell. These include ants, fleas, termites, centipedes, etc. Those having four senses of touch, taste, smell, and sight consists of wasps, flies, gnats, mosquitoes, butterflies, moths, scorpions, etc. The five-sensed beings have hearing capacity in addition to the prior four qualities and their category includes aquatic animals (fish, tortoise, crocodile), winged animals (birds), and terrestrials consisting of quadruples (horses, cows, bulls, elephant, lions, and reptiles).[28] The five-sensed beings can attain true spiritual insight which is the primary stage of *moksa*. They are able to follow *karma* same as the human beings who follow *anuvratas*. But an animal can not attain such advance stage of knowledge which is a pre-requisite for *moksa*.[29] In Jainism, ecological-domain humans are treated differently from others because they can attain *kaivalya* but others are not. After attainment of *moksa*, human can be free from the cycle of birth and death.[30] The *Tīrthānkaras* propound that only humans have the capability to learn and practice physical and mental austerities necessary for curtailing and wiping out all *ghatiya* (bad) *karmas*. After the removal of *ghatiya karmas* a person can attain *kevalajñana* (omniscience).[31]

Śanti Suri vividly illustrates living beings, starting with the Earth beings and ending with the *devas* and ordained persons. He provides a life span, occurrences of their appearances, and their characteristics. According to him, rocks can survive for 22,000 years, water body souls for 7,000, wind body souls have a life span of 3,000 years, and fire bodies could sustain for 3 days and 3 nights only.[32] Each such category of souls bears attributes of life, breath, energy, and sense of touch.[33] The *prithivikāyikas* or earth bodies consist of crystalline quartz jewels, gems, coral, vermilion, orpiment, realgar, mercury, gold, soda ash, and sea salt.[34] The *jalakāyikas* or water bodies are underground water, rain water, dew, ice, hail, water drops on green vegetables, and mist.[35] The *agnikāyikas* or fire bodies include burning coals, flames, inflamed cowdung, fire reflected in sky, spark originating from fire or from the sky, shooting stars, and lightening.[36] The *vayukāyikas* include wind bodies blowing up and down, whirl winds, wind coming from the mouth, melodious winds, rarified winds, etc.[37] The *prthvikāyikas*, *jalakāyikas*, *agnikāyikas*, and *vayukāyikas* possess four vitalities (*prānas*), viz., vitality of energy (*kayabalaprāna*), vitality of respiration (*ucchvasanisvasaprāna*), the vitality of life (*ayuprāna*), and the vitality of senses of touch (*sparsaprāna*). They may imbibe other vitalities of smell or sense of sight or of hearing. On the basis of their ability to adopt senses they are classified as one-, two-, three-, four-, or five-sensed beings.[38] As scientific and technological developments keep growing, the old ideas of co-existence keep fading away. The distinct advantage of Nature as a natural ally has been transformed into exploitation of Nature in name of wanton growth and development. Such manipulations have led to disruption of the entire complex of life forms.[39] Padmanabh Jaini comments that entrepreneurship for the preservation of the environment should not be relied on the Earth, water, fire, and air bodies but these elements should be considered as moral ombudsman. Each of such individual body can create the physical (*āudarika*) form for *ajīva* which may vary from others in *gunas* of consciousness or awareness.[40] A conscious soul may feel pleasure or pain through its single sense of touch and the vast paraphernalia elaborated through the Earth, water, fire, and wind bodies could be a better medium to learn and preserve the world.

Though Jain theological interpretations describe inter-connectedness of various elements of Nature, the inherent decay and downfall of human world is also considered. Jain literature mentions that human species will socially and ecologically decay and the world will be destroyed. After the decline, it will regenerate with the next cycle of time.[41] The Nature intervenes as disastrous actions of human beings erode the equilibrium of the Earth. It is said that if humankind is a catalyst in the degradation of Nature then Jain tradition also says that Nature is the vector for deterioration of the world.[42] But it seems as an extreme view because Jain cosmological assumptions expounds degeneration of the human world because of *karma* cycle. If human actions are at the level of dangerous propensity then due to interconnectivity of *prithvi*, *jala*, *agni*, and *vāyu* bodies are bound to be affected. The degeneration starts with humans and then spreads to other life forms. Environmental concerns cannot be separated from socio-economic concerns. If consumption pattern and resource mobilization are not in appropriate direction then calamity is bound to happen.[43] The solution for such problem is to accept the plurality of beings as recommended by Jainism.[44] It can prepare ground for an ecological ethics.

Jain cosmology divides the universe between *jīva* and *ajīva*. *Jīva* possesses consciousness and energy that may belongs to the Earth, water, fire and water bodies. *Ajīva* covers time and space in which *jīva* survives. They both are determined by *karma* or *dravya* and the nature of *karma* reflects their destinies both in this birth and future. *Karma* is considered to be source of channelization to relieve negative actions and an inspiration to endure for positive actions. The *jīva* or soul could be divided into *saṃsāri* (worldly) and *mukta* (emancipated). The *saṃsāri jīva* alludes to false notions and possessions. As a result souls become *bahirātman* or obscured. Such souls are potentially harmful for the ecological harmony. The second state is *antarātman* which shuns indulgences and strive for supreme knowledge. The third state is identified as *parātmana* which is free from bondages of *karma* and cycles of life and death. The *saṃsāri* souls can be categorized as *trasas* (mobile) and *sthavara* (immobile). The *sthavaras* are further segmented into the Earth, water, fire, air, and plants. Each one of them has one sense of touch.[45] All such souls are *karma* bound which has highly technical characteristics. The five colours (*lesya*) of *karma* have been associated with different personality types. Jagmander Lal Jaini categorizes them as:

A hungry person with the most negative black lesya karma uproots and kills an entire tree to obtain few mangoes. The person of the blue karma fells the tree by chopping the trunk, again merely to gain a handful of fruits–fraught with grey karma, a third person spares the trunk but cut off the major limbs of the tree. The one with orangish-red karma carelessly and heedlessly lops off several branches to reach the mangoes. The fifth exhibiting white karma merely kicks up the ripe fruits that has dropped to the foot of the tree.[46]

Such *karmas* in 148 possible forms identified as ranging from subversive delusions and passions to non-destructive positive notions form to be a *kevalinjana*.[47] The Jain *karma* responds to human actions and its response for their future. Kelly says:

Jain Acharyas were concerned about the pollution of the soul by karma, which is considered as a type of extremely subtle matter that is attracted to and bound with soul when ever are informed by passions (*kasayas*). This type of pollution causes the soul to undergo transformation that give rise to *mithyata* or false views of reality, and cause various types of improper conduct. Engaging the conduct that minimizes volitional action that cause harm (*himsa*) and pain or suffering (*vedana*) to other living beings also maximizes one's own suffering. Such actions result in binding of wholesome (*punyaprakritis*) of karmic matter that produce feelings of bodily pleasure (*salavedaniya karma*) and those karmas that lead to rebirth as a human (*manusya*) or a heavenly being (*deva*). Conversely harmful action causes one to bind unwholesome varieties of karma (*papa prakritis*) including karma that produces pain (*asatavedaniya karma*) and those karmas that lead to the rebirth as animal (*tryanca*) or hell being (*nārakī*).[48]

The *karma* theory in Jainism and various forms of *jīva* delineate some scope to form environmental ethics conducive to modern age. It gives scope not to indulge but to make adjustment with Nature. Jain ethics do not believe that everything including plants and animals have been created for the advantage of human beings. It gives a wider spectrum to move beyond the geographical space and embrace the whole universe. Though human beings live in a particular economic and cultural tradition but sympathetic attitude towards Nature is necessary. It is true that materialism and consumerism encourage tendency to accumulate wealth, and consumerism is relied on notion that the universe is a collection of material objects. Such assumptions always give way to depression and negativity in every consumer society where human beings find themselves surrounded by nothing but material objects.[49] Mahāvīra says that when a person is afflicted with lust and passion then he would be devoid of truth and reality.[50] Jainism preaches that the world is composed of substances of different kinds and essential character of such substances is the interconnectedness. It makes the world permanent and moving. The respect for this interconnectedness can provide a stability and perpetual harmony with Nature.

Unlike Jainism, Buddhism propounds that nothing is permanent in the universe and everything is momentary (*kśanikavāda*). The *Aṅguttara Nikāya* says:

Conditioned phenomenon are impermanent; conditioned phenomenon are unstable; conditioned phenomenon are unreliable. . . . Sineru, the king of mountains, 84,000 yojanas in length and 84,000 yojanas in width; it is submerged 84,000 in the great ocean and rises up 84,000 yojanas above the great ocean . . . when the great earth and Sineru, the king of mountain, are blazing and burning, neither ashes nor soot are seen.[51]

The Buddha talks about change and decay saying that everything originates from the same condition and disappears when the condition ceases to be. This idea is very much applicable to modern environmental ethics. If society is able to know the adverse affects of deforestation, then it can be checked. The Buddha always says that the world is always moving through alternate cycle evolution and dissolution and each of such cycle lasts after long periods of gestation and maturity. The natural process of evolution and dissolution are affected by morals of human beings. The *Aggañña Sutta* says that the first beings were feeding on delight and were self luminous, relishing their glory, and flew the skies, until greed entered in their minds. As the moral turpitude affected the internal environment, the flavoursome, fragrant substances completely disappeared. People started eating edible fungus (mushroom) and later on creepers. As they continued to feed on fungus and creepers, their bodies became coarser. The good-looking ones became ugly, arrogant and self-conceited. The female and male sex organs developed and became more prominent. Because of over jealous sexual preoccupation between the male and female, lust and passion aroused. Out of such negative actions, people became lazy and selfish. The indulgence developed lawlessness, crime, and violence. To curb this and provide equitable justice, class system was created. The kshatriyas became kings to sustain law and order, similarly brāhamanas, vaiśyas and śudras were also created to facilitate different works. The society became more complex and further moral degeneration began adversely affecting the Nature. The fertility of the Earth further diminished. At last, the Buddha says that the people who lead good life in body, speech, and thoughts attain good destiny in this life and future and that though change is inherent, human action (good/bad) accelerates and shapes that change.[52]

The *Cakkavati Sihanada Sutta* goes on to predict the future course of action. When human moral degenerates further, the life span of the people will be shortened from thousand years to 10 or 20 years. Girls will be marriageable at 5 years of age and flavoursome foods like ghee, butter, sesame, molasses, and salt would disappear. People will feed on coarse grains. There will be no rules and no respect for elders, ascetics, and brāhmans. Fierce enmity and hatred will prevail. But the Buddha again intervenes that by doing wholesome good like refraining from ill-taking, sexual misconduct, lying, slander, harsh speech, and ill will, the life span could be expanded.[53] Buddhism thus provides distinct idea of evolution. Buddha says that body, sensation, perception, disposition, and consciousness are impermanent and life is a series of manifestation of its becoming. He believes that everything is conditional and dependent and avoids extremes of eternalism and nihilism. He denied the ultimate reality of the empirical self but accepts the empirical reality. While Jainism believes in doctrine of manyness of reality, matter (*pudgala*), and soul (*jīva*). Both have diverse views on evolution of universe and its functioning but both emphasize upon the continuation and flourishing of the world.

Ahiṃsa as an Ecological Tool

Ahiṃsa is a sensitive and pragmatic response to environmentalism. Practically all religions accept that non-violent approach towards animal kingdom can deliver mutual respect between humans and other animals. The word *ahiṃsa* has been derived from the Sanskrit root *hims* meaning 'to kill or injure'. When prefixed with *a*, it signifies intention not to kill or injure.[54] The *śramanic* religions tremendously acknowledged and adopted the principle of non-violence. Jainism accepts that all lives are integrated and to harm other is to hurt the community as a whole.[55] The *Ācārāṅga*

Sutra says that all beings are fond of life and feel pleasure and pain.[56] The principle of *ahimsa* is found in the *Mahāvratas* as well as in the *Anuvratas*. It corresponds to mind, body, speech, and covers domains of intension as well as speech. It is a moral and ethical responsibility for harmful endeavour, and action.[57] The *Anuvratas* recommends non-violence (*ahimsa*), non-stealing (*asteya*), speaking truth (*satya*), non-possession (*aparigraha*), and celibacy (*brahmacharya*). The compassion for animals has been shown by strict vegetarianism.[58] Jain lay followers are told to avoid violent actions even at minute level. They can not adopt occupations, viz., production and sale of charcoal, cutting and sale of timber, construction and sale of carts, use of animals in transportation of goods, use of animal byproducts like ivory, bones, conch shells, trade in lacs and similar products, agriculture, etc.[59]

Jainism lays emphasis on sentiency and protection of plants. The intention to harm plants or animals will replicate in oneself.[60] It leads to unambiguous environmental ethics but such ethical considerations have not saved South Asia from facing environmental problems because of modern industrial development.[61] Mahāvīra says that trees have many good qualities and plants have life just like humans and animals.[62] The *Ācārāṅga Sutra* mentions vows to refrain from action that leads to injuring the plants.[63] The trees should be protected not destroyed.[64] Chapple says about plant ethics of Jains:

The first vow ahimsa requires respect for and protection of all life forms, stemming from the premise that even a blade of grass is not different from oneself in its essential vitality. Advocates of vegetarianism claim that abstention from eating meat not only spares the lives of animals but also helps contribute to a healthy ecosystem. The third vow, not stealing, means that one abstain from taking what does not belong to oneself. This can be particularly instructive for the people of developed world who continue to consume the majority of world's resource. . . . The fourth vow non-possession is tacitly environmental, as demonstrated by Acharya Tulsi; the less one owns, the less harm has been committed to one's eco sphere. On practical level the fifth vows sexual restrain can be seen as one way to hold down population growth.[65]

The *Ācārāṅga Sutra* tells that though hurting one-sense beings, which include plants, is not readily apparent through observation, their suffering is known when one cuts, strikes, or kills them.[66] They feel pain when harmed because their *jīva* is conscious (*mohaniya karma*). They also generate instincts of fear (*bhayasamjnas*), food (*āhārasamjnas*), reproduction (*maithunasamjna*), and accumulation of goods for future (*parigrahasamjna*).[67] The movement of *jīvas* for liberation establishes nodal point during the lifetime. *Ahiṃsa* leads to liberation from *karmic* bondage and its perception of *jīva* is highly ecological because it regards all form of life as a member of single community. It works like a vector for individual soul to absolve from *karmic* bond. This *karma* cycle begins *jīva's* passion for nourishment, reproduction, and accumulation. For *moksa*, it is pertinent to minimize craving that leads to harming of other life forms.[68] The rationale for *ahiṃsa* is based on belief that all life forms should be respected and not harmed. The *Ācārāṅga Sutra* mentions that injurious activities inspired by self interest always leads to evil and darkness. One corrupts oneself as soon as one intends to corrupt. One kills oneself as soon as one intends to kill other.[69] The Jains practise non-violence on plant life by not treading on green grass or harming a living plant. They protect *vāyū kāyās* by not fanning themselves and *agni kāyās* by not kindling or extinguishing fire. The protection of *jala kāyās* is done by not to take bath, swim or use water which is not boiled. The *pṛthvī kāyās* are protected by not involving in agricultural and other such pursuits. The *Pratikramana Sutra* seeks pardon from all living creatures and inculcates friendship with all beings and enmity with none.[70] The importance of *ahiṃsa* can be seen prayers discussed in such *sutras* recited twice by Śvetambara ascetics and once a year by the Jain *upāsaka*. It starts with prayer identifying and seeking absolution from karmic action of any form of violence caused to various lives. It says:

700,000 earth bodies, 700,000 water bodies, 700,000 fire bodies, 700,000 air bodies, 10,000,000 separate plant bodies, 1,400,000 aggregated plant bodies, 200,000 two-sensed beings, 200,000 three-sensed beings, 200,000 four-sensed beings, 400,000 divine five sensed beings, 400,000 infernal five sensed beings, 400,000 plant and animal five sensed beings, 1,400,000 humans: in this way there are 8,400,000 forms of existence. Whatever harm I have done, caused to be done, or approved of, by mind, speech, or body, against all of them: may be that harm be without consequence.[71]

The interconnectedness between humans and others has been demonstrated in other hymns of forgiveness given in Jain *sūtras*. One of such confessions says that:

I want to make pratikramana for injury on the path of my movement, in coming and in going, in treading on living things, in treading on seeds, in treading on green plants, in treading on dew, on beetles, on mould, on moist earth, and on cowwebs; whatever living organism with one or two, or three or four or five senses have been injured by me or knocked over or crushed or squashed or touched or hurt or affrighted or removed from one place to another ordeprived of life—may all that evil have been done in vain (micchāmidukkadam).[72]

Human beings damage Nature through their interaction for survival or ignorance depending upon their *karma*. Even an enlightened one cannot survive in this world without harming the living creatures. Jains evolved methods to deal with such situation. With avoidance and prohibitions, pragmatic approaches are also adopted which permits injury to living beings at moderate level that does not accrue negative *karma*. Haribhadra vividly discussed such situations and provided justifiable solutions. Though harming the plants and trees by cutting them for religious purposes accrue negative *karma* but using wood for making temple or flowers for worshipping the *Tīrthānkaras* earn better *karma* than previously-accrued negative *karma*.[73] He ponders over issues of violence involved in building of temples and argues that building activities should be linked to moral etiquettes since beginning.[74] He says that the wood that is bought for making the temple does not involve any destruction of life as it is purchased not cut.[75] Haribhadhra justifies such actions by giving analogy of a snake. A woman sees her child playing when a snake came out from the hole, the women pulled her child violently. The child experienced pain when being dragged by the mother but would experience more pain if he was bitten by the snake. In the same way, the harm done to the environment by cutting a tree for making of a temple is out-weighed by the virtues earned after making the temple for the worshipping of the *Tīrthānkaras*.[76] An ethics of intention involved in digging of well is for a greater good and a positive disposition for the society. The householder who harms the life of the creatures by digging is doing it for the survival of the society. Digging of wells or worshipping of *jinas* with flowers may be wrong in doctrinal terms but ethically it will bring positive dispositions for its meritorious actions.[77] Despite such ombudsman, humans are considered inhospitable to many forms of life. The day to day activities like pounding, grinding, cooking, etc., cause destruction of living creatures and are impediments in path to attain *kaivalya*.[78] The Jain *sutras* also say that some of the actions of human beings are not oriented for their livelihood or growth for lust or negative propensity. They destruct living creatures everywhere, whether they are walking, eating, sleeping or working. The more his movement are restricted, the fewer *trasa-jīva* or *sthavara-jīva* will perish.[79] The *Ācārāṅga Sutra* says that passion is the cause of mental perturbance.[80] Even harm is done to some of the beings unknowingly or unintentionally. The *Niryukti* says the Earth bodies do not manifest consciousness because of a constant coma of deep slumber producing *karma*. Ploughing, digging, and other such actions harm them.[81] The *Parigrahaparamanuvrata* prescribes limited possession for personal use. The lay followers are forbidden to indulge in malpractices like adulteration of goods, under weighing goods, supplying inferior products, overloading beasts of burden and harming other's means of livelihood.[82] Jainism always discourages violence encouraged by vicious mindset which purport to evil and darkness. It leads to bondage, delusion, death, and hell.

Jainism denounces violent action against any living beings even committed by laities and monks. Mahāvīra sent one of his *ganadhara* Indrabhuti to brāhmana Agnisharma to stop the performance of animal sacrifice in which thousands of animals were planned to kill. Agnisharma paid reverence for Mahāvīra and took vow not to kill animals for sacrifices.[83] Jain literature also mentions rewarding a Jain in his next birth if he sticks to Jain vows and harms no one. Padmanath Jaini cites many of such stories of getting rewards. Once Mahāvāra's soul was reborn as lion. When lion was preached by a Jain ascetic, he inculcated kindness and compassion and refrained from killing animals for food. Consequently, he died and was reborn as a human being and became *kevaljina*.[84] It also mentions the story of a pair of cobras named Dharmendra and Padmavati who saved the life of *Tīrthānkara* Parśvanātha in Vārānasī. They were hidden in heap of firewood being kindled by non-Jain ascetic. Parśvanātha tried to save their lives by extinguishing the fire but it was too late. When they were dying, Parśvanātha recited *Pancanamaskara mantra* for them. As a consequence, they were reborn as *yaksas* and were worshipped by the *jinas*.[85] In another story, an elephant was born as Prince Megha who became an eminent monk and disciple of Mahāvīra. The story says:

Long ago, there was a large forest fire, and all the animals of the forest fled and gathered around a lake, including a herd of elephants, deer, rabbits, squirrels, etc. For hours the animals crowded together in their small refuge, cowering from the fire. The leader of the elephant herd got an itch, and raised a leg to scratch himself. A tiny rabbit quickly occupied the space vacated by elephant's foot. The elephant out of an overwhelming desire not to hurt the rabbit, stood on three legs for more than three days until the fire died down and the rabbit scampered off. By then, his leg was numb and he toppled over. Still retaining a pure mind and heart, the elephant died. As a reward for his compassion, he overcome the need for embodiment as an animal and was born as a prince by the name of Megha and eventually became a disciple of Mahavira, taking the vows of a monk in hopes of transcending all forms of existence.[86]

These stories show animal abilities to respond to circumstances for compassionate actions and they expound the Jain ecological and practical tradition that animals can attain higher place and wisdom. Jain teachers are questioned when one argues about tolerance towards other contemporary religions and teachers. The *Syādavāda* or *Anekāntavāda* may be to accommodate many facets at one point of time but it was operational only at ethical level. John E. Cort calls it 'Intellectual Ahiṃsa' as the Jain thinkers did not acknowledge views of others as valid although they were committed to the Jain view.[87] Jains accord that all violence is intended and it is not possible that the person who does or thinks wrongs can be exempted from it. Even if his ignoranc lead to his intention of violence and wrongs.[88] Such examples are found in the Jain literature where arrogance and ignoble conducts have been shown towards other *sramānic* teachers. The Digambara tradition says that the destiny of the soul of the Ajivika teacher Makkhaliputta Gosala and others who preached false doctrines (against Jain teachings), would be born as *nigodas* in their next birth.[89] Sīha, the commander of Licchavis, was an ardent follower of Mahāvīra. When the Buddha visited Vaiśalī, he desired to visit him but was dissuaded by Mahāvīra by saying that the Buddha preached false doctrine. But Sīha visited the Buddha with his 500 soldiers. He discovered that he was one of the most generous teachers of his time who preached Sīha on condition that he would continue to support Jain ascetics. Impressed by his generosity, Sīha invited the Buddha to a meal but the Niganthas opposed it by spreading false rumours that beef had been served for the Buddha and other monks.[90] The *Abhayarājakumāra Sutta* mentions an episode of Prince Abhaya of Magadha who visited the Buddha and asked a number of uneasy questions suggested by Mahāvīra. The Buddha answered all the questions and Abhaya became his disciple.[91] However liberal views about other sects allowed Jains to maintain the correctness of their own view and to refute other's views as false. Even the *Tīrthānkara* Parśvanātha was generous and highly accommodating in framing of rules and teachings. Altogether Jains propose lesser use of resources with minimum desire and consumption. Accumulation of wealth and unbridled consumption are unequivocally declared sin in Jainism. The laities are always encouraged to recognize that superfluous life is harmful. Their fundamental teachings are deeply rooted in ethos pertaining to sustainable approach towards the Earth and environment.

Buddhism, like Jainism, has positive notion towards nature. Buddhist view on *ahiṃsa* is based on mutual respect and rightness. The *Samaññaphala Sutta* says that the monks should avoid killing of living beings and keep aloofness from the destruction of life. one should be merciful and compassionate to all creatures that have life.[92] Buddhism adheres that all living beings fear death, so one should neither kill nor cause to kill.[93] Despite such thoughts Buddhist view on sentiency of plants and place of animals in eye of human world are quite debatable. The life in plants is quite different from Jainism which propounds absolute structure about life form in plants. Buddhism vacillates in different phases to embrace a firm and common view point. Probably the aim of Buddhism was to accommodate more pragmatic view point as well as to endorse respect for plant life. The absolute idea that plant has life so should not be killed, can raise question that how human being can survive if one will not use plant resources. Similarly life in animal has been respected in Buddhism but at the same time meat eating is allowed to some extent under *tikotiparisuddha* rules.

Notes

1. *Tattvartha Sutra* (Umasvati), I.33, tr. Nathmal Jatia, San Francisco: Harpar Collins, 1994.
2. Christopher Key Chapple, *Jainism & Ecology: Nonviolence in the Web of Life*, New Delhi: Motilal Banarsidass, 2006, p. xvii.
3. John M. Koller, 'Jain Ecological Principles', in *Jainism & Ecology: Nonviolence in the Web of Life*, Christopher Key Chapple, New Delhi: Motilal Banarsidass, 2006, pp.19–34, see p. 20.
4. Thomas McEvilley, 'An Archaeology of Yoga', *RES*, no. 1, 1961, pp. 44–77 (Jyotendra Jaina and Eberhard Fisher also consider similarities between ascetics of Mohenjodaro and Jain *Tirthānkaras*. Jyotendra Jaina and Eberhard Fisher, *Jaina Iconography*, Leiden: Brill, 1978, p. 12.)
5. *Ācārānga Sutra*, II.15.25 tr. Herman Jaicobi, *Jain Sutras*, New York: Dover Press, 1884; repr. 1968.
6. Ibid., II.15.21.
7. B.B. Lal, *The Earliest Civilization of South Asia*, New Delhi: Aryan Books International, 1997, p. 224.
8. D. Srinivasan, 'The So-called Proto Siva Seal from Mohenjodaro: An Iconographical Assessment', *Archives of Asian Art*, vol. 29, 1975–6, pp. 47–58; D. Srinivasan, 'Unhinging Siva From the Indus Civilization', *Journal of Royal Asiatic Society of Great Britain and Ireland*, 1984, pp. 77–89.
9. McEvilley, 'An Archaeology of Yoga', p. 52.
10. Richard Lannoy, *The Spiriting Tree: A Study of Indian Culture and Society*, New York: Oxford University Press, 1971, p. 10.
11. B. Allchin and F.R. Allchin, *The Rise of Civilization in India and Pakistan*, Cambridge: Cambridge University Press, 1982, p. 215.
12. Katherine Anne Harper, *The Iconography of the Saptamatrkas: Seven Hindu Gooddesses of Spiritual Transformation*, New York: Edwin Mellen Press, 1989, pp. 3–11.
13. Lal, *The Earliest Civilization of South Asia*, p. 230.
14. W.A. Fairservis, 'An Epigraphic View of the Harappan Culture', in *Archaeological Thought in America*, ed. C.C. Lamberg-Karlovski, Cambridge: Cambridge University Press, 1989, pp. 205–17.
15. *Rigveda*, X.136.
16. Padmanabh S.Jaini, *The Jaina Path of Purification*, California: University of California, 1979, p. 33.

17. R.C. Majumdar, *The Age of Imperial Unity*, Bombay: Bharatiya Vidya Bhavan, 1980, p. 427.
18. Singh, *Buddhism at Sārnāth*, pp. 70–5.
19. Benoytosh Bhattacharya, *The Indian Buddhist Iconography*, Calcutta: M.L. Mukhopadhyaya, pp. 342–5.
20. *Rigveda*, X.121.
21. Ibid., X.90.
22. Christopher Key Chapple, 'The Living Earth of Jainism and the New Story: Rediscovering and Reclaiming a Functional Cosmology', in *Jainism & Ecology*, ed. Christopher Key Chapple, Delhi: Motilal Banarsidass, 2006, pp. 119–40.
23. Umasvati, *Tattvartha Sutra*, 2.21–2, tr. Nathmal Tatia, San Francisco: Harper Collins, 1994.
24. *Gommatasāra Jivakānda*, tr. J.L. Jaini, *Sacred Books of Jainas*, vol. 5, New Delhi: Today and Tomorrow Publications, 1990.
25. *Bhagvatī Sutra*, vol. I, p. 271; vol. III, p. 339, tr. K.C. Lalwani, Calcutta: Jain Bhawan, 1973–80.
26. *Prajnapana Sutra*, chap. 8.
27. Padmanabh S. Jaini, 'From Nigoda to Moksa: The Story of Marudevi', *Proceedings of International Conference on Jainism and Early Buddhism*, Lund University, 4–7 June 1998. (Śvetambara sources accept that soul of Marudevi, the mother of Rishabhanatha has such experience.)
28. *Tattvārtha Sutra*, 2.22–3.
29. Jaini, 'Indian Perspective on Spirituality of Animals', *Buddhist Philosophy & Culture: Essays in Honour of N.A. Jayawickrama*, ed. David J. Kalupahana and W.G. Weeraratne, Colombo: N.A. Jayawickrama Felicitation Committee, 1987, pp. 169–78.
30. Jaini, *The Jaina Path of Purification*, Delhi: Motilal Banarsidass, 2014, pp. 140–1.
31. Kristi L. Wiley, 'The Nature of Nature: Jain Perspective on the Natural World', *Jainism & Ecology*, ed. Christopher Key Chapple, Delhi: Motilal Banarsidass, 2006, pp. 35–62.
32. *Jivavicona Prakarnam* (Santi Suri), 34.
33. Ibid., 163.
34. Ibid., 3–4.
35. Ibid., 5.
36. Ibid., 6.
37. Ibid., 7.
38. *Sarvārthasiddhi*, 2.13–17.
39. Thomas Berry, *The Dream of the Earth*, San Francisco: Sierra Club Books, 1988, pp. 164–5.
40. Jaini, *The Jaina Path of Purification*, pp. 90–2.
41. *Painnayasuttaim*, Jain Agam Series, vol. I, no. 17, tr. Punyavijaya and Antlal Mohan Lal Bhajak, Bombay: Mahavira Jain Vidyalaya, 1984, pp. 409–523.

42. Paul Dundas, 'The Limits of Jain Environmental Ethics', in *Jainism &
    Ecology*, ed. Christopher Key Chapple, Delhi: Motilal Banarsidass,
    2006, pp. 95–117.
43. John E. Cort, 'Green Jainism: Notes and Queries toward a Possible
    Jain Environmental Ethics', in *Jainism and Ecology*, ed. Christopher
    Key Chapple, Delhi: Motilal Banarsidass, 2006, pp. 63–94, see p. 78.
44. J.C. Sikdar, 'The Fabric of Life as Conceived in Jaina Biology',
    Sambodhi, 3, 1974, pp. 1–10.
45. *Jīvasamacacadhikara*, 75–7.
46. Jagmander Lal Jaini, *The Outlines of Jainism*, Cambridge: Cambridge
    University Press, 1976, pp. 47–8.
47. Helmuth Von Glasenapp, *The Doctrine of Karman in Jaina Philosophy*, Bai
    Vijibai Jivanlal Pannalal Chairty Fund, 1942, p. 19.
48. Wiley, 'The Nature of Nature: Jain Perspective on the Natural World',
    pp. 35–6.
49. Briane Swimme, *The Hidden Heart of the Cosmos: Humanity and the New
    Story*, New York: Orbis Books, 1996, pp. 33–4.
50. *Ācārāṅga Sūtra*, I.I.I.
51. *Aṅguttara Nikāya*, IV.100.
52. *Dīgha Nikāya*, III.80.
53. Ibid., III.71–5.
54. Lois Dummont, *Homo Hierarchicus: The Caste System and its Implications*,
    Chicago: The University of Chicago Press, 1970, p. 148.
55. John M. Koller and Patricia J. Koller, *Asian Philosophies*, Saddle River,
    NJ: Printice Hall, 2002, pp. 32–3.
56. *Ācārāṅga Sūtra*, 1.2.3.
57. Cort, 'Green Jainism: Notes and Queries toward a Possible Jain
    Environmental Ethics', p. 74.
58. Wiley, 'The Nature of Nature: Jain Perspective on the Natural World',
    p. 45.
59. Padmanabh S. Jaini, 'Ecology, Economics, and Development in
    Jainism', in *Jainism & Ecology*, ed. Christopher Key Chapple, Delhi:
    Motilal Banarsidass, 2006, pp. 141–58, see pp. 143–4.
60. Harman Jacobi, ed., *Jain Sutras*, vol. 22, New Delhi: Motilal Banarsidass,
    1964, p. 10.
61. Harold Coward, 'The Ecological Implications of Karma Theory', in
    Purify the Earthly Body of God: Religion and Ecology in Hindu India, ed.
    Lance E. Nelson, Albany: State University of New York Press, 1998,
    pp. 39–40.
62. *Ācārāṅga Sūtra*, 2.4.2.
63. Ibid., 1.1.5.
64. Ibid., 2.4.2.
65. Christopher Key Chapple, *Nonviolence to Animals, Earth, and Self in Asian
    Traditions*, Delhi: Satguru Publications, 1995, p. 71.

66. *Ācārāṅga Sūtra*, 1.1.
67. *Prajnapana Sūtra*, chap. 8; *Gommatasāra Jīvakaṇḍa*, 134–9.
68. Padmanabh S. Jaini, 'Ecology, 'Economics, and Development in Jainism', p. 142.
69. *Ācārāṅga Sūtra*, 1.2.2; 1.5.5.
70. *Pratikramana Sutra*, V.49, tr. R Williams, in *Jaina Yoga: A Survey of Medieval Srāvakācāras*, London: Oxford University Press, 1963, p. 207.
71. *Sraddha-Pratikramana Sutra (Prabodha Tika)*, ed. Panyas Bhadrankarvijaygani and Muni Kalyanprabhavijay, vol. 2, Bombay: Jain Sahitya Vikas Mandal, pp. 120–1.
72. *Airyāpathikī Sutra*, III.124, tr. R. Williams, *Jaina Yoga: A Survey of Medieval Sravakacaras*, London: Oxford University Press, 1963, pp. 203–4. Kristi L. Wiley, 'The Nature of Nature: Jain Perspectives on the Natural World', in *Jainism & Ecology: Nonviolence in the Web of Life*, ed. Christopher Key Chapple, Delhi: Motilal Banarsidass, 2006, pp. 35–59, see p. 46.
73. *Āvasyaka Niryukti*, p. 2.
74. *Pāñcāsaka*, 7.42.
75. *Ṣodaśaka*, 6.7–8.
76. *Pāñcāsaka*, 7.37–41.
77. *Kūpadṛṣṭānta Visadīkāraṅa*, p. 70.
78. *Yoga Sutra*, 122.
79. Ibid., 100.
80. *Ācārāṅga Sūtra*, 1.1.2.
81. *Gommatasāra Karmakanda*, 23.16.
82. Bhagachandra Jain, 'Ecology and Spirituality in Jain Tradition', in *Jainism & Ecology: Nonviolence in the Web of Life*, ed. Christopher Key Chapple, Delhi: Motilal Banarsidass, 2006, pp. 168–80, see p. 177.
83. Sadhvi Shilapi, 'The Environmental and Ecological Teachings of Tirthankara Mahavira', in *Jainism & Ecology: Nonviolence in the Web of Life*, ed. Christopher Key Chapple, Delhi: Motilal Banarsidass, 2006, p. 163.
84. Padmanabh S. Jaini, 'Indian Perspectives on Spirituality of Animals', in *Buddhist Philosophy and Culture: Essays in Honour of N.A. Jayawikrema*, ed. David J. Kalupahana and W.G. Weeratna, Colombo: N.A. Jayawikrema Committee, 1987, pp. 169–78, see p. 169.
85. Ibid., pp. 173–4.
86. Ibid., pp. 174–5; Christopher Key Chapple, *Nonviolence to Animals, Earth, and Self in Asian Traditions*, New Delhi: Sri Satguru Publications, 1993, pp. 12–13.
87. John E. Cort, '"Intellectual Ahiṃsa" Revisited: Tolerance and Intolerance of Others', *Philosophy: East and West*, vol. 50, no. 3, 2000, pp. 324–47. (H.R. Kapadia and A.B. Dhrva propose the idea that Jains are hostile to views of other contemporary ideas and views of

Tīrthānkaras on *ahiṃsa* cannot be absolute. Mallisena, *Syadamanjari*, ed. A.B. Dhruva, Bombay: Bombay University, 1933, p. lxxiv. Haribhadra, *Anekantajyapataka*, ed. H.R. Kapadia, 2 vols., Baroda: Oriental Institue, 1947, p. cxiv. John E. Cort claims that Jains did not adhere to total relativity but it will be difficult to expect that they accept others views equal or superior to them.)

88. E. Phyllis Granoff, 'The Violence of Non-Violence: A Study of Some Jain Response to Non-Jain Religious Practices', *Journal of the International Association of Buddhist Association*, vol. 15, no. 1, 1992, pp. 1–43.

89. Kristi L. Wiley, 'The Nature of Nature: Jain Perspectives on the Natural World', in *Jainism & Ecology: Nonviolence in the Web of Life*, ed. Christopher Key Chapple, Delhi: Motilal Banarsidass, 2006, pp. 35–59, see p. 55.

90. *Vinaya Pitaka*, I.233ff; *Aṅguttara Nikāya*, IV.179ff.

91. *Majjhima Nikāya*, I.391ff.

92. *Dhammapada*, V.275.

93. Ibid., V.129.

6

Nature in Theragāthā *and* Therīgāthā

The *Theragāthā*, the eighth book, and the *Therīgāthā*, the ninth book, of the *Khuddaka Nikāya* of *Sutta Pitaka* consists of 264 poems in 1,279 verses and 73 poems in 522 verses, respectively. These texts recount the struggle and accomplishments of the various *bhikkhus* and *bhikkhunis* along their road to *arahathood*. In these *gāthas* regular descriptions of natural environments as a source of tranquility and enlightenment finds place. These poets demonstrate the Buddha's teaching as a catalyst for *arahathood* in the forest. They praised the appearance of uninhabited land, woods, lakes, or marshes. Their necessities and enjoyments have been sought in forests. The vast forests on mountain spurs and ridges, the fertilizing meadows and flowing rivers are subject of monk's creation. The investigation of Nature is the major concern for them. The beauty of Nature through which the monks proceeded to *arahathood*, their famous hermitages, the greatness of the Gijjhakuta and the other hills, and awesomeness of the surrounding of forests are immortalized in a beautifully articulated language of the *Theragāthā* and the *Therīgāthā*. These texts show that all the natural elements are divine and the monks are intermingled with these divine powers. Here the treatment of Nature is a realistic description with a moral lesson. The *Theragāthā* and the *Therīgāthā*, both versified compositions, bear witness to a multidimensional approach towards care of Nature. There are identifiable sensitivities to Nature, forest, hills in many of its verses, though considered overall these poetries are mediated through an overreaching Buddhist vision which eulogize the evanescence of things temporal. This is the most important phenomenon and consistently encountered feelings in the utterance of varying length and content gathered in these *gāthas*. The elements of Nature have been used as metaphor and they link this concept to the popular belief of bad *kamma* and *dukkha*.

Gijjhakuta and Other Hills

Gijjhakuta played a vital role in sustenance of various organism. During the age of the Buddha, it was thickly forested and served as sanctuary for diverse variety of living organism. It also acted as a protector from harsh weather conditions and during rainy season, the flowing streams of Gijjhakuta provided constant supply of fresh water to the plains of Rājagaha. It was surrounded by a ring of hills, scrubby jungles, and rocks. It is quite secluded with only few human beings; although there were plenty of non-humans, especially snakes and elephants. Impatient and ill-tempered people could not survive in rocks because they came into conflict with other creatures. In such odd circumstances *bhikkhus* faced a lot of discomfort, weariness, etc. Talputta was a *natagāminī* of Rājagaha. After the preaching of the Buddha, he entered the *saṃgha* and became an *arahat*.[1] Talputta excelled his name for his bright and cheerful poetry. He says that the peaks of mountains, their slopes, forests, and the caves are suitable places for meditation.[2] It is impossible to remove *anicca* when the mind is disillusionzed by material possessions, people, and other assignments. When all these entanglements and cravings are given up, there is a chance to ordain the truth. Talputta praises the natural beauty and serenity of Gijjhakuta (vulture's peak) of Rājagaha (*kadā mayūrassa sikhaṇḍino vane, Dijassa sutvā girigabbhare rutaṃ*).[3] The forest is full of snakes and beasts and in such places *metta* and *karuna* are essential to survive and live. The incessant rains in the hills give peace and sublimity which enable them to practice austerities for realization of *jhāna* (*Vivaramanupatanti vijjuta Vebhārassa ca pandavassa ca*).[4] Mahākassapa was one of the most eminent disciples of the Buddha. He was ordained by the Buddha himself at his *gandhakutī* at Veluvana.[5] The Buddha regarded him equal to himself in exhorting the monks to lead an active monastic life.[6] Mahākassapa praises the attributes of the mountains (*Yattha eke vihaññati āruhantā siluccayaṃ, tattha buddhassa dāyādo sampajāno patissato*).[7] He glorifies the steadfastness of the mountains and shows his resolution to climb the hill for attainment of the *jhāna*. Bhadda Kundalkesa was born in the family of the treasurer of Rājagaha. After her painful marriage to a robber, she joined the order of the *niganthas*, much to her dissatisfaction. She had prolonged the discussion with Sariputta. Later on, the Buddha ordained her. She had been there for 50 years wandering in Anga, Magadha, Kāsī, and Kośala.[8] The *Therīgāthā* includes several verses composed by her. She praised the Gijjhakuta hill of Rājagaha where she was ordained by the Buddha. After a deep meditation she obtained the *arahathood* (*Divāvihāra nikkhamma gijjhakutamhī pabbati, addasaṃ virajaṃ buddhaṃ*).[9] Dantika, another *arahat*, was born in Sāvatthī and joined the order under Prajapati Gotami. During her siesta on Gijjhakuta, she saw a well-tamed elephant and took inspiration (*Divāvihāra nikkhamma gijjhakutamhī pabbati*). Dantika saw that the elephant was tamed by the *mahout* and obeyed his command. She believed that if an animal could leaves its wild instincts under some supervision then one can attain *jhāna* to be in isolation by following austerities. Elephant is shown as mark of strength and show a way for detachment.

The caves and mountains are considered to be the repository of moral and spiritual truth of the monks and the nuns and a manifestation of the universal divine spirit through which *bhikkhu* can attain *nibbāna* (*Puriso aṅkusamādāya dehi pādanti yācati, Nāgo pasārayī pādaṃ puriso nāgamānihi*).[10] Vakkali Thera joined the *saṃgha* to serve the Buddha and always wanted to be associated with him. Seeing his obsession the Buddha preached him to look to *dhamma*. When he did not pay heed to this, the Buddha, instructed him to go to forest of Gijjhakuta hills to attain *jhāna*.[11] Vakkali practiced austerities at the hills and forests (*Vataragabhinito tvam Vihāram kanane vane*).[12] Later, the Buddha visited him and with his blessings he attained *arahathood*. The steadfastness of the Gijjhakuta hills became symbolic for the monks and nuns to develop their strength and insight (*Yadā ahaṃ pabbajito agārasmāna gāriyaṃ, Nābhijānamī saṅkappaṃ anariyaṃ dosasamhitam*).[13]

Forests and Plants

The forests are attractive when the Sun shines and the weather is warm but if one proposes to live there for long in all weathers,

there come several hardships to be faced. It encourages one
to curb greed, aversion, and delusion, the three roots of evils
(*Nilabbhavaṇṇa rucirā sītavārī sucinadharā, Indagopakasañchannā te seta
ramayanti manti*).[14] The wild forces has amenities or distraction,
nothing to take the mind away from the basic fear of seeing things
as they really are, empty of self. The Buddha declared Revata,
an *arahat*, immense among the forest-dwellers (*araññakanām*).[15]
He attained *arahathood* at Khadiravana (acacia forest).[16] Now he
was self-awakened and fully-endowed with the preachings of the
Buddha. Similarly, many such hills were instrumental for *jhāna*
(*Dharaṇī ca sincati vāti maluto vijjutā carati nabhe*).[17] Vimala, another
arahat, entered the order under the guidance of the Buddha
and lived in a hill cave of Kosala. It is said that because of his
rigorous penances, there was a vast cloud that burst in the sky
and rain started allaying his pain and discomfort, making him
an *arahat*. The forests induce the monks to adopt practices and
habits which reflect their motive, i.e. *nibbāna*, and contributes
to their liberation. Vanavaccha derives his name from the forest
whose name literally means 'woodland'. He was born in the
forest at Kapilvatthu. His name was Vaccha but because of his
affection for the forest he was known as Vanavaccha. In the forest
he performed deep meditation and attained *arahathood*. When
he returned to Kapilvatthu with the Buddha, he delivered a
lecture on the importance of the forest and its resources which
form a great wealth to obtain the truth of life.[18] But sometimes
living in the forests becomes vulnerable especially for the nuns.
The incidence with Subha Jivakambavanika may be cited as an
example here. Once while passing through the Jīvaka's mango-
grove, a goldsmith's son blocked her path and invited her for some
sensual pleasure; she refused to oblige him and seeing that he was
obsessed by the beauty of her eyes, she pulled off one of her eyes.
The man asked for forgiveness and later Subha recovered her
eye with the blessings of the Buddha. Mahā-Kottihika was the
foremost disciple of the Buddha. He was known for his logical
thinking (*patsambhidappatanam*).[19] He was born in Sāvatthī and the
Buddha himself gave him lessons on *anicca*, *dukkha* and *anatta*.[20] His
poetries on Nature are mentioned in *Theragāthā*. Mahā-Kottihika
says that the meditation in the forest has taught him power and
given him wisdom to realize the truth. The evil and aversion have

been separated from his mind just as the strong breeze separates the leaf from a tree (*Dhanāti pāpake dhamme dumapattaṃ va maluto ti*).[21] Vimalā Therī was a courtesan of Vaiśalī. In her poems, she describes that how she had left behind the life of a courtesan and joined the order. She was living on begging and spending her life in the forest under the trees which made her more contended and awakened. She took her abode under the tree and attained the bliss (*Nisinnā rukkhamūlamhī avitakkassa labhinī*). Ekavihariya Thera says that his lonely life is very pleasant in the forest and haunted by rutting elephants (*mattakuñjarasevitaṃ eko atthavasī khippaṃ pavisissāmī kānanṃ*). He renounced his material life and went to the forest for meditation. The blossoming flowers, the cool mountain gorges, and the dense forests are the refreshing delight in the Gijjhakuta (*Sitavane sītale girikandare*). Such environment encourages him to attain *jhāna*.[22] Singalapita describes how he took inspiration for *arahathood* in the Bhesakala forest of Sumsumargiri (*bhesakalāvana kevalam atthikasaññaya aphari pathavim imaṃ*). He left all his sensual and material pleasure and attained perfection.[23]

Sunita, another disciple, says that he practiced the teachings of the Buddha and one night he attained *arahathood* by following austerity, celibacy, restrain, and self-control. The monks show strength and wisdom to realize that all things while pursuing the *arahathood* are nothing but to follow the divine orders which are universally established. The order of the monks are to attain *nibbāna* and to live with humility and forbearance.[24] Vakkali Thera expresses the same view about his forest life (*sabbattha dummano bālo sīlesu asamāhito*). He mentions about the difficulties of the forest life and the limited opportunities of the alms. But the Thera enjoys this arduous life and makes up his mind, strength, and faculties to obtain *nibbāna*. He resolves to live in the forest with firmness and concord. In the forest he strives untiringly both day and night with awakened self and tamed spirit to attain *jhāna*.[25] Udayin compares *jhāna* with the blossoming lotus, full of the golden pollen and sweet fragrance, and speaks about the quality of an awakened one to thrive in the world of sensory experience without any clinging or attachment. Though the mundane life is rooted in the desires that gives rise to the development of selfhood, one can learn to live without being bounded by the impulses and cravings for pleasure and pain. It is the stage of the Buddhahood. The lotus emerging from the mud and blooming above the water is a popular way of expressing the Buddha's transcendence. Udayin says that as lotus blooms under the muddy water yet remains undrenched, in the same way the Buddha is born in this world, resides here but is free from all sorts of clinging and attachments (*No pālippati lokena toyena padumaṃ yathā*).[26] Sariputta or Upatissa wrote 37 verses in the praise and appreciation of Nature.[27] He says that *jhāna* of the Buddha cannot be compared with the mighty ocean, the depth of the Earth or the steadfastness of the mountains (*Ajalo jalasamāno sadā carati nibbuto*). To him, the teacher with his great wisdom keeps the *dhammacakka* rolling and just like the Earth, water, and fire, he is free from all types of attachments and delusions.[28] Mahākassapa, in his several poetries, shows the same appreciation for Nature (*Kārerimālā vitatā bhumibhāgā manoramā, kuñjarābhirndā rammā te selā ramayanti maṃ*).[29]

Talputta says that the creeper in the tropical forests are sometimes of enormous sizes. Craving, he says, is like that; it has the huge and disorient trunk of ignorance all twisted round and round with wrong perverted views of reality. The craving creeper is supported by the forest with the same impression. It blankets and strangulates true understanding of this world and of this mind and body, and its branches spread out further. Similarly, craving also has huge and hoary trunk of *avijja* all moulded with wrong and distorted views of knowledge. Generally people strive for making their craving creeper grow to monstrous proportion. Only the sword of the *jhāna* is able to cut the material possessions and cravings of desire.[30]

Matangaputta, in his poetry, criticizes the persons who seek excuses because of extreme seasons and says that those who accept it as a mere futile grass, are capable enough for *arahathood* (*Dabbam kusam potakilam usīram muñjababbajaṃ urasā pondudissāmi*).[31] Yasoja compares himself with a *kala* plant. He says that because of his moderate life and food, he became weak and lean yet he is practising the austere life. He is considered as ardent as the war elephant who is ready for the war (*brahāvane Nāgo saṅgāmasīseva sato*).[32] Bhalliya shows his commitment for attainment of *arahanthood* and compares himself with the bridge made of reed. He adopted symbolism in his poem and expresses himself as a strong bridge made of reed which is able to encounter the great deluge.[33] The *gāthā* text shows that the monks and nuns express their inclination towards Nature by adopting certain metaphor, similes, and symbolism. In majority of references, it is shown that the dawn, i.e. *jhāna*, remains hidden behind the darkness of the night; likewise happiness is always hidden behind the darkness of the sorrow and the *jhāna* always comes out at the appropriate and assigned time.

Animals and Birds

In the *gāthā* texts, the divine spirits has also been revealed through the activities and symbolism perceived from animals. Sometimes the animals and birds are represented as a positive step to attain *jhāna* but sometimes their negative traits are explained to counter the ignorance and passion. Talputta says that the lions are unafraid of other animals and the Buddha has been compared to lions, quite fearless and roaring. His wisdom sword is quick enough to cut all attachments. It is said that with their stern and penetrative vision one could encounter the evils of Māra and can attain *nibbāna*. Cittaka Thera says that the peacock with its attractive colours and gorgeous necks screams out in Karamvi forest in the winter (*Nīlā sugīvā sikhina morā kāraṃciyam abhinadanti*) and awakes the monks to prepare themselves for the meditation.[34] The plaintive call of the peacocks are vividly described by the monks and nuns. It is a favourite theme of the Nature poetry preserved in the *gāthā* text. The peacocks are also represented to symbolize illusion. Its strange cries amidst rocks and cliffs would be arresting. The Buddha, however, says that swan is better than the peacock despite its plain colour and because it is without any ornament. It can cover more distance than a peacock as a common man is burdened with the wealth and bondage because their spiritual flight is limited. On the other hand, the monks are without any possessions and are able to fly high and far, i.e. the attainment of *nibbāna*.[35]

Nandaka gives the balanced appreciation of the Nature that comes from the focused mind in meditation and relates his feelings and contemplation regarding the nature of mind and how to develop mindfulness leading finally to wisdom. He says that the monks should strive for meditation with all their effort and engage in the discovery of the truth and tread diligently on the path of the Buddha.[36] Vanavacch expresses same view about the animals and forests. He points that the hills and forest regions with the sources of fresh water and massive boulders which are frequented by the monkeys and deer and covered by water, weeds, etc., are refreshing (*Acchudikā puthusilā gonangulamigāyutā, Ambusevālasañjannā te selā ramyantī mānti).*[37] He put all his efforts for attainment of the *arahathood.*[38] Vijitasena compares the asceticism of the monks with the taming of the elephants. He says that his mind will be fastened in the way as the elephants are tamed by their *mahouts.* When the monks turn inwards for the contemplation of the abstract and subtle, from particular to concrete manifestations, they become aware of the similarities between the self and Nature.[39] Sona Potriyaputta says that the calm night garlanded with the zodiac stars is not for comfort and sleep but for staying awake. If one sleeps he will miss the opportunity and the situation will be highly dejecting and defeating just as the fall from the elephant and consequent death by trampling of the elephant and this would be better than the loss of intellect and knowledge.[40] The Buddha told Sariputta when he looked at Sumana, fetching water from the Anotatta Lake of the Himalayas, that he was reminded of the novice Anuruddha who was thoroughbred and well-trained. By following the norms of *samgha* he was to attain the *arahathood.*[41]

Rain, Cloud, Rivers, and Oceans

In the *gāthā* texts, rains, clouds, rivers, and oceans are also admired. The river is described as a traveller's unmindful of meandering on the way to his destination. Sometimes she is like an adorable and caring mother who puts an ill infant on her lap, patting, soothing, and giving solace. Kalu Udayin was the son of Suddhodhana's chief minister and the childhood companion of Siddhārtha; he later joined the Buddhist *samgha.* He wrote about 60 poetries on Nature but only a few verses are found. In his poetry, he especially praises the river Rohiṇī which runs through Śakya and Koliya *gana* gives the joyous recitation of the forest, flowers, and their fragrances.[42] Sankicca Thera, born in Sāvatthī and ordained by Sariputta, was instrumental in converting 500 robbers in *samgha* who tried to sacrifice him.[43] The *Theragāthā* has a series of verses spoken by Sankicca in praise of the charm of the forests in reply to an *upāsaka* who waited for him and requested him to dwell in the village. Like the monsoon winds drive the clouds in the rainy season, so the thought concerned with insight impels the monks for salvation (*yathā abbhāni verambo vāto nudati pāvuse*).[44] The *bhikkhus* accept the divine spirit of the ocean and all entities, living and non-living, as its waves. Similarly, the monks and Nature are different in appearance but they are interdependent and believe in co-existence. Subhuti, the younger brother of Anathpindika, mastered *Vinaya* and for the *dhyana*, he started living in the dense forest where he developed an insight and attained *nibbāna* on the basis of *mettajhāna*. He was declared the chief of those who lived in remote region and in peace (*aranaviharinam aggo*).[45] Subhuti praises the rain God to come and enhance their power to attain *arahathood*.[46] Annakondanna Thera, from a wealthy family of Donavatthu near Kapilvatthu, was one of the *paññcavaggiyas* and was ordained by the Buddha.[47] The Buddha praised him with the words: *annasi vata bho Kondanno*, so he came to be known as Annata Kondanna.[48] Because of rain, the flowers bloom along the rivers and drizzling of the rain, the dark night, and the lonely and sublime forests are considered ideal for the meditation and to attain *nibbāna*. The monks share their happiness and experiences of Nature just as the buds after blossoming share their fragrance with all.[49] Sometimes the natural surroundings also preach lesson to the nuns or the monks. Ubbiri, born in the rich family of Savatthi became insane when her daughter Jiva died and later she was preached by the Buddha who told her that at the same burial ground 84,000 of her daughters all named jīvā had been burnt. She thus learnt about the impermanence and joined the order of the Buddha.[50] Punnika Therī, a slave girl in the house of Anāthpindika, heard the *Sihanada Sutta* one day and became *Sotapañña*.[51] She also converted brāhman Sotthiya to Buddhism.

The *Theragāthā* and *Therīgāthā* exhibit that for the monks and nuns, Nature is a power, a motion, a spirit, a guide, and a philosopher which lead them to the infinite and towards the *nibbāna* permeating and preserving all the Universe. They are not the intruders of the natural resources but a devotee who searches for motivation and spirituality for the attainment of the *arahanthood*. Their adoration and regard for the forests, hills, rivers, flowers, etc., encourages the harmonious co-existence, vitality, and interdependence with the Nature. The *bhikkhus* and *bhikkhunis* found aesthetic sensibility, experience, and pleasure in the natural surroundings. They irresistibly draw themselves towards Nature as they realize natural beauty in perfection, abundance, and infinite multiplicity. The analytical and evaluative considerations relating to Nature establish distinct character which has been a stamp of Nature that comes to fore impressively at certain stage. It also preludes to a notable ethical dimension about positive mindset for planet Earth. It is also to ponder over that what can be adhered, is not only the elements related to classic evaluation of forest, hills, and rivers, but a striking delineation of the expressive transition in the consciousness which evolves at stage of novice and transformed to the spiritually attuned one. The recitation of natural elements is clearly the most important and consistently encountered features in the utterance of the *Therīgāthā* and the *Theragāthā*. It does not offer discourses or disquisitions on Buddhist view on Nature, but rather insights into Buddhism as practiced through subjective appropriation by the committed *bhikkhus* and *bhikkhunis*. These are texts which give holistic appreciation on emphatic understanding of the Buddha's view. The *gāthās* deserve recognition as one of the oldest religious reflective documents whose authors contributed immensely without any planned way of writing. The use of poetic craftsmanship to inculcate charming Buddhist sensitivity to environmental ethics indeed became admirable in *gāthās*. It would be optimistic to observe that the clash and contest between the spiritual commitment and worldly urgings that figures frequently in the *Theragāthā* and the *Therīgāthā* have been indicating positive notion for co-existence and environment-friendly ethics.

Notes

1. *Saṃyutta Nikāya*, IV.306ff. (The corresponding texts in Sanskrit are also mentioned as the *Sthaviragātha* and *Sthavirigatha*, Etienne Lamotte, *Historie du bouddhisme indien: Des Origins a lere Saka*, Bibliotheque du Museon, 43, Louvian: Universite de Louvain, 1958, pp. 177–8).
2. *Theragāthā*, V.1091.

3. Ibid., V.1108.
4. Ibid., V.41.
5. *Anguttar Nikāya*, I.23; *Majjhima Nikāya*, I.347, 354.
6. *Saṃyutta Nikāya*, II.205.
7. *Theragāthā*, VV.1060–5, 1082–5.
8. *Aṅguttara Nikāya*, I.25; *Dhammapadaṭṭakathā*, II.217ff.
9. *Theragāthā*, VV.107–11.
10. Ibid., VV.48-50.
11. *Manorathapūraṇī*, I.140f; *Dhammapadaṭṭakathā*, IV.118f. [*Therīgāthā Commentary* says that after his dismissal he lived on Gijjhakuta but could not attain *jhāna* because of his emotional nature (*saddha*). The Buddha visited him and uttered a verse to encourage him; *Theragāthā Commentary*, I.420; Vakkali recited four verses in reply, which won him arahanthood. The Buddha declared him foremost among those of implicit faith (*saddhadhimuttanam*); *Aṅguttara Nikāya*, I.25; *Divyavadāna*, 49.]
12. *Theragāthā*, VV.350–354.
13. Ibid., VV.645–8.
14. Ibid., V.13.
15. *Aṅguttara Nikāya*, I.24.
16. *Dhammapadaṭṭakathā*, II.188ff.
17. *Theragāthā*, V.50.
18. *Therīgāthā*, VV.366–99.
19. *Aṅguttar Nikāya*, I.24; *Dīpavamsa*, V.9.
20. *Saṃyutta Nikāya*, IV.145–7.
21. *Theragāthā*, V.2.
22. Ibid., VV.537–46.
23. Ibid., V.18.
24. Ibid., VV. 626–31.
25. Ibid., VV.330–4.
26. Ibid., VV.700–1.
27. Ibid., VV.991–2.
28. Ibid.. VV.1013–14.
29. Ibid., VV.1062–6.
30. Ibid., VV.1100–2.
31. Ibid., VV.231–3; Matangaputta Thera in his poetry criticizes the persons who seek excuses because of extreme seasons, etc. He says that those people who complain that it is too cold or too hot or too late in the evening to shirk from their assigned work are not to obtain knowledge. The persons who accept it as a mere futile grass are capable enough for arahanthood (*Dabbam kusam potakilam usīram muñjababbajaṃ urasā pondudissāmi*).
32. Ibid., VV.243–5.
33. Ibid., V.7.

34. Ibid., V.22.
35. Ibid., VV.1116–18.
36. Ibid., VV.173–4.
37. Ibid., V.113.
38. Ibid., V.49.
39. Ibid., VV.355–9.
40. Ibid., VV.193–4.
41. Ibid., VV.429–34. (Anotatta is one of the seven great lakes of Himalaya, the other being Kannamunda, Rathakāra, Chaddanta, Kunāla, Mandākinī, and Sihappapata. It is surrounded by five mountain peaks, viz., Sudassanakūta, Citrakūta, Kālakūta, Gandhamadana, and Kelāsa. All the rains that fall on the five peaks and all the rivers that rise in them flow into lake. The light of the sun and the moons falls only in reflections on the lake. Four channels open out in the direction of the four quarters: Sīhamukha, Hatthimukha, Assamukha, and Usabhamukha. *Aṅguttara Nikāya,* IV.101; *Suttanipāta,* I.66; II.407.)
42. Ibid., VV.527–9.
43. *Dhammapadaṭṭakathā,* II.240ff.
44. *Theragāthā,* VV.597–8.
45. *Aṅguttara Nikāya,* I.24.
46. *Theragāthā,* V.1.
47. *Manorathapūraṇī,* I.78–84.
48. *Vinaya Pitaka,* I.12.
49. Ibid., VV.522–6.
50. *Therīgāthā,* VV.51–3.
51. *Papañcasudanī,* I.347.

7

Ecology, Economy, and Buddhism

With the fructification of globalization various centrifugal and centripetal forces to regulate and determine world economics also emerged from its hibernation. The world is enlightened that globalization of economy is not only a heavenly boon but also have some thorny issues. It does ensure free flow of capital, technology, scientific innovations, albeit not without poverty, conflict, and discrimination. Since the Neolithic Age, *Homo sapiens* monopolized the resources of the Earth in the name of satisfying their needs. When these needs transformed from subsistence to industrialization, it also leads to destruction of forest, growing population, drying up of the rivers, melting of glaciers, and global warming. It has been argued that traditional religions are less significant and in today's world most valuable asset is consumerism. The market economy, in fact, is rapidly assimilating the globe into a common thread with consumerism as its dominant value system. David R. Loy says,

Market is becoming the truly world religion, binding all corners of the globe more and more tightly into a worldview and set of values whose religious role we overlook only because we insist on seeing them as 'secular'. So it is no coincidence that our time of ecological catastrophe also happens to be a time of extraordinary challenge to more traditional religions. Although it may offend our vanity, it is somewhat ludicrous to think of conventional religious institutions as we know them today serving a significant role in solving environmental crisis. . . . The result is that up to now they have been unable to offer what is most needed, a meaningful challenge to the aggressive proselytizing of market capitalism, which has already become the most successful religion of all time, winning more converts more quickly than any previous belief system or value system in human history.[1]

Till the nineteenth century, economics trampled subjects like ecology, moral values, and social ethics. When the world confronted with the modern problems, it is obvious to think about practical ethics recommended in religions to resolve critical economic impasse. Economists themselves started considering environmental factors in economic merchandises and transactions. The questions have been raised about probity and implication of rational thinking in economic production and distribution. Stephanie Kaza informs that much of the deforestation can be traced directly to human population. Ever expanding urbanization leads to loss of species, industrial manufacturing to air pollution, and factory farming to water pollution. Accordingly, the environmental impact can be reciprocal to rapidly rising population and increasingly efficient technology and consumption rate:

I = PAT (Environmental Impact = Population Size × Affluence × Technology)

Much of the debate has been focused on population and affluence with the buoyant optimum that technological innovations will resolve everything. The factors of greed and over-consumption impetuously encouraged by materialistic societies offer little choice to others but to compete. Buddhism has been engaged to develop well-conceived plans to help society to overcome competition for monopolizing the markets and protect emotional security that derives human beings.[2] E.F. Schumacher has considered slogans like 'Small is Beautiful' to lay the foundation for Buddhist Economics.[3] On the other hand, the disillusion caused by modern economics facilitated the concepts of 'Gross National Happiness'[4] and 'Sufficiency Economy'.[5] His majesty Jigme Singye Wangchuck, the king of Bhutan is credited with the coining of the term 'Gross National Happiness' in 1972. He defined development and economic growth in terms of people's happiness. In the growth factors, non-material development has also been counted which ensures improved quality of life. The happiness index has also been counted with other economic variables like production and consumption. The Bhutanese economy tries to balance materialism with spirtitaul factors especially Buddhism. The notion of 'Gross National Happiness' is based on four pillars—Economic Growth and Development, Preservation and Sustainable use of Environment, Preservation and Promotion of Cultural Heritage and Good Governance. In

1997, His Majesty Bhumibol Adulyadej, king of Thailand declared his economic vision 'Sufficiency Economy' which has been deeply influenced by teachings of the Buddha. It stresses self-reliance but does not believe in isolation. Its aim is to immunize the nation and society against internal and external volatility. Economic growth can be used by moderation, rationality, prudence and wisdom. It also encourages harmonious and constructive participation in globalization to optimally utilize appropriate knowledge and resources. It seeks to strengthen the symbiosis and harmony between men and his natural environment.

Contesting Issues

Ernst Friedrich Schumacher was invited to Myanmar as an economic advisor by U Nu when Sixth Synod or *Chattha Sangayana* to rewrite Pāli canons was going on. He pondered over no conflict between Buddhism and economic development and thought that spiritual values could be blended with modern technology for progress. He says that 'Right Livelihood' may be fundamental key to develop economics for well being of society. In developing these ideas his political assignments in Myanmar and wanderings in Myanmar and other South-East Asian nations helped a lot. With his idea of 'Buddhist Economics', Schumacher has earned a number of admirers and critics. He has been blamed for romanticizing the things without adequate planning and also praised to provide a sustainable alternative model. Inspired by Schumacher, Glen Alexandrin recommends 'b-elements', i.e. inculcation of Buddhist virtues in modern economics and economic planning. The 'b-entrepreneurs' will have to produce goods with mass engagement for the benefit of others. It would be called 'meditation in action'.[6] With mixing of Buddhist virtues in Western economic principles, all segments of modern economy like production, human resource, demand, and corporate responsibilities could be rationalized which can be helpful in planning, analysis, and implementation.[7] John B. Cobb, Jr. mentions that renaissance has changed the nature of labour from organic to machines. It transformed the world view of growth because human-induced work has some thought process while machines are operated by mechanical forces. Economists know that *Homo economicus* is an abstraction full of indulgence and appetite where human has been perceived as source of insatiable desires.

It is obvious that neither Buddhism nor Christianity can support this doctrine or the practice that follows from it. Buddhism emphasizes that true life comes from the abandonment of all craving. Our system posits and encourages limitless craving. Christianity sometimes suggests that craving for spiritual goods is desirable, but it gives no support to craving for unneeded material possessions and consumption. There could hardly be a flatter contradiction. The conflict is equally sharp with respect to the economist's view that human beings behave self-interestedly. Buddhists and Christians may agree that there is a strong tendency in this direction. But we deplore this and encourage other tendencies. Economists, on the other hand, call the selfish behaviour they describe 'rational'. They show that rational behaviour leads to greater wealth not only on the part of those individuals who practice it but also in society as a whole. At this point, they tend to forget that wealth is only one of many goods, and that other academic disciplines study some of these other goods. Many of them forget that from the point of view of these other disciplines, human community is a value.[8]

While linking Buddhism and economics, eyebrows have been raised regarding how Buddhism with aloofness from *saṁsāric* activities can resolve contentious economic issues. The modern economics has complex and crystallized principles with special ethical consequences centred on profits and markets. It has been assumed by a number of scholars that Buddhism is some other-worldly religion devoid of all social and material aspects of society. Max Weber hypothesized that Buddhism is apolitical and restricted only to the monk community. It always encourages laities to embrace a wandering life, that of active brotherhood, and leave the mundane world.[9] He says that *nibbanic* tradition of Buddhism is not conducive to society but is hallucinated by the psychic state devoid of any physical activity. Salvation is absolutely an individual performance and the society does not get any help from it. These spiritual practices may culminate in absolute flight from the world and such a contemplative renouncement is characteristic of ancient Buddhism.[10] Melford Spiro says that engagement of monks and nuns are totally out-worldly which is religiously perilous. Even good *kamma* leads to accumulation of merit and rebirth. The true Buddhists are those who abandon all

their social engagements and wander like the rhinoceros.[11] The
Vinaya was mainly for monks and nuns but was scantly applied
too on laities.[12] Ken Jones says that it would be unscholarly to
transfer the scriptural social teaching uncritically and without
careful consideration to modern societies or to announce that
the Buddha was a 'democrat and an internationalist'.[13] Thus,
the scholarly debates and comments about negative description
of Buddhism are nothing but ignorance of the real nature of
early and living tradition of Buddhism since their observations
are based on canonical texts and monastic cultures, rather living
traditions prevalent in India and all parts of Buddhist Asia.
Walpola Rahula says that Buddhism is not a parasitic religion and
it had a significant contribution in shaping the socio-economic
activities.

It is unfortunate that hardly any other section of the Buddha's teaching is so
much misunderstood as 'meditation' both by Buddhist and non-Buddhists.
The moment the word 'meditation' is mentioned, one thinks of an escapist
from daily activities of life, assuming a particular posture, like a statue in
some cave or cell in a monastery, in some remote place cut off from society,
and musing on, or being absorbed in, some kind of mystic or mysterious
thought or trance. True Buddhist meditation does not mean this kind of
escape at all.[14]

Payutto mentions that Buddhism has been described as an
ascetic religion but asceticism has been experimented, evolved
and refined by the Buddha before his enlightenment.[15] Frederic
Pryor also emphasizes that *kammic* strand of Buddhism is more
pragmatic for laities. The Buddha exhorts right from his first
preaching that the middle path is the best way to lead a happy
life and both extreme indulgence and asceticism are painful.[16]
Pryor adds that if seeking of *nibbāna* by maximum share of
population is goal, then planning should be derived for raising
material prosperity so that more monks could join the *saṃgha*.
The interdependence between *bhikkhus* and *upāsakas* will have
some implication which shows some sort of allegiance between
the *nibbānic* and *kammic* strands of Buddhism.[17] Weber reflects
that the characteristics of Buddhism varies from region to region
depending on the cultural milieu and local traditions. It does
not provide rational system of material prosperity and trade.
For them, the world is totally relenquised and it does not believe

in the rationalized ethical transformation of existing conditions necessary to galvanize economy. There was no development towards capitalism nor even any string in this direction.[18] Pryor counters Weber's idea that the later only emphasized on the monastic strand of Buddhism. If he might have examined tradition of laities, he must have discovered quite a different side of economic and social facets of Buddhism. Business and capital accumulation together with earning of merit by lay people have been the main features of Buddhism. Zen Buddhism, which has a wider impact on Japan has never restrained the capitalist economy of the Japanese society. Nevertheless, the relationship between 'other-worldly Buddhism' and socio-economic institutions are much more complicated than what Weber perceived.[19] Pryor examines that canonical literature could supply few guidelines in highly complicated and impersonal economic complexities but traditional doctrine could be extrapolated to meet the new situations and demands. It requires creation of small, interactive communities having considerable self-sufficiency without any class struggle and socio-economic discrimination. Buddhism ponders over inherent defects in capitalism vis-à-vis communism and argues that the doctrine of middle path could be drawn up as a possible new face of economy. It will help to balance between extreme materialism and penurial poverty which are the opposite but truth of modern world. Though lack of direct injection on economic affairs give opportunity to some scholars to call Buddhist economics incredibly naive but it his high time to seek some cogency between economic policies and religion.[20] Payutto questions if the concept of Buddhist economics exists because conceptual framework to define economy is Western; although some Buddhist perspectives must be incorporated in economics. The Buddhist economics is not considered to be a self-conceited science but a mix of a number of interdependent disciplines working to evolve a protective environment and welfare society.[21] Buddhism offers considerable insight into economic system and institutions but adoption of these insights flourish if one follows it as a 'practice' rather than purely theoretical or ethical.[22] With floating of ideas like 'Buddhist Economics', and 'Sufficiency Economy', etc. suspicions have been felt about its viability and efficacy. Can such models efficient and sufficient to provide alternative solutions to shuffle or replace the existing economic structure. If global economics embrace virtues of Buddhist economics then it will be a retrograde step or a looking forward to advancement. Is 'Buddhist Economics' helped in the growth of Myanmar? Is Bhutan really progressing under patronage and surveillance of 'Gross National Happiness'? How 'Sufficiency Economy' helped Thailand? The universal effectiveness and applicability of such models at global level is a big issue. The world is grappling with danger of consumerism and global warming, hence it will be a test for these models how they can rejuvenate the global society. The emphasis should be on effective use of canonical and non-canonical literature to prepare guidelines for effective economic growth and mutual co-existence between biotic and abiotic.

Needs and Coexistence

Earth is governed on the principles of maximization of profit and the planet is bearing the pain since the Industrial Development. Mankind is potent enough to do subtle damage to the Earth and she is not able to sustain the hazardous impact of it. The understanding of planetary ecology is not good enough to human beings who are outreaching its limit.[23] Sooner or later, the Earth is going to respond. Economics cannot be separated from other disciplines. It searches new paradigm of thought and methodology to restrict rampant consumerism and check environmental repercussions. Recent ecological happenings give thought that economics is not in touch with magnitude of causes and conditions that prelude to reality. It overemphasizes the basic economic segments like market, investment, consumer, pricing, but lacks the ideal vision of co-existence. Materialism formed the foundation on which modern economics operates and in this, various forces work closely. The foundation was laid during Industrial Revolution when tenets of free trade and Capitalism were propounded. Soon dialectical materialism was presented to oppose free capital regime. However, both the systems failed to understand the real demand of people. In this rapidly-changing age of globalization, the fundamental productive forces and environment as well as nuclear energy, chemical discoveries, pesticides, medical researches, etc., have changed the nature of the world. So models of socio-economic system should be adopted in consideration of these inventions and transitory conditions.[24] Schumacher observes that the present economic system is based on discriminatory measures of consumption rate and productive pattern. The acquisition of wealth is the highest form of virtue and money is considered to be the most powerful. It requires no justification and sometimes mutilates the self and Nature.[25] It has been argued that his views on Buddhist economics has opened new vistas for individual and society to imbibe the ideology and process for an effective state economy by applying the teachings of the Buddha.[26] Schumacher sees fundamental difference between modern economics and economics oriented by Buddhist ideals. In modern economics output is based on automation sources minimizing the human labour. The opportunity depends on specialization and paid in respect of monetary values. While economics oriented by Buddhism facilitates production involving masses, here the production is concerned with human progress rather than profit. This process is not aloof from machines but utilize it in proper manner to harness man's energy and provide them opportunity for their social engagements and leisure.[27] Schumacher was influenced by teachings of the Buddha who endorsed that all sentient beings are interdependent and orderly relation among them could be maintained with *metta* and *śila* and one should follow ideals of middle path.[28] He recommends the use of industries for the good of people and their proper engagement than to encourage cutthroat completion and conflict.[29] Modern economists consider consumption to be the sole end and that the purpose of all economic activities is to maximize human satisfaction by the optimal pattern of consumption. It is not oriented towards employment-generation or to fulfil the basic needs of the people. Buddhist economics tries to maximize consumption by optimal pattern of productive efforts. It can be encouraged from local resources for local requirement by maintaining less dependency on imports from far off areas. Modern economics also does not distinguish between renewable and non-renewable sources of energy and is accounted for profit only. Buddhist economics recommends ecologically sound practices for the use of resources and follow restrain in using the non-renewable sources of energy and opt for renewable sources of energy.[30]

The neoliberal capitalism endorses maximization of profit at the expense of human values and environmental sustainability. The multinational corporations or 'Transnational Tyrannies' have monopolized two-third of world trade and have become creators of the universe by possessing special rights and privileges. Their capitalist zeal treats environment as a sub-system of capitalism 'hence it is to be reaped in order to lubricate the wheels of the capitalist machine' with an insatiable desire for profit, perpetuating to greed, hatred, moral turpitude, and negligence towards environment.[31] The globalization of economy has also led to social and cultural crisis, poverty, and powerlessness in some pockets of the world. It has eroded the traditional community structure and accelerated the depletion of natural resources[32] The Third World economies have virtually succumbed to intensive consumerism mainly those produced by the transnational corporations. People have been induced to abandon their traditional way of life and culture evolved over thousands of years and most suitable to their local conditions and environment. The labourers are compelled to sacrifice their services at low wages in the name of industrialization. The peasantry has been displaced for the sake of large infrastructure projects. The people are taught to compete and indulge in excessive consumerism which encourages greed, violence, and delusion in the society. It is the globalization of *tanhā* or craving. It may be craving for the gratification of passions or eternity or for the success. The vast chunk of the population who are lured by the consumer oriented mercantilism will never have the means to acquire the commodities portrayed to them. So they consider themselves inferior, alienated, and culturally backward. The globalization brings about certain groups of people who are not currently capable of coping with the increased competitive pressure to compete with the rest of the world. With economic hegemony, the dominant nations control the political institutions and economy of the dependent nations who need their financial and economic support. In such bondage leads to enormous debts and erosion of traditional institution for the underdeveloped nations. At such circumstances new secular institutions preloaded with new social and cultural values have emerged. Due to the presence of industrialized market economy, traditional, social, and economic structure based on agrarian economy has been jeopardized. Buddhist world view has tried to transform itself by accommodating modern socio-economic values. It paves the way to prepare ground for not to succumb to the wrath of Modernization and Westernization.[33] The principle of interdependence may be a positive step aimed at curbing this deep rooted problem. It encourages the principle of equality and justice together with the rule of law for all nations. The *paticcasamuppada* explains that every existing thing is both conditional and that nothing can exist independently.[34] It recognizes the existing reality of a thing, a person, or a nation. It always tends to make a greatly united world in which all the people regardless of nation, religion, culture, etc., can co-exist and live independently and harmoniously. In the context of globalization, the interdependence also means that whatever principles, policies, and actions taken should have positive impact. The Buddhist teachings on non-discrimination and equality are related to this understanding. It recognizes the complexity of causation that produces conflicts and suffering and clarifies the issues that leads to reconciliation and solution to the problems.[35] The mindset of the Buddha was to establish equalitarian ethos which could cut across the tribalism and the distinction of race or religion. He asserts that lineage does not enter into man's being either good or bad, nor good look or wealth.[36] It provides a new way of thinking for current situation and act as potential and competent force for the process of globalization to cope with international competitiveness and challenges to meet global demand as well as develop cooperative working environment. Sulak Sivaraksa coined "small 'b' Buddhism" signifying Buddhist doctrine with transformative relevance and pragmatic methodology to engage with contemporary problems and their solutions. He argues suffering are incorrigible human tendencies about consumerism, materialism, and unwarranted possessions which are threatening the world. He visualizes that short term political and economic gain are creating chaos and suffering which can only be stopped with mindfulness and rational thinking. For it, he uses 'b' in place of 'B' for Buddhism to emphasize changed vision of Buddhism to counter self-conceited ideas engulfing the world.[37]

The economy oriented by consumerism always encourages new desires and demands among people. All such demands accentuates to suffering by causing frustration as their desire for lasting, and wholly-satisfying fulfilments are constantly disturbed by the changing and ever-producing world while the human mindset always wants things to be other than what they currently have. They also embolden to act on the various acts whose results lead to further disturbing situations and suffering.[38] Buddhist ideals constantly put forth that the society is based on reasoning, moderation, and harmony, a constant awareness of the primacy of Buddhist teaching, charity as a way of life, compassion, and wisdom. Buddhist virtues can encourage the making of co-operative societies with need-based, sustainable economies rather than greed-oriented profit market economies.[39] The society is a community of righteousness anywhere and everywhere uncensored by the rules of regional or national affiliation. It can be developed on *vissāsa* (mutual trust and cooperation in place of conflict and acquisitiveness), *ahasa* (non-violence), *samata* (equality of all human beings), etc. The Buddha says that who does not wish for his own prosperity by unfair means is wise, virtuous, and religious. The ideal society envisaged by the Buddha foresees that the State has the responsibility to wipe out discrimination and ensure the full employment for all sections of society. It repudiates a vision of future based on the notion of progress as an unlimited growth leading eventually to destructive consumerism, and strives for a just world order which will end hegemony and all other forms of hostilities. The role of *dhamma* here is to act as a custodian of moral and cultural values and to be an all-pervasive force. The growing economic interdependence, increased cultural reciprocation, rapid advancement in information technology, and geopolitical challenges are binding people and the biosphere more tightly in a single global system. This process also sprouts differences everywhere fuelled by regional and ethnic diversities and disparities. The ideological and religious conflict is taking a heavy toll on human lives. The *dhamma* preaches that greediness is the worst of disease and the contentment is the greatest wealth and trust is the best of relationship. It gives the notion of desirability of evolving a culture prelude to modern social, economic, and administrative institutions, and formulates the most consistent theory of human suffering known to mankind. The underdevelopment within a nation is characterized not only by the production of pseudo-values and non-values but also by mal-distribution of genuine credentials. The over-consumption by the privileged classes goes hand in hand with under-consumption by the masses.[40] The materialism is engulfing each and every society of the world and is eroding their vibrant cultural values. In a globalized world, to gain wealth, power, and to fulfil the insatiable sensual pleasure through undesirable means are becoming the most domineering values. The sustainable and traditional patterns are apparently fast changing. In the east, the traditional joint family structure is on the verge of collapse and is being replaced by the nuclear family structure. The monoculture of globalization has been promoting a system totally at odd with the existing values of the traditional societies. It encourages to negative direction of *kamma* leading to unemployment, disintegration of traditional family, community structure, and imbalance in ecosphere. When the society is facing such kind of difficulties motivated by unwholesome and evil roots, it will loose the healthy structure and will not be able to survive. Buddhism states such implications. The approval or disapproval of policies is to articulate the voice of the people, a nation has to make a serious effort to carve out both an alternative vision of the modern society and an indigenous path leading to it. The much of traditional knowledge and expertise have been lost in the name of modernity and science, depriving common people everywhere of help in the time of need.

Idealism and Pragmatism

Buddhist canonical literature mentions state as a patron and the king is head for the prosperity of the people. The Buddha saw no virtue in poverty and it is an impediment in the realization of truth.[41] It is this underlying principle which has been expressed in so many forms from the canonical literature to *Jātakas*, culminating in fixed maxim that the king is the head of the people, for their welfare. The aim of the state was to secure peace, material prosperity, facilitation of trade, protection of guilds, trade routes, etc. The Buddha was a great believer in economic and political wisdom who believed that economic greatness of the country is inherent in just and egalitarian policies. Human progress and economic development are the creation of circumstances and the right attitude of human being. The *Cakkavati Sihanada Sutta* says that the king must maintain a moral life for prosperity of the state and the subject. The king is duty-bound to remove poverty and maintain prosperity.[42] The *Kutadanta Sutta* instructs the king to eradicate corruption and protect his citizens. The security and prosperity of his subjects is the most important concern for the king.[43] The *Jātakas* inform abundant accounts of information on economic affairs. They present a systematic and exhaustive account of every aspect of economic life of people centred around domestication, agriculture, and trade. The *Dhammapadatthakathā* informs about the great *Uttarapatha* (great northen route) connecting Vārānasī and Takshaśila.[44] The *Sankha Jātaka* mentions trade voyages between Vārānasī and Suranabhumi.[45] The *Sudhabhojana Jātaka* alludes to merchants going across the sea with a hope to earn immense fortune.[46] Even certain marketing practices like pricing, haggling, etc., have also been mentioned in the *Jātakas*.[47] The State policies could be best exhibited in the welfare administration of Aśoka. His forefathers, under the genius of Kautilya, combined administration and welfare economics. The second was a corollary from first, so policy was directed to keep and develop the *varta* or national economy. To secure the economic prosperity of country, the people should be treated with particular attention and solicitude. His Separate Rock Edicts mention his policy of welfare governance in which he calls his subjects as his children (*sava-munā me pajā*).[48] He also planted trees on roadside, opened hospitals, and dug well at regular intervals *(duve chikisakā katā manusāchikisā chā pasu-chikisā chā, ... magesu lukhāni lopitāni udupānāni chā khānāpitani paṭibhogāye pasu-munisānaṃ).*[49] His policies were continued in later ages where the Kushanas, the Śakas, and the Indo-Greeks followed his policies and patronized their trade and commerce. It was not only in India but in the whole of Buddhist Asia, that the respective kings developed and followed economic policies for the progress and welfare of their country. The long span of peace and prosperity also developed the long standing monk-laity relationship in these regions. The monks reciprocated to subject by preaching and perpetuating moral policies guided by Buddhist ideals. Because of *dhammadāna* by the monks, the laities progress and ideal reciprocation between monk and laity inculcates virtue of prosperity and growth. Similarly, the king patronized monasteries by showering benevolence and ensuring material prosperity and trade.[50] Western model of economy has been criticized for too much counting on consumption and expenditure. If the attitude towards ecosystem is not changed, then human will be deprived from its own existence.[51] It is practically difficult to wipe out consumerism from this world but more moderate life could be offered as an alternative solution. It would mean to endure some form of employment in the name of economic development.[52] Buddhism supports full employment for everyone with considering maximization of employment or production. It would be a great departure from Buddhist tradition if too much emphasis is given on production and profit in place of human dignity and welfare.[53] Buddhist radiation principle ensures growth of economy through collective *dhammic* efforts of individuals. It is in sharp contrast to Adam Smith's economics which is individualistic in nature. It has been perceived that economy with egalitarian and non-discriminative ethos could be practiced through *dhammic* action and Buddhist teachings like *Brahma Vihāra* can play pivotal role in it.[54] Buddhadasa Bhikkhu speaks about *Dhammic Socialism* to cure evils of consumerism and discrimination. It conceives co-existence of mankind, animals, plants, and other ecological beings.[55] Buddhadasa Bhikkhu further says that birds consume as much as their stomach allow and can not hoard because they do not maintain granaries. Ants and insects eat to fill their appetite and trees absorb up their necessity. Nobody tries to transgress other's right or hoard what does not belong to them. All this is controlled by Nature and a form of natural socialism.[56] Schumacher says that Right Livelihood is one of the basic tenets of his noble eightfold path indicating that there is something like the Buddhist economics. It suggests to impart an individual a chance to utilize and develop his faculties to overcome his ego hassles for togetherness and co-existence. Also, leisure as an alternative to work is also not considered good since they should be complimentary to each other.[57] The Buddhist way of non-consumer attitude could be of a little help to restrain accelerating exhaustion of natural resources. *The paticcasamuppada* takes on a more inner scope to curtail the desires rather than more conditioning of consciousness. Nothing exists beyond Nature and whatever is associated with Nature cannot be separated. The controlling and conquering of Nature are fallacy. It should be treated as to be a determinant within cause and effect process. Mankind has no innate energy to create, independent of natural causes. It is a process of recognizing the factors required to manipulate a cause. Humankind's knowledge and action are an additional factor for natural process. The best way is to be friendly with Nature by realizing interdependence in both the physical and mental sense.[58] The teachings of the Buddha has been embedded in awareness of removal of self-centred confusion and craving. The *tanha* could be adequately understood as psychological drive that shows themselves in subjective state of anguish and these drives are imposed in the very economic structure that affect the lives of the majority of the people of the Earth.[59] Pryor discusses *anatta* in a different way, endorsing that though the self does not exist, the present understanding of *atta* (self) is cause of individual's separation from Nature. The self-conceited desire is transitory and accentuates selfishness and greed.[60] Stephanie Kaza says that human desires are infinitely soaring and there are numerous ways to succumb to their demand by creating new products.

The ideology of consumerism serves perhaps as the carrier virus, attaching to hosts whose immune resistance is weakened by colonialism, bankruptcy, malnutrition and war. The cause of this disease is craving or desire which broadly falls into three types, otherwise known as three poisons. The first, desire 'for sense pleasure' or greed is the cornerstone of marketing psychology. Advertisements urge consumers to increase their greed in as many arenas as possible; international trade negotiations do their best to open up markets overseas to further spread the competitive craving of greed. The second poison, the desire 'to get rid of' or aversion/hatred is equally central to marketing strategy. Pest control products get rid of hatred insects . . . consumers readily believe they will be happy if they can just get rid of the things they don't want. The third type is the desire 'to become' ignorance/delusion. This refers to deluded thinking that existence can somehow become other than what it actually is . . . All three poisons . . . to endless suffering, all to the profitable well-being of those who can take advantage of this.[61]

Sivaraksa says that Buddhist teachings can be moulded to manifest new ideas, like five precepts, of killing, intoxication, lying, stealing, and adultery in a different manner. Modern agriculture and use of chemical fertilizers and pesticides may kill rich micro-organism and deforestation for industrialization and the agrarian expansion may lead to loss of many kinds of biotic and abiotic species. In a similar way, radioactive nuclear wastes could destroy the whole human race. He further says that the application of *Brahama Vihāra* could be helpful to transform our economic and ecological visions. The right view could be initiated by *karuna* and *mudita*. The increasing disparities between rich and poor could be addressed not only by public action but also by compassionate action imbibed by society itself. The Buddhist virtues of *metta* and *upekkha* can develop indifference to success or failure.[62] The 1998 World Watch Report shows loss of forests directly linked to explosive growth in global consumption of paper and wood products. With almost half of the Earth's forest cover exploited, the demand is further increasing. Each year 16 million hectares are wiped out for wood products or agriculture. Habitat loss means loss of species and other organism. Without adequate sources of food, water, shelter, and reproduction sites, many animal species are on the verge of extinction.[63] Buddhism floats the idea before the society is general applicability cutting across the divisive tendencies and provide social adhesive to fuse the diverse ethnic cultural elements into harmonious social groups based on certain homogeneous and egalitarian principles. Environmental factors are considered both in economic transactions and in solving economic crisis, and the need of ethics in addressing the problems of conservation and the environment is becoming more and more apparent. This has led many economists to rethink about isolated specialized approach of economics. Modern engaged Buddhism with its value-loaded elements of generosity, compassion, and wisdom can comprehend social action and vision with radically imbibed tenets of contemporary sources and environmental virtues. The assimilation of Buddhist tenets with existing ecological thoughts could pave the way for more congenial way of living and development based on contentment rather than self-perpetuating desires.[64] The serious environmental repercussions of rampant consumerism have compelled economists to develop more ecological awareness. Buddhist virtues could be applied on values of goods, services, consumption production, pricing, and marketing. Here curtailment of *taṇha* and corresponding increase in *chanda* is more desirable. Consumption and economic wealth are necessary but not the goals in themselves. It should be treated merely as a foundation for human development and enhancement of quality of life.[65] Capitalism with its motive of maximizing the profit has caused economic, social, and ecological havoc not only in developing economies but also in the developed ones. Stephanie Kaza mentions:

women going blind over microscopes to make computer chips in Malaysia, boys crippled in carpet factories in Pakistan, banana workers sterilized by pesticides exposure in Costa Rica—the web is thick with suffering. Almost no act of consumption today does not involve some means of human or environmental abuse. To act ethically within this web is great challenge for both individuals and institutions. But incentive is for greater to act economically, i.e. for profit. This is the point where religious tradition can make a critical contribution, perhaps the very effort needed to turn the tide.[66]

Buddhism attempts to develop an economic model based on Buddhist virtues in retaliation of exploitative and destructive capitalist economic structure.[67] With its doctrine of middle path, it draws proper attention to avoid general materialism, spiritual sickness, and brings in the vision of an alternative society. Its moral content has been exemplified by the noble eightfold path in the particular context of right action and right livelihood. The major task is to differentiate and identify what parts of canon should be considered to construct models for modern economics. It accepts innovation and change in economics but not with a purpose to annihilate his opponents or accumulate abundance of wealth. Its intention is to derive mechanism for equal opportunity to all in terms of resources, opportunity, and rights. Buddhism is not averse to material prosperity but emphasizes on egalitarian views.[68] Parameters of modern economics could not be directly found in Buddhist scriptures because society and economy of the early India was quite different from modern age. The re-establishing faith and elasticity in economic system is only possible with change in values. Social values are the guiding force for science and technology, paradigm shift from hegemony and competition to cooperation and conservation, and from accumulation of wealth to inculcation of inner growth.[69] Buddhist virtues can be ushered in the system which believes less or no role of religion in economic pursuits. It will be taking cognizance of the right way of development—a middle path between hedonism and sustainability. It will begin conscious and systematic channel of planning and development that can be termed as 'intermediate technology'.[70] The restructuring of social values to be aware and moderate will transform attitude to be more environmentally sustainable and progressive. Understanding of nature to recognize its limitation will be more beneficial for achieving tranquility and forbearance. Contemplative action and meditation can also overcome deafening ideology of consumerism. The impact of suffering due to consumerism could be controlled by meditation and mindfulness and transformed into the state of equanimity. It is a psychological and metaphysical tool to create a space where visualization of distress could be coped with.[71] Buddhist virtues can facilitate four levels of freedom. These are indispensable—peace and happiness, physical freedom, social freedom, and emotional and intellectual freedom. The first may be related to the material world and physical environment which could absolve from paucity of basic needs. Social freedom covers freedom from violence, oppression, and exploitation. Emotional freedom saves a person from mental defilement and other forms of suffering. It can provide pure and peaceful mind, and finally intellectual freedom can be achieved through knowledge and wisdom. Buddhism also endorses right view on objectivity of mechanization and believes in mechanization which enhances skills and power but not enslaving the human being.[72]

Paticcasamuppada was the weapon of the Buddha which is sure to be effective under all challenging situations. Modern economics does not possess anything that can be viewed as decisively effective in all challenging situations. It is besieged with numerous problems, deficiencies, and defects, in relation to its capacity to handle human component of *samsāric* actions—the key ingredients of environmental crisis. The principle of interdependence gives methodology and tool to motivate sustainable development when humankind goes through depression and delusion on account of non-satisfaction. The

Buddha's mission was to incarnate responsibilities to deliver message to solve problems which has troublesome invincibility. The influence and impact of long-term economic evil and its wicked manifestation has been the main cause of human suffering. Here Buddhist virtues can be instrumental to frame rules and reform the shortcomings in addition to direct cleansing action. The traditional canonical and non-canonical teachings could be transformed and re-adjusted into a formidable fighting force in support of righteous and virtuous causes which profusely stress the significance of clearly-set objectives. The population is one aspect where the principle of interdependence can be properly utilized. The excessive growth in population is a burden for Earth and if it has rapid increase then there is fair chance of growth of consumerism and materialism because the catchment area of goods and services will be automatically increased. The other factor is if population growth is stabilized in coherence with the existing death rate, then there will be less pressure on resources. Infrastructure and awareness are two factors for growth and decline of population growth rate. In some of the developed nations with best infrastructures, there is negative growth rate of population because people are not willing to extend their families but at the same time some nations encourage for higher birth rate for utilization of better human capital resources. Similarly in poor countries higher birth rate are desired because children are considered as means to earn livelihood and because of high infant mortality rate. There are numerous other factors for population growth depending on geographical and economic necessities and if we are able to examine the real cause of such growth rate then population can be stabilized within stipulated time without any disproportionate distribution of population and it will help to sustain natural resources for future generation.

The doctrine of *kamma* extols the preferability of right action which leads to the essentiality of upholding *dhamma* in arena of economic affairs and righteous governance. Modern economy as matter of its competitive nature, remains in mode of perpetual change. In the turbulence of adverse conditions, Buddhism could attempt for new capabilities and modalities based on flexibility and responsiveness. Despite all the modern facilities, the world has failed to respond to the challenges of Nature. A perusal of life and teaching of the Buddha brings to light numerous instances which confirms that his perpetual experiments and thinking always strived for getting right answers for complex problems of the world which increase suffering. The missionary agenda that he had drawn was with a motive to encounter peoples suffering. The competitive and dynamic economic vibrancy is fair but it needs to shed what is harmful and avoidable and acquire what is discernable in pursuance of its specific objectives. The judicious and rewarding means of *brahma vihāras* can be greatly helpful to neutralize the present crisis, and *paticcasamuppada* is extremely pragmatic and approachable to counter the evil forces of Māra arriving in the form of global warming and acid rain, even 2,500 years after *mahāparinibbāna* of the Buddha.

Notes

1. David R. Loy, 'The Religion of the Market', *Journal of the American Academy of Religion*, Summer 1997, pp. 275–90, see pp. 275–6, <http://www.jstor.org/stable/1965766>.
2. Stephanie Kaza, 'Overcoming the Grip of Consumerism', *Buddhist-Christian Studies*, vol. 20, 2000, p. 23.
3. E.F. Schumacher, *Small is Beautiful: Economics as if People Mattered*, New York: Harper and Row, 1975, p. 246.
4. Ananda W.P. Gurge, 'Buddhist Economics—Myth and Reality', *Hsi Lai Journal of Humanistic Buddhism*, 2006, pp. 116–17.
5. Ibid., pp. 119–20.
6. Glen Alexandrin, 'Buddhist Economics: Demand and Decision Making', *The Eastern Buddhist*, n.s., vol. XXI, no. 2, 1988, pp. 36–53.
7. Alexandrin, 'Elements of Buddhist Economics', *International Journal of Social Economics*, vol. XX, no. 2, 1993, pp. 3–11.
8. John B. Cobb, Jr., 'A Buddhist-Christian Critiques of Neo-Liberal Economics', <http://www.smallisbeautiful.org/pdf/buddhist_economics/english.pdf>.
9. Max Weber, *The Religion of India: The Sociology of Hinduism and Buddhism*, New York: The Free Press, 1958, pp. 205–8.
10. Max Weber, *Sociology of Religion*, London: Lowe & Brydone, 1966, pp. 213, 266–7.
11. Melford E. Spiro, *Buddhism and Society: A Great Tradition and its Burmese Vicissitudes*, London: George Allen & Unwin Ltd., 1971, p. 427.
12. Heinz Bechert, 'Buddhism as Factor of Political Modernization:

The Case of Sri Lanka', in *Religion and Development in Asian Societies*, ed. Friedrich Nauman-Stiftung, Colombo: Marga Publication, 1974, pp. 1–11, see pp. 3–5.

13. Jones, *The Social Face of Buddhism*, pp. 66–7.
14. Walpola Rahula, *What the Buddha Taught*, London: Gordon Frazer, 1959, p. 98.
15. P.A. Payutto, 'Buddhist Economics: A Middle Way for Market Place', chap. IV, Bangkok: Buddhadharma Foundation, 1994.
16. Frederic L. Pryor, 'A Buddhist Economic System in Principle: Non Attachment to Worldly Thing Is Dominant but the Way of the Law Is Held Profitable', *American Journal of Economics and Sociology*, vol. 49, no. 3, July 1990, pp. 339–59.
17. Pryor, 'A Buddhist Economic System in Practice', *American Journal of Economics and Sociology*, vol. 50, no. 1, January 1991, pp. 17–33, see pp. 23–4.
18. Max Weber, *Economy and Society*, Berkeley: University of California Press, 1968, pp. 62–5.
19. Pryor, 'A Buddhist Economic System in Practice', pp. 25–6.
20. Ibid., pp. 28–9.
21. Payutto, 'Buddhist Economics', chap. I, pp. 1–3.
22. Simon Zadek, 'The Practice of Buddhist Economics? Another View', *American Journal of Economics and Sociology*, vol. 52, no. 4, 1993, pp. 433–45, see p. 433, <http:/www.jstor.org/stable/3487468>, accessed on 27 March 2012.
23. Timmerman, 'Western Buddhism and Global Crisis', p. 357.
24. Jan Tinbergen, 'Wise Management for More Human World', in *Solutions for a Troubled World*, ed. Marc Macy, London: Earthview Press, 1987, pp. 56–7.
25. Schumacher, *Small is Beautiful*, pp. 246–7.
26. Padmasri de Silva, *The Search for Buddhist Economics*, Kandy: BPS, 1975, p. 6.
27. Ananda W.P. Guruge, 'Buddhist Economics—Myth and Reality', pp. 72–130, see pp. 74–5.
28. Ibid., p. 86.
29. Ibid., pp. 76–8.
30. E.F. Schumacher, 'Buddhist Economics', *Manas*, vol. XXII, no. 33, August 1969, pp. 1–14, see pp. 3–5, <www.manasjournal.org/pdf>.
31. Sulak Sivaraksha, 'Economic Aspects of Social and Environmental Violence from a Buddhist Perspective', *Buddhist-Christian Studies*, vol. 22, 2002, pp. 47–60, see pp. 47–8, <http://www.jstor.org/stable/1390560>, accessed 23 April 2012.
32. Pracha Hulanuwatr and Janeb Rasbash, *Globalization from a Buddhist Perspective*, Bodhi Leaves, no. 146, Kandy: Buddhist Publication Society, 1998.

33. Swearer, 'Sulak Sivaraksa's Buddhist Vision for Renewing Society', p. 18.
34. S.C. Chatterji and D.M. Dutta, *An Introduction to Indian Philosophy*, Calcutta: Calcutta University Press, 1984, pp. 133–4.
35. Alfred Bloom, *Globalization and Buddhism*, <http://www.shindharmanet. com/wp-content/uploads/2012/pdf/Bloom-Globalization.pdf>, accessed 26 March 2014.
36. *Majjhima Nikāya*, II.179.
37. Swearer, 'Sulak Sivaraksa's Buddhist Vision for Renewing Society', pp. 43, 45.
38. Peter Harvey, 'Buddhist Reflections on "Consumer" and "Consumerism"', *Journal of Buddhist Ethics*, vol. 20, 2013, pp. 334–56, <http://blogs:dickinson.edu/buddhistethics>, accessed 25 March 2014.
39. Stephanie Kaza and Kenneth Kraft, *Dharma Rain: Source of Buddhist Environmentalism*, p. xvii.
40. Sachs Ignacy, 'Development, Maldevelopment and Industrialization of Third World Countries', *Development and Change*, vol. X, no. 4, 1979, pp. 635–46.
41. *Aṅguttara Nikāya*, III.352.
42. *Dīgha Nikāya*, III.62–5.
43. Ibid., I.140–2.
44. *Dhammapadaaṭṭhakathā*, I.10.123.
45. *Jātaka*, no. 442.
46. Ibid., no. 535.
47. Ibid., no. 5.
48. Hultzsch, *Corpus Inscriptionum Indicarum*, p. 113.
49. Ibid., pp. 27–8.
50. Frank E. Reynolds, 'Ethics and Wealth in Theravāda Buddhism: A Study in Comparative Religious Ethics', *Ethics, Wealth and Salvation: A Study in Buddhist Social Ethics*, ed. Russell F. Sizemore and Donald K. Swearer, Columbia, SC: University of South Carolina Press, 1990, pp. 59–76.
51. Richard B. Gregg, *A Philosophy of Indian Economic Development*, Ahmadabad: Navajivan Publishing House, 1958, pp. 140–1.
52. John K. Galbraith, *The Affluent Society*, Hamondsworth, Middlesex: Penguin, 1962, pp. 272–3.
53. Schumacher, 'Buddhist Economics', pp. 2–4.
54. Pryor, 'A Buddhist Economic System in Practice', p. 18.
55. Tavivat Puntarigvivat, 'Buddhadasa Bhikkhu and Dhammic Socialism', *The Chulalongkorn Journal of Buddhist Studies*, vol. 1, no. 2, 2003, pp. 189–207, see pp. 188–9.
56. Buddhadasa Bhikkhu, *Dhammic Socialism*, Bangkok: Interreligious Commission for Development, 1986, pp. 65–6.

57. Schumacher, 'Buddhist Economics', pp. 1–3.
58. J.W. Wikramasinghe, *Has the Apple Not Fallen: Neo-Classical Economics in Buddhist Perspectives*, Colombo: Godage International Publishers, 2010, pp. 202–3.
59. Stephan Batchelor, *Buddhism without Beliefs: A Contemporary Guide to Awakening*, New York: Riverhead Books, 1997, p. 112.
60. Pryor, 'A Buddhist Economic System in Principle', p. 341.
61. Stephanie Kaza, 'Overcoming the Grip of Consumerism', *Buddhist-Christian Studies*, vol. 20, 2000, p. 34.
62. Swearer, 'Sulak Sivaraksa's Buddhist Vision for Renewing Society', pp. 46–8.
63. Lester Brown, Christopher Flavin, Hilary French, and Linda Strake, eds., *The State of the World Report*, New York: W.W. Norton, 1998, pp. 25–6.
64. David Landis Barnhill, 'Good Work: An Engaged Buddhist Response to the Dilemmas of Consumerism', *Buddhist-Christian Studies*, vol. 24, 2004, pp. 55–63, see p. 56, http:/www.jstor.org/stable/4145564, accessed 21 March 2012.
65. Payutto, 'Buddhist Economics', chap. III.
66. Kaza, 'Overcoming the Grip of Consumerism', p. 27.
67. Tavivat, Puntarigvivat, 'Buddhist Economics: A Thai Theravāda Perspective', *World Buddhism: Journal of the World Buddhist University*, no. 1, 2004.
68. Proyer, 'A Buddhist Economic System in Practice', pp. 21–2.
69. Sivaraksa, 'The Religion of Consumerism', pp. 178–90.
70. E.F. Schumacher, 'Industrialization through Intermediate Technology', *Minerals and Industries*, vol. 1, no. 4, Calcutta, 1964.
71. Joanna Macy and Molly Young Brown, *Coming Back to Life: Practices to Reconnect Our lives, Our World*, Gabriola Island, BC: New Society Publishers, 1998, pp. 190–1.
72. Swearer, 'Sulak Sivaraksa's Buddhist Vision for Renewing Society', p. 50.

8

Happy Planet: Buddhist Pedagogy in Globalized Context

The happy planet concedes the notion that humans are part of the natural world and the limited resources of the Earth should not be used to meet their enormous ends and insatiable desires. The economic resources are not meant to be exploited wastefully. The scientists and social thinkers acknowledge that the mechanism to unbridled growth has far-reaching consequences and a dividing line should be drawn to avoid unforeseen happenings. The role of Buddhism in its new *avatāra* is no less vast, as changing demography, growing multicultural societies, and consequent sociocultural exchanges have generated enormous shift not only in congregational life but also in 'living Buddhism'. The realities of rapid economic interdependence and globalization have generated a state of affair which facilitate closer social contact and relationships than ever before. This increased contacts are not only a prelude to reciprocation of ideas and new alliances but also foster conflict and hostility. Every nation is under severe stress due to rising aspirations of people for good life in conjunction with emergence of marginal classes living in the fringes of every metropolitan. Avarice and acquisitive instincts are so high that people are adopting aggressive approach towards the Nature for short-term goals, without thinking its long-term consequences. The globalization and contemporary models of development create fissure between the affluent classes and the poor. Such discriminatory constellations have the potential to intensify divisiveness in contemporary societies and can damage the fragile network of relationship which knit them together.[1] The engaged and environmental landscapes of Buddhism has given due place to its dissenters, mystics, eclectic spiritualists, and restless philosophers. It invigorates the sociocultural milieu of oneness and the manyness and acts like a bridge to cross over from ignorance to knowledge for happy and peaceful living. It is viewed as one of the most important tools to develop the society and raise the living standard of the people. A progressive society imparts knowledge to make people educated and aware. This perspective has always been at the very heart of the Buddha and his teachings. Its recent manifestations could be seen as strengthening of such traditions in the light of contemporary social and economic conditions. There is a close and complex proximity between education, society, economy, and growth. The institution imparting the knowledge has been developed in such a way to facilitate knowledge and skill in terms of earning material prosperity, and a comfortable life without any personal demeanour. It is felt that such system is incompatible as it is measured on scale of money spent on institutions, research grants, placements, and earnings. Despite growing concerns and strategies chalked out by United Nations Social and Economic Council to promote universal respect of human rights and fundamental freedom for all without discrimination of race, sex, language, or religion, it has always been pondered over that universal egalitarianism is a distant dream for any state or nation because it is an ideal condition but any responsible nation must apprise to make its every citizen aware, dutiful, and self-earned. There is, however, a wide scale of discrimination, bias, and prejudice to emphasize the pervasive and critical nature of social inequality woven throughout social institutions as well as embedded within individual consciousness.[2] The pedagogical curriculum must include shared cultural ethos not only for economic well-being but also for safeguarding the Nature.

The alarming situation suggests that such catastrophic calamities are going to be a recurrent phenomenon. The traditional methods involve reforestation programmes, reduction of emissions of green house gases, etc. Only systemic change in human mindset inculcated by school curriculum can be the best solution. It is seen that when the worst natural disaster occurred, people across the region felt devastated and man-made alterations in eco-system have been made responsible for it. Humans are to learn the root causes and remedies of such disasters. The geography of ecological and socio-economic problems runs down the major parts of Asia, Africa, America, and Europe. The frequent drought and flood corridors have been deep bearings due to ill-conceived industrialization strategies. The frequency of cyclones is increasing as the century progresses. The voices for 'jal, jangal, jameen' (water, forest, and land) have been a rallying battle cry in India as small farmers have been marginalized or their land has been encroached by those who are destroying it in the name of the development. It is timidity or lack of awareness among the people to respond the callous approach of the successive governments to abandon the poor and facilitate predatory multinational corporations. These causes lead to declining agricultural production, depleting water resources, destroying nutrients of the soil accompanied by more use of fertilizers and pesticides to further multiply the problem. The modern curriculum trains people to earn and be instrumental in the process of development by contributing in inventions, health, trade, etc., but traditional learning always encourages development and progress with sustainability. Further increase in human population is bound to displace animals, water resources, and forests. The drastically-reduced forest cover will expand deserts, weaken the monsoon, raise the sea levels, and increase temperature between 2 °C and 3 °C in the next hundred years. Aftershocks of the growing population and senseless industrialization have already been noticed in India in the recent decades. The urbanization has been permitted along the rivers without considering the ecological after effects. The recent floods and waterlogging in cities and states like Bihar, Mumbai, Jammu & Kashmir, Delhi, Hardwar, and Chennai suggests that natural water flow of the rivers Koshi, Mithi, Jhelam, Yamuna, Ganga, and Adyar has either been arrested or encroached by large multiplexes, malls, and multistoreyed flats. The natural lakes and ponds surrounding them and sustaining their extra water since centuries have been buried under concrete jungles. Such problems exist everywhere; China, Thailand, and Myanmar are facing regular flood devastations while the Pacific countries and the Indian subcontinent are grappling with increased rate of earth quakes. Countries like Bangladesh and Vietnam are coping with the menace of rising sea level.

In this grim situation the pertinent question here is if the preaching on environmentalism, cutting green house gas emissions, switching from fossil fuels to renewable energy will work or is there an urgent need to change the world view of present economic process. Is it a philanthropy or a renewed effort to earn more profit to industrialize climate research that leads to spending of millions of dollars on planetary geo-engineering? There are apprehension among the scientists for unintended consequences even before starting such experiments. It is said that injecting sulphur into the stratosphere to cool the Earth surface may have disastrous effects on some natural occurrences, like, the South Asian monsoon will be completely killed. All such researches are, however, going to be hypothetical and dangerous as it does not address the root cause of the problem. The continuation of climatic catastrophe may also lead to massive internal and international relocation and dislocation. It will not be easy for nations to open their boundaries to the affected people and will prompt them to militarize their borders and increase surveillance as is happening in the case of migration of Central Asian refugees. Environmental threats have become a potent issue in international peace, security, and order. Environmental dilapidation and its consequences have posed tremendous stress upon politics, economy, and socio-cultural foundations of the society all across the world. This has been frequently causing displacement and migration, and inducing conflict sometimes of protracted nature in several regions of the world. Environmental menace has direct or indirect bearing on political upheaval and socio-economic disequilibrium. If people get displaced in quest of safe and secure condition to protect the vital core of their lives and avert the existential threat, they often tend to take refuge to the location they assume safe. There are two wide-ranging situations prevalent: first, within sovereign territorial boundary when there is systemic (political, economic, and social) robustness absent, structural discrepancies obstinately rooted, and scope for accommodation with rising concerns narrowly plaited, and people are compelled to look beyond their border and migration takes shape of international issue; second, insensitiveness towards transcendental (universal) concerns of the receiving nation-state compel to exhaust extraordinary measures, such as defending the boundaries through beefing up military shield. The second condition appears to be the easiest way out as it leaves no scope for universal concerns such as human rights, protection of life and dignity, and humanity as a whole. In such situation, militarization of border to neglect seer human concerns stemming from environmentally-induced challenges is the most inconsequential measure. This can be resolved by stressing upon profound tenets of Buddhism which gives numerous methods to settle such precarious situations.

Buddhism upholds the principles of cross-cultural unity, respect, and generous handling of sensitive issues related to environment, society and education. It endorses a socio-political doctrine with a pragmatic and distinct theory of man's place and role in the world. It carefully ponders that human societies in a particular socio-economic structure in terms of culturally deriven mechanism of role and status. The Buddhist pedagogical approach provides an alternative to rise above the thought of critical evaluation of its cultural values in comparison to others and accommodates views of different cultures comprising attributes and visions of good life. It helps to expand the moral and intellectual horizon of the society. Buddhism could be of immense help in the growth and strengthening of demographic constitution comprising multitude of races and ethnic group with diverse cultures. Such cultures continuously attempt to bring forth a common identity and consensual charter of interdependence, at the same time it has been strongly advocated that the complete harmony and coexistence among the diverse elements of society would hardly be possible. It has been argued that it is a totally futile exercise to get a normative characteristics of all cultures and religions, and instead to imbibe all in their own terms.[3] People have been excluded from positions of decision-making by putting them aloof either from education or construction of such discriminating standards based on religion, colour, or gender. Such phenomenon is percolating at individual and societal beliefs, behaviours, conscious, and unconscious ethos. It perpetuates implicit and explicit values that bind individuals and institutions, and illustrates that oppression appears in attitude and behaviour at individual and systemic levels. The attitude of individual and society describe the values, beliefs, ethos, and stereotypes that support and justify discrimination. The social identities can include ethnicity, gender, socio-economic status, caste, and religion. In a particular society there may be members of social identities who are disenfranchised, exploited, and victimized while there are some dominant sections of population who take unfair advantage in the society. These dominant groups define the rules, customs, and values which become acceptable to all and at the opposite end, the alienated group is considered deviant and defective. Such features in a society give understanding to learn the dynamics of complexities and alienation, and thus fair treatment and equal access to resources and education to all is absolutely necessary. John Rawls says:

Each person possesses an inviolability founded on justice that even the welfare of society as a whole cannot override. For this reason justice denies that the loss of freedom for some is made right by a greater good shared by others. It does not allow that the sacrifices imposed on a few are outweighed by the larger sum of advantages enjoyed by many. Therefore in a just society the liberties of equal citizenship are taken as settled; the rights secured by justice are not subject to political bargaining or to the calculus of social interests.[4]

Buddhism is accepted as a tool by many nations to attain absolute equality and interdependence by bounding them as a faith and as a way of life. It is originated from the Buddha's recognition that all sentient beings possess the innate wisdom and there is no inherent difference among them. It can provide altruistic education which is cognitive, effective, and behavioural. It can usher in transmission of experience, exploration of potential, and method to develop just society. The purpose of Buddhist way of thinking is constructive as well as earning for growth. Material growth is necessary but not at the cost of poverty, discrimination and environmental deterioration. The Buddha's teaching can be evolved in more humanistic way of education that leads to altruism, joyfulness, non-discrimination and self-cultivation. Buddhism has appeared sparingly in the social justice movement. It offers the image of the *bodhisattva* of compassion and as an image for social work. A cultural figure with a thousand eyes and hands—it symbolizes the ability to perceive suffering and respond appropriately. Buddhist notion of interconnectedness offers a new extension of social justice. The Buddhist concept of *sunyata* (emptiness) reflects the situation that social environment is a constantly-changing reality that has no true boundaries and it develops a non-attachment practice stance. This stance includes acceptance and openness to difference, the readiness to let go, and the appreciation of changes as opportunities for new possibilities. It is observed that our egos often trap into defined roles, precluding the possibility for authentic connection between people. Buddhism is a practice concerned with changing consciousness as a necessary condition for sustainable world. Not only is it necessary to change policies, procedures, and behaviours, but changing the frame of mind behind draconian social policies and practices is also necessary. This entails paying attention to the entire situation and all the players involved in a situation, particularly the egos of one's self and others. The developed and other nations are fighting over reduction of emission of green house gases as developed nations are adamant not to share responsibility for historical wrong-doings and sharing of technology for it. Their demand is that the incorrigible damage done to climate in long run of industrialization should not be made accountable. Countries like China, India, Brazil, and others are demanding that the West should transfer the technology and bear financial expense to check the deteriorating climatic condition. As advocates for systemic change, we are not individual islands. Injustice is much more than a wrong that has been perpetrated against someone; it is an entire situation that involves interdependent phenomena to which one must attend in its entirety. Buddhism entails an intricate dialectic between personal consciousness-raising and helping the world. Conceptualizing ideas in education such as advocacy of environmentalism, social justice, and social development are certainly challenging. Though there are exceptions, much of the writing in the social development and advocacy literature focuses on ends, rather than on processes or means. Buddhist social development practice provides an opportunity to look into the process and the most importantly to look into our interconnected selves. This can include looking into our blind spots, such as our subtly-colonialist attitudes, and looking at the overt and subtle ways that is inappropriately used as power with stakeholders, colleagues, and within other institutions. The primary Buddhist position on social action is one of total activism, an unswerving commitment to complete self-transformation and complete world transformation.[5]

Buddhism can be helpful to learn, introspect, evaluate, and regulate education and awareness for all because it is not mere a creedal faith but also an ethical agency to set the standard of social behaviour and virtues to encourage social justice. It can be a floating signifier whose enigma leads to identify social processes where differentiation and condensation happen synchronically. In early Buddhism, the aim of an ordained monk was to make effort through teachings of the Buddha to propagate equalitarian ethos. The duty of the monks was to uncover the duality between acceptance, not of logical entities, with a permissible domain and to chalk out strategies to narrow down diversity. The Buddha proclaims the *dhamma* which is beneficent at the beginning, in the middle, and also at the end, for both the divine and human.[6] The *saṃgha* became a divine preceptor, a personal councillor and social educator for the society. It gives the notion of desirability of evolving a culture that leads to sustenance of just socio-economic structure and administration. The idea put by Buddhism before society was of general applicability cutting across the diverse tendencies and provide social adherence to diverse ethnic cultural elements based on homogeneous and egalitarian principles.[7] What is common between Buddhism and environmentalism is that both perceive a vision of society in which the distribution of resources should be shared and equitable, and people should be physically and psychologically safe and secured. It envisages a society where members are self-determining and interdependent. It engages in social actions which have some belongings and social responsibility.[8] The Buddha has done the same by attempting to learn and understand the histories, traditions, and experiences of the people who had formerly been excluded and marginalized. His vision to access, retention, and understanding of the society began as a radical approach to create a homogenous society with heterogeneous cultures. Over the time he also examined that his efforts for awareness and social reformation have been challenged by deeply-embedded rigid and dogmatic system that disenfranchised people but he carried on his efforts to discover the root causes of the evils to wipe it out. He visualized that there are limitations to change culture, stereotypes, and prejudiced attitude which are maligning the people. Buddhism emphasizes the need to pursue the quest to find out a basis common among all members of the planet, otherwise it would be more prone to destruction and disaster. Its aim is to yield shared values which bind society together and may also give rise to consciousness of whole. The Buddha accepted that despite distances and differences in time and space the interrelatedness and continuity of traditions cannot be disregarded. It gives opportunity to revaluate the doctrine to make it contextually relevant. The Buddha utters that religious intolerance are held responsible for dividing societies into watertight compartments which makes intercultural dialogue difficult and undermines plurality of ideas.

Recently many models of disseminating learning and knowledge have been evolved, experimented, and practiced. It has been argued that discussion concerning diversity required to move beyond access and assimilation and efforts are going on to deliver equal opportunity of education and economic resources to all, regardless of race, religion, colour, or sex. Some of the problems like way to respect cultural differences and balancing one's culture verses developing a common culture have been experienced. It has been found that the notion of race and existence of racial hierarchy have been prevalent since the beginning of modern institutions.[9] A noticeable growth has been seen to provide equal access to opportunities to deprived members of society and it has been derived by a number of economic, political, and socio-cultural facets. The ideological view like multiculturism facilitates, admits, and welcomes people from all section of society. It has been universally deployed and invested with multitude of meanings relation to various dimensions of society. It emphasizes upon the idea that the dominant and subordinate values can swap positions to create belongingness and hybrid identity.[10] It shows an assumption about tolerance which includes a hegemonic culture with some other diverse entities which have to be understood, accepted, and mingled. The greatest predicament in this situation is to keep straight the balance of powers, because the dominant culture always desires to be hegemonistic. The motive behind shared ethics is to create community that protects the integrity of various groups and usher in general curriculum for all. It is a mode of learning dominantly representing a will to restructure academic

canons and to aspire for knowledge production and politico-
cultural norms that built heterogeneous societies. It has been
argued that multiculturism did not always challenge established
cultural prejudices as was envisioned. It is considered as fluid
enough to denote very different kind of cultural relations that is
critically challenged by many.[11] A movement for socio-cultural
change in the field of resource distribution and education should
be more than the representation of multi-faceted cultures. For a
just and judicious pedagogical strategy that can challenge biased
assumptions, practices, and norms incorporates a notion that one
live in a homogeneous society and have equal opportunity to all
means and ends. Sometimes, it is charged that the multicultural
approach did not look into the issues that lead to the unequal
social conditions and disparities in the society.[12] The mobilization
for structural change to provide equal accessibility should be
more than the representation of many cultures. Search for a
pedagogical strategy that challenges biased practices and thoughts
is utmost for an urgent requirement of modern pedagogy. It helps
to reduce social tension among the communities and help them
to improve without forfeiting their cultural ethos. It can be done
by diversifying the curriculum to bring educational equity for
low income and historically marginalized groups.[13] The norms of
compassionate justice has been enshrined in the Buddhist ethics
and moral order. It does not provide rational bias for ruthless
culture of greed and selfishness. The welfare of the community
depends upon equal accessibility of opportunity by highlighting
the importance of frugality, resourcefulness, and control over
excessive craving. The equal opportunity in the field of resources
and education can be exemplified by accepting communal
deliberations, face to face negotiations, free and frank discussions
among the community members. The Buddha emphasizes upon
reason and choice rather than dissenting customs and beliefs. It
was a form of deliberative democracy which was participating
and accommodating difference of opinion and even dissent
without imposing majority.[14]

The wider deliberations suggest that a comprehensive overhaul
of policymaking is necessary. Instead of witnessing the glory
and power of a historically mythicized humanity, a substantive
vision is required to raise the standard of human life. It is not the

demand that Buddhist virtues should get professionally inculcated, but paradoxically its strength resides in holistic approach for human kind and other beings. The fluctuation, oscillation, obliteration, and confrontation of values should be restricted and predominance of impartial values should be inculcated to avoid pitfalls. The values inherent in a particular culture are internally plural and reflect a continuing reciprocation between its different traditions and strand of thoughts. These values are not devoid of coherence but are fluid, plural, and imbibing. It grows out of conscious and unconscious interactions but also intends to self-determination and inner impulses. So, it is complimentary to know the target groups and educators, designing of outcome based activities and creation of facilities. The educators are to bring transformative learning experiences through an integrate process that incorporates cognitive and effective interpersonal and intrapersonal domain of learning for the holistic growth.[15] The internal and external pluralities should be properly judged as a society cannot appreciate the values of other cultures unless it respects the plurality within. Generally, the closed societies do not interact and reciprocate others because they define their own identity in terms of their differences with others and often feel suffocated and threatened by them. They safeguard their identity by resisting outside influence and contact. Being a good educator requires to inculcate willingness to open up to learn from others and it also includes setting up of a physical space for appropriate training and functioning with members to create opportunity to reflect on their salient learning experiences. Sometimes members of marginalized groups are free to participate in dominant cultural ethos but stay away because of deep sense of alienation. The aim is to establish an equilibrium between the emotional and cognitive components of learning process, and acknowledge the personal and societal dimensions of problems, experiences, and rectifications; the intention is to evolve a credible source of information, honest personal reflection, questioning the prior beliefs and assumptions and sustained critical thinking.[16] Such goals encourage more imperatives to create accessible and inclusive educational opportunities for under privileged at equal footing. It also challenges the assumption that all members of a society share a universally common culture that ensures equal access for resources and opportunities. It is vital to challenge rules protecting privileged and the aim of social-justice-embedded education is to explore and provide effective education to arouse critical consciousness, institutional, and societal changes. The remedy does not lie in the exercise alone but also in developing an understanding for transformative learning. The idea behind this is to reject the notion that education is a value neutral process. Instead, attempts should be made to inculcate socially transparent education with proper discourses, values and customs.[17] Environmental and social justice education requires awareness content, process and endurance to simultaneously participate in the process and step out to judge and intervene in ongoing interaction.[18] Early Buddhism has well developed view on social justice which remains a powerful template providing normative guidelines for the theory and practice for all dimension of statecraft in the domain of education, economy or governance.[19] The discrimination or misrecognition may have a cultural or material foundation and often recognition involves a cultural and political contestation. Mutual recognition permits a person and other to have freedom and agency in the development and attainment of their own self-consciousness, i.e. a cognitive awareness of the self and its relation to the other. It requires to find ways and means of reconciling the legitimate demands of the marginalized groups. It leads to true economic integration without mutilation of marginal and isolated cultures. Buddhism cherishes reconciliation of the legitimate demands of unity and diversity and attainment of economic integration without cultural uniformity. It avoids pollution of mind and cherishes belongingness and willingness to respect others which accentuate culturally neutral and socially transcendental society.

The investigation of right perception to discover the root cause of deception and discrimination is the first stage of recovery process. A member of social group is born and brought up in relation to ethnicity, gender, nationality, religion, and certain socio-economic structure. The social identity is primary criteria through which personality is groomed. The widespread pattern is found across the world to show instances of subjugation and intergroup dissonance. It embraces the notion that an individual has social identity in relation to particular religion and socio-cultural fabric. All these apprise that current problems relating to deterioration in every aspects of life can be transformed. The approach of educational method should be in form of commitment to equal partnership across the ethnic, religion, and gender lines. The personal expression of the Buddha and his method to resolve conflict could be instrumental here. The Buddha did not apply hegemonistic attitude to resolve any issue of the Buddhist *saṃgha* but always interested in amicable solutions. The dissent among the monks in Kośambi can be example where the monks were divided on certain issues and the Buddha could not settle it. Seeing the awkward situation, he left Kośambi but advised the monks to associate with friends who were righteous, mindful, wise and happy and abandon those who were in opposition nature. The Buddha left the scope of reconciliation and thus provided an opportunity to use their own wisdom.[20] When education fails to provide equal opportunity to underprivileged classes, the middle way is an approach to social well being. It constitutes normative guidelines for public policy in terms of ideals of material and moral welfare.

Naturally, derived choices are necessary to accommodate those who are not the part of dominant cultural ethos. The shared cultural ethic and commitment should be a stable and long-lasting mechanism to achieve well-being of the society. The policies facilitating education could be broadened comprising a system of public morality, social welfare, and environmentalism based on a robust analysis of the human conditions. It requires to pay adequate attention to social relations and make conscious use of reflections and expressions as a mechanism to counter subversive ideas and to promote pragmatic ethos. It rewards changes in awareness level that is impetus to personal growth and wisdom. It also facilitates discussions and brain storming and provide opportunity to common people to share their experience and evaluate their achievements. It is a complete task that should be undertaken with full knowledge of the context and determination because it builds authentic relationship by transgressing conflict and prejudice. Such efforts mirror just and unjust social relations by neutralizing problematic elements. Paulo Freire gives critical pedagogical view and practice and recommends a theoretical philosophy and pedagogy that serves as an impetus for thinking, liberation movements, critical educational work and social justice action. The goal of perfecting critical conscious is to learn and understand how relationship among social groups can be transformed to a more equitable tool.[21] Sukumar Dutt refers to a passage from *Aṅguttara Nikāya* that mentions the quality and pedagogical method for a good communicator.

A monk may learn new and unheard things relating to the dhamma without getting confused. The first condition is the teacher's own ability and range of knowledge. The teacher himself should have mastered the dhamma as set forth in the nine aṅgas as learnt, as mastered (by himself). He teaches other the dhamma in detail, as learnt, as mastered, he makes other repeat it in detail, as learnt, as mastered, he ever reflects, he ever ponder in his heart, mindful he pores over it. Thus is the instruction carried on by the teacher, himself accomplished in canonical lore, taking the monk learner through the whole of the canon until the trainee becomes 'much heard' (bahussuta) or learned (pandita).[22]

Education is the key to enhance the base of environmentalism and provide space for negotiations and reach to some standards for protection of planet. The act of discrimination makes categories of differences that hierarchically divide people as superior and inferior. The level of difference in any society is systemic and involves the unjust limitation of the prospects of self-development, realization of goals, and material success of one part of population for the unlimited benefits of other section of population. The institutional and cultural barriers that are created by such social dynamics are more complicated and it is propagated in the society under rubrics of cultural world view. Environmentalism orients towards reducing and resolving conflict among nations whether they are developed or developing and avoids failures or discord between groups of haves and have nots. It identifies disparities in societal opportunities, resources, and outcomes among the marginalized groups. The intention to provide accessibility of resources for all should be manifested with ideology and application. Education is the key to broaden the base of ecological response of humans and it leads to freedom at physical and intellectual level. It is primary condition for the quest of human completion.[23] One of the foci of such policy is to create opportunities for inter-group cooperation and activities that have the potential to take participants towards perspective of belongingness and shared values because they all have shared humanity and can focus on the common bond instead of their differences. It gives the idea that social alienation and marginalization are a superficial conflict. It shows circumstances under which social identities became important and also signifies the primary determinant of social perception and behaviour. It also specifies different strategies that society can employ to cope up with a deviant social occurrences. It is truly psychological and pertinent on social content as the key determinant of self-definition and behaviour. The response of the people could be understood in terms of subjective beliefs about the marginalized groups and nations, and their relation with other members of the society. Freire says that authentic thinking is concerned about reality and it does not take place in ivory-tower isolation but only in communication.[24] Eradication of discrimination and perpetuation of just norms necessitate to know profoundly the mechanism by which power is shared historically to silence and marginalize certain social groups through biased curriculum, poor infrastructure, or discrimination on various social parameters. Progressive educators commit to social justice to disrupt and problematize such social circumstances. Personal identity and ethnicity may not give an indication of individual's affiliation with a historical or cultural background because personal identification with one's own ethno-culture is an issue of personal choice. The parameters like race or caste are social constructions that divide people artificially into different hierarchies based on arbitrary socio-cultural and physical characteristics. Any scientific connection between visible difference and psychological attributes is delusion. Race is a political phenomenon brought into existence and made viable by socio-economic and political acumen. Such hierarchies of social groups sustain institutionalized system of power and privilege by sustenance of oppressed groups on one hand and the privileged on the other.[25]

The identity of a person in a nation is shaped by recognition or its absence often by the misrecognition of others. By instigating and perpetuating conflict one can inflict real damage and distortion to the people or society. Non-recognition may inflict harm and can be treated as a kind of oppression, impersonating a person in a false, disrespectful, and reduced mode of being.[26] Such repugnant ideas have been perpetuated in the society through cultural imposition and ideological subordination. The pedagogical view with egalitarianism can identify pronouncement of such beliefs and hateful invectives. To remove any sort of inferiority among the oppressed group is first stage of reformation. The damage done by foul words invokes millions of cultural ethos of inferiority that one has painfully repressed and that impinged upon as a badge of servitude and subservience.[27] The ideological balance is challenging and ultimately pedagogical objective is to examine and teach about the complexities of social conflict. Its main goal should be to sharpen the critical thinking skills in order to develop their thought and intension.[28] Buddhism can be helpful in the formation of such pedagogical theories because it recognizes existing realities of things and always strives to make a greatly-united world in which all the people, regardless of nation, religion, or culture, can live happily and flourish. In the context of climate change and interdependence, whatever principles, policies, and action taken should bear positive intension. The mindset of the Buddha was to establish equalitarian ethos which could cut across the distinction of race or religion. He says that lineage does not enter into man's being either good or bad.[29] The Buddha formulated his teachings at a time of profound social and economic upheaval and turmoil. He envisaged a new form of social and economic relations built around the shared values of equality and equanimity. The Buddha is often seen as the most enlightened classical teacher and his pragmatism could be seen in his willingness to listen, entertain, and consider dissenting points.

The pedagogical approach for sustenance and survival of planet invigorate culture to the extent to alleviate those social relations that functions to silence marginalized groups and nations. It avoids rather a negative view of all sorts of invasive cultures and attempts to reverse creed of unsympathy against human beings and Nature. The aim is to fight against all well-anchored beliefs related to the man's superiority. Beginning with effective interdependence is a methodological approach that is grounded in an understanding of the history and legacy of exclusion, discrimination, and a vision of systemic social changes. It is a complex task that should be facilitated with full knowledge of the elements that speed up learning, social justice, and commitment to transform the world view on environmental and social issues. It requires plasticity in approach formation, implementation and recovery. The early Buddhist monastic development can be one of the examples of it. The Theravāda monasteries in India were centres of faith and the novice monks had to go for *nisssaya* for monastic training.[30] In these monasteries custom developed among the monks holding discussions and debates among themselves. The learning was once to get expertise in canonical literature but gradually its scope was liberalized and extended. This type of method and transparency in pedagogical methods could offer approaches toward creating possible solutions. Emergence of Mahāvihāra tradition (monastic universities like Nālandā) on Buddhist horizon changed, modified, and innovated Buddhist education, its curriculum, literature, language of writing, and mode of education. The process was designed by a re-orientation of monastic learning whereby it liberalized its cloistered inbred character and turned into a learning that was liberal and multifaceted. It was not isolated from the larger life of the society. Similarly, in modern pedagogy, the experiences, intergroup contacts, dialogue opportunities can form a stage for critical self-reflection and freedom of expression on grounds of equality and non-discrimination. Buddhism propounds *maitree*, and *karunā* with an understanding of dependent co-arising, interconnectedness, and an understanding of the source of suffering. In the context of development of the proper environmental ethic in a globalized context, it is fairly easy to advocate for the oppressed and the underprivileged, but what is much more difficult is for true compassion to appear and to advocate for everyone, including those who enjoy privileges and those who are lacking. Loving kindness (*metta*) embarks upon to develop happiness for himself and keep free from enmity and affliction. Inadvertently, it develops a selfless person with a broader outlook.[31] The compassion (*karuna*) starts with feelings of disadvantages of not having it. It is directed towards four categories of the people, viz., the dear one, the unfortunates, the hostile, and the unbiased or neutral. The Buddha says that it should be first directed towards unfortunates or hostiles.[32] So it gives pervading scope to inculcate harmony into different warring or hostile groups and by doing this people can live peacefully with other's concern. The sympathetic joy (*muditā*) is to be unenvied upon success of others. It removes insecurity and envy, the two major factors of conflict.[33] It deprives the feeling of marginalization among the various groups of the people ethnic or religious. The equanimity (*upekkhā*) exhibits neutrality that encourages equality and respect for all beings.[34] The inclusion of these four elements in any pedagogical curriculum can transform the character and thought of the society. It produces good human beings full of invariable affection and free of anger or envy. It restricts mad rush for material gain and introduces socially standardized values irrespective of religion or ethnicity. It may be the most suited idea to generate a universal consensus to rationally evaluate the deep-rooted flaws of present discriminatory patterns existing in the globalized world.

It should be noted that Buddhism does not necessarily promote a particular political, economic or social ideology. Buddhism is compatible with progressive democratic ideas as well as economics based on sharing resources and controlled consumption. These ideas ought to be explored in more depth as a way to contribute to the substantive literature on sustenance. The historical-doctrinal viewpoints of Buddhism could be explored to educate the people. Buddhist pedagogical tradition comes up with a number of ingenious solutions to deal with problems inherent in process of globalization and consequential economic deprivation. Many of such solutions are based on skilful means (*upaya*) adopted to a particular circumstance to avoid the pitfalls of various development models. It sets up unique bridge and paradigm to facilitate objectivity and engagement. Buddhist view and practice of meditation can be adopted in curriculum to develop equanimity and selflessness in the society. Learning about the self and the nature of mind and its delusions are of central importance to the Buddhist endeavour. Meditation helps the practitioner to understand True Self which is beyond the categories of gender, caste, race, and religion, and yet it is not beyond these things. The self or mind can often manifest in dichotomous thinking and selfishness. Meditative practices can help individuals distinguish the True Self and recognize that the self is constantly changing and impermanent, and cut through the illusory separation between self and others. Early Buddhism avoids the debate of good and bad by taking a different approach.

The Buddha emphasized that we all have both wholesome and unwholesome traits. What is important is reducing our unwholesome characteristics including afflictive emotions. The pedagogical structure requires understanding of social and political content in which such phenomenon occurs. It identifies systemic forces and barriers which are related to each other and which jointly immobilizes institutions. It is a disclaimer that a particular type of economic system is incoherent or bizarre; it is, however, a well-considered notion that all kinds of thought and life have limitations. It cannot comprise the full range of attributes, complexity, and grandeur of our planet. For sustainable and blessed planet, homogenization of cultures are necessary but its plural and differentiated patterns must also be preserved and respected. For it, all kinds of centrism which isolate assimilative traditions of cultures must be avoided. A happy planet cherishes the diversity of cultures and shared economic values and always endorses coexistence, self-determination, and intellectual and moral sympathy.

Notes

1. Robert Hattam, 'Socially Engaged Buddhism as a Provocation for Critical Pedagogy in Unsettling Times', in *Cross-Cultural Studies in Curriculum: Eastern Thought and Educational Insights*, ed. Claudia Eppert and Hongyu Wang, London: Routledge, 2008, pp. 109–36, see p. 109.
2. Anand Singh, 'Buddhist Response to Educational Crisis: Locating Space for Creating and Sustenance of Just Society', *Buddhism and World Crisis*, Bangkok, 2015, pp. 427–57.
3. John B. Cobb, Jr., 'The Meaning of Pluralism for Christian Self-Understanding', in *Religious Pluralism*, ed. Leroy S. Rouncer, Notre Dame: University of Notre Dame, 1984, pp. 161–79.
4. John Rawls, *A Theory of Justice*, Cambridge, MA: Harvard University Press, 1999, pp. 3–4.
5. R.A.F. Thurman, 'Guidelines for Buddhist Social Activism Based on Nagarjuna's Jewel Garland of Royal Counsels', in *The Path of Compassion: Writings on Socially Engaged Buddhism*, ed. F. Eppsteiner and D. Maloney, Berkeley, CA: Parallax, 1985, pp. 46–65, see p. 46.
6. *Mahāvagga* I.I.

7. Anand Singh, 'Social Issues in Early Buddhism: Gender, Caste and Class', *The Mahabodhi*, vol. 116, no. 6, 2008–9, pp. 8–16.

8. M. Adams, L. Bell and P. Griffin, eds., *Teaching for Diversity and Social Justice: A Source Book*, New York: Routledge, 2007, p. 3.

9. D.B. Tyack, 'Constructing Difference: Historical Reflections of Schooling and Social Diversity', *Teachers College Record*, vol. 95, no. 1, 1993, pp. 8–34.

10. Barnor Hesse, *Un/Settled Multiculturism: Diasporas, Entanglements, Transruptions*, London: Zed Books, 2000, p. 8.

11. Chicago Studies Group, 'Critical Multiculturism', ed. D.T. Goldberg, *Multiculturism: A Critical Reader*, Oxford: Blackford, p. 115.

12. D.G. Smith et. al., *Diversity Works: The Emerging Picture of How Students Benefit*, Washington, D.C.: Associates of American Colleges and Universities, 1997, pp. 12–17.

13. J.A. Williamson, L. Rhodes and M. Dunson, 'A Selected History of Social Justice Education', *Review of Research in Education*, vol. 31, no. 11, 2007, pp. 195–224.

14. Laksiri Jayasuriya, 'Buddhism: Politics and Statecraft', *International Journal of Buddhist Thought and Culture*, vol. 11, 2008, pp. 54–5.

15. S.J. Quaye, 'Think Before You Teach: Preparing for Dialogue about Racial Realities', *Journal of College Student Development*, vol. 53, no. 4, 2012, pp. 542–62.

16. M. Adams, 'Pedagogical Framework for Social Education', in *Teaching for Diversity and Social Justice: A Source Book*, ed. M. Adams, L. Bell and P. Griffin, New York: Routledge, 2007, p. 32.

17. P. McLaren and H. Giroux, 'Radical Pedagogy as Cultural Politics: Beyond the Discourse of Critique and Anti-Utopianism', pp. 29–57.

18. P. Griffin and M.L. Ouellett, 'Facilitating Social Justice Education Courses', in *Critical Pedagogy and Predatory Culture: Oppositional Politics in Post Modern Era*, ed. P. McLaren, 1995, p. 90.

19. Tambiah, *World Conqueror and World Renouncer*, p. 25.

20. Nand Kishore Prasad, 'The Democratic Attitude of the Buddha', in *Buddha and Early Buddhism*, ed. Mahendra P. Mittal, New Delhi: LPP, 2006, p. 270.

21. Paulo Freire, *Pedagogy of the Oppressed*, New York: Continuum, 2006, pp. 10–11.

22. Sukumar Dutt, *Buddhist Monks and Monasteries in India*, New Delhi: Motilal Banarsidass, 2000, p. 322. (*Aṅguttara Nikāya*, VI.51.) (The nine *aṅgas* are *Sutta, Geyya, Veyyakarana, Gāthā, Udāna, Itivuttaka, Jātaka, Abbhutadhamma,* and *vedalla.*)

23. Freire, *Pedagogy of the Oppressed*, p. 4.

24. Ibid., p. 77.

25. Barbara Applebaum, 'Social Justice, Democratic Education and Silencing of the Words That Wounds', *Journal of Moral Education*, vol. 32, no. 2, 2003, p. 158.

26. C. Taylor, *Multiculturalism and the Politics of Recognition*, Princeton: Princeton University Press, 1992, p. 25.

27. C.R. Lawrence III, 'If He Hollers Let Him Go: Regulating Racist Speech on Campus', in *Words That Wounds: Critical Race Theory, Assaultive Speech and the First Amendment*, ed. M.J. Matsuda, C.R. Lawrence III, R. Delgado and K. Crenshaw, Boulder, CO: West View Press, pp. 17–51.

28. Aaron J. Hahn Tapper, 'A Pedagogy of Social Justice Education: Social Identity Theory, Intersectionality and Empowerment', *Conflict Resolution Quarterly*, vol. 30, no. 4, 2013, p. 433.

29. *Majjhima Nikāya*, II.179.

30. Ibid., I.32.

31. *Saṃyutta Nikāya*, I.75–7.

32. Ibid., I.77–9.

33. Ibid., IX.94–5.

34. Ibid., IX.96.

Bibliography

Primary Sources

Ācārāṅga Sutra, tr. Herman Jaicobi, *Jain Sutras*, New York: Dover Press, 1884; repr. 1968.

Airyāpathikī Sutra, tr. R. Williams, *Jaina Yoga: A Survey of Medieval Sravakacaras*, London: OUP, 1963.

Aṅguttara Nikāya, *The Book of Gradual Sayings*, tr. F.L. Woodward, Delhi: MLBD, repr. 2006.

Anekantajyapataka (Haribhadra), ed. H.R. Kapadia, 2 vols., Baroda: Oriental Institute, 1947.

Arthaśastra of Kautilya, ed. R. Shamsastri, Mysore: Wesleyan Mission Press, 1919.

Aśokavadana, tr. John S. Strong, *The Legend of King Aśoka: A Study and Translation of Aśokavadana*, Princeton: Princeton University Press; Delhi: MLBD, repr. 2010.

Atharvaveda, tr. W.D. Whitney, Cambridge, 1955; Delhi: LPP, repr. 2006.

Atthaśalinī of Buddhaghosa, ed. E.I. Muller, London: PTS, 1897.

Avadānaśataka, P.C. Bagchi, 'A Note on the Avadānaśataka and its Chinese Translations', *Visva-Bharati Annals*, 56–61, vol. 1, ed. P.C. Bagchi, Calcutta: Visva-Bharati, 1945.

Bhagvatī Sutra, tr. K.C. Lalwani, Calcutta: Jain Bhawan, 1973–80.

Buddhavaṃśa, ed. Richard Morris, London: PTS, 1882.

Buddhavaṃśa Commentery, I.B. Horner, London: PTS, 1978.

Cullavamśa, ed. W. Geiger, 2 vols., London: PTS, 1925–7.

Cullavagga, Vinaya Texts, ed. F. Max Müller, T.W. Rhys Davids and Herman Oldenberg, Delhi: LPP, repr. 2007.

Dhammapada, ed. O. Von Hinubur and K.R. Normon, Oxford: PTS, 1997, F. Max Müller, SBE, Oxford, 1898, Delhi: LPP, repr. 1996.

Dhammapadaṭṭhakathā of Buddhaghosa, ed. H.C. Norman, 4 vols., London: PTS, 1906–14.

Dīgha Nikāya, ed. T.W. Rhys Davids and T.E. Carpenter, 3 vols., London: PTS, 1890–1911; Delhi: MLBD, repr. 2010.

Dīpavaṃśa, tr. H. Oldenberg, London, 1879, Delhi: Asian Educational Services, repr. 2006.

Divyāvadāna, ed. P.L. Vaidya, Buddhist Sanskrit Text no. 20, Darbhanga: The Mithila Institute of Post-Graduate Studies, 1959.

Gommatasāra Jīvakānda, tr. J.L. Jaini, *Sacred Books of Jainas*, vol. 5, New Delhi: Today and Tomorrow Publications, 1990.

Guhyasamaja Tantra or the Tathgata Guhyaka, ed. Benoytosh Bhattacharya, *GOS*, no. 53, Baroda: Oriental Press, 1931.

Harivaṃśa, ed. R. Kinjawadekar, Poona, 1936.

Harshacarita (Banabhatta), tr. E.B. Cowell and F.W. Thomas, London: Royal Asiatic Society, 1897.

Jain Sutras, ed. Harman Jacobi, 22 vols., New Delhi: MLBD, 1964.

Jātaka, ed. E.B. Cowell, Delhi: LPP, repr. 1993.

———, ed. V. Fausball, London: Freebner and Co., 1872.

Jātakamālā, ed. H. Kern, Boston, 1891, tr. J.S. Sepeyer, *The Gātakamala or Garland of Birth Stories*, Aryasura, *Sacred Book of Buddhist*, London: OUP, 1895.

Jīvavicona Prakarnam (Santi Suri) *along with Pathaka Ratnakara's Commentary*, ed. Muni Ratna-Prabha Vijaya, tr. Jayant P. Thaker, Madras: Jain Mission Society, 1950.

Kathāvatthu, ed. A.C. Taylor, London: PTS, 1894.

Kātyāyana Śrauta Sūtra, ed. H.G. Ranade, Pune: Ranade Publication Series, 1978.

Lalitavistāra, ed. R. Mitra, Calcutta: Asiatic Society, 1877.

Lankavatāra Sutra, tr. Daisetz Teitaro Suzuki, Delhi: MLBD, 2004.

Mahābodhivaṃśa, ed. S.A. Strong, London: PTS, 1891.

Mahaprajnaparamita Sastra, tr. Etienne, Lamotte, 5 vols., Louvain, 1944–80.

Mahavaṃśa, ed. W. Geiger, Delhi: Asian Educational Services, repr. 2011.

Mahāvastu, ed. E. Senart, Paris, 1887–97.

Majjhama Nikāya, T.W. Rhys Davids, SBE, Oxford, 1881; Delhi: LPP, repr. 2006.

———, *The Collection of the Middle Length Sayings*, tr. I.B. Horner, Delhi: MLBD, 2004.

———, ed. V. Trenckner and R. Chalmers, PTS, London, 1888–1902; Delhi: MLBD, repr. 2004.

Manorathapuranī of Buddhaghosa, ed. Max Walleser, London: PTS, 1924.

Milindapañho, ed. T.W. Rhys Davids, SBE, Oxford, 1890; Delhi: LPP.

Painnayasuttaim, Jain Agam Series, no. 17, tr. Punyavijaya and Antlal Mohan Lal Bhajak, Bombay: Mahavira Jain Vidyalaya, 1984.

Papanchasudanī of Buddhaghosa, ed. J.H. Wood and D. Kosambi, London: PTS, 1922.

Paramatthajotika of Buddhaghosa, vol. I, ed. H. Smith, London: PTS, 1915; vol. II, 1916–18.

Paramārtthadīpanā of Dhammapala—

    on the *Vimānavattthu*, ed. E. Hardy, London: PTS, 1901.

    on the *Pettavatthu*, ed. E. Hardy, London: PTS, 1899.

on the *Therīgāthā*, ed. E. Mueller, London: PTS, 1893.

on the *Udāna*, ed. F.L. Woodward, London: PTS, 1926.

Pratikramana Sutra, tr. R William, *Jaina Yoga: A Survey of Medieval Srāvakācāras*, London: OUP, 1963

Puggalapannatti–Atthakathā of Buddhaghosa, ed. G. Landsberg and Rhys Davids, JPTS, 1913-14.

Rāmāyana (Vālmīkī), Ralph T.H. Griffith, Delhi: LPP, repr. 2003.

Rigveda–Samhita and *Pada* Text with Sayana's Comm, ed. F. Max Müller, SBE, vol. XXXII, Oxford, 1897; Delhi: LPP, repr. 2006.

Sadhanāmālā, ed. Benoytosh Bhattacharya, 2 vols., *GOS*, nos. 26, Baroda: Oriental Press, 1925–28, pp. 8–41.

Samantapāsadika of Buddhaghosa, ed. J. Takakusu, 2 vols., London: PTS, 1924.

Sammohavinodinī of Buddhaghosa, ed. T.W. Rhys Davids and T.E. Carpenter, London: PTS, 1986.

Saṃyutta Nikāya, *The Book of the Kindred Sayings*, ed. Rhys Davids and F.L. Woodward, 5 vols., London: PTS, 1917–30; Delhi: MLBD, repr. 2005.

Sarvārthasiddhi, ed. Pujyapada Shastri, Delhi: Bhartiya Jnanapitha, 1992.

Śatpatha Brāhmana, ed. A. Weber, London, 1885.

Sraddha-Pratikramana Sutra (*Prabodha Tīka*), ed. Panyas Bhadrankarvijaygani and Muni Kalyanprabhavijay, Bombay: Jain Sahitya Vikas Mandal.

Sumangalvilāsinī of Buddhaghosa, ed. T.W. Rhys Davids and T.E. Carpenter, London: PTS, 1886.

Suttanipāta, ed. D. Anderson and H. Smith, London: PTS, 1913.

Suttanipāta Commentary, ed. Helmer Smith, London: PTS, 1917.

Syadamanjari (Mallisena), ed. A.B. Dhruva, Bombay: Bombay University, 1933.

Tattvartha Sutra (Umasvati), tr. Nathmal Tatia, San Francisco: Harper Collins, 1994.

Theragātha–Psalms of the Brethren, ed. Rhys Davids, London: PTS, 1913.

Therīgātha Commentary, ed. E. Müller, London: PTS, 1893.

Therīgātha–Psalms of the Sisters, ed. Rhys Davids, London: PTS, 1909.

Udāna Commentary (Dhammapala), tr. Peter Masefield, vol. 2, London: PTS, 1995.

Vinaya Pitaka, ed. H. Oldenberg, London: PTS, 1879–83, tr. T.W. Rhys Davids and H. Oldenberg, SBE, Oxford, 1881–5; Delhi: LPP, repr. 2005.

Viśuddhimagga of Buddhaghosa, ed. C.A.F. Rhys David, 2 vols., London: PTS, 1920–1.

Chinese Sources

Beal, Samuel, *Si-yu-ki, Buddhist Records of the Western World*, tr. from the Chinese of Hiuen-Tsang, 2 vols., London, 1906; Delhi: LPP, repr. 1995.

Giles, H.A., *The Travels of Fa-hien or Record of Buddhist Kingdom*, Cambridge, 1923.

Julien, S., *Memoires sur les Contrees Occidentales*, tr. of Hiuen-Tsang, Paris, 1857–8.

Legge, J.H., *Record of the Buddhist Kingdoms, being an Account of the Chinese Monk Fa-hien's Travels*, Oxford, 1886.

Takakusu, J.A., *A Record of the Buddhistic Religion as Practiced in India and Malay Archipelago* (AD 671–695), Delhi: Munshiram Manoharlal, 2001.

Watters, Thomas, *On Yuan Chwang's Travels in India* (AD 629–645), ed. T.W. Rhys Davids and S.W. Bushell, 2 vols., London, 1904; Delhi: LPP, repr. 2000.

Tibetan Sources

Dhammasvami, *Biography of Dhammasvami* (*Chag lo tsa-baChosrje-dpal*): *A Tibetan Monk Pilgrim*, tr. George Roerich, Patna: K.P. Jaiswal Institute, 1959.

Sumpa, Khan (*Pag Sam Jon Zang* by Poyece Pal Jor), ed. Sarat Chandra Das, *History of Rise, Progress and Downfall of Buddhism in India*, Calcutta: Princeton Press, 1908.

Tāranātha, tr. Lama Chimpa and A. Chattopadhyaya, *Taranatha's History of Buddhism in India*, Shimla: Indian Institute of Advanced Study, 1970.

Bu-ston, tr. E. Obermiller, *The History of Buddhism in India and Tibet*, Delhi: Satguru Publications, 1999.

Secondary Sources

Adams, M., 'Pedagogical Framework for Social Education', in *Teaching for Diversity and Social Justice: A Source Book*, ed. M. Adams, L. Bell and P. Griffin, New York: Routledge, 2007, pp. 15–33.

Adams, M., L. Bell and P. Griffin, eds., *Teaching for Diversity and Social Justice: A Source Book*, New York: Routledge, 2007.

Agarwal, D.P., *Steps Towards Urban Revolution in Doab: Archaeological and Ecological Data*, Delhi, 1969.

Agrawal, V.S., *Studies in Indian Art*, Vārānasī: Vishwavidalaya Prakashan, 2003.

Allchin, B. and F.R. Allchin, *The Rise of Civilization in India and Pakistan*, Cambridge: Cambridge University Press, 1982.

Alexandrin, Glen, 'Buddhist Economics: Demand and Decision Making', *Eastern Buddhist*, n.s., vol. XXI, no. 2, 1988, pp. 36–53.

———, 'Elements of Buddhist Economics', *International Journal of Social Economics*, vol. XX, no. 2, 1993, pp. 3–11.

Analayo, Bhikkhu, 'Canonical Jātaka Tales in Comparative Perspective-The Evolution of Tales of the Buddha's Past Life', *Fuyan Buddhist Studies*, no. 7, 2012, pp. 75–100.

————, *The Genesis of the Bodhisattva Ideal*, Hamburg: Hamburg University Press, 2010.

Anderson, James N., *The Great Transformation*, Boston: Beacon Press, 1957.

Applebaum, Barbara, 'Social Justice, Democratic Education and Silencing of the Words That Wounds', *Journal of Moral Education*, vol. 32, no. 2, 2003, pp. 151–62.

Aramaki, Noritoshi, '*Shizen-hakaikarashizen-sasei e-Rekishe no Tenkainitsuiti*' (*From Destruction of Nature to Revival of Nature: On a Historical Conversion*), *Deai*, II(i), 1992, pp. 3–22.

Ariyaratne, A.T., *Collected Works*, vols. I–V, Moratuwa: Sarvodaya Research Institute, 1978–99.

————, *Peacemaking in Sri Lanka in the Buddhist Context*, Moratuwa: Sarvodaya Vishwa Lekha, 1987.

————, *The Power Pyramid and the Dhammic Cycle*, Moratuwa: Sarvodaya Vishwa Lekha, 1988.

Badiner, Allan Hunt, *Dharma Gaiya: A Harvest of Essays in Buddhism and Ecology*, California: Parallax Press, 1990.

Balbir, Nalini, 'Jain-Buddhist Dialogue: Material from the Pāli Scriptures', *Journal of Pāli Text Society*, vol. XXVI, 2000, pp. 1–42.

Bareau, Andre, *Recherches sur la biographie du Buddha* (*Research on the Biography of the Buddha*), Tome I, Paris, 1970.

Barnhill, David Landis, 'Good Work: An Engaged Buddhist Response to the Dilemmas of Consumerism', *Buddhist-Christian Studies*, vol. 24, 2004, pp. 55–63, http:/www.jstor.org/stable/4145564, accessed: 21 March 2012.

Batchelor, Martine, 'Even the Stones Smile', in *Buddhism and Ecology*, ed. Martine Batchelor and Kerry Brown, London and New York: Cassel, 1992, pp. 2–17.

Batchelor, Stephen, *The Awakening of the West*, Berkeley: Parallax Press, 1990.

————, 'The Sands of the Ganges', in *Buddhism and Ecology*, ed. Martine Batchelor and Kerry Brown, London and New York: Cassel, 1992, pp. 31–40.

————, 'The Buddhist Economics Reconsidered', in *Dharma Gaiya: A Harvest of Essays in Buddhism and Ecology*, ed. Allan Hunt Badiner, California: Parallax Press, 1990, pp. 178–82.

Bechert, Heinz, 'Buddhism as Factor of Political Modernization: The Case of Sri Lanka', in *Religion and Development in Asian Societies*, ed. Friedrich Nauman-Stiftung, Colombo: Marga Publications, 1974, pp. 1–11.

Bellah, Robert N., 'Epilogue: Religion and Progress in Modern Asia', in *Religion and Progress in Modern Asia*, ed. Robert N. Bellah, New York: Free Press, 1965, pp. 168–229.

Berry, Thomas, *The Dream of the Earth*, San Francisco: Sierra Club Books, 1988.

Bhattacharya, Benoytosh, *The Indian Buddhist Iconography*, Calcutta: M.L. Mukhopadhyaya, 1958.

Bhikkhu, Buddhadasa, *Dhammic Socialism*, tr. Donald K. Swearer, Bangkok: Thai Interreligious Commission for Development, 1981.

Bhikkhu, Panyananda, 'Buddhadasa Lives On: Recalling the Life of Buddhadasa Bhikkhu', *Crossroads: An Interdisciplinary Journal of Southeast Asian Studies*, vol. 8, no. 1, 1993, pp. 119–24, http://www.jstor.org/stable/40860932, accessed 28 March 2012.

Bhikkhu, Santikaro, 'Buddhadasa Bhikkhu: Life and Society through the Natural Eyes of Voidness', in *Engaged Buddhism: Buddhist Liberation in Asia*, ed. Christopher S. Queen and Sallie B. King, Albany: State University of New York Press, 1996, pp. 147–93.

Bidwell, R.G., *Plant Physiology*, New York: Macmillan, 1979.

Birch, Charles and John B. Cobb, Jr., *The Liberation of Life: From Cell to Community*, Denton, Texas: Environmental Ethics Books, 1990.

Bloom, Alfred, *Globalization and Buddhism*, http://www.shindharmanet.com/wp-content/uploads/2012/pdf/Bloom-Globalization.pdf, accessed 26 March 2014.

Bond, George D., 'A.T. Ariyaratne and the Sarvodaya Shramadana Movement in Sri Lanka', in *Buddhism: Buddhist Liberation Movements in Asia*, ed. Christopher S. Queen and Sallie B. King, Albany: State University of New York Press, 1996, pp. 121–46.

Boruah, Bijoy H., 'Environmental Wisdom', in *Readings in Environmental Ethics: Multidisciplinary Perspective*, ed. D.C. Srivastava, Delhi: Rawat Publications, 2005, pp. 23–8.

Bose, Sugata and Ayesha Jalal, *Modern South Asia*, New York: Routledge, 2004.

Brown, Kerry, 'In the Water there Were Fish and the Fields Were Full of Rice: Reawakening the Lost Harmony of Thailand', *Buddhism and Ecology*, ed. Martine Batchelor and Kerry Brown, London and New York: Cassel, 1992, pp. 87–99.

Brown, Lester, Christopher Flavin, Hilary French and Linda Strake, eds., *The State of the World Report*, New York: W.W. Norton, 1998.

Brown, Brian, 'Towards a Buddhist Ecological Cosmology', *Bucknell Review*, vol. 37, no. 2, 1993, pp. 124–37.

Burgress, James, *Buddhist Stūpas of Amaravati and Jaggayyapeta*, London: ASI, 1887.

Callicott, J. Baird, 'Conceptual Resources for Environmental Ethics in Asian Traditions of Thought: A Propaedeutic', *Philosophy East and West*, vol. 37, no. 2, April 1987, pp. 115–30, http://www.jstor.org/stable/1398732, accessed 21 March 2012.

———, The New New (Buddhist?), *Ecology*, 2005, pp. 1–24.

———, 'Traditional American Indian and Western European Attitude towards Nature: An Overview', *Environmental Ethics*, vol. 4, 1982, pp. 292–318.

Callicott, J. Baird and Roges T. Ames, *Nature in Asian Tradition of Thoughts: Essays in Environmrntal Philosophy*, Delhi: Satguru Publications, 1991.

Capra, Fritjof, *Uncommon Wisdom*, London: Century Hutchinson Ltd., 1987.

Chakravarti, Uma, 'Buddhism as a Discourse of Dissent?: Class and Gender', *Pravada*, vol. 1, no. 5, May 1992, pp. 12–18.

———, *The Social Dimensions of Early Buddhism*, Delhi: Munshiram Manoharlal, 1996.

Chakravarti, D.K. and Nayanjot Lahiri, 'The Iron Age in India, the Beginning and Consequences', *Puratattva*, vol. 24, 1994, pp. 12–32.

———, 'Animals and Environment in Buddhist Birth Stories', in *Buddhism and Ecology: The Interconnection of Dharma and Deed*, ed. Mary Evelyn Tucker and Duncan Ryuken Williams, Massachusetts: Harvard University Press, 1997, pp. 131–48.

Chapple, Christopher Key, *Ecological Prospects: Scientific, Religious and Aesthetic Perspectives*, Delhi: Satguru, 1995.

———, *Jainism and Ecology: Nonviolence in the Web of Life*, Delhi: MLBD, 2006.

———, *Nonviolence to Animals, Earth, and Self in Asian Traditions*, New Delhi: Sri Satguru, 1995.

———, 'The Living Earth of Jainism and the New Story: Rediscovering and Reclaiming a Functional Cosmology', in *Jainism and Ecology*, ed. Christopher Key Chapple, Delhi: MLBD, 2006, pp. 119–40.

Chatterji, S.C. and D.M. Dutta, *An Introduction to Indian Philosophy*, Calcutta: Calcutta University Press, 1984.

Chattopadhyaya, B.D., *D.D. Kosambi: Combined Methods in Indology and Other Writings*, Delhi: OUP, 2003.

Chaudhary, K.A., K.S. Saraswat and G.M. Buth, *Agriculture and Forestry in Northern India*, New Delhi, 1977.

Chow, Fa, 'Sukara-Maddava and the Buddha's Death', *Annalas of Bhandarkar Research Institute*, ed. R.N. Dandekar, 1942, pp. 127–33.

Clippard, Seth Devere, 'The Lorex Wears Saffron: Towards a Buddhist Environmentalism', *Journal of Buddhist Ethics*, vol. 18, 2011, pp. 212–44.

Cobb, John B., Jr., 'A Buddhist-Christian Critiques of Neo-Liberal Economics', *Eastern Buddhist*, vol. 34, no. 2, pp. 1–15, 2002, http://www.smallisbeautiful.org/pdf/buddhist_economics/english.pdf.

———, 'Process Theology and Environmental Issues', *The Journal of Religion*, vol. 60, no. 4, October 1980, pp. 440–58, http://www.jstor.org/stable/1202659.

Cobb, John B., Jr. and Charles Birch, *The Liberation of Life*, Denton: Cambridge University Press, 1990.

———, 'The Meaning of Pluralism for Christian Self-Understanding', in *Religious Pluralism*, ed. Leroy S. Rouncer, Notre Dame: University of Notre Dame, 1984, pp. 161–79.

Coomaraswamy, Ananda K., *Buddha and the Gospel of Buddhism*, Delhi: Asia Publishing House, 1956.

Coningham, Robin A.E., 'Monks, Caves and Kings: A Reassessment of the Nature of Early Buddhism in Sri Lanka', *World Archaeology*, vol. 27, no. 2, October 1995, pp. 222–42, http://www.jstor.org/stable/125083, accessed 26 March 2012.

Cort, John E., 'Green Jainism: Notes and Queries toward a Possible Jain Environment Ethics', in *Jainism and Ecology*, ed. Christopher Key Chapple, Delhi: MLBD, 2006, pp. 63–94.

———, 'Intellectual Ahiṃsa Revisited: Tolerance and Intolerance of Others', *Philosophy East and West*, vol. 50, no. 3, 2000, pp. 324–47.

Coward, Harold, 'New Theology on Population, Consumption, and Ecology', *Journal of the American Academy of Religion*, vol. 65, no. 2, pp. 259–73, http://jaar.oxfordjournals.org, accessed 21 March 2012.

———, 'The Ecological Implications of Karma Theory', in *Purify the Earthly Body of God: Religion and Ecology in Hindu India*, ed. Lance E. Nelson, Albany: State University of New York Press, 1998, pp. 39–40.

Cowell, E.B., ed., *The Jātaka or Stories of Buddha's Former Birth*, Delhi: LPP, repr. 1907.

Cumming, Mary, 'The Lives of the Buddha in Art and Literature of Asia', *Michigan papers on South and Southeast Asia*, 20, Ann Arbor: Centre for South and Southeast Asian Studies, Michigan, 1982, pp. 74–83.

Cunningham, Alexander, *The Ancient Geography of India*, Delhi: LPP, repr. 2006, pp. 350–1.

———, *The Stūpa of Bharhut*, London, 1879.

Darlington, Susan M., 'Buddhism and Development: The Ecology Monks of Thailand', in *Action Dharma: New Studies in Engaged Buddhism*, ed. Christopher S. Queen, Charles Prebish and Damien Keown, London: Routledge, 2003, pp. 96–109.

———, *Buddhism Morality and Change: The Local Response to Development in Thailand*, Ph.D. Dissertation, University of Michigan, 1990.

———, 'Not Only Teaching–The Work of Ecology Monk Phrakhru Pitak Nanthakhun of Thailand', *Forest, Trees and People Newsletter*, vol. 34, September 1997, pp. 17–20.

———, 'The Good Buddha and the Fierce Spirit Protecting the Northern Thai Forest', *Contemporary Buddhism*, vol. 8, no. 2, 2007, pp. 169–85.

———, 'Buddhism and Development: The Ecology Monks of Thailand', in *Action Dharma: New Studies in Engaged Buddhism*, ed. Christopher Queen, Charles Prebish and Damien Keown, London: Routledze, 2003, pp. 96–109.

———, 'The Ordination of a Tree: The Buddhist Ecology Movement in Thailand', *Ethnology*, vol. 37, no. 1, Winter 1998, pp. 1–15.

———, 'Tree Ordination in Thailand', in *Dharma Rain: Sources of Buddhist Environmentalism*, ed. Stephanie Kaza and Kenneth Kraft, Boston: Shambhala, 2000, pp. 198–205.

Darwin, Charles, *On the Origin of Species by Means of Natural Selection*, London: John Murray, 1859 (1964, reprint with introduction by Ernst Mayr).

Davids, T.W. Rhys., *Buddhist Suttas*, vol. XI, SBE, Delhi: LPP, repr. 2007.

———, *Dialogues of the Buddha*, 3 vols., Delhi: LPP, repr. 2001.

Deleanu, Florin, 'Buddhist Ethology in Pāli Canon: Between Symbol and Observation', *The Eastern Buddhist*, vol. XXXII, no. 2, 2000, pp. 79–127.

de Silva, Lily, 'The Hills Wherein My Soul Delights', in *Buddhism and Ecology*, ed. Martine Batchelor and Kerry Brown, London and New York: Cassel, 1992, pp. 18–30.

———, 'Early Buddhist Attitude Towards Nature', in *Dharma Rain: Sources of Buddhist Environmentalism*, ed. Stephanie Kaza and Kenneth Kraft, Boston: Shambhala, 2000, pp. 91–103.

de Silva, Padmasri, *Buddhism, Ethics and Society: The Conflicts and Dilemmas of Our Times*, Clayton: Monash Asia Institute, 2002.

———, *Environmental Philosophy and Buddhist Ethics*, New York: St. Martin's Press, 1998.

———, *Value Orientation and Nation Building*, Colombo: Lake House Investment, 1976.

Deitrick, James E., 'Engaged Buddhist Ethics: Mistaking the Boat for Share', in *Action Dharma: New Studies in Engaged Buddhism*, ed. Christopher S. Queen, Charles Prebish and Damien Keown, London: Routledge, 2003.

Devall, Bill, 'Deep Ecology and Political Activism', in *Dharma Rain: Sources of Buddhist Environmentalism*, ed. Stephanie Kaza and Kenneth Kraft, Boston: Shambhala, 2000, pp. 379–92.

Devall, Bill and George Session, *Deep Ecology*, Salt Lake City: Peregrive Smith Books, 1985.

Dhammika, S., *Nature and the Environment in Early Buddhism*, Singapore: Buddha Dhamma Mandala Society, 2015.

Di Zerega, Gus., 'Deep Ecology and Liberalism: The Greener Implications of Evolutionary Liberal Theory', *The Review of Politics*, vol. 58, no. 4, Autumn 1996, pp. 699–34.

Dube, S.N., *Cross Currents in Early Buddhism*, New Delhi: Manohar, 1980.

Dummont, Lois, *Homo Hierarchicus: The Caste System and its Implications*, Chicago: The University of Chicago Press, 1970.

Dundas, Paul, 'The Limits of a Jain Environmental Ethics', in *Jainism & Ecology*, ed. Christopher Key Chapple, Delhi: MLBD, 2006, pp. 95–117.

Dutt, N., 'Place of Laity In Early Buddhism', *Indian Historical Quarterly*, vol. 21, nos. 1–4, 1945, pp. 163–83.

Eckel, Malcom David, 'Is There a Buddhist Philosophy of Nature?', in *Buddhism and Ecology: The Interconnection of Dharma and Deeds*, ed. Mary Evelyn Tucker and Ducan Ryuken Williams, Cambridge, MA: Harvard University Press, 1997, pp. 327–49.

Elliot, H.M. and John Dowson, *The History of India as Told by Its Own Historians*, vol. III, Allahabad: Kitab Mahal, 1940.

Eppsteiner, Fred, *The Path of Compassion: Writings on Socially Engaged Buddhism*, Berkeley: Parallax Press, 1988.

England, Philippa, 'UNCED and the Implementation of Forest Policy in Thailand', in *Seeing Forests for Trees: Environment and Environmentalism in Thailand*, ed. Philip Hirsch, Chiang Mai: Silkworm Books, 1996, pp. 53–71.

Erdosy, George, 'The Origin of Cities in the Ganges Valley', *Journal of the Economic and Social History of Orient*, vol. 28, no. 1, 1985, pp. 85–109.

Fairservis, W.A., 'An Epigraphic View of the Harappan Culture', in *Archaeological Thought in America*, ed. C.C. Lamberg-Karlovski, Cambridge: Cambridge University Press, 1989, pp. 205–17.

Feddema, J.P., 'The "Lesser" Violence of Animal Sacrifice: A Somewhat Hidden and Overlooked (Ignored?) Reality in Sinhala Buddhism', *Anthropos*, Bd.90, H.1./3, 1995, pp. 133–48, http://www.jstor.org/stable/40463108, accessed 26 March 2012.

Fergusson, John, *War and Peace in World Religions*, New York: OUP, 1978.

Filliozat, Vasundhara, *Vijaynagar*, New Delhi: NBT, 1977.

Findly, Ellison Banks, 'Borderline Beings: Plant Possibilities in Early Buddhism', *Journal of the American Oriental Society*, vol. 122, no. 2, April–June 2002, pp. 252–63.

———, *Plant Lives: Borderline Beings in Indian Traditions*, Delhi: MLBD, 2008.

Flattery, David Stophlet and Martin Schwartz, *Haoma and Haomaline: The Botanical Identity of the Leagacy in Religion, Language and Middle Eastern Folklore*, Berkeley: University of California Press, 1989.

Foucher, A., *The Beginning of Buddhist Art and Other Essay in India and Central Asian Archaeology*, Delhi: Asian Educational Services, repr. 1994.

Freire, Paulo, *Pedagogy of the Oppressed*, New York: Continuum, 2006.

Fricke, Thomas, 'Introduction: Human Ecology in Himalayas', *Human Ecology*, vol. 17, no. 2, June 1989, pp. 131–45.

Fritsch, Albert J., *Environmental Ethics: Choices for Concerned Citizen*, Garden City New York: Anchor Books, 1980.

Fromm, Erich, *To Have or To Be?*, London: Continuum, 2008.

Fujimoto, Akira, 'Do Plants Have Lives? Two Kinds of Jivitindriya by the Theravadins', *NGBK*, vol. 68, 2003, pp. 87–109.

Gadgil, Madhav, 'Towards Ecological History of India', *Economic and Political Weekly*, vol. 20, nos. 45/47, November 1985, pp. 1909–18.

Gadgil, Madhav and Ramchandra Guha, *The Fissured Land: An Ecological History of India*, New Delhi: OUP, 1992.

Galbraith, John K., *The Affluent Society*, Hamondsworth, Middlesex: Penguin, 1962.

Gard, Richard A., *Buddhism*, New York: George Braziller, 1962.

Ghee, Lim Tech, *Reflections on Development in Southeast Asia*, Singapore: Institute of Southeast Asian Studies, 1988.

Glasenapp, Helmuth Von, *The Doctrine of Karman in Jaina Philosophy*, Bai Vijibai Jivanlal Pannalal Charity Fund, 1942.

Gordon, Wasson R. and Wendy Doniger O'Flaherty, 'The Last Meal of the Buddha', *Journal of American Oriental Society*, vol. 102, no. 4, October–December 1982, pp. 591–603.

Gombrich, Richard F., *Theravāda Buddhism: A Social History from Ancient Benares to Modern Colombo*, London & New York: Routledge and Kegan Paul, 1988.

Goudie, Andrew, *The Human Impact: On the Natural Environment*, Oxford: Basic Black Ltd., 1990.

Granoff, E. Phyllis, 'The Violence of Non-Violence: A Study of Some Jain Response to Non-Jain Religious Practices', *Journal of the International Association of Buddhist Association*, vol. 15, no. 1, 1992, pp. 1–43.

Gregg, Richard B., *A Philosophy of Indian Economic Development*, Ahmadabad: Navajivan Publishing House, 1958, pp. 140–1.

Griffin, P. and M.L. Ouellett, 'Facilitating Social Justice Education Courses', in *Teaching for Diversity and Social Justice*, ed. M. Adams, L.A. Bell and P. Griffin, New York: Routledge, 2007, pp. 89–113.

Griffith, John, *The Paintings in the Buddhist Cave Temples of Ajanta*, London: The Author, 1896.

Gross, Rita M., 'Buddhist Resources for Issues of Population, Consumption and the Environment', in *Population, Consumption and the Environment: Religious and Secular Responses*, ed. Harold G. Coward, Albany: State University of New York Press, 1995, pp. 291–312.

George, Grimm, *The Doctrine of the Buddha: The Religion of Reason and Meditation*, Leipzig: W. Drugulin, 1926.

———, 'Population, Consumption and Environment', in *Dharma Rain: Sources of Buddhist Environmentalism*, ed. Stephanie Kaza and Kenneth Kraft, Boston: Shambhala, 2000, pp. 409–22.

———, 'Toward a Buddhist Environmental Ethic', *Journal of American Acdemy of Religion*, vol. 65, no. 2, 1997, pp. 333–53.

Gurge, Ananda W.P., 'Buddhist Economics—Myth and Reality', *Hsi Lai Journal of Humanistic Buddhism*, 2006, pp. 71–130.

———, *Return to Righteousness: A Collection of Speeches, Essays and Letters of Anagarika Dhammapala*, Colombo: Government Press, 1965.

Gunn, Michael C., 'Cultural Ecology: A Brief Overview', *Nebraska Anthropologist*, vol. 5, 1980, pp. 19–27.

Gustafson, James M., *A Sense of Divine: The Natural Environment From a Theocentric Perspective*, Cleveland: Pilgrim Press, 1996.

Gyatso, Tenzin, H.H. Dalai Lama, 'A Tibetan Buddhist Perspective on Spirit in Nature', in *Sprit and Nature: Why the Environment is a Religious*

Issue, ed. Rocheteller Steven C. and John C. Elder Bostan: Becon Press, 1992, pp. 109–23.

Habib, Irfan, *Man and Environment: The Ecological History of India*, Delhi: Tulika Books, 2010.

———, *The Atlas of the Mughal Empire; Political and Economic Maps with Detailed Notes, Bibliography and Index*, Delhi: OUP, 1982.

Hakamaya, Noriaki, 'Shizen-hihen to-shite no Bukkyo' (*Buddhism as a Criticism of Physis/Natura*). *Kamazawa-daiguku Bukkyogakubu Ronshu*, vol. 21, 1990, pp. 380–3.

Halifex, Roshi Joan and Marty Peale, 'Interbeing: Precepts and Practices of an Applied Ecology', www.upaya.org/roshi/dox/interbing/pdf.

Hallisey, Charles and Anne Hansen, 'Narrative, Sub-Ethics, and the Moral Life: Some Evidence From Theravāda Buddhism', *The Journal of Religious Ethics*, vol. 24, no. 2, 1996, pp. 305–27.

Hanh, Michael, 'Buddhist Contribution to Indian Belles Letters', *Acta Orientalia Acadiamiae Scientiarum Hungaricae*, vol. 63, no. 4, December 2010, p. 455.

Hanh, Thick Nhat, *Vietnam: Lotus in a Sea of Fire*, New York: Hill and Wary, 1967.

———, 'The Last Tree', in *Dharma Gaia: Harvest of Essays in Buddhism and Ecology*, ed. Allan Hunt Badiner, California: Parallax Press, 1990, pp. 217–21.

———, 'The Sun My Heart', in *Dharma Rain: Sources of Buddhist Environmentalism*, ed. Stephanie Kaza and Kenneth Kraft, Boston, London: Shambhala, 2000.

Hargrove, Eugene, 'Weak Anthropocentric Intrinsic Value', in *After Earth Day*, ed. Max Oelschlaeger, Denton: University of North Texas Press, 1992.

Harper, Katherine Anne, *The Iconography of the Saptamatrkas: Seven Hindu Goddesses of Spiritual Transformation*, New York: Edwin Mellen Press, 1989.

Harris, Ian, 'Buddhism and Ecology', in *Contemporary Buddhist Ethics*, ed. Damien Keown, Richmund, Surrey: Curzon Press, 2000.

———, 'Buddhist Environmental Ethics and Detraditionalization: The Case of Eco Buddhism', *Religion*, vol. 25, 1995, pp. 199–211.

———, 'Getting the Grip with Buddhist Environmentalism: A Provisional Typology', *Journal of Buddhist Ethics*, vol. 2, 1995, pp. 173–90.

———, 'Causation and Telos: The Problem of Buddhist Environmental Ethics', *Journal of Buddhist Ethics*, vol. 1, 1994, pp. 46–59.

———, 'Ecological Buddhism?', in *Religion and the Environment: A Global Anthology Worldviews*, ed. Richard S. Foltz, Belmont, CA: Woodsworth, 2003, pp. 171–81.

Hattam, Robert, 'Socially Engaged Buddhism as a Provocation for Critical Pedagogy in Unsettling Times', in *Cross-Cultural Studies in Curriculum:*

Eastern Thought and Educational Insights, ed. Claudia Eppert and Hongyu Wang, London: Routledge, 2008, pp. 109–136.

———, 'How Environmentalist is Buddhism?', *Religion*, vol. 21, April 1991, pp. 101–14.

Harvey, Peter, 'Buddhist Reflections on "Consumer" and "Consumerism"', *Journal of Buddhist Ethics*, vol. 20, 2013, pp. 334–56.

———, *Introduction to Buddhist Ethics*, Cambridge: Cambridge University Press, 2000.

Hearn, Lafcadio, 'Buddhist Names of Plants and Animals', in *Buddhist Writings of Lafcadio Hearn*, ed. Kenneth Rexorth, Santa Barbara: Ross Erikson, 1977, pp. 202–13.

Hesse, Barnor, *Un/Settled Multiculturism: Diasporas, Entanglements, Transruptions*, London: Zed Books, 2000.

Hirsch, Philip, 'Environment and Environmentalism in Thailand: Material and Ideological Bases', in *Seeing Forest For Trees: Environment and Environmentalism in Thailand*, ed. Philip Hirsch, Chang Mai: Silk Worm Books, 1996, pp. 15–36.

Hirsch, Philip and Carol Warren, *The Politics of Environment in Southeast Asia: Resource and Resistance*, London: Routledge, 1998.

Horner, I.B., *Early Buddhism and Taking of Life*, Kandy: BPS, 2008.

Howard, Jonathan, *Darwin: A Very Short Introduction*, Delhi: OUP, 1982.

Hughes, J. Donal, 'Ecology in Ancient Greece', *Inquiry*, vol. 18, 1975, pp. 115–25.

———, *Ecology in Ancient Civilization*, Albuquerque, New Mexico: University of New Mexico Press, 1975.

———, 'The Environmental Ethics of Pythagoreans', *Environmental Ethics*, vol. 2, 1980, pp. 195–213.

Hultzsch, E., *Corpus Inscriptionum Indicarum (Inscriptions of Aśoka)*, Delhi: Indological Books, 1969.

Ignacy, Sachs, 'Development, Maldevelopment and Industrialization of Third World Countries', *Development and Change*, vol. X, no. 4, 1979, pp. 635–46.

Ives, Christopher, 'In Search of Green Dharma: Philosophical Issues in Buddhist Environmental Ethics', in *Destroying Mara Forever: Buddhist Ethics Essays in Honor of Damien Keown*, ed. John Power and Charles S. Prebish, Ithaca, New York: Snow Lion Publications, 2009, pp. 165–85.

———, 'Resources for Buddhist Environmental Ethics', *Journal of Buddhist Ethics*, vol. 30, 2013, pp. 541–71, accessed 23 April 2014.

Jaickson, Peter A., *Buddhism, Legitimation, and Conflict: The Political Findings of Urban Thai Buddhism*, Singapore: Institute of Southeast Asian Studies, 1989.

Jain, Bhagachandra, 'Ecology and Spirituality in Jain Tradition', in *Jainism & Ecology: Nonviolence in the Web of Life*, ed. Christopher Key Chapple, Delhi: MLBD, 2006, pp. 168–80.

Jaina, Jyotendra and Eberhard Fisher, *Jaina Iconography*, Leiden: Brill, 1978.

Jaini, Jagmander Lal, *The Outlines of Jainism*, Cambridge: Cambridge University Press, 1976.

Jaini, Padmanabh S., 'Ecology, Economics, and Development in Jainism', in *Jainism & Ecology*, ed. Christopher Key Chapple, Delhi: MLBD, 2006, pp. 141–58.

———, 'From Nigoda to Moksa: The Story of Marudevi', *Proceedings of International Conference on Jainism and Early Buddhism*, Lund University, 4–7 June 1998.

———, 'Indian Perspective on Spirituality of Animals', in *Buddhist Philosophy and Culture: Essays in Honour of N. A. Jayawickrama*, ed. David J. Kalupahana and W.G. Weeraratne, Colombo: N.A. Jayawickrama Felicitation Committee, 1987, pp. 169–78.

———, *The Jaina Path of Purification*, California: University of California, 1979.

Jayasuriya, Laksiri, 'Buddhism: Politics and Statecraft', *International Journal of Buddhist Thought and Culture*, vol. 11, September 2008, pp. 47–74.

Jha, D.N., *The Myth of the Holy Cow*, London: Verso, 2002.

Jones, Ken, 'Buddhism and Social Action: An Exploration', in *The Path of Compassion: Writings on Socially Engaged Buddhism*, ed. Fred Eppsteiner, Berkeley: Parallax Press, 1988, pp. 65–81.

———, *The Social Face of Buddhism: An Approach to Political and Social Activism*, London: Wisdom, 1992.

Jung, Hwa Yol, 'The Harmony of Man and Nature: A Philosophical Manifesto', *Philosophical Inquiry*, vol. 8, 1986, pp. 32–49.

Jung, Hwa Yol and Peter Jung, 'Gary Snyder's Ecopiety', *Environmental History Review*, vol. 14, no. 3, Autumn 1990, pp. 74–87, http://www.jstor.org/stable/3984727, accessed 21 March 2012.

Kabilsingh, Chatsumarn, 'Buddhist Monks and Forest Conservation', in *Radical Conservatism: Buddhism in the Contemporary World, Essays in Honour of Bhikkhu Buddhadasa's 84th Birthday*, ed. Sulak Sivaraksa, Bangkok: Sathirakoses-Nagapradipa Foundation, 1990, pp. 301–10.

———, 'Early Buddhist View on Nature', in *Dharma Gaia: Sources of Buddhist Environmentalism*, ed. Allan Hunt Badiner, Berkeley: Parallax Press, 1990, pp. 8–13.

Kalupahana, David J., *Buddhist Philosophy: A Historical Analysis*, Hawaii: University Press of Hawaii, 1976.

———, *Ethics in Early Buddhism*, New Delhi: MLBD, 1995.

———, *Karma and Rebirth: Foundations of The Buddha's Moral Philosophy*, Colombo: Buddhist Cultural Centre, 2009.

———, 'Man and Nature: Towards a Middle Path of Survival', *Environmental Ethics*, vol. 8, no. 4, 1986, pp. 371–80.

Kapleau, Philip, 'Responsibility and Social Action', in *Dharma Rain: Sources of Buddhist Environmentalism*, ed. Stephanie Kaza and Kenneth Kraft, Boston, London: Shambhala, 2000, pp. 241–5.

Kaza, Stephanie, 'Overcoming the Grip of Consumerism', *Buddhist-Christian Studies*, vol. 20, 2000, pp. 23–42.

Kaza, Stephanie and Kenneth Kraft, *Dharma Rain: Sources of Buddhist Environmentalism*, ed. Stephanie Kaza and Kenneth Kraft, Boston: Shambhala, 2000.

Kelley, A. Parkar, 'Pragmatism and Environmental Thought', in *Environmental Pragmatism*, ed. Andrew Light and Eric Katz, London: Routledge, 1996, pp. 21–37.

Keown, Damien, *Buddhism and Bioethics*, London: Macmillan and St. Martin Press, 1995.

———, *Contemporary Buddhist Ethics*, Richmond Surrey: Curzon Press, 2000.

Kemmerer, Lisa, 'Buddhist Ethics and Nonhuman Animals', *Peace Study Journal*, vol. I, issue I, Fall 2008, pp. 13–28.

Keys, Charles F., 'Communist Revolution and the Buddhist Past in Cambodia', in *Asian Visions of Authority: Religion and Modern States of East and Southeast Asia*, ed. Charles F. Keys, Laurel Kendall, Helen Hardacre, Honolulu: University of Hawaii Press, 1994.

King, Sallie B., 'Thich Nhat Hanh and the United Buddhist Church of Vietnam: Non-Dualism in Action', in *Buddhist Liberation Movements in Asia*, ed. Christopher S. Queen and Sallie B. King, Albany: State University of New York Press, 1996, pp. 321–64.

King, Winston L., *In the Hope of Nibbāna; An Essay in Theravada Buddhist Ethics*, Illinois: Open Court Publishing Company, 1964.

Kitagawa, Joseph M., 'Buddhism and Social Change: An Historical Perspective', in *Buddhist Studies in Honour of Walapola Rahula*, ed. Somaratna Balassoriya, Andre Bareau, Richard Gombrich, Siri Gunasingha, Udaya Mallawarachchi and Edmund Perry, London: Gordon Fraser, 1980, pp. 84–101.

Koller, John M., 'Jain Ecological Perspectives', in *Jainism & Ecology*, ed. Christopher Key Chapple, Delhi: MLBD, 2006, pp. 19–34.

Koller, John M. and Patricia J. Koller, *Asian Phillosophies*, UPPS Saddle River N.J.: Prentice Hall, 2002.

Kraft, Kenneth, *Inner Peace World Peace: Essays on Buddhism and Non-Violence*, Albany: State University of New York Press, 1992.

———, 'Nuclear Ecology and Engaged Buddhism', *Dharma Rain: Sources of Buddhist Environmentalism*, ed. Stephanie Kaza and Kenneth Kraft, Boston: Shambhala, 2000, pp. 393–408.

Kramrisch, Stella, 'The Mahavira Vessel and the Plant Putika', *Journal of American Oriental Society*, vol. 95, no. 2, April–June 1975, pp. 222–35.

Kuhn, Thomas S., *The Copernicus Revolution, Planetary Astronomy and the Development of Western Thought*, New York: Random House, 1959.

Lafleur, William R., 'Enlightenment for Plants and Tress', in *Dharma Rain: Sources of Buddhist Environmentalism*, ed. Stephanie Kaza and Kenneth Kraft, Boston, London: Shambhala, 2000, pp. 109–16.

———, 'Saigyo and the Buddhist Value of Nature', *History of Religion*, vol. 13, no. 2, 1974, pp. 93–128.

Lal, B.B., *The Earliest Civilization of South Asia, Rise, Maturity and Decline*, Delhi: Aryan Books International, 1997.

———, *The Homeland of Aryans: Evidence of Rigvedic Flora and Fauna and Archaeology*, Delhi: Aryan Books International, 2005.

Lal, Makkhan, *Archaeology of Population*, Vārānasī: BHU, 1984.

———, 'Summary of Four Season Explorations in Kanpur District, Uttar Pradesh', *Man and Environment*, vol. 8, 1984, pp. 61–80.

———, *Settlement History and the Rise of Civilization in the Ganga-Yamuna Doab*, New Delhi: B.R. Publishing, 1984.

———, 'Iron Tools, Forest Clearance, and Urbanization in Gangetic Plains', in *Iron and Social Change in Early India*, ed. B.P. Sahu, New Delhi: OUP, 2006, pp. 137–49.

Lama, Dalai, 'Five Point Peace Plan for Tibet', in *The Anguish of Tibet*, ed. Petra K. Kelly, Gert Bastian and Pat Aiello, Berkeley: Parallax Press, 1991, pp. 285–96.

———, 'A Tibetan Buddhist Perspective on Spirit in Nature', in *Spirit and Nature: Why the Environment is Religious Issue*, ed. Steven C. Rochoteller and John C. Elder, Boston: Becon Press, 1992, pp. 109–23.

———, 'Make Tibet a Zone of Peace', in *Dharma Rain: Sources of Buddhist Environmentalism*, ed. Stephanie Kaza and Kenneth Kraft, Boston, London: Shambhala, 2000, pp. 231–6.

Lamotte, Etienne, *Historie du bouddhisme indien: Des Origins a lere Saka*, Bibliotheque du Museon, vol. 43, Louvian: Universite de Louvain, 1958.

Lannoy, Richard, *The Spiriting Tree: A Study of Indian Culture and Society*, New York: OUP, 1971.

Lawrence, C.R. III, 'If He Hollers Let Him Go: Regulating Racist Speech on Campus', in *Words That Wounds: Critical Race Theory, Assaultive Speech and the First Amendment*, ed. M.J. Matsuda, C.R. Lawrence III, R. Delgado and K. Crenshaw, Boulder CO: Westview Press, 1993, pp. 17–51.

Leopold, Aldo, *The Land Ethics*, ed. Hugh La Follette, *Ethics in Practice: An Anthology*, Oxford: Blackwell, 1997, pp. 621–30.

———, *A Sand County Almanac and Sketches Here and There*, Oxford: Oxford University Press, 1997.

Levitt, Stephan Hillyer, 'New Considerations Regarding the Identity of Vedic Soma as the Mushroom Fly-Agaric', *Studia Orientalia*, vol. 111, 2011, pp. 105–18.

Loori, John Daido, 'River Seeing the River', in *Dharma Rain: Sources of Buddhist Environmentalism*, ed. Stephanie Kaza and Kenneth Kraft, Boston, London: Shambhala, 2000, pp. 141–9.

Lopez, Donald S., Jr., *Curators of the Buddha: The Study of Buddhism under Colonialism*, Chicago: University of Chicago Press, 1996.

Lovelock, James E., *Gaia: A New Look at Life on Earth*, New York: OUP, 1979.

Loy, David R., *Great Awakening: A Buddhist Social Theory*, Somerville: Wisdom Publications, 2003.

————, 'The Religion of the Market', *Journal of the American Academy of Religion*, vol. 65, no. 2, Summer 1997, pp. 275–90.

Macdermott, James P., 'Animal and Human in Early Buddhism', *Indo-Iranian Journal*, vol. 32, no. 2, 1989, pp. 269–80.

————, 'Is There Group Karma in Theravāda Buddhism?', *Numen*, vol. 23, Fasc. 1, April 1976, pp. 67–80, htttp://www.jstor.org/stable/3269557, accessed 8 February 2013.

Macy, Joanna, *Dharma and Development: Religion as Resource in the Sarodaya Self-Help Movement*, West Hartford: Kumarian Press, 1983.

————, 'Guarding the Earth', in *Dharma Rain: Sources of Buddhist Environmentalism*, ed. Stephanie Kaza and Kenneth Kraft, Boston: Shambhala, 2000, pp. 293–302.

————, 'The Greening of the Self', in *Dharma Gaia: A Harvest of Essays in Buddhism and Ecology*, ed. Alan Hunt Badiner, Berkely,: Parallax Press, 1990, pp. 53–63.

————, 'The Sounds of Bombs not Exploding', *Yes Magazine*, 30 June 2002, p. 53.

————, *World as Lover, World as Self*, California: Parallax Press, 1991.

Macy, Joanna and Molly Young Brown, *Coming Back to Life: Practices to Reconnect Our Lives, Our World*, Gabriola Island, BC: New Society Publishers, 1998.

Mahalingum, T.V., *Administration and Social Life under Vijaynagar*, Madras: University of Madras, 1940.

Majumdar, R.C., *The Age of Imperial Unity*, Bombay: Bharatiya Vidya Bhavan, 1980.

Malalasekera, G.P., *Dictionary of Pāli Proper Names.*, 2 vols., Delhi: MLBD, 2007.

Malandra, W.W., 'Atharvaveda 2.27: Evidence for a Soma-Amulet', *Journal of American Oriental Society*, vol. 99, 1979, pp. 220–4.

Mandal, K.K., 'Agricultural Technology in the Jātaka', *Proceedings of Indian History Congress*, 59th Session, 1998, pp. 97–107.

Marsh, G.P., *Man and Nature*, New York: Scribner, 1965.

Martin, Julia, *Ecological Responsibility: A Dialogue with Buddhism*, Delhi: D.K. Press, 1997.

Martin, Rafe, 'Thoughts on Jātakas', in *Dharma Rain: Sources of Buddhist Environmentalism*, ed. Stephanie Kaza and Kenneth Kraft, Boston, London: Shambhala, 2000, pp. 104–8.

Masuda, Jiryo, 'Origin and Doctrine of Early Indian Buddhist Schools', *Asia Major*, vol. II, 1925, pp. 1–78, see p. 21.

McHarg, Ian L., *Design With Nature*, New York: Double Day and Company, 1969.

McDermott, J.P., 'Animals and Humans in Early Buddhism', *Indo-Iranian Journal*, vol. 32, 1989, pp. 269–80.

McElroy, Michael B., *The Atmospheric Environment: Effects of Human Activity*, Princeton: Princeton University Press, 2002.

McEvilley, Thomas, 'An Archaeology of Yoga', *RES*, no. 1, 1961, pp. 44–77.

McLaren, P. and H. Giroux, 'Radical Pedagogy as Cultural Politics: Beyond the Discourse of Critique and Anti-Utopianism', in *Critical Pedagogy and Predatory Culture: Oppositional Politics in Post Modern Era*, ed. P. McLarenpp, 1995, pp. 29–57.

McMahan, David L., *The Making of Buddhist Modernism*, Oxford: Oxford University Press, 2008.

Merchant, Carolyn, *Ecology*, Delhi: Rawat Publications, 1996.

Miller, Cynthia, 'The Impact of Christianity on Buddhist Nonviolence in the West', *Inner Peace, World Peace: Essays on Buddhism and Nonviolence*, ed. Kenneth Kraft, Albany: State University of New York Press, 1992, pp. 91–110.

Mills, Martin A., Toni Huber and Poul Pedersen, 'Ecological Knowledge in Tibet', *The Journal of Royal Anthropological Institute*, vol. 4, no. 4, December 1998, pp. 783–6.

Milton, J. Gorden, *The Encyclopaedia of Religious Phenomenon*, Canton: Visible Ink Press, 2008.

Mittal, Mahendra P., *Buddha and Early Buddhism*, New Delhi: LPP, 2006.

Mookerjee, R.K., *Aśoka*, Delhi: MLBD, 2007.

Nakamura, Hujime, 'The Idea of Nature: East and West', *The Great Ideas Today, Encyclopedia Britannica*, 1980, pp. 235–302.

Naomi, Appleton, '*Jātakas*' *Oxford Research Encyclopedia of Religion*, August 2016, pp. 1–16.

Naess, Arne, 'Deep Ecology', ed. Carolyn Merchant, *Ecology*, Delhi: Rawat, 1996.

———, 'The Deep Ecology Movement: Some Philosophical Aspects', *Philosophical Inquiry*, vol. 8, 1986, pp. 10–31.

———, 'The Shallow and the Deep, Long Range Ecology Movement: A Summary', *Inquiry: An Interdisciplinary Journal of Philosophy and the Social Sciences*, vol. 16, 1973, pp. 95–100.

Neumann, Karl Eugen, *Die Reden Gotomo Buddho'saus des mittlerensammlung Majjhimanikayo des Pāli-kanons*, Leipzig, 1896.

Nishkar, Wes and Barbara Gates, 'The Third Turning of the Wheel—A Conversation with Joanna Macy', in *Dharma Rain: Sources of Buddhist Environmentalism*, ed. Stephanie Kaza and Kenneth Kraft, Boston, London: Shambhala, 2000, pp. 150–60.

Obeysekere, Gananath, 'Buddhism and Conscience', *Daedalus*, vol. 120, 1991, pp. 219–39.

———, 'Religious Symbolism and Political Change in Ceylon', in *The Two Wheels of Dharma: Essays on the Theravāda Tradition in India and Ceylon*, ed. Gananath Obeyesekere, Frank Renolds and Bardwell L. Smith, Chambersburg: *American Academy of Religion*, 1972, pp. 58–78.

Odum, Eugene P., *Ecology: The Link Between the Natural and the Social Sciences*, New York: Holt Rinehart and Winston, 1975.

Oldmeadow, Peter, 'Buddhist Yogacara Philosophy and Ecology', 2008, pp. 238–52, ojs-prod.library.usyd.edu.au/index/ssr/article/download/ 669/649, accessed 21 May 2013.

O'Flaherty, W.D., 'Epilogue: The Last Meal of the Buddha', *Journal of the American Oriental Society*, vol. 102, no. 4, 1982, pp. 591–603, see p. 603.

Okada, Mamiko, 'Eco-paradigm in Buddhist Narrative Literature: Plants and Tress and Ecoethics', *IBK*, vol. 93, no. 47.1, 1998, pp. 226–30.

Ophuls, William, 'Notes for a Buddhist Politics', *Dharma Rain: Sources of Buddhist Environmentalism*, ed. Stephanie Kaza and Kenneth Kraft, Boston: Shambhala, 2000, pp. 369–78.

Ostovari, Nasrin, Seyed Abolghasem Foruzani, Seyed Alireza Golshani and Sara Adloo, 'A Historical Survey on "Haoma" Plant in Ancient Iran and India', *Research on History of Medicine*, vol. 2, no. 4, 2013, pp. 129–34.

Pandey, G.C., *Studies in the Origin of Buddhism*, Delhi: Orient Books, 1974.

Parker, Kelly A., 'Pragmatism and Environmental Thought', *Environmental Pragmatism*, ed. Andrew Light and Eric Katz, London: Routledge, 1996, pp. 352–76.

Passmore, John, *Man's Responsibility for Nature: Ecological Problems and Western Traditions*, London: Duckworth, 1974.

———, 'The Treatment of Animals', *Journal of History of Ideas*, vol. 36, no. 2, April–May 1975, pp. 195–218.

Paul, Sherman, *In Search of Primitive*, Baton Rouge: Lousiana State University Press, 1986.

Payutto, P.A., *Buddhist Economics: A Middle Way for the Market Place*, tr. Dhammavijaya and Bruce Evans, Bangkok: Buddhadharma Foundation, 1994.

———, 'Buddhist Solution for the Twenty-First Century', *Dharma Rain: Sources of Buddhist Environmentalism*, ed. Stephanie Kaza and Kenneth Kraft, Boston: Shambhala, 2000, pp. 170–8.

———, *Khon Thai Kap Pa (Thais and the Forest)*, Bangkok: Association for Agriculture and Biology, 1994.

Peale, Marty and Joan Halifax, 'Interbeing: Precepts and Practices of an Applied Ecology', pp. 1–25, www.upaya.org/roshi/dox/Interbeing.pdf, accessed 1 May 2013.

Pedersen, Poul, Martin A. Mills and Toni Huber, 'Ecological Knowledge in Tibet', *The Journal of the Royal Anthropological Institute*, vol. 4, no. 4, December 1998, pp. 783–6.

Perry, Patricia Hunt and Lyn Fine, 'All Buddhism is Engaged: Thich Nhat Hanh and The Order of Inter-being', *Engaged Buddhism in the West*, ed. Christopher S. Queen, Sommervile: Wisdom Publications, 2000, pp. 35–66.

Pfanner, David E. and Jasper Ingersoll, 'Theravāda Buddhism and Village Economic Behaviour: A Burmese and Thai Comparison', *The Journal of Asian Studies*, vol. 21, no. 3, May 1962, pp. 341–61, http://www.jstor.org/stable/2050678, accessed 27 March 2012.

Pholpoke, Chayant, 'The Chiang Mai Cable Car Project: Local Controversy over Cultural and Eco-Tourism', *The Politics of Environment in Southeast Asia: Resources and Restrain*, ed. Philip Hirsch and Carol Wassen, London: Routledge, 1998, pp. 262–77.

Poething, Kathryn, 'Movable Peace: Engaging the Transnational in Cambodian Dhammyietra', *Journal for Scientific Study of Religion*, vol. 41, no. 1, March 2002, pp. 19–28.

Polanyi, Karl, *The Great Transformation*, Boston: Beacon Press, 1958.

Pracha, Hulanuwatr and Rasbash Janeb, *Globalization from Buddhist Perspective*, *Bodhi Leaves*, no. 146, Kandy: Buddhist Publication Society, 1998.

Prebish, Charles S., 'Ambiguity and Conflict in the Study of Buddhist Ethics: An Introduction', *Journal of Religious Ethics*, vol. 24, no. 2, 1996, pp. 295–303.

———, *Luminous Passage: The Practice and Study of Buddhism in America*, Berkeley: University of California Press, 1998.

Prime, Ranchor, *Hinduism and Ecology: Seed of Truth*, London: Cassel Publishers, 1992.

Pryor, Frederic L., 'A Buddhist Economic System in Practice: The Rules of State Policy Making of the Ideal Kings Sought a "Middle Way" between Right and Left', *American Journal of Economics and Sociology*, vol. 50, no. 1, January 1991, pp. 17–33.

———, 'A Buddhist Economic System in Principle: Non-attachment to Worldly Things is Dominant But the Way of the Law is Held Profitable', *American Journal of Economics and Sociology*, vol. 49, no. 3, July 1990, pp. 339–51.

Puntarigvivat, Tavivat, 'Buddhadasa Bhikkhu and Dhammic Socialism', *The Chulalongkorn Journal of Buddhist Studies*, vol. 2, no. 2, 2003, pp. 189–207, accessed 10 March 2014.

———, 'Buddhist Economics: A Thai Theravāda Perspective', *World Buddhism: Journal of the World Buddhist University*, no. 1, 2004.

Quaye, S.J., 'Think Before You Teach: Preparing for Dialogue About Racial Realities', *Journal of College of Student Development*, vol. 53, no. 4, 2012, pp. 542–62.

Queen, S. Christopher, ed., *Engaged Buddhism in the West*, Somerville: Wisdom Publications, 2000.

———, 'Introduction: The Shapes and Sources of Engaged Buddhism', in *Engaged Buddhism: Buddhist Liberation Movements in Asia*, ed. Christopher S.

Queen and Sallie B. King, Albany: State University of New York Press, 1996, pp. 1–44.

Queen, S. Christopher, Charles Prebish and Damien Keown, eds., *Action Dharma: New Studies in Engaged Buddhism*, London: Routledge, 2003.

Queen, S. Christopher and Sallie B. King, eds., *Engaged Buddhism: Buddhist Liberation Movements in Asia*, Abany: State University Press of New York, 1996.

Rahula, Walpola, *The Heritage of the Bhikkhu: A Short History of the Bhikkhu in Educational, Cultural, Social and Political Life*, New York: Grove Press, 1974.

———, *What the Buddha Taught*, London: Gordon Frazer, 1959.

Rajapakse, Vijitha, 'Early Buddhism and John Stuart Mill's Thinking in the Fields of Philosophy and Religion: Some Notes Toward Comparative Study', *Philosophy East and West*, vol. 37, no. 3, July 1987, pp. 260–85, http://www.jstor.org/stable/1398519, accessed 23 March 2012.

Ramakomud, Sriprinya, 'Theravāda Buddhist Values and Economic Development', *Crossroads: An Interdisciplinary Journal of Southeast Asian Studies*, vol. 2, no. 2, 1985, pp. 83–9, http://www.jstor.org/stable/40860204, accessed 28 March 2012.

Ramonan, K. Venkata, *Nagarjuna Philosophy*, Tokyo, 1966.

Ray, Reginald A., *Buddhist Saints in India: A Study in Buddhist Values and Orientations*, Oxford: Oxford University Press, 1994.

Raychaudhuri, Hemchandra, *Political History of Ancient India*, Calcutta: University of Calcutta, 1972.

Reynolds, Frank E., 'Ethics and Wealth in Theravāda Buddhism: A Study in Comparative Religious Ethics', in *Ethics, Wealth and Salvation: A Study in Buddhist Ethics*, ed. Russel F Sizemore and Donald K. Swearer, Columbia: University of South Carolina Press, 1990, pp. 59–76.

Reynolds, Frank E. and Regina T. Clifford, 'Sangha, Society, and the Struggle for Social Identity: Burma and Thailand', in *Transition and Transformation in the History of Religion*, ed. Frank Reynalds and Ludwig Theodore, Leiden: Brill, 1980, pp. 56–91.

Ray, Reginald A., *Buddhist Saints in India: A Study in Buddhist Values and Orientations*, Oxford: Oxford University Press, 1994.

Rawls, John, *A Theory of Justice,* London: Oxford University Press, 1973.

Ricoeur, Paul, 'Imagination in Discourses and in Action', in *Rethinking Imagination: Cultural Creativity*, ed. Gillian Robinson and John Rundell, London: Routledge, 1994, pp. 118–35.

Rigg, Jonathan, ed., *Counting the Costs: Economic Growth and Environmental Change in Thailand*, Singapore: Institute of Southeast Asian Studies, 1995, pp. 3–24.

Robert, Elizabeth, 'Gaian Buddhism', in *Dharma Gaia: A Harvest of Essays in Buddhism and Ecology*, ed. Allan Hunt Badiner, Berekely: Parallax Press, 1999, pp. 147–54.

Roshi, Robert Aitken, *The Mind of Clover: Essays in Zen Buddhist Ethics*, San Francisco: North Point Press, 1984.

Ruegg, D. Seyfrot, 'Ahiṃsa and Vegetarianism in the History of Buddhism', *Buddhist Studies in Honour of Rahula Walapola*, ed. Somaratna Balasooriya, London: Gorden Frazer, 1980, pp. 234–41.

Rupp, George, 'The Relationship between Nirvana and Samsara: An Essay on the Evolution of Buddhist Ethics', *Philosophy of East and West*, vol. 21, no. 1, January 1971, pp. 55–67.

Russell, Josiah C., 'The Population of Ancient India: A Tentative Pattern', *Journal of Indian History*, University of Kerala, 1973, pp. 267–81.

———, 'The Population of Hiuen Tsang's India (AD 629–645)', *Journal of Indian History*, vol. XLVII, no. 1, 1969, pp. 367–83.

Saddhatissa, H., *Buddhist Ethics: Essence of Buddhism*, London: George Allen and Unwin Ltd., 1970.

Sahni, Pragati, *Environmental Ethics in Buddhism: A Virtue Approach*, New York: Routledge, 2008.

———, 'Environmental Ethics in the Jātakas: Further Reflections', *Buddhist Approach to Environmental Crisis*, Bangkok: MCU, pp. 129–45.

Salgado, Nirmala, *The Structure of Evil and Ethical Action in the Jātakatthavaṅṅanā*, unpublished thesis, Northwestern University, 1992.

Sandell, Klas, *Buddhist Perspectives on the Ecocrisis*, Kandy: BPS, 1987.

Santikaro, Bhikkhu, 'Buddhadasa Bhikkhu: Life and Society through the Natural Eyes of Voidness', in *Engaged Buddhism: Buddhism Libration Movements in Asia*, ed. Christopher S. Queen and Sallie B. King, Albany: SUNY, MA, 2000, pp. 147–93.

Sarao, K.T.S., 'Ancient Indian Buddhism and Ahijsa', www.purifymind.com.

Sasse, Rolien, *Evaluation of the Dhammayeitra*, Cambodia: Centre for Peace and Non-Violence, 1999, http//www.igc.apc.org.

Shaeffaer, Francis A., *Pollution and the Death of Man: The Christian View of Ecology*, Wheaton, Illinois: Tyndale House, 1971.

Shilapi, Sadhvi, 'The Environmental and Ecological Teachings of Tirthankara Mahavira', in *Jainism & Ecology: Nonviolence in the Web of Life*, ed. Christopher Key Chapple, Delhi: MLBD, 2006, pp. 159–67.

Schmithausen, Lambert, *Buddhism and Nature*, Studia Philologia Buddhica, vol. VII, Tokyo: The International Institute of Buddhist Studies, 1991.

———, *Plants in Early Buddhism and the Far Eastern Idea of the Buddha-Nature of Grasses and Trees*, Lumbini: Lumbini International Research Institute, 2009.

———, 'The Early Buddhist Tradition and Ecological Ethics', pp. 9–10, dharmaflower.net.

———, *The Problems of Sentience of the Plants in Early Buddhism*, Studia Philologica Studia, vol. VI, Tokyo: The International Institute of Buddhist Studies, 1991.

Schumacher, E.F., 'Buddhist Economics', *Manas*, vol. XXII, no. 33, 1969, pp. 1–15.

———, *Small is Beautiful: Economics As if People Mattered*, New York: Harper and Row, 1975.

———, 'Industrialization through Intermediate Technology', *Minerals and Industries*, vol. 1, no. 4, Calcutta, 1964.

Seed, John, 'Rain Forest as a Teacher', in *Dharma Rain: Sources of Buddhist Environmentalism*, ed. Stephanie Kaza and Kenneth Kraft, Boston: Shambhala, 2000, pp. 293–302.

Seed, John, Joanna Macy, Pat Flemming and Arne Nash, *Thinking Like a Mountain: Towards a Council of All Beings*, Philadelphia: New Society Publications, 1988.

Sessions, Robert, 'Deep Ecology verses Ecofeminism: Healthy Differences or Incompatible Philosophies?', *Hypatia*, vol. 6, no. 1, *Ecological Feminism*, Spring 1991, pp. 90–107.

Shaida, S.A., 'Environmental Ethics: A Historical, Intellectual Background', in *Readings in Environmental Ethics: Multidisplinary Perspecticve*, ed. D.C. Srivastava, Delhi: Rawat Publications, 2005, pp. 3–13.

Sharma, R.S., *Material Culture and Social Formation in Ancient India*, Delhi: Macmillan, 2001.

———, *India's Ancient Past*, Delhi: Oxford University Press, 2005.

Shively, Donald H., 'Basho—The Man and the Plant', *Harvard Journal Asiatic Studies*, vol. 16, 1953, pp. 146–61.

———, 'Buddhahood for the Nonsentient: A Theme in the Plays', *Harvard Journal of Asiatic Studies*, vol. 20, 1957, pp. 135–61.

Shrimali, Krishna Mohan, 'Religion, Ideology and Society', *Social Scientist*, vol. 16, no. 12, December 1988, pp. 14–60.

———, *The Age of Iron and the Religious Revolution (700–350 BC)*, New Delhi: Tulika Books, 2010.

Sikdar, J.C., 'The Fabric of Life as Conceived in Jaina Biology', *Sambodhi*, vol. 3, 1974, pp. 1–10.

Singer, Peter, *Practical Ethics*, Cambridge: Cambridge University Press, 2000.

Singh, Anand, *Buddhism at Sārnāth*, Delhi: Primus Books, 2014.

———, 'Buddhist Response to Educational Crisis: Locating Space for Creating and Sustaining of Just Society', *Buddhism and World Crisis*, Bangkok: MCU, 2015, pp. 447–57.

———, 'Ecological Consciousness in Buddhist Theism and Their Role in Recovery of Global Ecological Crisis', *Global Recovery: The Buddhist Perspective*, Bangkok: MCU, 2010, pp. 3–13.

———, 'Ecological and Environmental Concerns amongst the Buddhist Communities of Ladakh: A Case Study', in *Buddhist Virtues in Socio-Economic Development*, Bangkok: MCU, 2011, pp. 428-40.

————, 'Social Issues in Early Buddhism: Gender, Caste and Class', *The Mahabodhi*, vol. 116, no. 6, 2008–9, pp. 8–16.

Singh, Dhruvasen and Ajai Mishra, 'Gangotri Glacier Characteristics, Retreats and Processes of Sedimentation in the Bhagirathi Valley', *Natural Symposium . . . Science Integrated and Related Societal Issues: Geological Survey of India*, no. 65, 2001, pp. 17–20.

Sivaraksa, Sulak, 'Being in the World: A Buddhist Ethical and Social Concern', *Buddhist-Christian Studies*, vol. 11, 1991, pp. 200–10.

————, 'Buddhism with Small b', in *Dharma Rain: Sources of Buddhist Environmentalism*, ed. Stephanie Kaza and Kenneth Kraft, Boston: Shambhala, 2000, pp. 177–24.

————, *Conflict, Culture, and Change: Engaged Buddhism in a Globalizing World*, Somerville: Wisdom Publications, 2005.

————, 'Development As if People Mattered', in *Dharma Rain: Sources of Buddhist Environmentalism*, ed. Stephanie Kaza and Kenneth Kraft, Boston, London: Shambhala, 2000, pp. 183–90.

————, 'Economic Aspects of Social and Environmental Violence from a Buddhist Perspective', *Buddhist-Christian Studies*, vol. 22, 2002, pp. 47–60.

————, 'The Religion of Consumerism', in *Dharma Rain: Sources of Buddhist Environmentalism*, ed. Stephanie Kaza and Kenneth Kraft, Boston, London: Shambhala, 2000, pp. 178–82.

————, *Seeds of Peace: A Buddhist Vision for Renewing Society*, Berkeley: Parallax Press, 1993.

Sizemore, Russell F. and Donald K. Swearer, eds., *Ethics, Wealth and Salvation: A Study in Buddhist Social Ethics*, Columbia: University of South Carolina Press, 1990.

Skidmore, Monique, 'The Politics of Space and Forms: Cultural Idioms of Resistance and Re-Membering in Cambodia', *Santi Culture Health*, vol. 10, no. 2, 1993–4, pp. 35–59.

Smith, D.G. et al., *Diversity Works: The Emerging Picture of How Students Benefit*, Washington DC: Associates of American Colleges & Universities, 1997.

Snyder, Gary, 'Blue Mountains Constantly Walking', in *Dharma Rain: Sources of Buddhist Environmentalism*, ed. Stephanie Kaza and Kenneth Kraft, Boston, London: Shambhala, 2000, pp. 125–40.

Spenglar, Oswald, *The Decline of the West*, New York: Oxford University Press, 1991.

Spiro, Melforde, *Buddhism and Society: A Great Tradition and its Burmese Vicissitude*, Berkeley: University of California Press, 1982.

Sponberg, Alan, 'Green Buddhism and the Hierarchy of Compassion', in *Buddhisn and Ecology: The Interconnection of Dharma and Deeds*, ed. Mary Evelyn Tucker and Duncan Ryuken Williams, Cambridge, MA: Harvard University Press, 1997, pp. 351–76.

————, 'The Buddhist Conception of an Ecological Self', *The Sound of Liberating Truth: Buddhist-Christian Dialogue in Honour of Frederick J. Streng*, ed. Sallie B. King and Paul O. Ingram, Ricmond Surrey: Curzon Press, 1999, pp. 116–18.

Srinivasan, D., 'The So Called Proto Siva Seal from Mohenjodaro: An Iconographical Assessment', *Archives of Asian Art*, vol. 29, 1975–6, pp. 47–58.

———, 'Unhinging Siva From the Indus Civilization', *Journal of Royal Asiatic Society of Great Britain and Ireland*, 1984, pp. 77–89.

Steward, Julian H., *Theory of Cultural Change: Methodology of Multilinear Evolution*, Urbana: University of Illinois Press, 1995.

———, 'Cultural Ecology', in *International Encyclopedia of Social Sciences*, vol. 4, 1968, pp. 337–44.

Steward, James J., 'The Question of Vegetarianism and Diet in Pāli Buddhism', *Journal of Buddhist Ethics*, vol. 17, 2010, pp. 100–40.

Strandberg, Elisabeth, 'Fausboll and the Pāli Jātaka', *The Journal of the International Association of Buddhist Studies*, vol. 3, no. 2, 1980, pp. 95–101.

Stutley, Margaret, *Ancient Indian Magic and Folklore: An Introduction*, London: Routledge and Kegan Paul, 1980.

Suksamran, Somboon, 'A Buddhist Approach to Development: The Case of "Development Monks" in Thailand', in *Reflections on Development in Southeast Asia*, ed. Lim Tech Ghee, Singapore: Institute of Southeast Asian Studies, 1988, pp. 26–48.

———, *Political Buddhism in Southeast Asia: The Role of Saṃgha in Modernization of Thailand*, London: C. Hurst and Co., 1977.

Swearer, Donald K., 'An Assessment of Buddhist Eco Philosophy', *Harvard Theological Review*, vol. 99, no. 2, 2006, pp. 123–37.

———, 'Principles and Poetry, Places and Stories: The Resources of Buddhist Ecology', *Daedilus*, vol. 130, no. 4, 2001, pp. 225–47.

———, 'Sulak Sivaraksa's Buddhist Vision for Renewing Society', *Crossroads: An Interdisciplinary Journal of Southeast Asian Studies*, vol. 6, no. 2, 1991, pp. 17–57, http://www.jstor.org/stable/40860347, accessed 28 March 2012.

———, 'The Hermeneutics of Buddhist Ecology in Contemporary Thailand: Buddhadas and Dhammapitaka', in *Buddhism and Ecology: The Interconnection of Dharma and Deeds*, ed. Mary Evelyn Tucker and Duncan Ryuken Williams, Cambridge, MA: Harvard Universirty Press, pp. 21–44.

———, 'Three Legacies of Bhikkhu Buddhadasa', in *Quest for New Society*, ed. Sulaka Sivaraksa, Bangkok: Thai Interreligious Commission for Development, Santi Pracha Dhamma Institute, 1994.

Swimme, Briane, *The Hidden Heart of the Cosmos: Humanity and the New Story*, New York: Orbis Books, 1996.

Takahashi, Ayako, 'The Shaping of Gary Snyder's Ecological Consciousness', *Comparative Literature Studies*, vol. 39, no. 4, East-West Issue, 2002, pp. 314–25.

Tambiah, S.J., *Buddhism Betrayed? Religion, Politics, and Politics in Sri Lanka*, London: The University of Chicago Press, 1992.

———, *The Buddhist Saints of the Forests and the Cult of Amulets*, Cambridge: Cambridge University Press, 1984.

———, *World Conqueror and World Renouncer: A Study of Buddhism and Polity in Thailand Against a Historical Background*, Cambridge: Cambridge University Press, 1976.

Tapper, Aaron J. Hahn, 'A Pedagogy of Social Justice Education: Social Identity Theory, Intersectionality and Empowerment', *Conflict Resolution Quarterly*, vol. 30, no. 4, 2013, pp. 411–45.

Tatia, Nathmal, 'The Jain Worldview and Ecology', *Jainism & Ecology*, ed. Christopher Key Chapple, Delhi: MLBD, 2006, pp. 3–18.

Taylor, C., *Multiculturalism and the Politics of Recognition*, Princeton: Princeton University Press, 1992.

Tenner, Edward, *Why Things Bite Back: Technology and the Revenge of Unintended Consequences*, New York: Alfred A. Knopf, 1996.

Thapar, Romila, 'Sacrifice, Surplus and Soul', *Cultrual Past: Essay in Early Indian History*, ed. Romila Thapar, Delhi: Oxford University Press, 2004, pp. 809–31, see pp. 816–18.

———, 'The Evolution of State in Ganga Valley in the Mid First Millennium BC', in *Cultrual Past: Essay in Early Indian History*, ed. Romila Thapar, Delhi: Oxford University Press, 2004, pp. 377–95.

Thily, Frank, *A History of Philosophy*, Allahabad: Central Publication House, 2007.

Thomas, E.J., 'Buddha's Last Meal', *Indian Culture*, vol. XV, nos. 1–4, 1948–9, pp. 1–3.

Thurman, R.A.F., 'Guidelines for Buddhist Social Activism Based on Nagarjuna's Jewel Garland of Royal Counsels', in *The Path of Compassion: Writings on Socially Engaged Buddhism*, ed. F. Eppsteiner and D. Maloney, Berkeley, CA: Parallax Press, 1985, pp. 46–65.

Timmerman, Peter, 'Western Buddhism and Global Crisis', in *Dharma Gaia: Sources of Buddhist Environmentalism*, ed. Stephanie Kaza and Kenneth Kraft, Boston: Shambhala, 2000, pp. 557–68.

Tinbergen, Jan, 'Wise Management for More Human World', in *Solutions for a Troubled World*, ed. Marc Macy, London: Earthview Press, 1987, pp. 56–7.

Tucker, Mary Evelyn and Duncan Ryuken Williams, *Buddhism and Ecology: The Interconnection of Dharma and Deeds*, Cambridge, MA: Harvard University Press, 1997.

Tyack, D.B., 'Constructing Difference: Historical Reflections of Schooling and Social Diversity', *Teachers College Record*, vol. 95, no. 1, 1993, pp. 8–34.

Tworkow, Helen, *Zen in America: Five Teachers and the Search for an American Buddhism*, New York: Kondansha International, 1994.

Udomittipong, Pipob, 'Thailand's Ecology Monk', *Dharma Rain: Sources of Buddhist Environmentalism*, ed. Stephanie Kaza and Kenneth Kraft, Boston, London: Shambhala, 2000, pp. 191–7.

Vetter, Tilmann, 'The Khandha Passage in the Vinaya Pitaka and Four Main Nikāyas', Wien: QAW, 2000, p. 132.

Waldau, Paul, *Buddhism and Animal Rights*, *Contemporary Buddhist Ethics*, ed. Damien Keown, Richmond Surrey: Curzon Press, 2000, pp. 81–112.

———, *Speciesism in Christianity and Buddhism*, University of Oxford, 1998.

———, *The Specter of Speciesism: Buddhist and Christian Views of Animals*, Oxford: Oxford University Press, 2001.

Waley, Arthur, 'Did Buddha die of Eating Pork?: With a Note on Buddha's Image', *Melanges Chinois et bouddhiques*, vol. 1931–32, Juillet, 1932, pp. 343–54, http://buddhism.lib.ntu.edu.tw.

Wang, Sally A., 'Can Man Go Beyond Ethics?: The System of Padmasambhava', *The Journal of Religious Ethics*, vol. 3, no. 1, Spring 1975, pp. 141–55, http://www.jstor.org/stable/40017721, accessed 28 March 2012.

Weber, Max, *Economy and Society*, Berkeley: University of California Press, 1968.

———, *Sociology of Religion*, London: Lowe and Brydone, 1966.

———, *The Religion of India: The Sociology of Hinduism and Buddhism*, New York: The Free Press, 1958.

Welbon, G. Richard, 'On Understanding of the Buddhist Nirvana', *History of Religions*, vol. 5, no. 2, Winter 1966, pp. 300–26.

Weiner, Mathew, 'Mahaghosananda as a Contemplative Social Activist', in *Action Dharma: New Studies in Engaged Buddhism*, ed. Christopher S. Queen, Charles Prebish and Damien Keown, London: Routledge, 2003, pp. 110–27.

Wezler, Albircht, 'Cattle Field and Barley: A Note on Mahabhasya', *Brahmavidya: Adyar Library Bulletin*, vol. I, no. 337, 1986, pp. 24–7.

———, 'A Notes on Sanskrit Bhruna and Bhrunahatya', in *Festschrft Klaces Bruhn*, ed. Nalni Balbir and Joalhem K. Boulze, Reenbek: Dr Inge Wezler, 1994, pp. 623–46.

White, James W., *The Soka Gakai and Mass Society*, Stanford: Stanford University Press, 1970.

White, Lynn, Jr., 'The Historic Roots of Our Ecological Crisis', *Science*, vol. 155, no. 3767, 10 March 1967, pp. 1203–7.

Whittal, James, 'Buddhism and Virtues', in *Contemporary Buddhist Ethics*, ed. Damien Keown, Richmond: Curzon Press, 2000, pp. 17–36.

Wickramasinghe, J.W., *Has the Apple not Fallen . . . !: Neo-Classical Economics in the Buddhist Perspective*, Colombo: Godage International Publishers, 2010.

Wiley, Kristi L., 'The Nature of Nature: Jain Perspective on the Natural World', in *Jainism & Ecology*, ed. Christopher Key Chapple, Delhi: MLBD, 2006, pp. 35–62.

Williamson, J., A.L. Rhodes and M. Dunson, 'A Selected History of Social Justice Education', *Review of Research in Education*, vol. 31, no. 11, 2007, pp. 195–224.

Windfuhr, Gernot L., 'Haoma/Soma: The Plant', *Acta Iranica*, vol. 25, E.J. Brill: Leiden, 1985, pp. 699–726.

Wohlberg, Joseph, 'Haoma-Soma in the World of Ancient Greece', *Journal of Psychology Drugs*, vol. 22, no. 3, July–September 1990, pp. 333–42.

Yamamoto, Shuichi, 'Environmental Ethics in Mahāyāna Buddhism: The Significance of Keeping Precepts (Sila-paramita) and Wisdom (Prajna-Paramita)', pp. 137–55.

Yarnall, Thomas Freeman, 'Engaged Buddhism: New and improved? Made in the USA of Asian Materials', in *Action Dhrama: A New Studies in Engaged Buddhism*, ed. Christopher S. Queen, Charles Prebish and Damien Kewon, London: Routledge, 2003, pp. 286–344.

Yu-lan, Fung, *A History of Chinese Philosophy*, 2 vols., Princeton: Princeton University Press, 1953.

Zadek, Simon, 'The Practice of Buddhist Economics? Another View', *American Journal of Economics and Sociology*, vol. 52, no. 4, October 1993, pp. 433–45, http://www.jstor.org/stable/3487468, accessed 27 March 2012.

Zsolnai, Laszio, 'Western Economics Verses Buddhist Economics', *Society and Economy*, vol. 29, no. 2, August 2007, pp. 145–53, http://www.jstor.org/stable/41472078, accessed 25 July 2013.

Zysk, Kenneth G., *Asceticism and Healing in Ancient India: Medicine in the Buddhist Monastery*, Delhi: MLBD, 2010.

Gazetteer

The Imperial Gazetteer Atlas of India, Delhi: LPP, 1931; repr. 2007.

Index